CW01217142

ELIZABETH CARY

The Tragedy of Mariam
The History of the Life, Reign and Death of Edward II

AEMILIA LANYER

Salve Deus Rex Judaeorum

RENAISSANCE WOMEN

The Plays of Elizabeth Cary

The Poems of Aemilia Lanyer

Edited with Introduction and Notes by
DIANE PURKISS

LONDON
WILLIAM PICKERING
1994

Published by Pickering & Chatto (Publishers) Limited
21 Bloomsbury Way, London WC1A 2TH

2252 Ridge Road, Brookfield, Vermont 05036, USA

www.pickeringchatto.com

All rights reserved.
No part of this publication may be reproduced,
stored in a retrieval system, or transmitted in any form or by any means,
electronic, mechanical, photocopying, recording, or otherwise
without prior permission of the publisher.

Copyright © Pickering & Chatto (Publishers) Limited 1994
Introduction and notes to this edition copyright © Diane Purkiss 1994

BRITISH LIBRARY CATALOGUING IN PUBLICATION DATA
A catalogue record for this title is available from the British Library.

LIBRARY OF CONGRESS CATALOGING-IN-PUBLICATION DATA
A catalogue record for this title is available from the Library of Congress

ISBN 1 85196 029 5

∞
This publication is printed on acid-free paper that conforms to
the American National Standard for the Permanence of Paper for
Printed Library Materials

Converted to digital print, 2002

CONTENTS

Introduction	vii
Acknowledgements	xlviii
Select Bibliography	xlix
Glossary	lviii
The Tragedy of Mariam, The Fair	1
The History of the Life, Reign, and Death of Edward II	79
Salve Deus Rex Judaeorum	239

To my parents

INTRODUCTION

The phrase 'Renaissance man' is familiar enough, but what can it mean to speak of 'Renaissance women'? Did women even *have* a Renaissance? Joan Kelly's question asks us to give up the idea of 'Renaissance women' as 'Renaissance men' in petticoats, and to consider the possibility that the movements which we call 'the Renaissance' impacted differently upon women than upon men.[1] First posed in 1977, Kelly's question has stimulated a comprehensive rethinking and reinvestigation of the place of gender in the phenomenon called the Renaissance, and this rethinking has called into question assumptions about that phenomenon. In this volume, the work of two women writers is represented, and to those who read this work it will become clear that to call Elizabeth Cary and Aemilia Lanyer 'Renaissance women writers' is to say more than that they were contemporaries of Shakespeare and Jonson and Milton. It is also not to say that either was Judith Shakespeare; neither woman was Shakespeare in drag, and neither was as comprehensively silenced as Virginia Woolf's tragic heroine. Both women wrote, but neither had full access to the financial, intellectual, and literary resources that make writing easy and pleasant, that make it a taken-for-granted possibility.

On the other hand, neither Cary nor Lanyer wrote in a separate sphere marked exclusively by gender; both women and their works were part of the literary system of Renaissance England. Nevertheless, both women were uneasy and uncomfortable in that system. Both Cary and Lanyer were products of a culture which marked women as absent, silent, other; both were constructed by a culture which had not been constructed by them. Both led lives and published works which express the paradox of being a 'Renaissance woman'. As subjects in history, Cary and Lanyer were caught up in and produced by that series of political, cultural and intellectual phenomena we call 'the Renaissance'.[2] As writers, their texts were shaped by familiar currents in literary, political and intellectual movements. But as women, they were excluded from the entitlements which the 'Renaissance man' could take for granted. The process of fashioning a self in the Renaissance depended on the notion that an individual was able to speak publicly and authoritatively, to enter the republic of letters by circulating writings, to participate in political and church life. Women were not excluded from all these spaces, but were often seen as marginal or out-of-place in them. Women could speak, but their speech was not authoritative and might be read as an indecorum which signified sexual looseness or availability; women could write, but publication might be read as transgressive, too open, and thus uncontrolled or disorderly; women could participate in life at court, but the notion of a powerful woman made contemporaries anxious; women could practise religion, but had little power within the church. Although Elizabeth Cary was given a humanist education, directed towards fashioning a person able to hold power and persuade others in the public realm, she was not entitled to make use of her learning in political or courtly life, as men were. As shall be demonstrated, the complications and instabilities of being both inside culture and excluded from it left traces in both women's lives, as well as in their works.

ELIZABETH CARY: LIFE

Because Elizabeth Cary was a noblewoman, the daughter and the wife of prominent men, we know a reasonable amount about her life. But what we know is refracted through the prism of these and other familial relations; state papers give accounts of her husband's career and of her acrimonious separation from him, and thus define her public identity as a noblewoman and as a recusant, but necessarily say little about how those identities overflowed into or intertwined with her identity as a writer.[3] However, our principal source for Cary's life is a biography by one of her daughters, probably Mary, a work which is itself a significant example of early modern women's writing.[4] Modern scholars handle this text cautiously, principally because they read it as dominated by the generic codes of counter-reformation hagiography.[5] Actually, Mary Cary breaks frequently with those codes, often dramatising their clash with the more sceptical and rational codes of humanist biography. In its juxtaposition of the discourses of Catholic sainthood with the playful tradition of humanist biography, the text's antecedent seems to be the *Life of Thomas More* rather than the lives of recusant saints as described in seventeenth-century counter-reformation panegyric.[6] The shibboleths of family morality are often bracketed or questioned by the text's teasing humour; it records that Cary's filial obedience extended to kneeling in the presence of her parents, but then adds that she 'was but an ill kneeler, and a worse riser'.[7] The comically inconvenient aspects of saintly dislocation from worldly affairs are mapped; Cary's financial improvidence and inability to deal with minor domestic details are sketched affectionately, with implicit appeal to a model of woman which is not commensurate with either the mother of the bourgeois household or the unworldly saint. Rather, the text's ideal seems to be the humanist goal of competent and virtuous self-government, or as we might say, independence. This implicit goal differentiates the *Life* sharply from hagiography such as the *Life of Margaret Clitherow*, which valorises its female object as a defiant but self-abnegating vessel for a divine message. At the same time, just because the sceptical and comic aspects of Cary's *Life* are more seductive for us than the norms of counter-reformation domestic discourse, it is tempting to valorise them as the 'truth' about Cary. These sceptical reflections, however, are also a product of discourse; the humanist milieu from which they come illustrates the complex way in which both Cary and her daughter were involved in humanist and intellectual projects usually believed to be wholly masculine by modern critics. Cary's *Life* therefore acts as a note of caution about overly simplistic answers to the question 'Did women have a Renaissance?' But for all its appeal to an intellectual model of the self-governing subject, the *Life* is about Cary the Catholic convert, not Cary the writer. The intersections between Cary's diverse identities as scripted in biographical texts remain undisclosed: Cary appears alternately as wife, mother, daughter, recusant, 'learned lady', writer, published author, but the task of analysing how and when these identities overlap or conflict has been left to modern feminist scholarship.

Elizabeth Tanfield, later Cary, was born in 1585 or 1586 at Burford Priory in Oxfordshire, the daughter of Elizabeth Symondes Tanfield and Lawrence Tanfield, a lawyer who later became Sir Lawrence Tanfield, Lord Chief Baron of the Exchequer. Little is known about Cary's mother; she was better-born than her husband, and this may have disturbed the normative balance of power in the household. The *Life* gives the impression that Cary's relations with her mother were not cordial; nonetheless, Elizabeth Symondes Tanfield seems to have been interested in court drama (a portrait of her survives in masque dress)[8] and in writing (she seems to have composed some verses for the tomb of her husband in Burford Church). Elizabeth Symondes Tanfield was extraordinarily unpopular with the people of Burford; a local legend is that if the river at Burford falls below a certain point, the Tanfields will return from hell; when the river threatened to sink below this level in the eighteenth century, the locals turned out to pour water into it to prevent such a dreadful occurrence.[9] These scraps of information together suggest that Elizabeth Symondes Tanfield was a woman of strong personality, interested in writing and in court drama; in these ways, Elizabeth Symondes may have influenced her daughter, despite their later animosity. Lawrence Tanfield's influence appears more obliquely; in the *Life*, there is a telling story about the young Elizabeth's defence of a woman charged with witchcraft. While the woman was being cross-questioned by Elizabeth's barrister father, Elizabeth noticed that she was simply admitting to whatever she was asked, and thus proved that her confessions of witchcraft were false.[10] The story

Introduction

illustrates the *Life*'s commitment to sceptical rationalism in the face of superstition, but may also illustrate Elizabeth's early involvement in those humanist discourses.

According to the *Life*, she was something of a child prodigy, learning French, Spanish, Italian, Latin, Hebrew and Transylvanian (p. 4); the emphasis on modern languages reflects the gendering of her education. Michael Drayton may have been one of her tutors, or she may have encountered him because he was in her father's employment; he dedicated an epistle to her in 1597, when she was eleven, in which he praises her facility in French and Italian and speaks of her judgement and reading as 'to be wondered at'.[11] She translated Ortelius's *Miroir du Monde* from French, dedicating the MS to her great-uncle, Sir Henry Lee, and also translated Seneca's *Epistles* from Latin.[12] According to her daughter, she was such an avid reader that she amassed an enormous debt to the servants for candles, which she used for reading in bed. (*Life*, pp. 6–7)

When she was fifteen, Elizabeth Tanfield was married to Sir Henry Cary, later created Viscount Falkland. Henry Cary was the son of the Master of the Royal Jewel House; the marriage was a made-to-order Renaissance trade-off, in which he got a substantial dowry and the Tanfields got a son-in-law connected to the nobility. Such marriages between prosperous upper-middle class families like the Tanfields and impoverished nobles like the Carys were a standard feature of the period: Elizabeth Cary was herself a product of a similar union.[13] At first Elizabeth moved in with Henry Cary's mother, but the two women did not get on. Punished by being sent to her room, Cary read continuously and contentedly until her mother-in-law removed all her books; 'then', her daughter says, 'she set herself to make verses' (p. 8). Cary's identity as a writer was thus born of deprivation after plenty. Her mother-in-law removed the signs and instruments of her role as learned lady, and she made verses to keep that role.

It was a role acknowledged publicly by a number of dedications. With the exceptions of Mary Sidney, Countess of Pembroke, and Lucy Countess of Bedford, Elizabeth Cary seems to have been the only Renaissance Englishwoman with a publicly acknowledged position as a writer and a patron within the discourses of Protestant humanism. The public creation of Cary's role in the world of letters began with Michael Drayton's dedication to her; Drayton acknowledges her learning, but foregrounds her place as a member of her father's household rather than as a subject in her own right. However, Cary was soon the co-recipient of a much more remarkable dedication, one which seems at first glance to contradict much of the received wisdom about the gendering of humanist discourse in the English Renaissance. It was produced by John Davies of Hereford in his volume *The Muses Sacrifice*, first published in 1612.[14] Davies was a writing master and calligrapher who produced the beautiful manuscript of the Sidney psalm translations; he could have been another of Cary's tutors. The dedicatory poem is addressed jointly to Lucy, Countess of Bedford, Mary Sidney, Countess of Pembroke, and Elizabeth Cary, Viscountess Falkland. Lucy, Countess of Bedford was one of the most significant woman patrons of the Renaissance era.[15] Mary Sidney was one of the principal woman writers and patrons of the age.[16] In grouping Cary with these prominent women, Davies was inviting her to share a new and potentially authoritative space for women in the realm of letters.

In writing about these three women, Davies uses the language of patronage normally assumed to be gendered male as if it needs no rewriting for them. He describes their bright eyes of virtue, suns which will add lustre to any object on which they look. As Lorna Hutson has recently argued, this metaphor is usually a homosocial one which constructs bonds between men; here it is used to describe the power of the female look.[17] In this poem, however, Davies uses this language as if it were uncontested that women might bestow virtue as well as men. In constructing an image for them as givers of virtue to the public, he directly compares all three women with Sir Philip Sidney, and furthermore represents them as Sidney's heirs.[18] Finally, he positively urges all of them to impart virtue to the corrupt procedures of the literary marketplace by publishing their writings;

in other words, he sees all three women as always already participating in the humanist project of imparting virtue to the commonwealth through literary persuasion.[19] Admittedly this last exhortation is accompanied by a metaphor which Margaret Ferguson has found equivocally sexual.[20] 'You press the Press with little you have made', Davies complains, and figures those more eager than the ladies as the profligate parents of print children 'basely got, conceived and born'. In this line, the class privilege of the three addresses guarantees their separation from the 'base' sexualisation of the print appearances of others; the conceit of urging a noble to reproduce himself, familiar from Shakespeare's sonnets, is applied to the women who are Davies's objects of address. They too are invited to duplicate themselves and thus do good, and this is metaphorised as a wifely duty of fertility, an avoidance of barrenness. In this way, the discourse of humanist writing becomes *particularly* applicable to women; the process of reproducing virtue is part of their role rather than at odds with it. No-one knows whether Cary was the one who chose to publish *The Tragedy of Mariam*, but, if she did, it may have been a response to Davies's poem.

Cary's role in the literary world was further shaped and acknowledged by Richard More's dedicatory sonnet in the second edition of *Englands Helicon*, published in 1614.[21] The final couplet echoes Shakespeare's Sonnet 18; just as Shakespeare's text assigns mutually constructing power to the patron and the poem, so More asserts that Cary has the same power: 'Then cherish thee (fair Stem)/ So shall they live by thee, and thee by them'. In Ireland, too, Cary attracted a client. Richard Belling dedicated his *Sixth Book to the Countess of Pembroke's Arcadia* to her in 1624, renewing the public link between Cary and Mary Sidney publicly established by John Davies's poem and by the publication of *Mariam* with its Senecan antecedents.[22] Like her other clients, Belling seemed to wish to claim a public place for Cary and through her a public place for himself.

This tenuous position in the world of letters was, however, threatened by events within the Cary household. Having spent Cary's dowry on Henry's ransom from the Netherlands, the couple finally set up house together. After a seven-year period of infertility, Cary gave birth to eleven children. This debilitating pattern of continual pregnancy took its toll: after the births of her second and fourth children, Cary temporarily lost her reason, suffering from melancholy and an inability to eat. The period of spectacular fecundity almost certainly slowed her literary output.[23] We don't know of any writings between *Mariam*, probably written between 1603 and 1604, and 1627, the alleged date of *Edward II*. As well, the first of many family disputes began. Lawrence Tanfield had settled a substantial jointure on his daughter; jointures were intended to provide income in case of the husband's death, and no doubt Tanfield was well aware of Henry Cary's numerous debts. Cary, however, seems to have mortgaged this jointure to enable her husband to take up the post of Lord Deputy of Ireland in 1622. Her father promptly disinherited her in favour of her son, Lucius Cary. Although Henry Cary later claimed that Tanfield was motivated by disgust at Cary's moves towards recusancy, it's equally possible that this quarrel dramatises another conflict, a conflict between the cautious bourgeois values of the Tanfields and the aristocratic profligacy of the Carys. In other words, class rather than gender or religion may have been the determining factor here. Caught between two patriarchal imperatives, Cary characteristically resolved the situation by rebelling against one in order to throw in her lot with the other, a move proleptic of her eventual religious conflicts and a move dramatised in the persons of both Isabella and Mariam.

The exact date of Cary's conversion to Catholicism is unknown. The *Life* attempts to argue that she was always already Catholic, as did Henry Cary after the separation, but this seems unlikely. Mary Cary presents her mother's religious thought as rational conclusions struggling against social conditioning, but it may be that the decisive moment occurred during Cary's stay in Ireland. While there she learned Gaelic (perhaps from Richard Belling) and also tried to help the impoverished locals by setting up a kind of craft cooperative for them. Although the venture was not a success, it brought her into contact with the Irish, and thus with a predominantly Catholic people.[24] Whatever influenced her, she was formally received into the Catholic Church shortly after her return from Ireland in November, 1626. She may have intended to keep her conversion a secret, but if so her aim was frustrated by her friend Lady Denbigh, sister of the Duke of Buckingham. Lady Denbigh had herself been flirting with Catholicism, and Cary seems to have confided in her.[25] Lady Denbigh promptly informed her brother of Cary's conversion, and he as promptly informed the King. The matter created a stir at court, largely because of Cary's rank and because of the increase in anti-Catholic prejudice in the 1620s.[26] The immediate result was that Henry Cary announced that he wished to separate from his wife; he also refused her a subsistence and even sent his servants to remove stores of food and firewood from her house.

In this, and in his persistent reluctance to provide any support for his wife, Henry Cary has been portrayed as a typical patriarch.[27] In fact, his reaction was excessive by seventeenth-century standards, largely because in enacting religious difference he was ignoring the laws of class. The idea of a noblewoman living in complete penury was repugnant to the court. The attitude a husband should take up towards a recusant wife was in any case a matter of some controversy in early modern England. Since a husband was legally responsible for his wife's behaviour, he was implicated in her actions, a matter of particular concern to a career courtier like Henry Cary, recently appointed to a position in Ireland. But the question of how a husband could force his wife to conform to Protestantism exposed a weakness at the heart of patriarchy. Some husbands took a tolerant line, like the man who explained plaintively that he had no means to make his wife conform; others resorted to violence, some dragging their wives physically to church.[28] Henry Cary did not appear to attempt to compel his wife to obey him by any means; he seems to have abrogated patriarchal power in his eagerness to distance himself from his wife's unacceptable behaviour. Ironically, his one suggestion was that Cary might be made to return to her mother, who he argued could perhaps persuade her to renounce Rome; the spectacle of seventeenth-century male familial authority relying on its mother-in-law to enforce its will demonstrates how questions of religion revealed the contradictions in seventeenth-century patriarchy.[29] When Cary refused this plan, Henry Cary insisted on instant separation and refused her financial support, suggesting a wish to remove himself completely from the scene of Roman Catholicism. In the end, this represented an attempt to sacrifice private to public authority.

The issues of obedience to authority versus liberty of conscience, debated fiercely and eloquently in *Mariam*, thus never arose publicly in the final breakdown of Cary's marriage. We should therefore be cautious about attempts to read the play in the light of Cary's marital breakdown over religion. It may be worth considering the possibility that writing a Senecan play about the difficult moral contradictions between the public and the private for women helped to inspire Cary to convert, and gave her a discursive model for doing so. As well, Cary's conversion is emblematic of her uneasy attempts to negotiate patriarchal authority and of the uncertainty and fragility of that authority. Cary's conversion is both a rebellion against and a submission to authority. The same tension is apparent in her numerous letters to Viscount Conway and others, pleading that they intercede with the King so that he will persuade Henry Cary to give her an allowance.[30] Unlike Aemilia Lanyer, Cary did not seek to convert her writing into cash; probably printers were reluctant to produce the work of a notorious Papist. But though she may have eschewed this kind of publicity, her letters are full of the assurance of her public position as a noblewoman. Their rhetoric of pleading was effective; Henry was eventually compelled by Charles to support her.

But becoming a recusant meant giving up the public role as patron of literary clients which Cary had begun to establish. No dedications were made to her between her conversion in 1625 and 1633; there were no more pleas for edifying moral works from the Sidney circle and its hangers-on. The only dedication she received after her conversion was that of Marston's *Collected*

Works in 1633.[31] Disowned by their author, who insisted that his name be removed from the title page, the work does not suggest that Cary had regained the status she had lost in the literary world by her conversion.[32] The dedication reveals the printer's concern to distance himself from the scandal of William Prynne's attack on women's involvement with the stage, published that year, by dedicating a volume of plays to a close friend of Henrietta Maria's. Although Cary's recusancy marked a break with wifely obedience and with the private sphere of the home, it also cut her off from the public sphere of letters as patron and also as writer. Her translation of Du Perron was printed at Douai, and was allegedly called in by the censor;[33] the *Life* reports that she could not find a printer for the remainder of her translations; her verse lives of Mary Magdalene, Elizabeth of Portugal and St Agnes have not survived.

Nor did her marital separation end her family troubles. Though Charles I arranged for the couple to be briefly reconciled, Henry Cary died shortly afterwards in a hunting accident. Another struggle for Cary's children began; this time it was her eldest son Lucius who tried to exercise authority over his younger siblings, removing them from their mother and installing them at his own residence at Great Tew in a bid to bring them up as Protestants. Lucius was too late; the children were willing to be smuggled to the Continent where the girls entered convents and the boys seminaries. This row shows the way Cary's recusancy at once affirmed and troubled patriarchal notions of the family. In teaching her children religion Cary was acting out her role as mother in accordance with ideology, but that enactment had become a form of rebellion. This practice of opposition through subordination, manifest in Cary's remarkable life-story, is explored in her dramatic works.

Cary died in 1639, and was buried in Henrietta Maria's private chapel at St James's. The burial-place marks the last trace of her public role: her friendship with the Catholic queen, about which the *Life* is almost silent. Cary's conversion to Roman Catholicism cost her her role as public woman of letters, and ironically has also silenced posterity, which until recently saw her solely in terms of her religion. Thanks to the efforts of feminist studies, she can now be re-placed in literary and cultural history.

The Tragedy of Mariam

Elizabeth Cary's *Tragedy of Mariam* is the first surviving play known to be written by a woman printed in English.[34] *Mariam* was listed in the Stationer's Register on 17 December 1612, and was printed in 1613. Two copies survive with a dedicatory sonnet to 'my worthy sister Mistress Elizabeth Cary' (A1); this leaf is taken out of most of the surviving copies.[35] It may be that this dedicatory verse is the one referred to in the *Life*; Cary's daughter speaks of verses stolen from her sister-in-law's room and printed without her consent (p. 9). Greg suggests that this verse was removed because it gave away the identity of the author too clearly, but Cary seems to have been well-known as the author in any case; Davies congratulates her on bringing to life the scenes of Syracuse and Palestine.[35] It may be that the leaf was bound in only with the dedication copies. The dedicatee, another Elizabeth Cary, was Cary's sister-in-law, the wife of Philip Cary, knighted in 1604/5. This event is used by Greg and others to date the play; since a dedication written after Philip's knighthood would address the dedicatee as Lady Elizabeth rather than Mistress Elizabeth.[37] This suggests an early date, of approximately 1603/4, possibly while Cary was still living with Henry's family. The dedication to a member of that family bears this out, as do the references to a previous dedication to Henry[38] and to Henry's absence; Henry was in the Low Countries in the early years of the marriage.

Like her contemporary Mary Sidney's translation of Garnier's *Marc-Antoine*, Cary's play was influenced by French Senecan drama, produced to be read privately rather than acted on the public stage.[39] However, in other ways *Mariam* is connected with the realm of letters and the circulation of ideas, discourses and writings. First, it shows the influence of Senecan drama and of Stoic ideas, making references to Seneca and even Montaigne.[40] Secondly, the principal source for *Mariam* is Thomas Lodge's translation of Josephus's *History of the Jewish People*, published in 1602; if the play was written during the years 1603-5, Cary's use of this work suggests her contact with new developments in the world of learning and publication.[41] Thirdly, *Mariam* is part of a group of plays which deal with the figure of Herod as a means to explore the political issues of monarchy, authority, tyranny and subject obedience to king and conscience.[42] In any case, *Mariam* is itself a powerful work, which takes up questions of gender and power in a way which demonstrates their relation.

Mariam's dilemma, figured at the beginning of the action as a choice between wifely duty and familial loyalty, becomes a more complex ontological and dramatic question about the (im)possibility for a woman of both being and seeming virtuous.[43] As many feminist critics have noted, the play dramatizes this dilemma in terms of the problem of the woman as speaking subject. In order to articulate virtue, Mariam must constantly breach the law of wifely silence, or as Sohemus puts it: 'Unbridled speech is Mariam's worst disgrace/ And will endanger her without desert' (ll. 1147–8).[44] The key words here are 'without desert'; in the very act of displaying her virtue, Mariam has lost it, but without such display how can she seem what she is? How can she be virtuous without seeming to be? This is the dilemma Lanyer explores for the woman writer addressing the woman patron, but Cary by contrast stages this dilemma as a series of moments of dramatic action or choice.

What dooms Mariam is not merely the speech of another woman who chooses to be outspoken in a manner the play equates with vice and sexual profligacy, but the fact that Herod equates Mariam's speaking with sexual looseness. 'She's unchaste;/ Her mouth will ope to every stranger's ear' (ll. 1646–7), he exclaims, equating the opening of the mouth with the availability of the body.[45] Ironically, however, Mariam's verbal openness also has another meaning. Her openness is a sign of her virtue because her speeches clearly reflect that virtue, open it to the listener; they are logocentrically understood, both being and seeming. By contrast, Salome speaks deceptively or theatrically, not disclosing virtue but misdirecting her speech to deceive and entrap her male auditors; what her speech makes her seem is radically disjunct from what she is. In Salome's case, a gap is opened between the 'I' who speaks and the 'I' who is the subject of speaking. Unlike Mariam, Salome is not punished.[46] In the light of Cary's subsequent ironic and bitter reflections on the operations of power in *Edward II*, this should be read less as an endorsement of Salome than as a reflection of a stoic disdain for the operations of the world upon virtue. Overtly, that is, for in another respect Salome also represents a dark fantasy about the possibility of using female speech not as a high-stakes wager on virtue, but as a means of power.

A fantasy resolution is eventually offered through the last act, which, as Elaine Beilin argues, reconfigures the death of Mariam as a representation of the crucifixion of Christ.[47] Like Lanyer, Cary turns from the perplexing paradoxes of the resources of language towards religious contemplation as a space for less problematic interpretation of virtue. But for woman to be an *imitatio christi* was not exactly unproblematic if it literally required a public death, even though the figure of the abused Christ was easily feminised, as Lanyer was to show. As Margaret Ferguson points out, the beheaded Mariam conjures the ghosts of Mary Queen of Scots and Anne Boleyn, as well as Christ, figures of precisely the same excessive and disordered sexuality of which Mariam stands accused.[48] In the end, the problem of Mariam's virtue and her speech can only be resolved by her ultimate silencing, so that others may speak for her and about her. Her ultimate value lies in the mouths of others, and cannot be articulated by her. She can only act it out by going to her death, becoming a symbol instead of a subject. This, the ultimate tragedy of the play, reflects the difficulty of answering the question Cary asks in the context of her time.

Introduction xxi

The History of the Life, Reign, and Death of Edward II

While *Mariam*'s attribution to Cary has been accepted for some ninety years, resting securely on the careful scholarship of Dunstan and Greg, the attribution of *Edward II* to her is much more doubtful. This attribution was first suggested by Donald Stauffer in 1935; recently it has been endorsed by Betty Travitsky and Tina Krontiris, both of whom claim that Stauffer proved the work to be Cary's, though neither presents any fresh evidence.[49] Unfortunately, both Travitsky and Krontiris exaggerate Stauffer's claims, as Elaine Beilin points out.[50] Matters have been complicated still further by D. Woolf's work, which takes no account of Stauffer but puts forward claims of its own.[51] Woolf argues that *Edward* does not belong to the 1620s at all, but is a forgery of the Exclusion Crisis era in which it was printed. A response from Isobel Grundy uses Stauffer's argument to address Woolf's, but does not review all the points Woolf makes.[52] It seems important to present an overview of the arguments and evidence both for and against Cary's authorship of *Edward*, and both for and against the date of 1627.

The situation is complicated by the existence of two texts whose relation to each other is by no means clear. The first is a folio volume, entitled *The History of the Life, Reign, and Death of Edward II...Written by E.F. in the Year 1627, and Printed Verbatim From the Original*, (London: J.C. for Charles Harper et al, 1680, hereafter F). F is a mixture of blank verse printed as prose and prose history. The second is an octavo, printed the same year, entitled *The History of the Most Unfortunate Prince King Edward II. With Choice Political Observations on him and his Unhappy favourites, Gaveston and Spencer*, (London: A. G. and J. P., 1680, hereafter 8vo). The relationship between the two volumes is difficult to determine. F's title page asserts that the work is 'written by E. F. in the year 1627' and 'printed verbatim from the original'. 8vo on the other hand asserts that the work is authored by Henry Cary, Viscount Falkland, and that it was found among his papers. Taken together, the two claims present strong evidence for Elizabeth Cary's authorship, and it is on these two claims that attribution is generally based. The initials are hers, and although the printed *Mariam* is signed E.C. she does use E. F. for letters. 8vo.'s claim that the MS was found among Henry Cary's papers links Cary to the MS, and permits the conjecture that her MSS may have been among his papers. However, this argument depends on taking the contradictory claims of F and 8vo together, despite the fact that the relations between the two issues and their counterclaims is by no means clear. It assumes that both printers had access to the same MS and to similar information; this is not necessarily the case. 8vo. is often said to be a shortened version of F; in fact there are few close parallels between them, as Stephanie Wright has recently pointed out.[53] This makes the relationship between the two texts less clear than has been assumed. Moreover, it seems possible that 8vo's printers simply attribute the 8vo. to Henry Cary on no real grounds whatsoever, a possibility strengthened by the fact that 8vo's preface has Henry Cary confused with his son Lucius, referring erroneously to what sounds like the Great Tew circle. After the Restoration Lucius Cary became an emblem of loyal but critical and rational humanism, largely through the writings of his friend Clarendon, and this may have been the printer's reason for invoking the name of Cary in publishing a work critical of the doings of a monarch and his favourites. On the other hand, the printers may have attributed a separate history of *Edward* to Henry Cary because they had seen or heard of the publication of the folio volume attributed to E.F. In the absence of MS or MSS, these matters must remain doubtful, but the connection between F and 8vo is by no means so clear or so unambiguous as to form the basis for attribution in the way it has.

Other evidence has been adduced to support *Edward*'s attribution to Cary, largely by Donald Stauffer. Many feminist critics do not appear to realize that Stauffer's essay is largely taken up with an argument about the date of *Edward*; he devotes only four pages to discussing the question of authorship, and of these

Introduction xxiii

three consist of the argument that a masculine figure like Henry Cary would not have shied away from visceral descriptions of violence, as the F-text of *Edward* does. This feebly essentialist argument is unlikely to appeal to feminist readers.[54] Elsewhere, too, Stauffer slides into essentialism; commenting on the 'emotional yet reticent nature' of the author of F's preface to the reader, he overlooks the fact that Cary's Preface to her translation of Du Perron is neither emotional nor reticent. Apart from arguments of this kind, Stauffer produces seven substantive arguments for attributing *Edward* to Elizabeth Cary:

1. that it stems from the stage tradition rather than from prose history;
2. that the grammatical constructions suggest a knowledge of Latin;
3. that absolute constructions occur often at the beginnings of sentences;
4. that the work contains passages of uncontrolled rhetoric;
5. that lines are almost invariably end-stopped;
6. that lines end with feminine endings almost invariably;
7. that the metre is regular to the point of monotony.

Most of these points apply only to the verse in *Edward* and not to the intervening prose. Even given this limitation, 1. and 2. are extremely general; 3. does not apply to *Mariam*, Cary's known dramatic work; 4. does not apply to *Mariam* and may be another instance of Stauffer's essentialist bias (women are uncontrolled). Similarly, feminine endings are very rare in *Mariam* and the fact that they are common in Edward points away from Cary as author, not towards her. However, end-stopped lines and metrical regularity are both features of *Mariam*, but as Elaine Beilin points out, they are also features of numerous other plays rather than features unique to Cary. Moreover, the metre of the verse sections of *Edward* is not as regular as that of *Mariam*, though this may reflect the unfinished state of the former. In short, Stauffer produces no convincing stylistic argument for attributing *Edward* to Cary.

Recently, Tina Krontiris has drawn attention to a series of

thematic parallels between *Edward* and Cary's life as recounted by her daughter, and also between *Edward* and *Mariam*. Of the former, she points out that in *Edward* Isabel is treated much more sympathetically than in Marlowe's play or in any of the chronicles. This rewriting of history in favour of a maligned female figure of power also takes place in *Mariam*, where Cary reverses Josephus' condemnation of the queen. This parallelism is persuasive, lending support to Krontiris's claims for Cary's authorship of *Edward*, but taken alone does not fully justify the attribution.

Still other arguments have been advanced. Elaine Beilin points out that there is a parallel between the Preface to Cary's translation of Du Perron and the Preface of F; in Du Perron, the Preface announces: 'One woman, in one month, so large a book/ In such a full emphatic stile to turn', while in F. the Preface announces 'nor fear I censure, since at the worst, 'twas but one month expended'. Even though the Perron prefatory poem is not by Cary, the statements about works composed in a month are a point of resemblance. More recently, Danielle Clarke has argued for an overlap between Cary's doctrine of historical change in *Edward* and Du Perron's argument as translated by her. Clarke's argument is the most convincing linkage so far made between *Edward* and Du Perron, though others have made less substantive links between *Edward* and *Mariam*. Two arguments for Cary's authorship have not been advanced. First, in *Mariam* Cary shows a decided partiality for obscure and unusual words, and there are also many such in the F-text of *Edward*. Secondly, *Edward* in places shows clear evidence of Catholic authorship, especially in the passage concerning the papal envoys and their peacekeeping mission.[55] Taken together with the other arguments, these factors strongly suggest that Cary is indeed the author.

On the other hand, the *Life* does not mention *Edward* at all, and in fact states unequivocally that apart from translation Cary never wrote anything in prose; though F is partly blank verse, there are lengthy prose passages. However, Mary Cary also mentions her mother's late-blossoming interest in history (*Life*,

p. 113), a point to which I will return again with regard to the date of the work. Moreover, Mary Cary does not mention *Mariam* either, and it may be that she did not know of all her mother's literary activities.

The question of authorship is necessarily bound up with the equally cloudy question of the date of *Edward*. Both F and 8vo were printed in 1680, and both publications plainly arise from the circumstances of the Exclusion crisis.[56] As Woolf points out, a number of dramatic and prose histories were produced at this time as covert warnings to Charles II, and frequent comparisons were made between the onset of the English Civil War some forty years earlier and events surrounding the crisis. The question is whether *Edward* is an early work printed because of the Exclusion Crisis, or a forgery of 1680 as Woolf argues. The title-page of F asserts that *Edward* was written in February 1627, but this is not in itself conclusive. Woolf points to the publication of *The Bishop of Carlisle's Speech Concerning the Deposing of Princes*, 1674, which was said to be a genuine fourteenth-century document but was in fact a forgery. Similarly, the Civil War years had seen the regular invention of 'ancient prophecies' like those of Mother Shipton and Merlin; their 'antiquity' granted them authenticity, but they were forgeries with polemical purposes. Such inventions drew on early modern notions of history as a series of moral or political exempla which could be deployed in the interests of instructing persons of today. In the case of *Edward*, the selection of 1627 as the date of composition might have been intended to warn Charles II through the example of his father, who ignored all warnings with disastrous consequences. In February 1627 the Duke of Buckingham was at the height of his power, and by 1680 some Civil War historians were arguing that his overmightiness had been a predisposing cause of conflict. However, it is notable that both the Civil War and Exclusion Crisis forgeries tend to claim medieval or still earlier origins rather than offering dates of less than seventy years ago.

Of course if *Edward* is an Exclusion Crisis forgery then it cannot have been written by Elizabeth Cary. However, arguments about the printer's choice of February 1627 can be reversed to make out a case for this date. The parallel between the situation the text describes (a weak king neglects the kingdom and his queen for a series of lover-favourites) and the events of the 1620s is very evident. Just as Edward's reign was destabilised by his powerful favourites Gaveston and Spencer, so in 1627 Charles I was under the thumb of the Duke of Buckingham. Just as Edward neglected Isabel, so Charles neglected his queen Henrietta Maria. Since *Edward* seems especially interested in Isabel, this parallel is especially significant, and does not apply to the Exclusion Crisis. Moreover, Buckingham's ascendancy over James I and Charles I inspired at least one other verse life of Edward and Gaveston: Sir Francis Hubert's poem, which the author of *Edward* may have used.[57]

If *Edward* was written in February 1627 as a response to Buckingham's role at court, what effect does this have on the attribution of it to Cary? At first glance, it makes the attribution to her less likely. Buckingham was Henry Cary's patron, and may have been responsible for his appointment as Lord Deputy of Ireland. Buckingham's sister, the Countess of Denbigh, was as we have seen Cary's friend and confidante. Moreover, Cary may be the author of one of the few really favourable elegies on Buckingham's death, one which asks the reader to take the word of two kings against one slave.[58] As well, Cary had separated from Henry Cary in 1625, and both Buckingham and the Duchess of Buckingham are among those she cites as her supporters in her bid to get an allowance from her estranged spouse.[59] In the light of all this, it seems extremely unlikely that she would simultaneously write a secret history which glances unfavourably at Buckingham's role at court. Moreover, in February 1627 Cary was thoroughly embroiled in bitter disputes with Henry Cary over her penurious situation.[60] At this point she was existing on a diet of crusts stolen by her maid from other people's wastepails. It seems unlikely that she would have chosen this moment to begin and end a complex and demanding work like *Edward*, and one which probably demanded a good deal of reading,[61] but the possibility cannot be ruled out,

Introduction xxvii

especially if she indeed began *Mariam* as a result of adversity. On the other hand, the *Life* asserts that Cary's interest in history occurred late in her life rather than in the 1620s. Moreover, Danielle Clarke's argument about connections between the political arguments about kingship and secular power in du Perron and *Edward* suggests that *Edward* was not finalised until after Cary's acquaintance with Du Perron's text, an acquaintance which seems to have begun in the late 1620s.[62] If Cary was the author of Edward, the work may have been begun in 1627, but it is on balance unlikely to have reached its present form then. The printed text of F may well represent Cary's attempt to rework an earlier play in the light of her new interest in history and the political doctrines of counter-reformation thought. Presumably, F's claim is based on a date on the MS from which *Edward* was printed; this date may not necessarily refer to the work's completion, if indeed it is complete.

Given the conjecture that *Edward* reached its present form later than 1627, we can look again at the work's possible connection with the relations between Charles and Buckingham in a new light. True, Lady Denbigh was one of Cary's friends, but she also betrayed Cary's conversion to the Duke, who in turn told the king. The Buckingham family were thus directly responsible for the financial and familial woes which dogged Cary for the rest of the decade. Much more importantly, *Edward* focuses not solely on Gaveston or Edward, but on the figure of Isabel, the queen demonised by Marlowe, Hubert, Holinshead and other writers on Edward II whom Cary had read. In the late 1620s and 1630s, Cary became very close to Henrietta Maria, dedicating her translation of Du Perron to the queen, and eventually being buried in her private chapel. If we accept the possibility that Cary may have worked on *Edward* after 1627, her view of Buckingham may gradually have been influenced by her sympathy for Henrietta. Henrietta had of course been completely sidelined by Buckingham's influence over her husband. It is the way *Edward* rewrites history for the benefit of Isabel which ultimately presents the strongest argument for a woman's authorship, and Cary's involvement with the queen is highly significant in this context. The fact that Isabel's rebellion is not presented entirely favourably need not militate against an argument for Henrietta's influence on the work; Cary may have wished to contrast Henrietta's Griselda-like resignation with Isabel's impetuous rebellion.

Plainly, *Edward*'s publication was the result of the Exclusion Crisis, and the passages in which Woolf finds the concerns of the Restoration *may* have been updated. Nonetheless, it does manifest some of the same political questions as *Mariam*, notably the question of what constitutes tyranny and when obedience to the ruler/husband can legitimately be replaced by defiance and rebellion. As treated in *Edward*, these questions are just as characteristic of Jacobean and Caroline political theory as of post-Restoration theory. In conclusion, then, it seems probable that the F-text of *Edward* is primarily a product of the pre-Civil War period, and thus may well be authored by Elizabeth Cary.

This does not solve the problem of the state of the F-text reprinted here. Blank verse is mixed with strongly rhythmical prose, and with prose far removed from blank verse; there is also the odd octosyllabic couplet. It is not at all clear whether the work was intended as a drama or a long narrative poem; although most of the speeches are in or are close to blank verse, large sections of narrative are also in verse, while generally passages of argument are in prose. There are two possibilities: Cary turned a verse drama or long poem into a prose history; the printer turned Cary's verse drama with prose interludes into a work of prose. In either case, the work may not be the finished piece as Cary intended, and we must bear this in mind especially when talking about its mixture of genres. Nor do we know whether Cary ever intended to publish it, or for whom it was written.

In her pathbreaking articles on Cary's *Edward*, Tina Krontiris implies that the work is strongly focused on the figure of Isabel, Edward's queen.[63] In fact, although Isabel is important in the latter part of the work, she is barely mentioned until halfway through the book, when Cary returns to the theme of

Mariam, the virtuous wife who confronts her husband's moral errors and must choose between wifely obedience and obedience to reason and morality, exploring this again through a different historical narrative. In the first third of the work, those questions of private versus public, of subversion of order, and of what can be said to count as good order in public and private realms alike are played out in *Edward* through Cary's exploration of Edward's relations with his favourites Gaveston and Spencer, and through his relations with his critical and dissatisfied nobility. Modern readers may well find Cary's handling of the former theme obnoxiously blind to the possibility of a homosexual subjectivity as explored by Marlowe; rather, the move she makes repeatedly is to create conflict between the supposed norms of monarchic behaviour and Edward's isolation, loneliness and feminisation. But her focus is always on the operations of court corruption and their interaction with conflict between the monarch and the aristocracy, or between the political principles of absolutism and the historic independence of the nobility.

It was precisely these issues which seemed crucial to the political debates of the seventeenth century, especially during the reigns of James I and Charles I.[64] In Cary's analysis, the virtuous and patriotic nobility, who stand for tradition and historical continuity, are opposed to the urban world of the corrupt court, in which ambitious young men sacrifice honesty for flattery and thus worsen rule to produce their own advancement. This recapitulates one of the central themes of *Mariam* without explicit reference to gender; how is it possible to display virtue through the tongue? The honest nobles like Lincoln are sidelined by Edward's preference for flattery, leaving the kingdom to go to an always unspecified rack and ruin without the benefit of their advice. Virtuous transparency of speech is misinterpreted by Edward as *lese-majeste*, while flattery misrepresents itself as proper respect. Edward's failures of interpretation are enclosed in a general chronicle narrative of his reign, with due emphasis on the disaster of Bannockburn, but what is distinctive about this chronicle is its admixture with issues of court virtue and court corruption, explicitly discussed. These often ironic and cogent bursts of argument suggest a growing interest in political philosophy on Cary's part, an interest which may have stemmed from her involvement in counter-reformation circles, and represent as well a very early instance of a woman writer engaged with politics and with the nature of history. Ultimately, this is where the value of *Edward II* lies.

AEMILIA LANYER

Aemilia Lanyer is the author of a poem about difficulties of interpretation, and particularly about the interpretation of women's reputations through sexual slander and scandal. Yet most of what we 'know' about her life is itself scandal and defamation. Aemilia Lanyer was christened on 27 January 1569 at St Botolph's Church, London. She was the daughter of Baptista Bassani, an Italian Jewish court musician who seems to have come to England to perform at the coronation of Edward VI in 1547, and Margaret Johnson, who died in 1587 and of whom nothing further is known.[65] Baptista Bassani died in 1576, leaving Lanyer a dowry of £100 to be paid to her when she was twenty-one.

In her poem to Susan Bertie, Dowager Countess of Kent and daughter of the Duchess of Suffolk, Lanyer calls Bertie 'the noble guide of my ungoverned days', suggesting that she may have been in the Suffolk household; while in her poem to Queen Anne of Denmark, she refers to the time when 'Great Eliza's favour blest my youth', suggesting some acquaintance with the court of Elizabeth I. She also claims to have been presented to Arabella Stuart in her poem to Arabella: 'Great learned lady, whom I long have known', again suggesting a familiarity with court circles.

Apart from Lanyer's poems and a few documents, our only source for her life is a few entries in Simon Forman's diary. Forman was an astrologer and physician consulted by many fashionable and ordinary women in Elizabethan London, but he

Introduction xxxi

was also a notorious figure, imprisoned for unlicenced medical practice, and subsequently revealed to be sexually involved with the court ladies who had been consulting him. Forman's sexual interest in women, which extended to fantasies about Elizabeth I, dominates his comments on Lanyer, and the issue has been further obfuscated by the careless transcription of A. L. Rowse in pursuit of his untenable theory about Lanyer and Shakespeare's sonnets.[66] Forman's impressions of Lanyer and the information he records about her are governed by the discourses of sexuality he uses. Lanyer first consulted him on 17 May 1597, and on this occasion he writes:

> She hath had hard fortune in her youth in that... her father died when she was young and so had misfortune... She was paramour to my old Lord of Hunsdon that was L. Chamberlain and was maintained in great pride... and it seems that being with child she was for colour married to a minstrel.[67]

Like his later interpreter Rowse, Forman's attention is given mostly to Lanyer's sexual activities and status, reflecting precisely the values given to women of which she complains in her poem to Margaret Clifford. When she visited him again on 3 June, he recorded:

> She was brought up in the country of Kent, and hath been married 4 years. The old Lord Chamberlain kept her longer. She was maintained in great pomp. She is high-minded. [She has] something in her mind she would have done for her. She hath 40 a year & was wealthy to him that married her in money and jewels. She can hardly keep secret. She was very brave in youth. She hath many false conceptions. She has a son, Henry.[68]

For Forman, Lanyer represented the figure of the sexually disorderly woman; she was not only the paramour of an elderly nobleman, married for colour, and loose with her tongue, but also extravagant in speech and with money, not able to enclose herself within the restraints of the doctrine of chastity. Having invented this figure, having 'penetrated' her secrets, Forman represented her to himself as sexually available to him, attempting to persuade her to have sex with him on a number of occasions and growing increasingly aggrieved when she refused.⁶⁹ Yet although Forman sees Lanyer in highly sexual terms, those critics who have echoed his view betray inattention to the content of his comments on her; for example, he writes that

> the present [i.e. Forman] sent his servant by who she sent word that if his master came he should be welcome, and he went and supped with her and stayed all night, and she was familiar and friendly with him in all things. But only she would not halek [Forman's code for penetrative sex]. Yet he told all parts of her body willingly and kissed her often but she would not do in any wise.⁷⁰

Plainly, Forman failed to seduce Aemilia Lanyer, and the notion of her uncontrolled sexuality is therefore his own fantasy.

The musician to whom she was married 'for colour' was Alfonso Lanyer, and the marriage was recorded on 18 October 1592. Alfonso Lanyer was initially a client of the Earl of Southampton, one of Shakespeare's patrons, and also served in Ireland and under the Lord Chancellor; he obtained a suit for the weighing of hay and straw about London, which he kept until his death. Alfonso Lanyer seems to have supported his wife's literary endeavours, since the Chapin Library copy of *Salve Deus Rex Judaeorum* is inscribed on the title-page 'The gift of Mr Alfonso Lanyer 8 No[vember] 1610/ Tho. Jones.'⁷¹ Thomas Jones was at that time Lord Chancellor of Ireland and Archbishop of Dublin. However, Forman reports that he spent her revenue, and Lanyer in a later court deposition claimed that he had spent 'a great part of her estate in the service of the late Queen in her wars of Ireland and other places'.⁷² She may have been wealthy to him, but it seems he dissipated her wealth, since after Alfonso Lanyer's death, Aemilia Lanyer seems to have opened a school 'for educating noblemen and gentlemen's children of great worth' at some point before 1617. The project became financially difficult, and Lanyer was forced to sue her landlord for repairs in 1617 and again in 1619; it is in one of these suits that she claims her husband squandered her inheritance.

Like Elizabeth Cary, Lanyer was disadvantaged by the marriage laws which meant that it was difficult for a wife to control property. Later she made repeated applications for her husband's licence for the weighing of hay, between 1635 and 1638, but did not get it.[73] She was buried at Clerkenwell on 3 April 1645. According to Rowse, she was described as a pensioner in the burial records, so it may be that her writings or other activities eventually gained her an income.[74]

Feminist approaches to *Salve Deus Rex Judaeorum* have been enthusiastic about parts of the poem while embarrassed about other parts. There has been a tendency, fostered by anthologies, to take the defence of Eve out of its difficult context and to present it alone as a piece of protofeminist rhetoric, while ignoring the patronage encomia at the beginning of the volume.[75] Comments on these have tended to focus on their interest in women patrons on the one hand and on their 'embarrassing' aspects on the other. From the carefully-planned and organised presentation copies of *Salve Deus*, it is clear that Lanyer was hoping to gain immediate financial rewards, as well as attracting a patron willing to see her as a permanent client.[76] However, there is no special reason to find this embarrassing; one might wish to argue instead that Lanyer is beginning to work on and within the image of the professional author, an image evolving in literary culture at the time she wrote, and that her project is an attempt to reshape that emerging role as a woman writer.[77] Feminist embarrassment springs in part from a general anxiety about patronage poetry, which cuts across (anachronistic) ideals of the Romantic artist, but also from an unwillingness to accept that the praise of noblewomen from whom one might expect a monetary reward is compatible with what women academics have wished to call a feminist stance.[78] This mistaken sense of incompatibility stems from a partial and ahistorical apprehension of the rhetoric of defences of women in the seventeenth century and before; such defences were often predicated on the construction of lists or catalogues of famous women and their virtues as exempla of a more general female virtue. What Lanyer does is to combine these catalogues with the rhetoric of patronage in which the patron-figure exceeds all historical or legendary figures, so becoming in a defence of women a new and spectacular exemplum of female virtue. One of the most innovative aspects of Lanyer's work is its generic and discursive experimentation; far from being an incoherent ragbag, *Salve Deus Rex Judaeorum* is a carefully-structured and organised attempt to put together the discourses of patronage, encomium, religious verse, defences of women, and the evocation of nature in a new way to create a new means of praising women and a new system of interpretation.

Feminist readings of Lanyer have been aided by the work of Lorna Hutson, whose essay on Lanyer shows how our expectations about what counts as truthful poetry are shaped by Shakespeare to an extent which makes Lanyer difficult for us to read.[79] Hutson shows how even feminist critics have been puzzled by the protocols of *Salve Deus*, taking refuge in equating its 'interested' pleas for patronage with the dark secrets of Lanyer's private life. Whore of her tongue equals whore of her body; Forman too makes this connection, since for him Lanyer cannot keep a secret as well as having a dubious sexual reputation. In fact, as Hutson shows, the innovative structure of *Salve Deus* represents a woman writer's hesitant approach to resolving the difficulties with which humanist discourses on virtue confront the woman writer. The poem is 'about' trying to find an appropriate way to counter the display of woman as a disclosed scandal (as Forman himself displays Lanyer) while praising a female virtue which cannot simply be equated with chastity, a female virtue envisaged as an interpretive procedure which allows women in particular to arrive at spiritual truth. Read as a rhetorical project of considerable complexity, Lanyer's poem can be seen not as a desperate attempt to link patronage to religion, but as a series of stories about the protocols of interpretation and reading. Just as Jesus's accusers misread him, whereas the women of Jerusalem interpret him correctly, so Lanyer struggles to find a way in which female virtue can be written and read without misinterpretation, or as she puts it, without scandal and rumour.

One of Lanyer's key strategies is to assemble a group of virtuous women, an interpretive community of female virtue who can give affirmation to her work and enter into a productive relation with the figure of the suffering and crucified Christ, also a feminised if not a feminine figure in Lanyer's hands. This interpretive community assembles the leading women patrons of the early seventeenth century, from Queen Anne of Denmark and her daughter Elizabeth of Bohemia to literary figures like Lucy Countess of Bedford, and Mary Sidney Countess of Pembroke.[80] This is not, or not solely, an attempt to get a dedication fee from each woman; it is also a way of bringing together the power of women as readers in order to register and display that power. The poem's principal dedicatee, however, is Margaret Clifford, Dowager Countess of Cumberland, and it is her skills in reading and decoding which form the real subject of the poem. The Countess is asked to embark on a kind of interpretive journey of learning in order to reach the point where she, like the women of Jerusalem, can read the crucifixion correctly. This is made possible both by Lanyer's correct interpretation of the Countess's virtues, and by the Countess's interpretation of Lanyer's poem. In order to read the poem correctly, the Countess is asked to perceive its virtue through a deceptive net of mortal frailties and disguises, and thus to perfect it. In this the Countess is to emulate the women of Jerusalem, who are able to see and understand the virtue of Christ despite his self-presentation as a poor criminal.

Lanyer thus compares her writing and herself with the figure of the persecuted, suffering Christ. Her poem, like Christ, is a virtue hidden in apparent inadequacy, a virtue which can only be revealed by the skilful reader. But the figure of the poet/ writer in Lanyer also resembles Christ. For while the women of Jerusalem are able to read Christ's virtue and reflect it, the men who condemn him fail in perception, seeing only vice and thus reflecting vice. This recalls Lanyer's remarks about scandal in her poem to Lady Anne Clifford: she writes that 'this poor work of mine shall be defended/ From any scandal that the world can frame.'

By reading the poem correctly, Clifford will be able to defend it from the world's scandal, a scandal to which Lanyer refers again in her introductory encomium to Margaret Clifford, condemning those 'who with their tongues the righteous souls do slay':

> As venomous as serpents is their breath,
> With poisoned lies to hurt in what they may
> The innocent: who as a dove shall fly
> Unto the lord, that he his cause may try.

The final masculine pronouns connect abstract lines on the evils of slander as misinterpretation with the figure of Christ, also misinterpreted by his accusers, but read correctly by virtuous women. This move, which lies at the centre of the section concerning Christ's passion, has the effect of feminising Christ's victimisation in a new way. Rather than having simple recourse to the images of Christ as mother, Lanyer comes close to representing him as a figure feminised because scandalised and held up – literally – to public opprobrium.[81]

In this context, Lanyer's justly celebrated landscape poem 'To Cookeham' becomes a final act of interpretation which attempts to reconcile and bring together the previous workings-out of the tangled questions she has raised earlier. Just as the women of Jerusalem's correct reading of Christ is their virtue, so the landscape's reading of the Clifford women is its virtue and ultimately theirs, since its virtue derives from them. This ingenious conceit, unprecedented in English poetry, prefigures the development of the country-house poem as a means of representing the interaction between virtuous reading and virtuous writing.[82] Often read in isolation, 'To Cookeham' makes sense in the light of the interpretive procedures sketched by Lanyer in the remainder of the volume.

It is characteristic of Lanyer that the final note in the volume offers the poem itself as her interpretation of a dream in which the words *'salve deus rex judaeorum'* feature prominently. Yet she does not figure her work as a direct response to a command from God, but as the beginning of a process of exegesis which the poem takes up, a moment when she begins to inscribe for herself a place, however equivocal, in Renaissance discourses of desire, religion and patronage.

Like her contemporary, Elizabeth Cary too wrestles with the difficulties of speech, silence and virtue, and with the problem of public virtue versus private life in relation to gendered discourses of scandal. In addressing and marking these issues of female subjectivity, both women begin the long task – still ongoing – of creating a space for the female subject in English literature. For both women, to be Renaissance women writers was to be involved in a culture in which their place was always already contested and contradictory. The accounts given here of the lives and works of both women, together with the works themselves, begin to answer the question of what it meant to be a 'Renaissance woman'. Both Cary and Lanyer were at once products of their culture and excluded from it; both struggled to make a space for their own writings within the contradictory position they occupied.

Both women were part of a patronage network which involved many other women writers and readers; both were empowered and constrained by the generic structures, rhetorics and discourses of Renaissance literature; both were writing through and about religion and the religious controversies of the day; both were influenced by the Sidney circle and both had connections with it; both were also influenced by the writings of the male writers who were their contemporaries.[83] Yet these contexts, though shared, operated differently on the two women, making generalisations about what it means to be a Renaissance woman writer look less simple. Though both were involved in patronage, Cary was largely a patron and Lanyer a client; they are connected by the stellar name of Mary Sidney, Countess of Pembroke, with whom Elizabeth Cary shared the dedication of a poem by John Davies, but to whom Lanyer addressed a patronage poem. Though both were caught up in religious issues, Lanyer was a militant Protestant, anxious to obliterate her father's Jewish ancestry from her public identity, while Cary began her literary life as a Protestant, but through her conversion to Catholicism was expelled from the literary system. Above all, the two women are divided by class, a form of division between women on which Lanyer comments herself, with bitterness. The different ways the two women were treated when in need of money illustrates that both inhabited the same patriarchal system in which property accrued to men, but also illustrates their class difference. Although Elizabeth Cary may well have needed money after her husband had violently repudiated her conversion to Catholicism, she could call on powerful supporters at court to press her claims for an income from him; these supporters were in turn motivated by a wish not to see a noblewoman starving. Lanyer, made a widow, complained that her husband had impoverished her, and could not even obtain rights to her husband's licence for hay. Although she died a pensioner, we do not know whether this was the result of her literary efforts.

Despite differences of class, religion and perhaps education, both women shared the difficulties of being a woman within the class system, and both had firsthand experience of the equivocal position women occupied within the structure of social identity. Both had to struggle to establish some right to an income independent of married life; Cary had to fight for an income from Henry Cary after her separation from him, and Lanyer made repeated applications for Alfonso Lanyer's licence to weigh hay after his death in 1613. As well, both women are concerned in their works with the place of women in society and women's dis-placement from subjectivity and control over language. In both *The Tragedy of Mariam* and *Edward II*, Elizabeth Cary investigates the place of queens connected with husbands whose behaviour revolts the women's consciences; in this way, she explores the questions of wifely obedience, wifely identity and wifely dissent. Lanyer's interrogation of the way in which rhetoric interprets woman as a scandal to be disclosed arises from a concern with the significance of female reputation, and results in a new way of representing an interpretive community of virtuous women. Both women published, made public their writings, though in neither case do we know how this came about, or how far the decision to publish was their own choice.

To publish is to offer a work to the public, to make it available, to move your name and your writing across a crucial dividing line; the line between public and private, a division increasingly gendered in the seventeenth century.[84] By becoming public, by appealing to the public, both women were moving out of that private sphere designated feminine; they sent their books out of the domestic and into the republic of letters, where they might form connections, have effects, trace or create relations which might go beyond the spaces of family and kinship designated proper to women. Publication could also designate a wish to influence the other public realms of politics and religion, but women's capacity to inspire virtue was supposed to be limited to the domestic sphere of piety.

In these ways, publication itself denoted participation in the Renaissance, in the sense that by publishing their work both women included themselves in the literary system and the world of letters.[85] But publication also signified women's exclusion from these realms by its very transgressiveness. When Lady Mary Wroth published her *Countess of Mountgomeries Urania* in 1621, she was attacked by Edward Denny, Baron of Waltham, who was convinced that one of *Urania*'s many plotlines was a slander upon himself and his family. Denny's attack stigmatized Wroth as 'hermaphrodite in show, in deed a monster/ As by thy words and works all men may conster', and he tells her to 'leave idle books alone/For wise and worthier women have writ none'.[86] The terms of Denny's attack suggest the gendered and sexualized impropriety of publication for women. At the same time, Denny also urges Wroth to produce a large volume of religious poetry, like that of her aunt Mary Sidney, thus implying that some forms of literary activity were deemed appropriate for women.

The lives and works of both the women represented here illustrate the difficulties and diffidences which beset women writers in such a culture, but also illustrate the way women could begin to prise open the contradictions and ambiguities of that culture in order to make a space within it for themselves. That space, soon to be refigured and reoccupied by women as diverse as Anna Trapnel, Aphra Behn, and Mary Astell, was first broached by women whose place within it was always uneasy, and who reaped little reward, pecuniary or otherwise, for their courageous endeavours. In restoring their works to the public sphere of letters which they occupied so uncomfortably, they may continue to unsettle fixed and simplistic notions of what counts as 'the Renaissance'.

NOTES

[1] Joan Kelly, 'Did Women Have A Renaissance?' in *Women, History and Theory: The Essays of Joan Kelly*, Chicago: Chicago University Press, 1984, 1st published 1977, pp. 19–50.

[2] For a recent attempt to address the question of what 'the Renaissance' was, see David Norbrook's preface in *The Penguin Book of Renaissance Verse*, ed. David Norbrook and H. R. Woudhuysen, Harmondsworth: Penguin, 1992, pp. xxi–xxvi, and his introduction to the same volume, pp. 1–12.

[3] The following account of Cary's life draws on these primary sources: Mary Cary's *The Lady Falkland: Her Life, From an MS in the Imperial Archive at Lille*, ed. R[ichard] S[impson], London: Catholic Publishing and Bookselling Company, 1861, hereafter called *Life* in text; Calendar of State Papers Domestic 1627–8, p. 109. CSPD Ireland 1625–32, pp. 279, 344–5, 354; CSPD 1634–5 pp. 159–60; 1635–6, pp. 431–2, 444, 451–2. The biographies of Cary I have consulted lean heavily on her daughter's *Life*; Kenneth P. Murdock, *The Sun At Noon: Three Biographical Sketches*, New York: Macmillan, 1939, esp. pp. 1–38; Georgiana Fullerton, *The Life of Elisabeth Lady Falkland, 1585–1639*, London: Burns and Oates, 1883. I have also used two biographies of Cary's eldest son Lucius: J. A. Marriot, *The Life and Times of Lucius Cary, Viscount Falkland*, London: Methuen, 1908; and Kurt Weber, *Lucius Cary, Second Viscount Falkland*, New York: Columbia University Press, 1940.

[4] See n. 3 above. For the literary value of the *Life*, see Isobel Grundy, 'Women's history? Writings by English nuns' in *Women/Writing/History*, ed. Isobel Grundy and Susan Wiseman, London: Batsford, 1992. Patrick Cary, the author's brother, went through the *Life* erasing passages which he considered 'too feminine'; these included a passage where Cary is said to be always 'either with child or giving suck' (*Life*, p. 15).

[5] For these codes, see Marie Rowlands, 'Recusant Women, 1560–1640' in *Women in English Society 1500–1800*, ed. Mary Prior, London: Methuen, 1985,

149–80. See also *Life of Mrs Dorothy Lawson of St Antony's Near Newcastle on Tyne*, ed. W. Palmes, 1851; *Philip Howard, Earl of Arundel and Anne Dacre his wife*, London, 1857; A. C. Southern, *An Elizabethan Recusant House*, 1950; M. Norman, 'Dame Gertrude More and the English Mystical Tradition', *Recusant History*, 13, 1975–6, p. 196.
[6] Grundy, 'Women's history?'.
[7] *Life*, p. 11.
[8] *Portrait of a Lady in Masque Dress, Said to be Lady Tanfield*, Tate Gallery.
[9] I am indebted to the rector of Burford Parish Church for this information.
[10] *Life*, pp. 5–6.
[11] Michael Drayton, *Englands Heroicall Epistles* (1597) in *The Works of Michael Drayton*, eds. J. W. Hebel, K. Tillotson and B. Newdigate, 5 vols, corrected, Oxford: Oxford University Press, 1961, v. 123–4.
[12] The MS of *Miroir du Monde* is normally kept at Burford, but is on loan to the Bodleian; for Seneca, see *Life*, p. 4.
[13] For an account of the marriage in Renaissance context, see Margaret W. Ferguson, 'Running on With Almost Public Voice: The Case of "E. C."' in *Tradition and the Talents of Women*, ed. Florence Howe, Urbana and Chicago: University of Illinois Press, 1991, 37–67.
[14] *The Muses Sacrifice or Divine Meditations*, London: Norton, 1612, sig. 2Rff.
[15] On Lucy, Countess of Bedford, see Barbara K. Lewalski, 'Lucy, Countess of Bedford: Images of a Jacobean Courtier and Patroness' in *Politics of Discourse: The Literature and History of Seventeenth-Century England*, ed. Kevin Sharpe and Steven Zwicker, Berkeley: University of California Press, 1987, 52–77; see also notes on Lanyer's poem to her in this volume.
[16] David Bergeron, 'Women as Patrons of English Renaissance Drama' in *Patronage in the Renaissance*, ed. Guy Fitch Lytle and Stephen Orgel, Princeton: Princeton University Press, 1981; Margaret Patterson Hannay, *Philip's Phoenix: Mary Sidney, Countess of Pembroke*, New York and Oxford: Oxford University Press, 1991. See also the note on Mary Sidney appended to Lanyer's poem to her in this volume.
[17] Lorna Hutson, 'Why the Lady's Eyes are Nothing Like the Sun' in *Women, Texts and Histories 1558–1760*, eds. Clare Brant and Diane Purkiss, London and New York: Routledge, 1992, 13–38.
[18] A conceit repeated by Aemilia Lanyer in her praise of Mary Sidney; see her poem in this volume, p. 251.
[19] On this aspect of the humanist project, see Victoria Kahn, *Rhetoric, Prudence and Scepticism in the Renaissance*, Ithaca: Cornell University Press, 1985, and Lorna Hutson, *Thomas Nashe in Context*, Oxford: Clarendon, 1989.
[20] Ferguson, pp. 44–5; see also 'The Spectre of Resistance: *The Tragedy of Mariam*' in *Staging the Renaissance*, ed. Peter Stallybrass and David Scott Kastan, London and New York: Routledge, 1992, 235–50.
[21] *Englands Helicon or the Muses Harmony*, printed for Richard More, 1614. The poem is signed 'Your honours ever to command Richard More'.
[22] Richard Belling, *Sixth Booke to the Countesse of Pembrokes Arcadia*, Dublin, 1624.
[23] *Life*, p. 11; Cary's children were Catherine, b. 1609, d. 1626 (in childbirth); Lucius, b. 1610; Lorenzo, b. 1613; Anne, b. 1614, professed as a nun 1639;

Edward, b. 1615?, d. 1616; Elizabeth, b. 1617, professed as a nun 1638; Lucy, b. 1619, professed 1638; Victoria, b. 1620; Mary, b. 1622, professed as a nun 1638; Patrick, b. 1624; Henry, b. 1625, professed as Father Placidus. On the dramatic effects of pregnancy and childbirth in early modern England see Patricia Crawford, 'The construction and experience of maternity in seventeenth-century England', in *Women as Mothers in pre-industrial England: essays in memory of Dorothy McLaren*, ed. Valerie Fildes, London and New York: Routledge, 1989, 3–38, and Linda A. Pollock, 'Embarking on a rough passage: the experience of pregnancy in early modern society', in Fildes, pp. 39–67.

[24] It may be significant that Cary's son born in Ireland was given the very Irish name of Patrick.

[25] Susan Feilding, first Countess of Denbigh, eventually became a Catholic while in exile with Henrietta Maria in Paris in 1651, after the Civil War. Richard Crashaw directed a poem to her, urging her to convert; see his *Carmen Deo Nostro, te decet hymnus*, Paris 1652, sigs. a3V–4R.

[26] On this see Peter Lake, 'Anti-Popery: The Structure of a Prejudice', in *Conflict in Early Stuart England*, ed. Richard Cust and Ann Hughes, London: Longman, 1989, 72–106. On Catholicism in this period, see William Raleigh Trimble, *The Catholic Laity in Elizabethan England*, Cambridge, Mass: Bellknap Press, 1964; Christopher Haigh, 'The Continuity of Catholicism in the English Reformation', *Past and Present*, 93, 1981, 37–69; John Bossy, *The English Catholic Community 1570–1850*, London: Darton, Longman and Todd, 1975.

[27] See for example Sandra K. Fischer, 'Elizabeth Cary and Tyranny, Domestic and Religious', in *Silent But For the Word: Tudor Women as Patrons, Translators and Writers of Religious Works*, ed. Margaret Patterson Hannay, Kent, Ohio: Kent State University Press, 1985, 225–37

[28] On this controversy see Rowlands, and Ferguson, 'Running On'.

[29] For Elizabeth Symondes Tanfield's severe response to her daughter's conversion, see her letter to Elizabeth Cary in *CSPD* Charles I, May 6 1627.

[30] Several of Cary's and Henry Cary's letters are reprinted in the Calendars of State Papers; see Calendar of State Papers Domestic 1627–8, p. 109; CSPD Ireland 1625–32, pp. 279, 344–5, 354; CSPD 1634–5 pp. 159–60; 1635–6, pp. 431–2, 444, 451–2.

[31] *The Workes of Mr J Marston*, London, 1633

[32] Marston may have removed his name from the title-page because of the printer's dedication to Cary and/or attack on Prynne; he was by that time an Anglican cleric.

[33] *The replye of the Most Illustrious Cardinall of Perron, to the... King of Great Britaine* (Jacques Davy du Perron), Douay: Martin Bogart, 1630. Dedicated to Henrietta Maria. 'Allegedly' because so many copies of it survive, making it less likely to have been called in immediately. I'm grateful to Danielle Clarke for informing me about her research on Cary's translation of Du Perron, which argues for strong links between the politics of that work and those of *Edward*.

[34] For the authorship of *Mariam*, see W. W. Greg; Lady Mary Wroth's pastoral tragicomedy, 'Loves Victorie', circulated in manuscript after 1621.

[35] *The Tragedie of Mariam, The Faire Queene of Jewry*, London; Thomas Creede

for Richard Hawkins, 1613. STC 4613. The Harvard and Huntington copies contain a dedicatory sonnet on A1R (to Cary's sister-in-law Elizabeth Cary) and a list of speakers on A1V, removed in the other issue. The Argument is on A2R–V, and the text begins on A3R. There are at least 15 instances of the second issue in which A1 is removed; one of the Bodleian copies contains a stub of A1. There has been one edition this century: *The Tragedie of Mariam*, 1613, ed. A. C Dunstan, W. W. Greg, Oxford: Oxford University Press, 1914, reissued as *The Tragedy of Mariam, 1613*, ed. A. C. Dunstan and W. W. Greg, with a supplement by Marta Straznicki and Richard Rowland, Oxford and New York: Oxford University Press, 1992.

[36] 'Thou makst Melpomen proud, and my Heart great/ of such a pupil, who, in Buskin fine,/ With Feet of State, dost make thy Muse to mete/ The scenes of Syracuse and Palestine'.

[37] *The Tragedie of Mariam*, ed. A. C. Dunstan; W. W. Greg, *A Bibliography of English Printed Drama to the Restoration*, 4 vols, (London; 1939–58), i. 449 (item 308).

[38] 'My first was consecrated to *Apollo*'; this work may be the lost tragedy of *Tamburlaine* mentioned in the *Life*, or the missing tragedy set in Syracuse to which Davies refers.

[39] Mary Sidney, Countess of Pembroke, *Antonie*, 1592, edited as *The Countess of Pembroke's Antonie*, Literarhistorische Forschungen, 1987; this usage of the term Senecan provokes confusion with the term's application to the blood and thunder plays of earlier years, notably Shakespeare's *Titus Andronicus*. Here it refers to drama which takes up Stoic themes of withdrawal from the world of active life to contemplation, and interrogates the practices of active life.

[40] It has been suggested by Marta Straznicki and Richard Rowland in their reissue of Dunstan's edition that the first soliloquy of Mariam seems indebted to Montaigne, *Essays* 1. 37.

[41] Thomas Lodge, (trans.) *The Famous and Memorable Works of Josephus*, 1602.

[42] For a survey of tragedies on Herod, see Rebecca W. Bushnell, *Tragedies of Tyrants: Political Thought and Theatre in the English Renaissance*, Ithaca: Cornell University Press, 1990. See also Maurice J. Valency, *The Tragedies of Herod and Mariamne*, New York: AMS Press, 1966, 1st pub. 1940.

[43] 'What she thought was required in this she expressed in this motto (which she caused to be inscribed in her daughter's wedding-ring) *Be and Seem*'. *Life*, p. 16.

[44] On the play as an exploration of the impossibility of female subjectivity, see Catherine Belsey, *The Subject of Tragedy*, London: Methuen, 1983.

[45] On this common equation in the Renaissance, see Lisa Jardine, *Still Harping on Daughters: Women and Drama in the Age of Shakespeare*, Brighton: Harvester, 1983.

[46] On the contrast between the two women see also Ferguson, in 'The Spectre of Resistance'.

[47] Cary introduces a series of parallels with Christ's death not present in Josephus; the butler who betrayed her hangs himself, like Judas, and Mariam is compared to a phoenix, a common type of Christ. Elaine V. Beilin, *Redeeming Eve: Women Writers of the English Renaissance*, Princeton: Princeton University Press, 1987.

[48] Ferguson, 'Spectre', p. 245.
[49] Donald Stauffer, 'A Deep and Sad Passion' in *The Parrot Presentation Volume*, ed. Hardin Craig, London, 1935; Betty Travitsky, *The Paradise of Women*, New York: Columbia University Press, 1989; Tina Krontiris, 'Style and Gender in Elizabeth Cary's *Edward II*' in *The Renaissance Englishwoman In Print: Counter-balancing the Canon*, ed. Anne Haselkorn and Betty Travitsky, Amherst: Massachussetts University Press, 1990, and *Oppositional Voices: Women as Writers and Translators of Literature in the English Renaissance*, London: Routledge, 1992. Barbara Lewalski discusses the attribution of *Edward II* in detail in her *Writing Women in Jacobean England*, Cambridge, Mass.: Harvard University Press, 1993, Appendix A, pp. 317–20. I regret that this book arrived too late for me to take its arguments into account, but Lewalski's conclusions are broadly similar to my own.
[50] Beilin, *Redeeming Eve*.
[51] D. R. Woolf, 'The True Date and Authorship of Henry, Viscount Falkland's History of the Life, Reign and Death of Edward II', *Bodleian Library Record*, 12, 1988, 440–52.
[52] *Bodleian Library Record*, 13, October 1988, 82–3
[53] Stephanie Wright, unpublished paper delivered at Oxford Women Text and History Seminar 1992. I am very grateful to Stephanie Wright for permission to cite her important findings.
[54] Lady Mary Wroth, for example, hardly shies from violence in *Urania*, and indeed as Helen Hackett points out some scenes in *Urania* fetishise violence to an extent which makes them uncomfortable reading for many feminists; see Helen Hackett, '"Yet Tell Me Some Such Fiction": Lady Mary Wroth's *Urania* and the 'Femininity" of Romance' in Brant and Purkiss, pp. 57–8.
[55] Barbara Lewalski also mentions the pro-Catholic passages in *Edward*, remarking correctly that they are inconceivable from Henry Cary; Lewalski, *Writing Women*, p. 319.
[56] The Exclusion Crisis arose from the proposal to exclude James, Duke of York from the succession to the throne on the grounds that he was a Roman Catholic. For an introductory account, see J. R. Jones, *Country and Court: England 1658–1714*, London: Edward Arnold, 1978, chapter 10.
[57] Francis Hubert, *The Deplorable Life and Death of Edward the Second, King of England*, 1628; revised and corrected the following year as *The History of Edward the Second, surnamed Carnarvan, one of our English Kings, together with the fatal downfall of his two unfortunate favourites Gaveston and Spencer*, 1629. Hubert claimed that the first edition was printed surreptitiously; histories of previous reigns could be political dynamite in this period, as Annabel Patterson shows in *Censorship and Interpretation: The Conditions of Writing and Reading in Early Modern England*, Madison: University of Wisconsin Press, 1984. Because Hubert's work clearly influenced Cary, Woolf uses the date of these works to argue that *Edward* is a late forgery, but it may simply be that its date of completion is later than 1627, as I suggest. Michael Drayton also wrote a verse life of Piers Gaveston, *Piers Gaveston of Cornwall, His Life, Death and Fortune*, 1593. Given his connection with Cary, this may be significant as a general inspiration, though I have not found any exact parallels with Cary's *Edward*.
[58] This elegy is attributed to 'the countess of Faukand' in BM MS Egerton

2725. f. 60; in another MS version it was said to have been copied from a commemorative statue of Buckingham in Plymouth (BM MS Add. 18044 f. 81). The elegy seems to have been extremely well-known; at least half a dozen MS versions of it are extant, but only MS Egerton attributes it to Cary. The MS Egerton text reads in full: 'Reader, stand still and see, lo here I am,/ Who was of late the mighty Buckingham;/God gave to me my being and my breath;/ Two kings their favours, and a slave my death;/ Now for my fame I challenge, and not crave/ That thou believe two kings, before one slave.' There are evident similarities with the blank verse of *Mariam*, and with Cary's MS dedicatory poem to Henrietta in the Beinecke Library copy of Du Perron (reprinted in *Kissing the Rod: An Anthology of Seventeenth-Century Women's Verse*, ed. Germaine Greer et al., London: Virago, 1988, pp. 59–60); nonetheless the attribution does depend on one MS only.

[59] Like Cary, Katherine (Manners) Villiers, Duchess of Buckingham was a Catholic, though she agreed to conform to the Church of England and to keep her religion private when she married Buckingham. The Countess of Denbigh did not take the plunge until after Cary's death; see note 25.

[60] Cary was received into the Roman Catholic Church in November 1626, whereupon the king confined her to her rooms for six weeks while Anglican divines tried to reconvert her (*Life*, 29–30). Since Henry Cary had cut off her allowance, she had no food, fuel or money (*Life*, 31–3). In July 1627 he was still refusing her an allowance (Letter, *CSP* Ireland, p. 245)

[61] It seems clear that Cary used Holinshead's Chronicle: Raphael Holinshead, *The Laste Volume of the Chronicles of England Scotland and Ireland*, 1577; she may also have used Robert Fabyan, *Chronycle of England*, 1533, and John Stow, *The Annales*, 1615, as well as the poems by Hubert and Drayton, and perhaps Marlowe's play; Woolf suggests that Cary also used the anonymous *Vita et Mors Edwardi Secundi*, which like *Edward II* makes Gaveston an Italian.

[62] *The replye of the Most Illustrious Cardinall of Perron*. A prefatory poem claims that the translation only took one month.

[63] Krontiris, 'Style and Gender' and *Oppositional Voices*. Stephanie Wright's important forthcoming study of both texts of Edward provides a much more balanced account.

[64] For an account of debates about monarchic theory, see J. P. Sommerville, *Politics and Ideology in England 1603–1640*, London and New York: Longman, 1986.

[65] On Baptista Bassani and Lanyer's husband Alfonso Lanyer, see Roger Prior, 'Jewish Musicians at the Tudor Court', *Musical Quarterly*, 69, 1983, 253–65; H. C. de Lafontaine, *The King's Musick: A Transcript of Records Relating to Music and Musicians 1460–1700*, London: 1909.

[66] On Forman, see Keith Thomas, *Religion and the Decline of Magic*, Harmondsworth: Penguin, 1971, pp. 362–3, and for A. L. Rowse's use of his diaries *The Poems of Shakespeare's Dark Lady*, London: Cape, 1976, introduction. Rowse does assemble some useful information on Lanyer, though he puts it entirely to the service of his absurd theory about her connection with the *Sonnets* of Shakespeare; the evidence for the connection is nil. For refutations of Rowse's theory, see Stanley Schoenbaum, 'Shakespeare, Dr Forman and Dr Rowse' in *Shakespeare and Others*, London: Scholar, 1985, pp. 54–79, and also

in *Shakespeare News*, 23, May 1973, September 1973; *Shakespeare Quarterly* 25, 1974, 131–33.
[67] Bodleian Library MS Ashmole 226, entry for 17 May 1597. I have modernised the spelling and punctuation, in keeping with the texts in this edition. Lord Hunsdon was Lord Chamberlain, briefly patron of Shakespeare's acting company.
[68] Bodleian Library MS Ashmole 226, entry for 3 June 1597. Rowse mistranscribes this entry as 'brown in youth'. Lanyer's son Henry may have been Lord Hunsdon's son; Forman said she had had many false conceptions, which may mean not miscarriage, but that she believed herself to be pregnant when she was not; this suggests irregular periods, and it may be that this was part of what she consulted Forman about; astrology could help to predict good moments for successful conception. It may be significant that Lanyer had a daughter, Odillya, who was baptized in 1598; she lived less than a year, and was buried at St Botolph's Church, Bishopgate in September 1599. See *The Parish Registers of St Margaret's Westminster 1539–1660*, ed. A. M. Burke, London: Eyre and Spottiswoode, 1914, p. 62, and *The Registers of St Botolph's Bishopgate*, trans. A. W. C. Hallam, 1889, 2 vols, vol I, p. 324. Her son Henry, who became a musician in the family tradition, had two children; he died in 1633 (*A True Register of All the Christenings, Mariages, and Burialls in the Parish of St James, Clerkenwell*, ed. R. Hovenden, 6 vols, London: 1884, vol. IV, p. 210).
[69] MS Ashmole 354, September 20 1597; see also entries for September 23, and his horoscope of Lanyer in MS Ashmole 236, f. 5.
[70] MS Ashmole 354, September 20 1597, f. 250.
[71] Chapin Library copy; MS inscription 'The guift of Mr Alfonso Lanyer 8 No: 1610/Tho: Jones'. I am grateful to the librarian at the Chapin Library for supplying me with this information, and with a full collation of this copy of *Salve Deus*.
[72] Rowse, p. 34.
[73] Calendar of State Papers Domestic, Charles I, February 19 1634–5, pp. 516–7.
[74] *A True Register of St James, Clerkenwell*, vol. IV, p. 263.
[75] See for example, Betty Travitsky, *The Paradise of Women: Writings by Englishwomen of the Renaissance*, New York: Columbia University Press, 1989.
[76] The presentation copies include the Chapin Library copy, which omits all dedications except those to the royal family, 'all virtuous ladies', the Countess of Cumberland, and the Countess of Dorset; the British Library copy, in which the dedications to Arabella Stuart and the countesses of Kent, Pembroke and Suffolk, and all but he last seven stanzas of the Dorset dedication are missing; the Dyce Collection copy at the Victoria and Albert, which omits dedications to Arabella Stuart, the Countess of Suffolk, the Countess of Pembroke and the Countess of Kent; this copy is bound in vellum with Prince Henry's emblem of ostrich-feathers, and may have been presented to him. The Bodleian copy omits 'To Cookeham'. Most critics have seen these omissions as political (note the frequency with which Arabella Stuart is dropped) but this can scarcely apply to the Countess of Pembroke; it may be that the motive was commercial rather than strictly political. All the presentation copies omit the feminist 'To the Virtuous Reader'.

[77] On the role of the writer, see Richard Helgerson, *Self-Crowned Laureates: Spenser, Jonson, Milton and the Literary System*, Berkeley: University of California Press, 1983, and John Guillory, *Poetic Authority: Spenser, Milton and Literary History*, New York: Columbia University Press, 1983.
[78] See my 'Material girls; The Seventeenth Century Woman Debate' in Brant and Purkiss, pp. 69–101.
[79] Lorna Hutson, 'Why the Lady's Eyes Are Nothing Like the Sun' in Brant and Purkiss, pp. 13–38. The reading I offer here is indebted to Hutson.
[80] Everyone who reads Lanyer is indebted to Barbara Lewalski's careful assemblage of evidence about these patrons in 'Of God and Good Women: The Poems of Aemilia Lanyer', in *Silent But For the Word*, ed. Margaret Patterson Hannay, Kent, Ohio: Kent State University Press, 1985, 203–24. Lewalski also gives an account of Lanyer in *Writing Women*, pp. 213–42.
[81] On medieval women's feminisations of the suffering Christ, see Caroline Walker Bynum, *Jesus as Mother: Studies in the Spirituality of the High Middle Ages*, Berkeley: University of California Press, 1982.
[82] Greer et al. suggest possible sources for 'To Cookeham' in Virgil's first eclogue, and in Veronica Franco's '*In Lode di Fumato*', p. 51. The notion of a landscape mourning for the loss of a resident is a staple of pastoral elegy, but figures even more in medieval love complaint, where winter and spring reflect the feelings of the singer; see for example Peter of Blois, '*Sevit aure spiritus*'. Lanyer could have known the trope from courtly songs. On the relation between Lanyer's poem and Ben Jonson's 'Penshurst', see Ann Baines Coiro, 'Writing in Service: Sexual Politics and Class Position in the Poetry of Aemilia Lanyer and Ben Jonson', *Criticism*, 35, 1993, 357–76. I regret that this article arrived too late for me to take its arguments into consideration, and I am grateful to Cedric Brown for pointing it out to me.
[83] On women patrons, see David Bergeron, 'Women as Patrons of English Renaissance Drama' in *Patronage in the Renaissance*, eds. Guy Fitch Lytle and Stephen Orgel, Princeton: Princeton University Press, 1981; on women and religion see Margaret Patterson Hannay, 'Introduction' in *Silent But For the Word: Tudor Women as Patrons, Translators and Writers of Religious Works*, ed. Margaret Patterson Hannay, Kent, Ohio: Kent State University Press, 1985; on the Sidney circle see Katherine Duncan Jones, *Sir Philip Sidney: Courtier Poet*, London: Hamish Hamilton, 1991.
[84] On this point, see Wendy Wall, 'Disclosures in print: the "violent enlargement" of the Renaissance voyeuristic text', *Studies in English Literature*, 29, 1989, 35–59.
[85] Circulation in MS was still considered more suitable by some, and not just for women; it may be relevant that Cary was addressed by Michael Drayton, a notable advocate of publication.
[86] See Hackett, pp. 47–8.

ACKNOWLEDGEMENTS

I would like to thank the following for their generous help during the preparation of this edition: the librarians of the Huntington Library, the Chapin Library, the Folger Shakespeare Library, the British and Bodleian Libraries, especially the manuscripts staff, the Victoria and Albert Museum Library, the National Portrait Gallery staff who kindly answered numerous enquiries about Elizabeth Cary and surviving portraits of her, and the equally patient and sagacious staff at the Courtauld Institute who tracked down the portrait which appears on the cover. Rosalind Ballaster, Clare Brant, Danielle Clarke, Lorna Hutson, Alison Shell, Stephanie Wright, and (as always) Ivan Dowling gave needed help and encouragement. I would also like to thank the general editor Janet Todd for her patience, and the publisher's editor Katherine Bright-Holmes for her help.

I first saw the likeness of Elizabeth Cary at Burford Church with my mother and father, Phillip and Fay Purkiss. This book is for them.

ELIZABETH CARY
SELECT BIBLIOGRAPHY

WORKS
Lost Works Mentioned in Life
Translation of Seneca's *Epistles*, Life of Tamberlaine, lives of female saints (St Agnes Martyr, St Elizabeth of Portugal, St Mary Magdalene).

MS
'Epitaph on the Duke of Buckingham', BL MS Egerton 2725, f. 60.
'The Mirror of the World', translation of Ortelius, *Miroir du Monde*, MS Burford Church, on loan to the Bodleian Library.

Original Printings
The History of the Life, Reign, and Death of Edward II...Written by E.F. in the Year 1627, and Printed Verbatim From the Original, London: J.C. for Charles Harper et al, 1680, folio, Wing F 313, attrib. to Henry Cary, 1st Viscount Falkland, BM.
The History of the Most Unfortunate Prince King Edward II. With Choice Political Observations on him and his Unhappy favourites, Gaveston and Spencer, London: A. G. and J. P., 1680, Wing F 314.
The Tragedie of Mariam, The Faire Queene of Jewry, London: Thomas Creede for Richard Hawkins, 1613, STC 4613.
The replye of the Most Illustrious Cardinall of Perron, to the... King of Great Britaine (Jacques Davy du Perron) Douay: Martin Bogart, 1630, STC 6385, dedicated to Henrietta Maria.

EDITIONS

The Tragedie of Mariam, 1613, eds A. C. Dunstan, W. W. Greg, Oxford: Oxford University Press, 1914.

The Tragedy of Mariam, 1613, eds A. C. Dunstan and W. W. Greg, supplement by Marta Straznicki and Richard Rowland, Oxford and New York: Oxford University Press, rept. 1992.

The History of the Most Unfortunate Prince, King Edward II, in *Harleian Miscellany*, 1808, rept. New York: AMS Press, 1965.

DEDICATIONS TO CARY BY OTHERS

Belling, Richard, *Sixth Booke to the Countesse of Pembrokes Arcadia*, Dublin, 1624.

Davies, Sir John, *The Muses Sacrifice or Divine Meditations*, London: Norton, 1612, sig. 2R.

Drayton, Michael, 'Englands Heroicall Epistles' (1597), *The Works of Michael Drayton*, eds J. W. Hebel, K. Tillotson and B. Newdigate, 5 vols, corrected, Oxford: Oxford University Press, 1961, v. pp. 123—4.

Marston, John, *The Workes of Mr J Marston*, London, 1633, Dedicatory letter to Cary.

Williams, Franklin B, *Index of Dedications and Commendatory Verses in English Books Before 1641*, London: Bibliographical Society, 1962.

BIOGRAPHY

Bossy, John, 'The English Catholic Community 1603—1625', *The Reign of James VI and I*, ed. A. G. R. Smith, London: 1973, pp. 91–106.

—— *The English Catholic Comunity 1570—1850*, London: Darton, Longman and Todd, 1975.

Calender of State Papers Domestic 1627–8, p. 109.

Calender of State Papers Domestic Ireland 1625–32, pp. 279, 344–5, 354.

Calender of State Papers Domestic 1634–5 pp. 159–60; 1635–6, pp. 431–2, 444, 451–2.

[Cary, Mary], ed. S[impson], R[ichard], *The Lady Falkland, Her Life from an MS in the Imperial Archives at Lisle*, London: Catholic Publishing and Bookselling, 1861.

Fullerton, Georgiana, *The Life of Elisabeth Lady Falkland, 1585–1639*, London: Burns and Oates, 1883.
Haigh, Christopher, 'The Continuity of Catholicism in the English Reformation', *Past and Present*, 93, 1981, pp. 37–69.
Hogrefe, Pearl, *Tudor Women: Queens and Commoners*, Ames: Iowa State University Press, 1975, p. 135.
Kennedy, Gwynne, 'Feminine Subjectivity and the English Renaissance: The Writings of Elizabeth Cary, Lady Falkland, and Lady Mary Wroth', PhD Diss., University of Pennsylvania.
Lake, Peter, 'Anti-Popery: The Structure of a Prejudice', in *Conflict in Early Stuart England*, eds Richard Cust and Ann Hughes, London: Longman, 1989, pp. 72–106.
Marriot, J. A., *The Life and Times of Lucius Cary, Viscount Falkland*, London: Methuen, 1908.
Murdock, Kenneth P, *The Sun At Noon: Three Biographical Sketches*, New York: Macmillan, 1939, esp. pp. 1–38.
Norman, M, 'Dame Gertrude More and the English Mystical Tradition', *Recusant History*, 13, 1975–6, p. 196.
Pearse, Nancy Cotton, 'Elizabeth Cary: Renaissance Playwright', *Texas Studies in Language and Literature*, 18, 1977, pp. 601–8.
Rowlands, Marie, 'Recusant Women, 1560–1640', *Women in English Society 1500–1800*, ed. Mary Prior, London: Methuen, 1985, pp. 149–80.
Shapiro, Arlene Iris, 'Elizabeth Cary: Her Life, Letters and Art', PhD Diss., SUNY-StonyBrook 1984.
Travitsky, Betty, *The Paradise of Women*, New York: Columbia University Press, 1989.
Weber, Kurt, *Lucius Cary, Second Viscount Falkland*, New York: Columbia Univeristy Press, 1940.

TEXTUAL SCHOLARSHIP

Greg, W. W., *A Bibliography of English Printed Drama to the Restoration*, 4 vols, (London: 1939–58), i, p. 449 (item 308).
Grundy, Isobel, *Bodleian Library Record*, 13, October 1988, pp. 82–3.
Krontiris, Tina, 'Style and Gender in Elizabeth Cary's *Edward II*',

The Renaissance Englishwoman In Print: Counterbalancing the Canon, eds Anne Haselkorn and Betty Travitsky, Amherst: Massachussetts University Press, 1990.

Lumley, Lady Joanna, *Iphigenia in Aulis*, ed. Harold Child, Malone Society Reprints, 1909.

Stauffer, Donald, 'A Deep and Sad Passion', *The Parrot Presentation Volume*, ed. Hardin Craig, 1935.

Woolf, D. R., 'The True Date and Authorship of Henry, Viscount Falkland's History of the Life, Reign and Death of Edward II', *Bodleian Library Record*, 12, 1988, pp. 440–52.

CRITICISM

Beilin, Elaine V., *Redeeming Eve: Women Writers of the English Renaissance*, Princeton: Princeton University Press, 1987.

Belsey, Catherine, *The Subject of Tragedy*, London: Methuen, 1983.

Bergeron, David, 'Women as Patrons of English Renaissance Drama', *Patronage in the Renaissance*, eds Guy Fitch Lytle and Stephen Orgel, Princeton: Princeton University Press, 1981.

Braden, Gordon, *Renaissance Tragedy and the Senecan Tradition*, New Haven: Yale University Press, 1985.

Bushnell, Rebecca W., *Tragedies of Tyrants: Political Thought and Theatre in the English Renaissance*, Ithaca: Cornell University Press, 1990.

Dunstan, A. C., *Examination of Two English Dramas: The Tragedie of Mariam by Elizabeth Cary and The True Tragedie of Herod and Antipater with the Death of Fair Mariam by Gervase Markham and William Sampson*, Konigsburg, Germany: Hartungsche Buchdruckerei, 1908.

Ferguson, Margaret W., 'A Room Not Their Own: Renaissance Women as Readers and Writers', *The Comparative Perspective on Literature*, eds Clayton Koelb and Susan Noakes, Ithaca: Cornell University Press, 1988, pp. 93–116.

—— 'Running on With Almost Public Voice: The Case of "E. C."', *Tradition and the Talents of Women*, ed. Florence Howe, Urbana and Chicago: University of Illinois Press, 1991, pp. 37–67.

Select Bibliography　　　　　　　　　　　　　　　　　　　　liii

— 'The Spectre of Resistance: *The Tragedy of Mariam*', *Staging the Renaissance*, eds. Peter Stallybrass and David Scott Kastan, London and New York: Routledge, 1992, pp. 235–50.

Fischer, Sandra K., 'Elizabeth Cary and Tyranny, Domestic and Religious', *Silent But For the Word: Tudor Women as Patrons, Translators and Writers of Religious Works*, ed. Margaret Patterson Hannay, Kent, Ohio: Kent State University Press, 1985, pp. 225–37.

Goreau, Angeline, 'Two English women in the seventeenth century: notes for an anatomy of female desire', *Western Sexuality: practice and precept in past and present times*, eds Philippe Aris and André Béjin, trans. Anthony Forster, Oxford: Blackwell, 1985, pp. 103–13.

Grundy, Isobel, 'Women's history? Writings by English nuns', *Women/Writing/History*, eds Isobel Grundy and Susan Wiseman, London: Batsford, 1992.

Gutierrez, Nancy A., 'Valuing Mariam: Genre study and feminist Analysis', *Texas Studies in Women's Literature*, forthcoming.

Hannay, Margaret Patterson, *Philip's Phoenix: Mary Sidney, Countess of Pembroke*, New York and Oxford: Oxford University Press, 1991.

Holdsworth, R. W. 'Middleton and the Tragedy of Mariam', *Notes and Queries*, 231, 1986, pp. 379–80.

Krontiris, Tina, 'Style and Gender in Elizabeth Cary's *Edward II*', *Renaissance Englishwomen in Print: Counterbalancing the Canon*, eds Anne M. Haselkorn and Betty S. Travitsky, Amherst: Massachusetts University Press, 1990.

— *Oppositional Voices: Women as Writers and Translators of Literature in the English Renaissance*, London: Routledge, 1992.

Lawson, Mildred Smoot, 'Elizabeth Tanfield Cary and *The Tragedie of Mariam*', *DAI* 45, 1985, 2886A.

Levin, Richard, 'A Possible Source for *A Fair Quarrell*', *Notes and Queries*, 228, 1983, pp. 152–3.

Lipking, Joanna, 'Fair Originals: Women Poets in Male Commendatory Poems', *ECLIfe*, 12, 1988, pp. 58–72.

Lunn, David, 'Elizabeth Cary, Lady Falkland (1586/7–1639)', *Royal Stuart Papers*, 11, 1977.

Shapiro, Arlene Iris, 'Elizabeth Cary: Her Life, Letters and Art', *DAI* 45 (1984), 1762A.

Sidney, Mary, Countess of Pembroke, *Antonie*, 1592, *The Countess of Pembroke's Antonie*, Literarhistorische Forschungen, 1987.

Travitsky, Betty, 'The *Feme Coverte* in Elizabeth Cary's *Mariam*', *Ambiguous Realities: Women in the Middle Ages and the Renaissance*, eds Carole Levin and Jeanie Watson, Detroit: Wayne State University Press, 1987, pp. 184–97.

Valency, Maurice J., *The Tragedies of Herod and Mariamne*, 1940, rept. New York: AMS Press, 1966.

AEMILIA LANYER
SELECT BIBLIOGRAPHY

WORKS

Texts

Salve Deus Rex Judaeorum, 1611, AT LONDON / Printed by Valentine Simmes for Richard Bonian and / are to be sold at his shop in Paules Church- / yard. Anno 1611, STC 15227, Huntington. First issue.

Salve Deus Rex Judaeorum, 1611, AT LONDON/ Printed by Valentine Simmes for Richard Bonian, and are / to be sold at his Shop in Paules Churchyard, at the / Signe of the Floure de Luce and / Crowne, 1611, STC 15227.5.

EDITIONS

Lanyer, Aemilia, *Salve Deus Rex Judaeorum*, 1611, ed. A. L. Rowse in *The Poems of Shakespeare's Dark Lady: Salve Deus Rex Judeorum by Emilia Lanyer*, London: Cape, 1976.

BIOGRAPHY AND PATRONS

MS Ashmole 226: *Simon Forman's Casebook*, entry for 17 May 1597, also June 3 and June 16 1597.

Ashton, Robert, *James I by His Contemporaries*, London: Hutchinson, 1969.

Bradley, E. T., *Life of the Lady Arbella Stuart*, London, 1889.

Byard, Margaret M, 'The Trade of Courtiership: The Countess of Bedford and the Bedford Memorials: A Family History from 1585 to 1607', *History Today*, January 1979, pp. 20–28.

Calender of State Papers Domestic James I August 23 1604, p. 146; November 23 1613, p. 210; November 22 1616, p. 407; Charles I February 19 1634–5, pp. 516–17.

Clifford, D. J. H., ed., *The Diaries of Lady Anne Clifford*, London: Alan Sutton, 1990.
De Lafontaine, H. C., *The King's Musick: A Transcript of Records Relating to Music and Musicians 1460–1700*, London: Dent, 1909.
Duncan-Jones, Katherine, *Sir Philip Sidney*, Oxford: Oxford University Press, 1991.
Hannay, Margaret Patterson, *Philip's Phoenix: Mary Sidney, Countess of Pembroke*, Oxford: Oxford University Press, 1990.
Lamb, Mary Ellen, 'The Countess of Pembroke's patronage', *English Literary Renaissance*, 12, 1982, pp. 162–79.
Lanyer, Aemilia, *Salve Deus Rex Judaeorum*, Chapin Library copy; MS inscription.
Lewalski, Barbara K. 'Lucy, Countess of Bedford: Images of a Jacobean Courtier and Patroness', *Politics of Discourse: The Literature and History of Seventeenth-Century England*, ed. Kevin Sharpe and Steven Zwicker, Berkeley: University of California Press, 1987, pp. 52–77.
Oman, Carola, *Elizabeth of Bohemia*, London: Hodder and Stoughton, 1938.
Prior, Roger, 'Jewish Musicians at the Tudor Court', *Musical Quarterly*, 69, 1983, pp. 253–65.
Rowse, A. L., *Simon Forman: Sex and Society in Shakespeare's Age*, London: Weidenfeld and Nicolson, 1974.
—— *The Poems of Shakespeare's Dark Lady: Salve Deus Rex Judeorum by Emilia Lanyer*, London: Cape, 1976.
Sackville-West, Vita, *The Diary of the Lady Anne Clifford*, London, 1923.
Schoenbaum, Stanley, 'Shakespeare, Dr Forman and Dr Rowse', *Shakespeare and Others*, London: Scholar, 1985, pp. 54–79.
Stationers Register 2 October 1610.
Steen, Sara Jayne, 'Fashioning an Acceptable Self: Arbella Stuart', *Women in the Renaissance: Selections from English Literary Renaissance*, eds Kirby Farrell, Elizabeth H. Hageman, and Arthur F. Kinney, Amherst: University of Massachusetts Press, 1990, pp. 136–53.
Thomson, Patricia, 'John Donne and the Countess of Bedford', *Modern Language Review*, 44, 1949, pp. 329–40.

Williams, Franklin B., *Index of Dedications and Commendatory Verses in English Books Before 1641*, London: Bibliographical Society, 1962.

Williamson, George C., *George, Third Earl of Cumberland 1558–1605: his Life and Voyages*, Cambridge: Cambridge University Press, 1920.

— *Lady Anne Clifford, Countess of Dorset, Pembroke and Montgomery*, Kendal: Titus Wilson and Son, 1922.

CRITICISM

Beilin, Elaine V., *Redeeming Eve: Women Writers of the English Renaissance*, Princeton: Princeton University Press, 1987.

Hutson, Lorna, 'Why the lady's eyes are nothing like the sun', *Women, Texts and Histories 1575–1760*, eds Clare Brant and Diane Purkiss, London and New York: Routledge, 1992.

Jones, Ann Rosalind, 'Assimilation with a Difference: Renaissance Women Poets and Literary Influence', *Yale French Studies*, 62, 1981, pp. 135–53.

— *The Currency of Eros; Women's Love Lyric 1520–1640*, Bloomington: Indiana University Press, 1991.

Krontiris, Tina, *Oppositional Voices; Women as Writers and Translators of Literature in the Renaissance*, London: Routledge, 1992.

Lewalski, Barbara K., 'Of God and Good Women: The Poems of Aemilia Lanyer', *Silent But For the Word*, ed. Margaret Patterson Hannay, Kent, Ohio: Kent State University Press, 1985, pp. 203–24.

— 'Rewriting Patriarchy and Patronage: Margaret Clifford, Anne Clifford and Aemilia Lanyer', *YES*, 21.

— 'The Lady of the Country House Poem', *The Fashioning and Functioning of the British Country House*, eds Gervase Jackson-Stops, Gordon J. Schochet, Lena Cowen Orlin and Elisabeth Blair McDougall, 1989, pp. 261–75.

Wright, Louis B., 'The Reading of Renaissance Englishwomen' *Studies in Philology*, 28, 1931, pp. 139–57.

GLOSSARY

Actaeon   Caught sight of the goddess Artemis/Diana bathing, and was punished by being turned into a stag by the angry goddess, and torn to pieces by his own hounds.
Aesop   Ancient Greek writer of animal fables.
Andrew   Saint and apostle, was said to be martyred by crucifixion.
Antonius   see Cleopatra
Argus   Hundred-eyed monster sent by Juno to guard Io from Jupiter.
Cleopatra   The last queen of Egypt, mistress of Julius Caesar and Mark Antony, she killed herself after Antony's death and Egypt's conquest by Rome. Lanyer's source may be North's translation of Plutarch, also used by Shakespeare.
Cynthia   Another name for the moon goddess, and the epithet by which Walter Ralegh addressed Elizabeth I in his poems.
Daphne   Nymph pursued by Apollo; to preserve her from rape she was turned into a laurel, and is a symbol of chastity.
Deborah   A prophetess who launched a military campaign to save Israel from the Canaanites, helped by Jael (q.v.). Deborah sings a praise-song to the Lord and thus may represent the woman writer.
Elysian fields, Elysium   The home in the afterlife of virtuous heroes in classical myth.
Ganymede   A beautiful boy kidnapped by Jove and made his cupbearer; hence a name for a gay partner.
Graces   Three daughters of Jupiter, often attendants on goddesses, the personifications of grace, beauty and pleasure in classical mythology.
Haman   see Hester

Glossary

Harpy   Mythical monster with the body of a bird of prey and the face of a woman, it defiled what it fed on.

Helen of Troy   The most beautiful woman in the world, wife of Menelaus of Sparta, her abduction by the Trojan prince Paris (q.v.) caused the Trojan war.

Hedalyan groves   Dwelling-place of the Graces.

Hester, or *Esther*   Saved the Israelites from Ahasuerus and his counsellor Haman by enchanting the king with her beauty; she became his queen, with the result that Haman was killed.

Holofernes   see Judith

Jael   Old Testament heroine. Killed the Canaanite general Sisera by driving a tent-peg through his head while he was asleep in her tent. See also Deborah.

Judith   Old Testament heroine who saved the city of Bethulia by devising a scheme to kill Holofernes, the Assyrian general who was besieging the town. Judith gained access to Holofernes by using her beauty and by pretending to be a deserter; when she was alone with him she got him drunk and cut his head off with a sword. In the Renaissance, a symbol of resistance to tyranny.

Lawrence, Saint   Martyr (AD 258), roasted on a gridiron. Famously remarked to his torturers; 'Turn me over, I'm done on this side'.

Lucrece   In Roman legend, the wife of Tarquinius Superbus, the ruler of Rome; hearing of her beauty and virtue, he visited her and, when he was unable to win her consent to adultery, raped her. She killed herself and her family wiped out the Tarquins, ending their tyranny.

Matilda   Virgin in legend ravished by King John.

Minerva   Roman goddess of wisdom and martial valour.

Morpheus   Greek god of sleep and dreams.

Octavia   Sister of Octavius, later Augustus Caesar, and wife of Mark Antony; deserted by him for Cleopatra.

Pallas   see Minerva

Paris   Son of Priam, king of Troy, he was asked to adjudicate in a quarrel between three powerful goddesses over which should receive the Apple of Discord, inscribed with the words, 'For the Fairest'. Minerva/Athene offered wisdom;

Juno/Hera offered power, but Paris chose Venus/Aphrodite, who offered him the most beautiful woman in the world: Helen of Troy. This began the Trojan War. The judgement of Paris was often moralised in the Renaissance as a choice between intellectual, political and sensual life.

Phaeton The son of Apollo, he begged to be allowed to drive the chariot of the sun, but failed to control the immortal horses, and scorched the earth in the confusion, finally falling to his death.

Phoebe Another name for the moon goddess Diana, and hence an epithet of Elizabeth I.

Phoebus Apollo the sun god.

Phoenix Mythic bird, the only one of its kind; it reproduces by immolating itself in a fire from which it is reborn.

Rosamund The mistress of Henry II. When his queen Eleanor of Aquitaine discovered the affair, she is said to have approached Rosamund and offered her the choice between a dagger and a cup of poison. Rosamund chose the poison.

Sheba, Queen of Legendary queen who visited Solomon, king of Israel, hoping to test his wisdom. Traditionally identified as the woman in the Song of Songs (Canticles), which Christian tradition reads as an allegory of Christ as the bridegroom of the church.

Stephen One of Christ's disciples and the first martyr, he was stoned to death.

Susanna The wife of a merchant, she was secretly desired by two elders who plotted to seduce her; she used to bathe in her garden, and the elders stationed themselves to watch her, springing on her as soon as she was alone, and telling her that if she did not agree to adultery with them they would tell everyone that they had caught her with another man. Susanna spurned their advances, and the men carried out their threat with the result that Susanna was condemned to death for adultery. Her innocence was proved by the young Daniel. Hence, like Lucrece, a symbol of married chastity, and of preferring death to dishonour.

Tarquin see Lucrece

Venus Roman goddess of love, sexuality and beauty.

THE TRAGEDY OF MARIAM, THE FAIR

Queen of Jewry
Written by that learned,
virtuous, and truly noble Lady,
E. C.

LONDON
Printed by Thomas Creede, for Richard
Hawkins, and are to be sold at his shop
in Chancery Lane, near unto
Sargeants Inn.
1613

TO DIANA'S EARTHLY DEPUTESS, AND MY WORTHY SISTER, MISTRESS ELIZABETH CARY[1]

When cheerful Phoebus his full course hath run,
His sister's fainter beams our hearts doth cheer:
So your fair brother is to me the sun,
And you his sister as my moon appear.

You are my next belov'd, my second friend, 5
For when my Phoebus' absence makes it night,
Whilst to th'Antipodes his beams do bend,
From you, my Phoebe, shines my second light.

He like to Sol, clear-sighted, constant, free,
You Luna-like, unspotted, chaste, divine; 10
He shone on Sicily, you destined be[2]
T'illumine the now obscured Palestine.
My first was consecrated to Apollo,
My second to Diana now shall follow.

E.C.

DRAMATIS PERSONAE[3]

Herod, King of Judaea.
Doris, his first wife.
Mariam, his second wife.
Salome, Herod's sister.
Antipater, his son by Salome.
Alexandra, Mariam's mother.
Silleus, Prince of Arabia, [lover of Salome].
Constabarus, husband to Salome.
Pheroras, Herod's brother.
Graphina, his love.
Babus first son.
Babus second son.
Ananell, the high priest.
Sohemus, a counsellor to Herod, [Mariam's guardian].
Nuntio [messenger].
Bu[*tler*], another messenger.
Silleus' man.
Soldier.
Chorus, a company of Jews.

THE ARGUMENT[4]

Herod the son of Antipater (an Idumean), having crept by the favour of the Romans into the Jewish monarchy, married Mariam, the granddaughter[5] of Hircanus, the rightful king and priest, and for her (besides her high blood, being of singular beauty) he repudiated Doris, his former wife, by whom he had children.[6]

This Mariam had a brother called Aristobolus, and next him and Hircanus his grandfather, Herod in his wife's right had the best title. Therefore to remove them, he charged the first with treason and put him to death, and drowned the second under colour of sport. Alexandra, daughter to the one, and mother to the other, accused him for their deaths before Antony.

So when he was forced to go answer this accusation at Rome, he left the custody of his wife to Josephus his uncle, that had married his sister Salome, and out of a violent affection (unwilling any should enjoy her after him) he gave strict and private commandment, that if he were slain, she should be put to death. But he returned with much honour, yet found his wife extremely discontented, to whom Josephus had (meaning it for the best, to prove Herod loved her) revealed his charge.

So by Salome's accusation he put Josephus to death, but was reconciled to Mariam, who still bore the death of her friends exceedingly hard.

In this meantime Herod was again necessarily to revisit Rome, for Caesar having overthrown Antony his great friend, was likely to make an alteration of his fortune.

In his absence, news came to Jerusalem that Caesar had put him to death; their willingness it should be so, together with the likelihood, gave this rumour so good credit, as Sohemus that

had succeeded Josephus' charge, succeeded him likewise in 30
revealing it. So at Herod's return, which was speedy and unexpected, he found Mariam so far from joy, that she showed apparent signs of sorrow. He still desiring to win her to a better humour, she being very unable to conceal her passion, fell to upbraiding him with her brother's death. As they were thus 35
debating, came in a fellow with a cup of wine, who, hired by Salome, said first it was a love potion, which Mariam desired to deliver to the king; but afterwards he affirmed that it was a poison and that Sohemus had told her somewhat, which procured the vehement hate in her. 40

The king hearing this, more moved with jealousy of Sohemus than with this intent of poison, sent her away, and presently after by the instigation of Salome, she was beheaded. Which rashness was afterwards punished in him, with an intolerable and almost frantic passion for her death. 45

ACT I, SCENE I

Mariam sola.

Mar.   How oft have I with public voice run on?
  To censure Rome's last hero for deceit
  Because he wept when Pompey's life was gone,
  Yet when he lived, he thought his name too great.
  But now I do recant, and Roman lord   5
  Excuse too rash a judgement in a woman:
  My sex pleads pardon, pardon then afford;
  Mistaking is with us but too too common.
  Now do I find by self experience taught
  One object yields both grief and joy:[7]   10
  You wept indeed, when on his worth you thought,
  But joyed that slaughter did your foe destroy.
  So at his death your eyes true drops did rain,
  Whom dead you did not wish alive again.
  When Herod lived, that now is done to death,   15
  Oft have I wished that I from him were free;
  Oft have I wished that he might lose his breath,
  Oft have I wished his carcase dead to see.
  Then rage and scorn had put my love to flight,
  That love which once on him was firmly set;   20
  Hate hid his true affection from my sight
  And kept my heart from paying him his debt.
  And blame me not, for Herod's jealousy
  Had power even constancy itself to change:
  For he by barring me from liberty,   25
  To shun my ranging, taught me first to range.
  But yet too chaste a scholar was my heart,
  To learn to love another than my lord;

To leave his love, my lesson's former part,
I quickly learned, the other I abhorred.   30
But now his death to memory doth call
The tender love that he to Mariam bore,
And mine to him; this makes those rivers fall,
Which by another thought unmoistened are.
For Aristobolus the loveliest[8] youth   35
That ever did in angel's shape appear
The cruel Herod was not moved to ruth,
Then why grieves Mariam Herod's death to hear?
Why joy I not the tongue no more shall speak,
That yielded forth my brother's latest doom?   40
Both youth and beauty might thy fury break
And both in him did ill befit a tomb.
And worthy grandsire ill did he requite,
His high assent alone by thee procured,
Except he murdered he to free the sprite   45
Which still he thought on earth too long immured.
How happy was it that Sohemus' mind[9]
Was moved to pity my distressed estate!
Might Herod's life a trusty servant find,
My death to his had been unseparate.   50
These thoughts have power, his death to make me bear,
Nay more, to wish the news may firmly hold,
Yet cannot this repulse some falling tear,
That will against my will some grief unfold.
And more I owe him for his love to me,   55
The deepest love that ever yet was seen,
Yet had I rather much a milk-maid be,
Than be the monarch of Judea's queen.
It was for nought but love he wished his end
Might to my death but the vaunt-courier[10] prove;   60
But I had rather still be foe than friend
To him that saves for hate, and kills for love.
Hard-hearted Mariam, at thy discontent
What floods of tears have drenched his manly face?
How canst thou then so faintly now lament   65

The Tragedy of Mariam

Thy truest lover's death, a death's disgrace?
Aye, now mine eyes you do begin to right
The wrongs of your admirer. And my lord,
Long since you should have put your smiles to flight,
Ill doth a widowed eye with joy accord. 70
Why now me thinks the love I bore him then,
When virgin freedom left me unrestrained,
Doth to my heart begin to creep again,
My passion now is far from being feigned.
But tears fly back, and hide you in your banks, 75
You must not be to Alexandra seen:
For if my moan be spied, but little thanks
Shall Mariam have from that incensed queen.

ACT I, SCENE II

[Enter] Alexandra.

Alex. What means these tears? My Mariam doth mistake,
    The news we heard did tell the tyrant's end; 80
    What weep'st thou for thy brother's murd'rer's[11] sake,
    Will ever wight a tear for Herod spend?
    My curse pursue his breathless trunk and spirit,
    Base Edomite the damned Esau's heir:
    Must he ere Jacob's child the crown inherit?[12] 85
    Must he, vile wretch, be set in David's chair?
    No, David's soul within the bosom placed
    Of our forefather Abram was ashamed
    To see his seat with such a toad disgraced,
    That seat that hath by Judah's race been famed.[13] 90
    Thou fatal enemy to royal blood,
    Did not the murder of my boy suffice
    To stop thy cruel mouth that gaping stood?
    But must thou dim the mild Hircanus' eyes,
    My gracious father, whose too ready hand 95
    Did lift this Idumaean from the dust,
    And he ungrateful caitiff did withstand

The man that did in him most friendly trust.
What kingdom's right could cruel Herod claim,
Was he not Esau's issue, heir of hell? 100
Then what succession can he have but shame?
Did not his ancestor his birth-right sell?
O yes, he doth from Edom's name derive
His cruel nature which with blood is fed,
That made him me of sire and son deprive; 105
He ever thirsts for blood, and blood is red.[14]
Weep'st thou because his love to thee was bent?
And read'st thou love in crimson characters?
Slew he thy friends to work thy heart's content?
No: hate may justly call that action hers. 110
He gave the sacred priesthood for thy sake
To Aristobolus. Yet doomed him dead
Before his back the ephod warm could make
And ere the mitre settled on his head.
Oh had he given my boy no less than right, 115
The double oil should to his forehead bring
A double honour, shining doubly bright,
His birth annointed him both priest and king.
And say my father, and my son he slew,
To royalize by right your prince-born breath: 120
Was love the cause, can Mariam deem it true,
That Herod[15] gave commandment for her death?
I know by fits he showed some signs of love,
And yet not love, but raging lunacy;
And this his hate to thee may justly prove, 125
That sure he hates Hircanus' family.
Who knows if he, unconstant wavering lord,
His love to Doris had renewed again?
And that he might his bed to her afford,
Perchance he wished that Mariam might be slain. 130
Mar.[16]   Doris – alas her time of love was past;[17]
Those coals were raked in embers long ago,
If Mariam's love and she was now disgraced,
Nor did I glory in her overthrow.

He not a whit his first-born son esteemed, 135
Because as well as his he was not mine:
My children only for his own he deemed,
These boys that did descend from royal line.
These did he style his heirs to David's throne;
My Alexander, if he live, shall sit 140
In the majestic seat of Solomon,
To will it so, did Herod think it fit.

Alex. Why? Who can claim from Alexander's brood
That gold-adorned lion-guarded chair?
Was Alexander not of David's blood? 145
And was not Mariam Alexander's heir?[18]
What more than right could Herod then bestow,
And who will think except for more than right:
He did not raise them, for they were not low,
But born to wear the crown in his despite. 150
Then send those tears away that are not sent
To thee by reason, but by passion's power;
Thine eyes to cheer, thy cheeks to smiles be bent,
And entertain with joy this happy hour.
Felicity, if when she comes she finds 155
A mourning habit and a cheerless look,
Will think she is not welcome to thy mind,
And so perchance her lodging will not brook.
Oh, keep her whilst thou hast her; if she go
She will not easily return again. 160
Full many a year have I endured in woe,
Yet still have sued her presence to obtain;
And did not I to her as presents send
A table, that best art did beautify
Of two, to whom heaven did best feature lend, 165
To woo her love by winning Antony.
For when a prince's favour we do crave,
We first their minions' loves do seek to win:
So I, that sought felicity to have,
Did with her minion Antony begin. 170
With double sleight[19] I sought to captivate

> The warlike lover, but I did not right:
> For if my gift had borne but half the rate,
> The Roman had been over-taken quite.
> But now he fared like a hungry guest, 175
> That to some plenteous festival is gone;
> Now this, now that, he deems to eat were best:
> Such choice doth make him let them all alone.
> The boy's large forehead first did fairest seem,
> Then glanced his eye upon my Mariam's cheek, 180
> And that without comparison did deem,
> What was in either but he most did seek.[20]
> And thus distracted, either's beauties' might
> Within the other's excellence was drowned:
> Too much delight did bar him from delight, 185
> For either's love, the other's did confound.
> Where if thy portraiture had only gone,
> His life from Herod Antony had taken.
> He would have loved thee, and thee alone,
> And left the brown Egyptian clean forsaken. 190
> And Cleopatra then to seek had been
> So firm a lover of her waned face;
> Then great Antonius' fall we had not seen,
> By her that fled to have him hold the chase.[21]
> Then Mariam in a Roman's chariot set 195
> In place of Cleopatra might have shown:
> A mart of beauties in her visage met,
> And part in this, that they were all her own.

Mar. Not to be empress of aspiring Rome
    Would Mariam like to Cleopatra live: 200
    With purest body will I press my tomb,
    And with no favours Antony could give.

Alex. Let us retire us, that we may resolve
    How now to deal in this reversed state.
    Great are th'affairs that we must now resolve, 205
    And great affairs must not be taken late.

ACT I, SCENE III

[Enter] Salome.

Sal. More plotting yet? Why, now you have the thing
   For which so oft you spent your suppliant breath,
   And Mariam hopes to have another king,
   Her eyes do sparkle joy for Herod's death.   210
Alex. If she desired another king to have,
   She might before she came in Herod's bed
   Have had her wish. More kings than one did crave
   For leave to set a crown upon her head.
   I think with more than reason she laments,   215
   That she is freed from such a sad annoy:
   Who is't will weep to part from discontent,
   And if she joy, she did not causeless joy.
Sal. You durst not thus have given your tongue the rein
   If noble Herod still remained in life: 220
   Your daughter's betters far I dare maintain
   Might have rejoiced to be my brother's wife.
Mar. My betters far, base woman 'tis untrue:
   You scarce have ever my superiors seen,
   For Mariam's servants were as good as you,   225
   Before she came to be Judea's queen.
Sal. Now stirs the tongue that is so quickly moved.
   But more than once your choler have I borne:
   Your fumish[22] words are sooner said than proved,
   And Salome's reply is only scorn.   230
Mar. Scorn those that are for thy companions held;
   Though I your brother's face had never seen,
   My birth thy baser birth so far excelled,
   I had to both of you the princess been.
   Thou party Jew and party Edomite,   235
   Thou mongrel: issued from rejected race,
   Thy ancestors against the heavens did fight
   And thou like them wilt heavenly birth disgrace.

Sal.   Still twit you me with nothing but my birth,
     What odds betwixt your ancestors and mine?   240
     Both born of Adam, both were made of earth,
     And both did come from holy Abraham's line.
Mar.   I favour thee when nothing else I say;
     With thy black acts I'll not pollute my breath,
     Else to thy charge I might full justly lay   245
     A shameful life, besides a husband's death.
Sal.   'Tis true indeed, I did the plots reveal,
     That passed betwixt your favourites and you:
     I meant not I, a traitor to conceal,
     Thus Salome your minion Joseph slew.   250
Mar.   Heaven, dost thou mean this infamy to smother?
     Let slandered Mariam ope thy closed ear:
     Self-guilt hath ever been suspicion's[23] mother,
     And therefore I this speech with patience bear.
     No, had not Salome's unsteadfast heart   255
     In Josephus' stead her Constabarus placed,
     To free herself, she had not used the art
     To slander hapless Mariam for unchaste.
Alex.   Come Mariam, let us go: it is no boot
     To let the head contend against the foot.[24]   260

[*Exeunt Mariam and Alexandra.*]

ACT I, SCENE IV

Sal.   Lives Salome to get so base a style
     As foot to the proud Mariam; Herod's spirit
     In happy time for her endured exile,
     For did he live she should not miss her merit.
     But he is dead, and though he were my brother,   265
     His death such store of cinders cannot cast
     My coals of love to quench: for though they smother
     The flames a while, yet will they out at last.
     Oh blest Arabia, in best climate placed,
     I by the fruit will censure of the tree;   270

'Tis not in vain, thy happy name thou hast,
If all Arabians like Silleus be.
Had not my fate been too too contrary
When I on Constabarus first did gaze,
Silleus had been object to mine eye,   275
Whose looks and personage must all eyes[25] amaze.
But now, ill-fated Salome, thy tongue
To Constabarus by itself is tied,
And now except I do the Hebrew wrong,
I cannot be the fair Arabian's[26] bride.   280
What childish lets are these? Why stand I now
On honourable points? 'Tis long ago
Since shame was written on my tainted brow,
And certain 'tis that shame is honour's foe.
Had I upon my reputation stood,   285
Had I affected an unspotted life,
Josephus' veins had still been stuffed with blood,
And I to him had lived a sober wife.
Then had I never cast an eye of love
On Constabarus' now detested face,   290
Then had I kept my thoughts without remove,
And blushed at motion of the least disgrace.
But shame is gone, and honour wiped away,
And impudency on my forehead sits.
She bids me work my will without delay,   295
And for my will I will employ my wits.
He loves, I love; what then can be the cause
Keeps me from[27] being the Arabian's wife?
It is the principle[28] of Moses' laws,
For Constabarus still remains in life.   300
If he to me did bear as earnest hate
As I to him, for him there were an ease:
A separating bill might free his fate
From such a yoke that did so much displease.
Why should such privilege to man be given?   305
Or, given to them, why barred from women then?
Are men than we in greater grace with heaven?

Or cannot women hate as well as men?
I'll be the custom-breaker, and begin
To show my sex the way to freedom's door, 310
And with an off'ring will I purge my sin –
The law was made for none but who are poor.
If Herod had lived, I might to him accuse
My present lord. But for the future's sake,
Then would I tell the king he did refuse 315
The sons of Babus in his power to take.
But now I must divorce him from my bed,
That my Silleus may possess his room.
Had I not begged his life, he had been dead;
I curse my tongue the hind'rer of his doom, 320
But then my wand'ring heart to him was fast,
Nor did I dream of change. Silleus said
He would be here, and see he comes at last;
Had I not named him, longer had he stayed.

ACT I, SCENE V

[Enter] Silleus.

Sil.   Well found, fair Salome, Judea's pride. 325
     Hath thy innated wisdom found the way
     To make Silleus deem him deified,
     By gaining thee, a more than precious prey?
Sal.   I have devised the best I can devise.
     A more imperfect means was never found, 330
     But what cares Salome; it doth suffice
     If our endeavours with their end be crowned.
     In this our land we have an ancient use,
     Permitted first by our law-giver's head:
     Who hates his wife, though for no just abuse, 335
     May with a bill divorce her from his bed.
     But in this custom women are not free,
     Yet I for once will wrest it; blame not thou
     The ill I do, since what I do's for thee,

The Tragedy of Mariam

    Though others blame, Silleus should allow.   340
Sil.   Thinks Salome, Silleus hath a tongue
    To censure her fair actions: let my blood
    Bedash my proper brow, for such a wrong,
    The being yours, can make even vices good.
    Arabia joy, prepare thy earth with green,   345
    Thou never happy wert indeed till now;
    Now shall thy ground be trod by beauty's queen,
    Her foot is destined to depress thy brow.
    Thou shalt, fair Salome, command as much
    As if the royal ornament were thine: 350
    The weakness of Arabia's king is such,
    The kingdom is not his so much as mine.
    My mouth is our Obodas' oracle,
    Who thinks not aught but what Silleus will.
    And thou rare creature, Asia's miracle,   355
    Shalt be to me as it: Obodas still.
Sal.   'Tis not for glory I thy love accept,
    Judea yields me honours worthy store;
    Had not affection in my bosom crept,
    My native country should my life deplore.   360
    Were not Silleus he with whom[29] I go,
    I would not change my Palestine for Rome;
    Much less would I a glorious state to show,
    Go far to purchase an Arabian tomb.
Sil.   Far be it from Silleus so to think;   365
    I know it is thy gratitude requites
    The love that is in me, and shall not shrink
    Till death do sever me from earth's delights.
Sal.   But whist; methinks the wolf is in our talk,
    Begone Silleus, who doth here arrive?   370
    'Tis Constabarus that doth hither walk;
    I'll find a quarrel, him from me to drive.
Sil.   Farewell, but were it not for thy command,
    In his despite Silleus here would stand.

                [*Exit Silleus.*]

ACT I, SCENE VI

[Enter] Constabarus.

Const. Oh Salome, how much you wrong your name, 375
Your race, your country, and your husband most!
A stranger's private conference is shame;
I blush for you, that have your blushing lost.
Oft have I found, and found you to my grief,
Consorted with this base Arabian here; 380
Heaven knows that you have been my comfort chief,
Then do not now my greater plague appear.
Now by the stately carved edifice
That on Mount Sion makes so fair a show,
And by the altar fit for sacrifice, 385
I love thee more than thou thyself dost know.
Oft with a silent sorrow have I heard
How ill Judea's mouth doth censure thee,
And did I not thine honour much regard,
Thou shouldst not be exhorted thus for me. 390
Didst thou but know the worth of honest fame,
How much a virtuous woman is esteemed,
Thou wouldst like hell eschew deserved shame,
And seek to be both chaste and chastely deemed.
Our wisest prince did say, and true he said, 395
A virtuous woman crowns her husband's head.[30]
Sal. Did I for this uprear thy low estate?
Did I for this requital beg thy life,
That thou hadst forfeited? – hapless fate,
To be to such a thankless wretch the wife! 400
This hand of mine hath lifted up thy head,
Which many a day ago had fall'n full low,
Because the sons of Babus are not dead,
To me thou dost both life and fortune owe.
Const. You have my patience often exercised; 405
Use made my choler keep within the banks.

The Tragedy of Mariam

  Yet boast no more, but be by me advised:
  A benefit upbraided, forfeits thanks.
  I prithee Salome, dismiss this mood,
  Thou dost not know how ill it fits thy place: 410
  My words were all intended for thy good,
  To raise thine honour and to stop disgrace.
Sal. To stop disgrace? Take thou no care for me,
  Nay do thy worst, thy worst I set not by:
  No shame of mine is like to light on thee,   415
  Thy love and admonitions I defy.
  Thou shalt no hour longer call me wife:
  Thy jealousy procures my hate so deep,
  That I from thee do mean to free my life,
  By a divorcing bill before I sleep.   420
Const. Are Hebrew women now transformed to men?
  Why do you not as well our battles fight,
  And wear our armour? Suffer this, and then
  Let all the world be topsy-turvied quite!
  Let fishes graze, beasts swim,[31] and birds descend,   425
  Let fire burn downwards whilst the earth aspires,
  Let winter's heat and summer's cold offend,
  Let thistles grow on vines, and grapes on briars,
  Set us to spin or sow, or at the best
  Make us wood-hewers, water-bearing wights,   430
  For sacred service let us take no rest:
  Use us as Joshua did the Gibonites.[32]
Sal. Hold on your talk, till it be time to end,
  For me I am resolved it shall be so:
  Though I be first that to this course do bend,   435
  I shall not be the last, full well I know.
Const. Why then, be witness heav'n, the judge of sins,
  Be witness spirits that eschew the dark,
  Be witness angels, witness cherubins,
  Whose semblance sits upon the holy ark,   440
  Be witness earth, be witness Palestine,
  Be witness David's city, if my heart
  Did ever merit such an act of thine,

    Or if the fault be mine that makes us part.
    Since mildest Moses, friend unto the Lord, 445
    Did work his wonders in the land of Ham,[33]
    And slew the first-born babes without a sword,
    In sign whereof we eat the holy lamb,
    Till now that fourteen hundred years are past,
    Since first the law with us hath been in force: 450
    You are the first, and will I hope be last,
    That ever sought her husband to divorce.
Sal.   I mean not to be led by precedent;
    My will shall be to me instead of law.
Const.   I fear me much you will too late repent, 455
    That you have ever lived so void of awe.
    This is Silleus' love that makes you thus
    Reverse all order: you must next be his.
    But if my thoughts aright the cause discuss,
    In winning you, he gains no lasting bliss; 460
    I was Silleus, and not long ago
    Josephus then was Constabarus now:
    When you became my friend you proved his foe,
    As now for him you break to me your vow.[34]
Sal.   If once I loved you, greater is your debt, 465
    For certain 'tis that you deserved it not.
    And undeserved love we soon forget,
    And therefore that to me can be no blot.
    But now fare ill my once beloved lord,
    Yet never more beloved than now abhorred. 470

                [*Exit Salome.*]

Const.   Yet Constabarus biddeth thee farewell.
    Farewell, light creature. Heaven forgive thy sin!
    My prophesying spirit doth foretell
    Thy wavering thoughts do yet but new begin.
    Yet I have better 'scaped than Joseph did; 475
    But if our Herod's death had been delayed,
    The valiant youths that I so long have hid
    Had been by her, and I for them, betrayed.

Therefore in happy hour did Caesar give
The fatal blow to wanton Antony;   480
For had he lived, our Herod then should live,
But great Antonius' death made Herod die.
Had he enjoyed his breath, not I alone
Had been in danger of a deadly fall,
But Mariam had the way of peril gone,   485
Though by the tyrant most beloved of all -
The sweet-faced Mariam, as free from guilt
As heaven from spots; yet had her lord come back,
Her purest blood had been unjustly spilt,
And Salome it was would work her wreck.   490
Though all Judea yield her innocent,
She often hath been near to punishment.

[*Exit Constabarus.*]

Chorus.

Those minds that wholly dote upon delight,
Except they only joy in inward good,
Still hope at last to hop upon the right,   495
And so from sand they leap in loathsome mud.
Fond wretches, seeking what they cannot find,
For no content attends a wavering mind.

If wealth they do desire, and wealth attain,
Then wondrous fain would they to honour leap;   500
If[35] mean degree they do in honour gain,
They would but wish a little higher step.
Thus step to step and wealth to wealth they add,
Yet cannot all their plenty make them glad.

Yet oft we see that some in humble state   505
Are cheerful, pleasant, happy and content,
When those indeed that are of higher state
With vain additions do their thoughts torment.
Th'one would to his mind his fortune bind,
Th'other to his fortune frames his mind.   510

To wish variety is sign of grief,
For if you like your state as now it is,
Why should an alteration bring relief?
Nay, change would then be feared as loss of bliss.
That man is only happy in his fate 515
That is delighted in a settled state.

Still Mariam wished she from her lord were free,
For expectation of variety;
Yet, now she sees her wishes prosperous be,
She grieves, because her lord so soon did die. 520
Who can those vast imaginations feed,
Wherein a property, contempt doth breed?

Were Herod now perchance to live again,
She would again as much be grieved at that;
All that she may, she ever doth disdain, 525
Her wishes guide her to she knows not what.
And sad must be their looks, their honour sour,
That care for nothing, being in their power.

ACT II, SCENE I

[Enter] Pheroras and Graphina.

Pher. 'Tis true Graphina, now the time draws nigh,
    Wherein the holy priest with hallowed right 530
    The happy long-desired knot shall tie,
    Pheroras and Graphina to unite.
    How oft have I with lifted hands implored
    This blessed hour, till now implored in vain,
    Which hath my wished liberty restored 535
    And made my subject self my own again.
    Thy love, fair maid, upon mine eye doth sit,
    Whose nature hot doth dry the moisture all,
    Which were in nature and in reason fit

    For my monarchal brother's death to fall.   540
    Had Herod lived, he would have plucked my hand
    From fair Graphina's palm perforce, and tied
    The same in hateful and despised band,
    For I had had a baby to my bride:
    Scarce can her infant tongue with easy voice   545
    Her name distinguish to another's ear,
    Yet had he lived, his power and not my choice
    Had made me solemnly the contract swear.
    Have I not cause in such a change to joy?
    What? though she be my niece, a princess born: 550
    Near blood's without respect, high birth a toy,
    Since love can teach blood and kindred scorn.[36]
    What booted it that he did raise my head
    To be his realm's co-partner, kingdom's mate,
    Withall he kept Graphina from my bed,   555
    More wished by me than thrice Judea's state.
    Oh, could not he be skillful judge in love,
    That doted so upon his Mariam's face?
    He, for his passion, Doris did remove;
    I needed not a lawful wife displace.   560
    It could not be but he had power to judge,
    But he that never grudged a kingdom's share,
    This well known happiness to me did grudge
    And meant to be therein without compare.
    Else had I been his equal in love's host;   565
    For though the diadem on Mariam's head
    Corrupt the vulgar judgements, I will boast
    Graphina's brow's as white, her cheeks as red.
    Why speaks thou not, fair creature? Move thy tongue,
    For silence is a sign of discontent: 570
    It were to both our loves too great a wrong,
    If now this hour do find thee sadly bent.
Graph.   Mistake me not, my lord; too oft have I
    Desired this time to come with winged feet,
    To be enwrapped with grief when 'tis too nigh.   575

You know my wishes ever yours did meet:
If I be silent, 'tis no more but fear
That I should say too little when I speak.
But since you will my imperfections bear,
In spite of doubt I will my silence break; 580
Yet might amazement tie my moving tongue,
But that I know before Pheroras' mind.
I have admired your affection long
And cannot yet therein a reason find.
Your hand hath lifted me from lowest state 585
To highest eminency, wondrous grace,
And me your handmaid have you made your mate,
Though all but you alone do count me base.[37]
You have preserved me pure at my request,
Though you so weak a vassal might constrain 590
To yield to your high will, then last not best
In my respect, a princess you disdain:
Then need not all these favours study crave,
To be requited by a simple maid?
And study still you know must silence have, 595
Then be my cause for silence justly weighed,
But study cannot boot nor I requite,
Except your lowly handmaid's steadfast love
And fast obedience may your mind delight,
I will not promise more than I can prove. 600
Pher. That study needs not let[38] Graphina smile,
And I desire no greater recompense.
I cannot vaunt me in a glorious style,
Nor shew my love in far-fetched eloquence,
But this believe me: never Herod's heart 605
Hath held his prince-born beauty-famed wife
In nearer place than thou fair virgin art
To him that holds the glory of his life.
Should Herod's body leave the sepulchre
And entertain the severed ghost again,[39] 610
He should not be my nuptial hinderer,
Except he hindered it with dying pain.

Come, fair Graphina, let us go in state
This wish-endeared time to celebrate.

[*Exeunt Pheroras and Graphina.*]

ACT II, SCENE II

[*Enter*] *Constabarus and Babus' Sons.*

1 Son.   Now, valiant friend, you have our lives redeemed,   615
Which lives, as saved by you, to you are due:
Command and you shall see yourself esteemed,
Our lives and liberties belong to you.
This twice six years with hazard of your life,
You have concealed us from the tyrant's sword;   620
Though cruel Herod's sister were your wife,
You durst in scorn of fear this grace afford.
In recompense we know not what to say;
A poor reward were thanks for such a merit,
Our truest friendship at your feet we lay,   625
The best requital to a noble spirit.
Const.   Oh how you wrong our friendship, valiant youth:
With friends there is not such a word as debt;
Where amity is tied with bond of truth,
All benefits are there in common set.   630
Then is the golden age with them renewed;
All names of properties are banished quite;
Division and distinction are eschewed:
Each hath to what belongs to other's right.
And 'tis not sure so full a benefit,   635
Freely to give, as freely to require:
A bounteous act hath glory following it,
They cause the glory that the act desire.
All friendship should the pattern imitate
Of Jesse's son and valiant Jonathan,   640
For neither sovereign's nor father's hate
A friendship fixed on virtue sever can.

>   Too much of this, 'tis written in the heart
>   And needs[40] no amplifying with the tongue:
>   Now may you from your living tomb depart,   645
>   Where Herod's life has kept you over-long.
>   Too great an injury to a noble mind,
>   To be quick buried, you had purchased fame
>   Some years ago, but that you were confined.
>   While thousand meaner did advance their name,   650
>   Your best of life, the prime of all your years,
>   Your time of action, is from you bereft.
>   Twelve winters have you overpassed[41] in fears;
>   Yet if you use it well, enough is left.
>   And who can doubt but you will use it well?   655
>   The sons of Babus have it by descent,
>   In all their thoughts each action to excel,
>   Boldly to act, and wisely to invent.
>
> *2 Son.*   Had it not like the hateful cuckoo been,
>   Whose riper age his infant nurse doth kill,   660
>   So long we had not kept ourselves unseen,
>   But Constabarus' safety[42] crossed our will.
>   For had the tyrant fixed his cruel eye
>   On our concealed faces, wrath had swayed
>   His justice so, that he had forced us die.   665
>   And dearer price than life we should have paid,
>   For you our truest friend had fall'n with us,
>   And we much like a house on pillars set
>   Had clean depressed our prop, and therefore thus
>   Our ready will with our concealment met.   670
>   But now that you, fair lord, are dangerless,
>   The sons of Babus shall their rigour show,
>   And prove it was not baseness did oppress
>   Our hearts so long, but honour kept them low.
>
> *1 Son.*   Yet do I fear this tale of Herod's death   675
>   At last will prove a very tale indeed:
>   It gives me strongly in my mind, his breath
>   Will be preserved to make a number bleed.
>   I wish not therefore to be set at large,

The Tragedy of Mariam

  Yet peril to myself I do not leer:[43]   680
  Let us for some days longer be your charge,
  Till we of Herod's state the truth do hear.
Const. What, art thou turned a coward, noble youth,
  That thou beginst to doubt undoubted truth?
1 Son. Were it my brother's tongue that cast this doubt,   685
  I from his heart would have the question out
  With this keen falchion,[44] but 'tis you, my lord,
  Against whose head I must not lift a sword,
  I am so tied in gratitude.
Const.   Believe,
  You have no cause to take it ill;[45]   690
  If any word of mine your heart did grieve,
  The word dissented from the speaker's will.
  I know it was not fear the doubt begun,
  But rather valour and your care of me:
  A coward could not be your father's son.   695
  Yet know I doubts unnecessary be:
  For who can think that in Antonius' fall,
  Herod his bosom friend should 'scape unbruised;
  Then Caesar we might thee an idiot call,
  If thou by him shouldst be so far abused.   700
2 Son. Lord Constabarus,[46] let me tell you this:
  Upon submission, Caesar will forgive,
  And therefore though the tyrant did amiss,
  It may fall out that he will let him live.
  Not many years ago it is since I,   705
  Directed thither by my father's care,
  In famous Rome for twice twelve months did lie,[47]
  My life from Hebrews' cruelty to spare.
  There, though I were but yet of boyish age,
  I bent mine eye to mark, mine ears to hear,   710
  Where I did see Octavius then a page,
  When first he did to Julius'[48] sight appear:
  Methought I saw such mildness in his face
  And such a sweetness in his looks did grow,
  Withall, commixed with so majestic grace,   715

       His phisnomy[49] his fortune did foreshow.
       For this I am indebted to mine eye,
       But then mine ear received more evidence,
       By that I knew his love to clemency,
       How he with hottest choler could dispense.   720
Const.   But we have more than barely heard the news,
       It hath been twice confirmed. And though some tongue
       Might be so false, with false report t'abuse,
       A false report hath never lasted long.
       But be it so that Herod have his life,   725
       Concealment would not then a whit avail,
       For certain 'tis, that she that was my wife
       Would not to set her accusation fail.
       And therefore now as good the venture give,
       And free ourselves from blot of cowardice,   730
       As show a pitiful desire to live,
       For who can pity but they must despise?
1 Son.   I yield, but to necessity I yield.
       I dare upon this doubt engage mine arm:
       That Herod shall again this kingdom wield   735
       And prove his death to be a false alarm.
2 Son.   I doubt it too – God grant it be an error!
       'Tis best without a cause to be in terror,
       And rather had I, though my soul be mine,
       My soul should lie, than prove a true divine.   740
Const.   Come, come, let fear go seek a dastard's nest;
       Undaunted courage lies in a noble breast.

              [*Exeunt omnes.*]

ACT II, SCENE III

          [*Enter*] Doris *and* Antipater.

Doris.   You[50] royal buildings bow your lofty side
       And scope to her that is by right your queen;
       Let your humility upbraid the pride   745

Of those in whom no due respect is seen.
Nine times have we with trumpets' haughty sound,
And banishing sour leaven from our taste,
Observed the feast that takes the fruit from ground,
Since I fair city did behold thee last;   750
So long is it since Mariam's purer cheek
Did rob from mine the glory, and so long
Since I returned my native town to seek,
And with me nothing but the sense of wrong.
And thee my boy, whose birth though great it were,   755
Yet have thy after fortunes proved but poor.
When thou wert born, how little did I fear
Thou shouldst be thrust from forth thy father's door.
Art thou not Herod's right-begotten son?
Was not the hapless Doris Herod's wife?   760
Yes: ere he had the Hebrew kingdom won,
I was companion to his private life.
Was I not fair enough to be a queen?
Why, ere thou wert to me false monarch tied,
My lake of beauty might as well be seen,   765
As after I had lived five years thy bride.
Yet then thine oath came pouring like the rain,[51]
Which all affirmed my face without compare,
And that if thou might'st Doris' love obtain,
For all the world besides thou didst not care.   770
Then was I young, and rich, and nobly born,
And therefore worthy to be Herod's mate:
Yet thou ungrateful cast me off with scorn,
When heaven's purpose raised your meaner fate.
Oft have I begged for vengeance for this fact,   775
And with dejected knees, aspiring hands,
Have prayed the highest power to enact
The fall of her that on my trophy stands.
Revenge I have according to my will,
Yet where I wished this vengeance did not light: 780
I wished it should high-hearted Mariam kill,
But it against my whilom lord did fight.

With thee sweet boy I came, and came to try
If thou before his bastards might be placed
In Herod's royal seat and dignity. 785
But Mariam's infants here are only graced,
And now for us there doth no hope remain.
Yet we will not return till Herod's end
Be more confirmed; perchance he is not slain.
So glorious fortunes may my boy attend, 790
For if he live, he'll think it doth suffice
That he to Doris shows such cruelty:
For as he did my wretched life despise,
So do I know I shall despised die.
Let him but prove as natural to thee 795
As cruel to thy miserable mother,
His cruelty shall not upbraided be
But in thy fortunes; I his faults will smother.
Ant. Each mouth within the city loudly cries
That Herod's death is certain; therefore we 800
Had best some subtle hidden plot devise,
That Mariam's children might subverted be,
By poison's drink, or else by murderous knife,
So we may be advanced, it skills not how:
They are but bastards, you were Herod's wife, 805
And foul adultery blotteth Mariam's brow.
Doris. They are too strong to be by us removed,
Or else revenge's foulest-spotted face
By our detested wrongs might be approved,
But weakness must to greater power give place. 810
But let us now retire to grieve alone,
For solitariness best fitteth moan.

[*Exeunt Doris and Antipater.*]

ACT II, SCENE IV

[Enter] Silleus and Constabarus.

Sil.   Well met, Judean lord, the only wight
  Silleus wished to see. I am to call
  Thy tongue to strict account.
Const.   For what despite   815
  I ready am to hear, and answer all.
  But if directly at the cause I guess
  That breeds this challenge, you must pardon me,
  And now some other ground of fight profess,
  For I have vowed; vows must unbroken be.   820
Sil.   What may be your exception?[52] Let me know.
Const.   Why? Aught concerning Salome,[53] my sword
  Shall not be wielded for a cause so low,
  A blow for her my arm will scorn t'afford.
Sil.   It is for slandering her unspotted name,   825
  And I will make thee in thy vow's despite
  Suck up the breath that did my mistress blame
  And swallow it again to do her right.
Const.   I prithee give some other quarrel ground
  To find beginning: rail against my name,   830
  Or strike me first, or let some scarlet wound
  Inflame my courage, give me words of shame;
  Do thou our Moses' sacred laws disgrace,
  Deprave our nation, do me some despite:
  I'm apt enough to fight in any case,   835
  But yet for Salome I will not fight.
Sil.   Nor I for aught but Salome. My sword
  That owes his service to her sacred name
  Will not an edge for other cause afford;
  In other fight I am not sure of fame.   840
Const.   For her, I pity thee enough already;
  For her, I therefore will not mangle thee:
  A woman with a heart so most unsteady

      Will of herself sufficient torture be.
      I cannot envy for so light a gain,   845
      Her mind with such inconstancy doth run:
      As with a word thou didst her love obtain,
      So with a word she will from thee be won.
      So light as her possessions for most day
      Is her affections lost, to me 'tis known: 850
      As good go hold the wind as make her stay,
      She never loves, but till she call her own.
      She merely is a painted sepulchre,
      That is both fair and vilely foul at once;
      Though on her outside graces garnish her,   855
      Her mind is filled with worse than rotten bones.[54]
      And ever ready lifted is her hand
      To aim destruction at a husband's throat:
      For proofs, Josephus and myself do stand,
      Though once on both of us she seemed to dote.   860
      Her mouth, though serpent-like it never hisses,
      Yet like a serpent, poisons where it kisses.
Sil.   Well, Hebrew, well, thou bark'st, but wilt not bite?
Const.   I tell thee still, for her I will not fight.
Sil.   Why then, I call thee coward.
Const.   From my heart,   865
      I give thee thanks. A coward's hateful name
      Cannot to valiant minds a blot impart,
      And therefore I with joy receive the same.
      Thou know'st I am no coward: thou wert by
      At the Arabian battle th'other day,   870
      And saw'st my sword with daring valiancy
      Amongst the faint Arabians cut my way.
      The blood of foes no more could let it shine,
      And 'twas enamelled with some of thine.
      But now have at thee; not for Salome   875
      I fight, but to discharge a coward's style.
      Here 'gins the fight that shall not parted be,
      Before a soul or two endure exile.[55]

The Tragedy of Mariam 33

[They fight.]

Sil.   Thy sword hath made some windows for my blood,
   To show a horrid crimson phisnomy. 880
   To breathe for both of us methinks 'twere good;
   The day will give us time enough to die.
Const.   With all my heart, take breath; thou shalt have time,
   And, if thou list, a twelvemonth: let us end.
   Into thy cheeks there doth a paleness climb; 885
   Thou canst not from my sword thyself defend.
   What needest thou for Salome to fight?
   Thou hast her, and may'st keep her; none strives for her:
   I willingly to thee resign my right,
   For in my very soul I do abhor her. 890
   Thou seest that I am fresh, unwounded yet;
   Then not for fear I do this offer make:
   Thou art with loss of blood to fight unfit,
   For here is one, and there another take.
Sil.   I will not leave as long as breath remains 895
   Within my wounded body: spare your words.
   My heart in blood's stead courage entertains;
   Salome's love no place for fear affords.
Const.   Oh could thy soul but prophesy like mine,
   I would not wonder thou shouldst long to die: 900
   For Salome, if I aright divine,
   Will be than death a greater misery.
Sil.   Then list, I'll breathe no longer.
Const.   Do thy will;
   I hateless fight, and charitably kill.

They fight.[56]

Pity thyself, Silleus, let not death 905
Intrude before his time into thy heart.
Alas, it is too late to fear, his breath
Is from his body now about to part.
How farest thou, brave Arabian?
Sil.   Very well,

My leg is hurt; I can no longer fight. 910
It only grieves me that so soon I fell,
Before fair Salom's wrongs I came to right.
Const.   Thy wounds are less than mortal. Never fear,
Thou shalt a safe and quick recovery find.
Come, I will thee unto my lodging bear; 915
I hate thy body, but I love thy mind.
Sil.   Thanks, noble Jew, I see a courteous foe,
Stern emnity to friendship can no art.
Had not my heart and tongue engaged me so,
I would from thee no foe, but friend depart. 920
My heart to Salome is tied too[57] fast,
To leave her love for friendship; yet my skill
Shall be employed to make your favour last
And I will honour Constabarus still.
Const.   I ope my bosom to thee, and will take 925
Thee in, as friend, and grieve for thy complaint;
But if we do not expedition make,
Thy loss of blood I fear will make thee faint.

[*Exeunt Constabarus and Silleus.*]

Chorus.

To hear a tale with ears prejudicate,
It spoils the judgement, and corrupts the sense; 930
That human error given to every state,
Is greater enemy to innocence.
It makes us foolish, heady, rash, unjust;
It makes us never try before we trust.

It will confound the meaning, change the words, 935
For it our sense of hearing much deceives;
Besides no time to judgement it affords,
To weigh[58] the circumstance our ear receives.
The ground of accidents it never tries,
But makes us take for truth ten thousand lies. 940

Our ears and hearts are apt to hold for good,
That we ourselves do most desire to be,
And then we drown objections in the flood
Of partiality, 'tis that we see
That makes false rumours long with credit past,   945
Though they like rumours must conclude at last.

The greatest part of us prejudicate,
With wishing Herod's death do hold it true;
The being once deluded does not bate,
The credit to a better likelihood due.   950
Those few that wish it not, the multitude
Do carry headlong, so they doubts conclude.

They not object the weak uncertain ground,
Whereon they built this tale of Herod's end,
Whereof the author scarcely can be found,   955
And all because their wishes that way bend.
They think not of the peril that ensu'th,
If this should prove the contrary to truth.

On this same doubt, on this so light a breath,
They pawn their lives and fortunes. For they all   960
Behave them as the news of Herod's death
They did of most undoubted credit call.
But if their actions now do rightly hit,
Let them commend their fortune, not their wit.

ACT III, SCENE I

[Enter] Pheroras [and] Salome.

Pher.   Urge me no more Graphina to forsake,   965
   Not twelve hours since, I married her for love;
   And do you think a sister's power can make
   A resolute decree, so soon remove?
Sal.   Poor minds they are that honour not affects.

Pher.   Who hunts for honour, happiness neglects.   970
Sal.   You might have been both of felicity
    And honour too in equal measure seized.
Pher.   It is not you can tell so well as I,
    What 'tis can make me happy, or displeased.
Sal.   To match for neither beauty nor respects   975
    One mean of birth, but yet of meaner mind,
    A woman full of natural defects,
    I wonder what your eye in her could find.
Pher.   Mine eye found loveliness, mine ear found wit,
    To please the one, and to enchant the other;   980
    Grace on her eye, mirth on her tongue doth sit,
    In looks a child, in wisdom's house a mother.
Sal.   But say you thought her fair, as none thinks else:
    Knows not Pheroras, beauty is a blast,
    Much like this flower which today excels,   985
    But longer than a day it will not last.
Pher.   Her wit exceeds her beauty.
Sal.   Wit may show
    The way to ill as well as good, you know.
Pher.   But wisdom is the porter of her head
    And bars[59] all wicked words from issuing thence.   990
Sal.   But of a porter, better were you sped,
    If she against their entrance made defence.
Pher.   But wherefore comes the sacred Ananell,
    That hitherward his hasty steps doth bend?

                    [*Enter Ananell.*]

    Great sacrificer y'are arrived well,   995
    Ill news from holy mouth I not attend.

ACT III, SCENE II

Ana.   My lips, my son, with peaceful tidings blessed,
    Shall utter honey to your list'ning ear;
    A word of death comes not from priestly breast,

	I speak of life: in life there is no fear.	1000
	And for the news I did the heavens salute,	
	And fill the temple with my thankful voice:	
	For though that mourning may not me pollute,	
	At pleasing accidents I may rejoice.	
Pher.	Is Herod then revived from certain death?	1005
Sal.	What? Can your news restore my brother's breath?	
Ana.	Both so, and so the king is safe and sound,	
	And did such grace in royal Caesar meet,	
	That he, with larger style than ever crowned,	
	Within this hour Jerusalem will greet.	1010
	I did but come to tell you, and must back	
	To make preparatives for sacrifice:	
	I knew his death your hearts like mine did rack,	
	Though to conceal it, proved you wise.[60]	

[Exit Ananell.]

Sal.	How can my joy sufficiently appear?	1015
Pher.	A heavier tale did never pierce mine ear.	
Sal.	Now Salome of happiness may boast.	
Pher.	But now Pheroras is in danger most.	
Sal.	I shall enjoy the comfort of my life.	
Pher.	And I shall lose it, losing of my wife.	1020
Sal.	Joy heart, for Constabarus[61] shall be slain.	
Pher.	Grieve soul, Graphina shall from me be ta'en.	
Sal.	Smile cheeks, the fair Silleus shall be mine.	
Pher.	Weep eyes, for I must with a child combine.	
Sal.	Well brother, cease your moans; on one condition	1025
	I'll undertake to win the king's consent:	
	Graphina still shall be in your tuition	
	And her with you be ne'er the less content.	
Pher.	What's the condition? Let me quickly know,	
	That I as quickly your command may act,	1030
	Were it to see what herbs in Ophir[62] grow,	
	Or that the lofty Tyrus[63] might be sacked.	
Sal.	'Tis not[64] so hard a task. It is no more	
	But tell the king that Constabarus[65] hid	

              The sons of Babus, done to death before,   1035
              And 'tis no more than Constabarus[66] did.
              And tell him more that I[67] for Herod's sake,
              Not able to endure his brother's foe,
              Did with a bill our separation make,
              Though loth from Constabarus[68] else to go.   1040
Pher.   Believe this tale for told: I'll go from hence,
              In Herod's ear the Hebrew to deface;
              And I that never studied eloquence,
              Do mean with eloquence this tale to grace.

                           Exit [Pheroras.]

Sal.   This will be Constabarus' quick dispatch,   1045
              Which from my mouth would lesser credit find:
              Yet shall he not decease without a match,
              For Mariam shall not linger long behind.
              First jealousy; if that avail not, fear
              Shall be my minister to work her end: 1050
              A common error moves not Herod's ear,
              Which doth so firmly to his Mariam bend.
              She shall be charged with so horrid crime,
              As Herod's fear shall turn his love to hate:
              I'll make some swear that she desires to climb,   1055
              And seeks to poison him for his estate.
              I scorn that she should live my birth t'upbraid,
              To call me base and hungry Edomite;
              With patient show her choler I betrayed,
              And watched the time to be revenged by sleight.   1060
              Now tongue of mine with scandal load her name,
              Turn hers to fountains, Herod's eyes to flame.
              Yet first I will begin Pheroras' suit,
              That he my earnest business may effect,
              And I of Mariam will keep me mute,   1065
              Till first some other shall her name detect.

                         [Enter Silleus' man.]

         Who's there? Silleus' man? How fares your lord,

The Tragedy of Mariam

  That your aspects do bear the badge of sorrow?
Silleus' man. He hath the marks of Constabarus' sword,
  And for a while desires your sight to borrow.   1070
Sal. My heavy curse the hateful sword pursue,
  My heavier curse on the more hateful arm
  That wounded my Silleus. But renew
  Your tale again. Hath he no mortal harm?
Silleus' man. No sign of danger doth in him appear,   1075
  Nor are his wounds in place of peril seen:
  He bids[69] you be assured you need not fear,
  He hopes to make you yet Arabia's queen.
Sal. Commend my heart to be Silleus' charge.
  Tell him, my brother's sudden coming now   1080
  Will give my foot no room to walk at large,
  But I will see him yet ere night I vow.

    [*Exeunt Salome and Silleus' man.*]

ACT III, SCENE III

[*Enter*] *Mariam and Sohemus.*

Mar. Sohemus, tell me what the news may be
  That makes your eyes so full, your cheeks so blue?
Soh. I know not how to call them. Ill for me,   1085
  'Tis sure they are; not so I hope for you.
  Herod
Mar.   Oh, what of Herod?
Soh.   Herod lives.
[*Mar.*] How! Lives? What, in some cave or forest hid?[70]
Soh. Nay, back returned with honour. Caesar gives
  Him greater grace than ere Antonius did.   1090
Mar. Foretell the ruin of my family,
  Tell me that I shall see our city burned,
  Tell me I shall a death disgraceful die,
  But tell me not that Herod is returned.
Soh. Be not impatient, madam, be but mild,   1095

　　　　His love to you again will soon be bred.
Mar.　　I will not to his love be reconciled,
　　　With solemn vows I have forsworn his bed.
Soh.　　But you must break those vows.
Mar.　　　　　　　　　　　　　　I'll rather break
　　　The heart of Mariam. Cursed is my fate.　　　　　　1100
　　　But speak no more to me, in vain ye speak,
　　　To live with him I so profoundly hate
Soh.　　Great queen, you must to me your pardon give:
　　　Sohemus cannot now your will obey.
　　　If your command should me to silence drive,　　　　1105
　　　It were not to obey, but to betray.
　　　Reject and slight my speeches, mock my faith,
　　　Scorn my observance, call my counsel naught:
　　　Though you regard not what Sohemus saith,
　　　Yet will I ever freely speak my thought.　　　　　　1110
　　　I fear ere long I shall fair Mariam see
　　　In woeful state, and by herself undone:
　　　Yet for your issue's sake more temp'rate be,
　　　The heart by affability is won.
Mar.　　And must I to my prison turn again?　　　　　1115
　　　Oh, now I see I was an hypocrite:
　　　I did this morning for his death complain,
　　　And yet do mourn, because he lives, ere night.
　　　When I his death believed, compassion wrought,
　　　And was the stickler 'twixt my heart and him;　　　1120
　　　But now that curtain's drawn from off my thought,
　　　Hate doth appear again with visage grim
　　　And paints the face of Herod in my heart,
　　　In horrid colours with detested look;
　　　Then fear would come, but scorn doth play her part,　1125
　　　And saith that scorn with fear can never brook.
　　　I know I could enchain him with a smile
　　　And lead him captive with a gentle word.
　　　I scorn my look should ever man beguile,
　　　Or other speech, than meaning to afford;　　　　　1130
　　　Else Salome in vain might spend her wind,

In vain might Herod's mother whet her tongue,
In vain had they complotted and combined,
For I could overthrow them all ere long.
Oh, what a shelter is mine innocence, 1135
To shield me from the pangs of inward grief:
'Gainst all mishaps it is my fair defence,
And to my sorrows yields a large relief.
To be commandress of the triple earth,[71]
And sit in safety, from a fall secure, 1140
To have all nations celebrate my birth,
I would not that my spirit were impure.
Let my distressed state unpitied be,
Mine innocence is hope enough for me.

Exit [Mariam.]

Soh. Poor guiltless queen! Oh, that my wish might place 1145
A little temper now about thy heart:
Unbridled speech is Mariam's worst disgrace,
And will endanger her without desert.
I am in greater hazard. O'er my head,
The fatal axe doth hang unsteadily; 1150
My disobedience once discovered,
Will shake it down: Sohemus so shall die.
For when the king shall find we thought his death
Had been as certain as we see his life,
And marks withall I slighted so his breath 1155
As to preserve alive his matchless wife,
Nay more, to give to Alexander's hand[72]
The regal dignity, the sovereign power;
How I had yielded up at her command
The strength of all the city, David's tower, 1160
What more than common death may I expect,
Since I too well do know his cruelty:
'Twere death, a word of Herod's to neglect,
What then to do directly contrary?
Yet life I quit thee with a willing spirit, 1165
And think thou could'st not better be employed:

I forfeit thee for her that more doth merit,
Ten such were better dead than she destroyed.
But fare thee well, chaste queen, well may I see
The darkness palpable, and rivers part;   1170
The sun stand still. Nay more retorted be,
But never woman with so pure a heart.
Thine eyes' grave majesty keeps all in awe,
And cuts the wings of every loose desire;
Thy brow is table to the modest law,   1175
Yet though we dare not love, we may admire.
And if I die, it shall my soul content,
My breath in Mariam's service shall be spent.

[*Exit Sohemus.*]

Chorus.

'Tis not enough for one that is a wife
To keep her spotless from an act of ill;   1180
But from suspicion she should free her life,
And bare herself of power as well as will.
'Tis not so glorious for her to be free,
As by her proper self restrained to be.

When she hath spacious ground to walk upon,   1185
Why on the ridge should she desire to go?
It is no glory to forbear alone
Those things that may her honour overthrow.
But 'tis thankworthy, if she will not take
All lawful liberties for honour's sake.   1190

That wife her hand against her fame doth rear,
That more than to her lord alone will give
A private word to any second ear,
And though she may with reputation live.
Yet though most chaste, she doth her glory blot,   1195
And wounds her honour, though she kills it not.

The Tragedy of Mariam

When to their husbands they themselves do bind,
Do they not wholly give themselves away?
Or give they but their body not their mind,
Reserving that, though best, for others' prey?[73]   1200
No sure, their thoughts no more can be their own
And therefore should to none but one be known.

Then she usurps upon another's right,
That seeks to be by public language graced,
And though her thoughts reflect with purest light,   1205
Her mind, if not peculiar, is not chaste.
For in a wife it is no worse to find
A common body, than[74] a common mind.

And every mind, though free from thought of ill,
That out of glory seeks a worth to show,   1210
When any's ears but one therewith they fill,
Doth in a sort her pureness overthrow.
Now Mariam had, but that to this she bent,
Been free from fear, as well as innocent.

ACT IV, SCENE I

Enter Herod and his attendants.

Herod.   Hail, happy city, happy in thy store   1215
   And happy that thy buildings such we see;
   More happy in the temple where w'adore
   But most of all that Mariam lives in thee.

Enter Nu[n]tio.

Art thou returned? How fares my Mariam?[75]
Nun.   She's well, my lord, and will anon be here   1220
   As you commanded.
Herod.   Muffle up thy brow
   Thou day's dark taper. Mariam will appear.
   And where she shines, we need not thy dim light,

Oh haste thy steps rare creature, speed thy pace
And let thy presence make the day more bright, 1225
And cheer the heart of Herod with thy face.
It is an age since I from Mariam went;
Methinks our parting was in David's days,
The hours are so increased by discontent;
Deep sorrow Joshua-like the season stays. 1230
But when I am with Mariam, time runs on:
Her sight can make months minutes, days of weeks,
An hour is then no sooner come than gone,
When in her face mine eye for wonders seeks.
You world-commanding city, Europe's grace, 1235
Twice hath my curious eye your streets surveyed,
And I have seen the statue-filled place
That once if not for geese[76] had been betrayed.
I all your Roman beauties have beheld,
And seen the shows your aediles did prepare, 1240
I saw the sum of what in you excelled,
Yet saw no miracle like Mariam rare.
The fair and famous Livia, Caesar's love,
The world's commanding mistress did I see,
Whose beauties both the world and Rome approve; 1245
Yet Mariam, Livia is not like to thee.
Be patient but a little, while mine eyes
Within your compassed limits be contained;
That object straight shall your desires suffice,
From which you were so long a while restrained. 1250
How wisely Mariam doth the time delay,
Lest sudden joy my sense should suffocate;
I am prepared, thou needst no longer stay;
Who's there, my Mariam, more than happy fate?
Oh no, it is Pheroras, welcome brother, 1255
Now for a while, I must my passion smother.

ACT IV, SCENE II

[Enter] Pheroras.

Pher.　All health and safety wait upon my lord,
And may you long in prosperous fortune live
With Rome-commanding Caesar at accord,
And have all honours that the world can give.　　　　1260
Herod.　Oh brother, now thou speakst not from thy heart.
No, thou hast struck a blow at Herod's love,
That cannot quickly from my memory part,
Though Salome did me to pardon move.
Valiant Phasaelus, now to thee farewell,　　　　　　1265
Thou wert my kind and honourable brother.
Oh hapless hour, when you self-stricken fell,
Thou father's image, glory of thy mother.
Had I desired a greater suit of thee
Than to withold thee from a harlot's bed,　　　　　1270
Thou wouldst have granted it; but now I see
All are not like that in a womb are bred.
Thou wouldst not, hadst thou heard of Herod's death,
Have made his burial time thy bridal hour;
Thou wouldst with clamours, not with joyful breath,　1275
Have showed the news to be not sweet but sour.
Pher.　Phasaelus' great worth I know did stain
Pheroras' petty valour, but they lie
(Excepting you yourself) that dare maintain
That he did honour Herod more than I.　　　　　　1280
For what I showed, love's power constrained me show,
And pardon loving faults for Mariam's sake.
Herod.　Mariam, where is she?
Pher.　　　　　　　　Nay, I do not know,
But absent use of her fair name I make;
You have forgiven greater faults than this,　　　　　1285
For Constabarus that against your[77] will
Preserved the sons of Babus, lives in bliss,
Though you commanded him the youths to kill.

Herod. Go, take a present order for his death,
  And let those traitors feel the worst of fears; 1290
  Now Salome will whine to beg his breath,
  But I'll be deaf to prayers and blind to tears.
Pher. He is, my lord, from Salome[78] divorced,
  Though her affection did to leave him grieve;
  Yet was she by her love to him enforced, 1295
  To leave the man that would your foes relieve.
Herod. Then haste them to their death. I will requite
  Thee, gentle Mariam. Salome,[79] I mean;
  The thought of Mariam doth so steal my spirit,
  My mouth from speech of her I cannot wean. 1300

Exit [*Pheroras*].

ACT IV, SCENE III

[*Enter*] *Mariam.*

Herod. And here she comes indeed; happily met
  My best and dearest half; what ails my dear?
  Thou dost the difference certainly forget
  Twixt dusky habits and a time so clear.
Mar. My Lord, I suit my garments to my mind, 1305
  And there no cheerful colours can I find.
Herod. Is this my welcome? Have I longed so much
  To see my dearest Mariam discontent?
  What is't that is the cause thy heart to touch?
  Oh speak, that I thy sorrow may prevent. 1310
  Art thou not Jewry's queen, and Herod's too?
  Be my commandress, be my sovereign guide;
  To be by thee directed I will woo,
  For in thy pleasure lies my highest pride.
  Or if thou think Judaea's narrow bound 1315
  Too strict a limit for thy great command,
  Thou shalt be empress of Arabia crowned,
  For thou shalt rule, and I will win the land.
  I'll rob the holy David's sepulchre

The Tragedy of Mariam

  To give thee wealth, if thou for wealth do care,   1320
  Thou shalt have all they did with him inter,
  And I for thee will make the temple bare.
Mar. I neither have of power nor riches want,
  I have enough nor do I wish for more;
  Your offers to my heart no ease can grant   1325
  Except they could my brother's life restore.
  No, had you wished the wretched Mariam glad
  Or had your love to her been truly tied;
  Nay, had you not desired to make her sad,
  My brother nor my grandsire had not died.   1330
Herod. Wilt thou believe no oaths to clear thy lord?
  How oft have I with execration sworn?
  Thou art by me beloved, by me adored,
  Yet are my protestations heard with scorn.
  Hircanus plotted to deprive my head   1335
  Of this long-settled honour that I wear,[80]
  And therefore I did justly doom him dead,
  To rid the realm from peril, me from fear.
  Yet I for Mariam's sake do so repent
  The death of one whose blood she did inherit,   1340
  I wish I had a kingdom's treasure spent,
  So I had ne'er expelled Hircanus' spirit.
  As I affected that same noble youth,
  In lasting infamy my name enroll[81]
  If I not mourned his name with hearty truth.   1345
  Did I not show to him my earnest love,
  When I to him the priesthood did restore?
  And did for him a living priest remove,
  Which never had been done but once before.
Mar. I know that moved by importunity,   1350
  You made him priest, and shortly after die.
Herod. I will not speak unless to be believed,
  This froward humour will not do you good;
  It hath too much already Herod grieved,
  To think that you on terms of hate have stood.   1355
  Yet smile, my dearest Mariam, do but smile,

And I will all unkind conceits exile.
Mar.   I cannot frame disguise, nor never taught
   My face a look dissenting from my thought.
Herod.   By heaven you vex me; build not on my love.   1360
Mar.   I will not build on so unstable ground.
Herod.   Nought is so fixed but peevishness may move.
Mar.   'Tis better slightest cause than none were found.
Herod.   Be judge yourself, if ever Herod sought
   Or would be moved a cause of change to find;   1365
   Yet let your look declare a milder thought,
   My heart again you shall to Mariam bind.
   How oft did I for you my mother chide,
   Revile my sister, and my brother rate;
   And tell them all my Mariam they belied,   1370
   Distrust me still, if these be signs of hate.

ACT IV, SCENE IV

[Enter Butler.]

Herod.   What hast thou here?
But.   A drink procuring love;
   The queen desired me to deliver it.
Mar.   Did I? Some hateful practice this will prove,
   Yet can it be no worse than heavens permit.   1375
Herod.   Confess the truth, thou wicked instrument
   To her outrageous will;[82] 'tis passion sure;
   Tell true, and thou shalt 'scape the punishment,
   Which if thou dost conceal thou shalt endure.
But.   I know not, but I doubt it be no less,   1380
   Long since the hate of you her heart did cease.
Herod.   Knowst thou the cause thereof?
But.   My lord, I guess
   Sohemus told the tale that did displease.
Herod.   Oh, heaven! Sohemus false! Go, let him die,
   Stay not to suffer him to speak a word.   1385

[Exit Butler.]

Oh damned villain, did he falsify
The oath he swore e'en of his own accord?
Now do I know thy falsehood, painted devil,
Thou white enchantress. Oh, thou art so foul,
That hyssop cannot cleanse thee, worst of evil. 1390
A beauteous body hides a loathsome soul;
Your love, Sohemus, moved by his affection,
Though he have ever heretofore been true,
Did blab forsooth, that I did give direction,
If we were put to death, to slaughter you. 1395
And you in black revenge attended now
To add a murder to your breach of vow.
Mar. Is this a dream?
Herod. Oh heaven, that t'were no more;
I'll give my realm to who can prove it so;
I would I were like any beggar poor,[83] 1400
So I for false my Mariam did not know.
Foul pith contained in the fairest rind,
That ever graced a cedar. Oh, thine eye
Is pure as heaven, but impure thy mind,
And for impurity shall Mariam die. 1405
Why didst thou love Sohemus?
Mar. They can tell
That say I loved him; Mariam says not so.
Herod. Oh, cannot impudence the coals expel
That for thy love in Herod's bosom glow;
It is as plain as water, and denial 1410
Makes of thy falsehood but a greater trial.
Hast thou beheld thyself, and couldst thou stain
So rare perfection; even for love of thee
I do profoundly hate thee. Wert thou plain,
Thou shouldst the wonder of Judaea be. 1415
But oh, thou art not. Hell itself lies hid
Beneath thy heavenly show. Yet, wert thou chaste,[84]
Thou mightst exalt, pull down, command, forbid,
And be above the wheel of fortune placed.
Hadst thou complotted Herod's massacre, 1420

That so thy son a monarch might be styled,
Not half so grievous such an action were,
As once to think that Mariam is defiled.
Bright workmanship of nature sullied o'er
With pitched darkness now thine end shall be;   1425
Thou shalt not live, fair fiend, to cozen more,
With heav'nly[85] semblance as thou coz'nedst me.
Yet must I love thee in despite of death,
And thou shalt die in the despite of love;
For neither shall my love prolong thy breath,   1430
Nor shall thy loss of breath my love remove.
I might have seen thy falsehood in thy face:
Where couldst thou get thy stars that served for eyes?
Except by theft, and theft is foul disgrace.
This had appeared before were Herod wise,   1435
But I'm a sot, a very sot, no better;
My wisdom long ago a-wandering fell;
Thy face encountering it, my wit did fetter,
And made me for delight my freedom sell.
Give me my heart, false creature; 'tis a wrong   1440
My guiltless heart should now with thine be slain;
Thou hadst no right to lock[86] it up so long,
And with usurper's name, I Mariam stain.[87]

Enter Bu[tler].

Herod. Have you designed Sohemus to his end?
But. I have, my lord.
Herod.   Then call our royal guard   1445
To do as much for Mariam; they offend,
Leave ill unblamed, or good without reward.

[Enter Soldiers.]

Here, take her to her death. Come back, come back;
What, meant I to deprive the world of light,
To muffle Jewry in the foulest black,   1450
That ever was an opposite to white?
Why, whither would you carry her?

The Tragedy of Mariam

Soldiers.   You bade
   We should conduct her to her death, my lord.
Herod.   Why, sure I did not; Herod was not mad,
   Why should she feel the fury of the sword?   1455
   Oh, now the grief returns into my heart,
   And pulls me piecemeal; love and hate do fight;
   And now hath love[88] acquired the greater part,
   Yet now hath hate, affection conquered quite.
   And therefore bear her hence; and Hebrew why   1460
   Seize you with lion's paws the fairest lamb
   Of all the flock?[89] She must not, shall not die,
   Without her I most miserable am.
   And with her more than most; away, away,
   But bear her but to prison, not to death.   1465
   And is she gone indeed? Stay, villains, stay,
   Her looks alone preserved your sovereign's breath.
   Well, let her go; but yet she shall not die;
   I cannot think she meant to poison me;
   But certain 'tis she lived too wantonly,   1470
   And therefore shall she never more be free.

   [*Exeunt Herod and Soldiers with Mariam.*]

ACT IV, SCENE V

But.   Foul villain, can thy pitchy-coloured soul
   Permit thine ear to hear her causeless[90] doom?
   And not enforce thy tongue that tale control
   That must unjustly bring her to her tomb?   1475
   Oh, Salome! Thou hast thyself repaid
   For all the benefits that thou hast done;
   Thou art the cause I have the queen betrayed,
   Thou hast my heart to darkest falsehood won.
   I am condemned, heaven gave me not my tongue   1480
   To slander innocents, to lie, deceive,
   To be the hateful instrument to wrong,
   The earth of greatest glory to bereave.

My sin ascends and doth to heaven cry,
It is the blackest deed that ever was;   1485
And there doth sit an angel notary
That doth record it down in leaves of brass.
Oh, how my heart doth quake: Achitophel,
Thou found a means thyself from shame to free;
And sure my soul approves thou didst not well;   1490
All follow some, and I will follow thee.[91]

[*Exit Butler.*]

ACT IV, SCENE VI

[*Enter*] *Constabarus, Babus' Sons, and their guard.*

Const.   Now here we step our last, the way to death,
   We must not tread this way a second time;
   Yet let us resolutely yield our breath:
   Death is the only ladder, heaven to climb.   1495
1 Son.   With willing mind I could myself resign,
   But yet it grieves me with a grief untold,
   Our death should be accompanied with thine,
   Our friendship we to thee have dearly sold.
Const.   Still wilt thou wrong the sacred name of friend?   1500
   Then shouldst thou never style it friendship more,
   But base mechanic traffic that doth lend
   Yet will be sure they shall the debt restore.
   I could with needless compliment return,
   'Tis for thy ceremony, I could say   1505
   'Tis I that made the fire your house to burn,
   For but for me she would not you betray.
   Had not the damned woman sought mine end,
   You had not been the subject of her hate;
   You never did her hateful mind offend,   1510
   Nor could your deaths have freed your nuptial fate.
   Therefore fair friends, though you were still unborn,
   Some other subtlety devised should be,

The Tragedy of Mariam

Whereby my life, though guiltless, should be torn;
Thus have I proved, 'tis you that die for me. 1515
And therefore should I weakly now lament,
You have but done your duties: friends should die
Alone their friends' disasters to prevent,
Though not compelled by strong necessity.
But now farewell, fair city, never more 1520
Shall I behold your beauty shining bright;
Farewell of Jewish men the worthy store,
But no farewell to any female wight.
You wavering crew: my curse to you I leave,
You had but one to give you any grace; 1525
And you yourselves will Mariam's life bereave,
Your commonwealth doth innocency chafe.
You creatures made to be the human curse,
You tigers, lionesses, hungry bears,
Tear-massacring hyenas; nay, far worse, 1530
For they for prey do shed their feigned tears.
But you will weep (you creatures cross to good)
For your unquenched thirst of human blood;
You were the angels cast from heaven for pride,
And still do keep your angels' outward show, 1535
But none of you are inly beautified,
For still your heaven-depriving pride doth grow.
Did not the sins of many[92] require a scourge,
Your place on earth had been by this withstood;
But since a flood no more the world must purge, 1540
You stayed in office of a second flood.
You giddy creatures, sowers of debate,
You'll love today, and for no other cause,
But for you yesterday did deeply hate;
You are the wreck of order, breach of laws; 1545
You, best, are foolish, froward, wanton, vain,
Your worst, adulterous, murderous, cunning, proud;
And Salome attends the latter train,
Or rather she[93] their leader is allowed.
I do the sottishness of men bewail, 1550

That do with following you enhance your pride;
'Twere better that the human race should fail,
Than be by such a mischief multiplied.
Cham's servile curse[94] to all your sex was given,
Because in Paradise you did offend; 1555
Then do we not resist the will of heaven
When on your wills like servants we attend?
You are to nothing constant but to ill,
You are with naught but wickedness indued;
Your loves are set on nothing but your will, 1560
And thus my censure I of you conclude.
You are the least of goods, the worst of evils,
Your best are worse than men; your worst than devils.
2 Son. Come, let us to our death; are we not blest?
Our death will freedom from these creatures give, 1565
Those trouble quiet sowers of unrest;
And this I vow that had I leave to live,
I would forever lead a single life,
And never venture on a devilish wife.

[*Exeunt omnes.*]

ACT IV, SCENE VII

[*Enter*] *Herod and Salome.*

Herod. Nay, she shall die. Die, quoth you; that she shall; 1570
But for the means. The means! Methinks 'tis hard
To find a means to murder her withal.
Therefore I am resolved she shall be spared.
Sal. Why, let her be beheaded.
Herod. That were well;
Think you that swords are miracles like you? 1575
Her skin will every cutlass-edge repel,[95]
And then your enterprise you well may rue.
What if the fierce Arabian notice take
Of this your wretched weaponless estate;
They answer when we bid resistance make, 1580

The Tragedy of Mariam

    That Mariam's skin their falchions did rebate.[96]
    Beware of this; you make a goodly hand,
    When you of weapons do deprive our land.
Sal.   Why, drown her then.
Herod.   Indeed a sweet device;
    Why, would not every river turn her course,   1585
    Rather than do her beauty prejudice?
    And be reverted to the proper source,
    So not a drop of water should be found,
    In all Judaea's quondam fertile ground.
Sal.   Then let the fire devour her.
Herod.   'Twill not be;   1590
    Flame is from her derived into my heart;
    Thou nursest flame, flame will not murder thee,
    My fairest Mariam, fullest of desert.
Sal.   Then let her live for me.
Herod.   Nay, she shall die;
    But can you live without her?
Sal.   Doubt you that?   1595
Herod.   I'm sure I cannot, I beseech you try;
    I have experience but I know not what.
Sal.   How should I try?
Herod.   Why, let my love be slain,[97]
    But if we cannot live without her sight,
    You'll find the means to make her breathe again,   1600
    Or else you will bereave my comfort quite.
Sal.   Oh aye, I warrant you.

            [*Exit Salome.*]

Herod.   What, is she gone?
    And gone to bid the world be overthrown;
    What? Is her heart's composure hardest stone?
    To what a pass are cruel women grown?   1605

            [*Enter Salome.*]

    She is returned already; have you done?
    Is't possible you can command so soon

A creature's heart to quench the flaming sun,
Or from the sky to wipe away the moon?
Sal.   If Mariam be the sun and moon, it is;   1610
For I already have commanded this.
Herod.   But have you seen her cheek?
Sal.   A thousand times.
Herod.   But did you mark it too?
Sal.   Aye, very well.
Herod.   What is't?
Sal.   A crimson bush, that ever limes
The soul whose foresight doth not much excel.[98]   1615
Herod.   Send word she shall not die. Her cheek a bush;
Nay, then I see indeed you marked it not.
Sal.   'Tis very fair, but yet will never blush,
Though foul dishonours do her forehead blot.
Herod.   Then let her die, 'tis very true indeed,   1620
And for this fault alone shall Mariam bleed.
Sal.   What fault, my lord?
Herod.   What fault is't? You that ask,
If you be ignorant, I know of none;
To call her back from death shall be your task;
I'm glad that she for innocent is known.   1625
For on the brow of Mariam hangs a fleece,
Whose slenderest twine is strong enough to bind
The hearts of kings; the pride and shame of Greece,
Troy-flaming Helen's, not so fairly shined.
Sal.   'Tis true indeed; she lays them out for nets,   1630
To catch the hearts that do not shun a bait;
'Tis time to speak, for Herod sure forgets,
That Mariam's very tresses hide deceit.
Herod.   Oh, do they so? Nay then, you do but well;
In sooth I thought it had been hair;[99]   1635
Nets, call you them? Lord, how they do excel;
I never saw a net that showed so fair.
But have you heard her speak?
Sal.   You know I have.
Herod.   And were you not amazed?

Sal.   No, not a whit.
Herod.   Then 'twas not her you heard; her life I'll save
    For Mariam hath a world-amazing wit.
Sal.   She speaks a beauteous language, but within
    Her heart is false as powder, and her tongue
    Doth but allure the auditors to sin,
    And is the instrument to do you wrong.
Herod.   It may be so; nay, 'tis so; she's unchaste;
    Her mouth will ope to every stranger's ear.
    Then let the executioner make haste,
    Lest she enchant him, if her words he hear;
    Let him be deaf, lest she do him surprise,
    That shall to free her spirit be assigned;
    Yet what boots deafness if he have his eyes;
    Her murderer must be both deaf and blind.
    For if he sees, he needs must see the stars
    That shine on either side of Mariam's face,
    Whose sweet aspect will terminate the wars,
    Wherewith he should a soul so precious chase.
    Her eyes can speak, and in their speaking move;
    Oft did my heart with reverence receive
    The world's mandates. Pretty tales of love
    They utter, which can human bondage weave.
    But shall I let this heaven's model die?
    Which for a small self-portraiture she drew;
    Her eyes like stars, her forhead like the sky,
    She is like heaven, and must be heavenly true.
Sal.   Your thoughts do rave with doting on the queen;
    Her eyes are ebon-hued, and you'll confess
    A sable star hath been but seldom seen,
    Then speak of reason more, of Mariam less.
Herod.   Yourself are held a goodly creature here,
    Yet so unlike my Mariam in your shape,
    That when to her you have approached near,
    My self have often ta'en you for an ape.
    And yet you prate of beauty; go your ways,
    You are to her a sunburnt blackamoor;

       Your paintings cannot equal Mariam's praise,[100]
       Her nature is so rich, you are so poor.
       Let her be stayed from death, for if she die,
       We do we know not what to stop her breath,
       A world cannot another Mariam buy.   1680
       Why stay you lingering? Countermand her death.
Sal.   Then you'll no more remember what hath passed;
       Sohemus' love, and hers, shall be forgot.
       'Tis well in truth; that fault may be her last,
       And she may mend, though yet she love you not.   1685
Herod.   Oh God, 'tis true. Sohemus: earth and heaven,
       Why did you both conspire to make me cursed?
       In coz'ning me with shows, and proofs uneven?
       She showed the best, and yet did prove the worst.
       Her show was such as had our singing king,   1690
       The holy David, Mariam's beauty seen,
       The Hittites had then felt no deadly sting,
       Nor Bethsabe[101] had never been a queen.
       Or had his son, the wisest man of men,
       Whose fond delight did most consist in change,   1695
       Beheld her face, he had been stayed again,
       No creature having her can wish to range.
       Had Asuerus seen my Mariam's brow
       The humble Jew, she might have walked alone,[102]
       Her beauteous virtue should have stayed below,   1700
       While Mariam mounted to the Persian throne.
       But what avails it all; for in the weight
       She is deceitful, light as vanity;
       Oh, she was made for nothing but a bait,
       To train some hapless man to misery.   1705
       I am the hapless man that have been trained
       To endless bondage. I will see her yet;
       Methinks I should discern her if she feigned.
       Can human eyes be dazed by woman's wit?
       Once more these eyes of mine with hers shall meet,   1710
       Before the headsman do her life bereave;
       Shall I for ever part from thee, my sweet,

The Tragedy of Mariam

    Without the taking of my latest leave?
Sal.   You had as good resolve to save her now;
    I'll stay her death, 'tis well determined,   1715
    For sure she never more will break her vow,
    Sohemus and Josephus both are dead.
Herod.   She shall not live, nor will I see her face,
    A long-healed wound a second time doth bleed;
    With Joseph I remember her disgrace,   1720
    A shameful end ensues a shameful deed.
    Oh, that I had not called to mind anew
    The discontent of Mariam's murmuring heart;
    'Twas you, you foul-mouthed ape, none but you,
    That did the thought hereof to me impart.   1725
    Hence from my sight, my black tormentor, hence!
    For hadst not thou made Herod insecure,
    I had not doubted Mariam's innocence,
    But still had held her in my heart for pure.
Sal.   I'll leave you to your passion; 'tis no time   1730
    To purge me now, though of a guiltless crime.

        Exit [*Salome*].

Herod.   Destruction take thee; thou hast made my heart
    As heavy as revenge; I am so dull,
    Methinks I am not sensible of smart,
    Though hideous horrors at my bosom pull.   1735
    My head weighs downwards; therefore will I go
    To try if I can sleep away my woe.

        [*Exit Herod.*]

ACT IV, SCENE VIII

        [*Enter*] *Mariam.*

Mar.   Am I the Mariam that presumed so much,
    And deemed my face must needs preserve my breath?
    I, I it was that thought my beauty such   1740
    As[103] it alone could countermand my death.

Now death will teach me; he can pale as well
A cheek of roses as a cheek less bright;
And dim an eye whose shine doth most excel
As soon as one that casts a meaner light. 1745
Had not myself against myself conspired,
No plot, no adversary from without
Could Herod's love from Mariam have retired
Or from his heart have thrust my semblance out.
The wanton queen that never loved for love, 1750
False Cleopatra, wholly set on gain,
With all her slights did prove, yet vainly prove
For her the love of Herod to obtain.
Yet her allurements, all her courtly guile,
Her smiles, her favours and her smooth deceit, 1755
Could not my face from Herod's mind exile,
But were with him of less than little weight.
That face and person that in Asia late
For beauty's goddess, Paphos' queen was ta'en,[104]
That face that did captive great Julius' fate, 1760
That very face that was Antonius' bane,
That face that to be Egypt's pride was born,
That face that all the world esteemed so rare,
Did Herod hate, despise, neglect and scorn,
When with the same, he Mariam's did compare. 1765
This made that I improvidently wrought
And on the wager even my life did pawn;
Because I thought, and yet but truly thought,
That Herod's love could not from me be drawn.
But now though out of time, I plainly see 1770
It could be drawn, though never drawn from me;
Had I but with humility been graced,
As well as fair I might have proved me wise;
But I did think because I knew me chaste,
One virtue for a woman might suffice. 1775
That mind for glory of our sex might stand,
Wherein humility and chastity
Doth march with equal paces hand in hand,

    But one if single seen, who setteth by?
    And I had singly one, but 'tis my joy,   1780
    That I was ever innocent, though sour;
    And therefore can they but my life destroy,
    My soul is free from adversaries' power.

Enter Doris.

    You princes great in power, and high in birth,
    Be great and high: I envy not your hap;   1785
    Your birth must be from dust, your power on earth;
    In heaven shall Mariam sit in Sarah's lap.[105]
Doris.   In[106] heaven? Your beauty cannot bring you thither;
    Your soul is black and spotted, full of sin:
    You in adultery lived nine years together,   1790
    And heaven will never let adultery in.
Mar.   What art thou that dost poor Mariam pursue?
    Some spirit sent to drive me to despair,
    Who sees for truth that Mariam is untrue;
    If fair she be, she is as chaste as fair.   1795
Doris.   I am that Doris that was once beloved,
    Beloved by Herod, Herod's lawful wife;
    'Twas you that Doris from his side removed,
    And robbed from me the glory of my life.
Mar.   Was that adultery? Did not Moses say   1800
    That he that being matched did deadly hate,
    Might by permission put his wife away,
    And take a more beloved to be his mate?
Doris.   What did he hate me for? For simple truth?
    For bringing beauteous babes for love to him?   1805
    For riches? Noble birth? Or tender youth?
    Or for no stain did Doris' honour dim?
    Oh, tell me Mariam, tell me if you know,
    Which fault of these made Herod Doris' foe?
    These thrice three years have I with hands held up   1810
    And bowed knees fast nailed to the ground,
    Besought for thee the dregs of that same cup,
    That cup of wrath that is for sinners found.

   And now thou art to drink it; Doris' curse
   Upon thyself did all this while attend,   1815
   But now it shall pursue thy children worse.
Mar. Oh, Doris, now to thee my knees I bend;
   That heart that never bowed to thee doth bow;
   Curse not mine infants; let it thee suffice
   That heaven doth punishment to me allow.   1820
   Thy curse is cause that guiltless Mariam dies.
Doris. Had I ten thousand tongues, and every tongue
   Inflamed with poison's power, and steeped in gall,
   My curses would not answer for my wrong,
   Though I in cursing thee employed them all.   1825
   Hear thou that did Mount Gerarim command[107]
   To be a place whereon with cause to curse;
   Stretch thy revenging arm; thrust forth thy hand,
   And plague the mother much, the children worse.
   Throw flaming fire upon the base-born heads   1830
   That were begotten in unlawful beds.
   But let them live till they have sense to know
   What 'tis to be in miserable state;
   Then be their nearest friends their overthrow,
   Attended be they by suspicious hate.   1835
   And Mariam, I do hope this boy of mine,
   Shall one day come to be the death of thine.

       Exit [*Doris*].

Mar. Oh, heaven forbid! I hope the world shall see
   This curse of thine shall be returned on thee;
   Now, earth farewell, though I be yet but young,   1840
   Yet I, methinks, have known thee too too long.

       Exit [*Mariam*].

       Chorus

The fairest action of our human life
Is scorning to revenge an injury;

For who forgives without a further strife
His adversary's heart to him doth tie.
And 'tis a firmer conquest truly said,
To win the heart, then overthrow the head.

If we a worthy enemy do find,
To yield to worth, it must be nobly done;
But if of baser metal be his mind,
In base revenge there is no honour won.
Who would a worthy courage overthrow
And who would wrestle with a worthless foe?

We say our hearts are great and cannot yield;
Because they cannot yield it proves them poor;
Great hearts are tasked beyond their power, but seld
The weakest lion will the loudest roar.
Truth's school for certain does this fame allow,
High-heartedness doth sometimes teach to bow.

A noble heart doth teach a virtuous scorn,
To scorn to owe a duty overlong;
To scorn to be for benefits forborne,
To scorn to lie, to scorn to do a wrong;
To scorn to bear an injury in mind,
To scorn a free-born heart slave-like to bind.

But if for wrongs we needs revenge must have,
Then be our vengeance of the noblest kind;
Do we his body from our fury save
And let our hate prevail against our mind?
What can 'gainst him a greater vengeance be,
Than make his foe more worthy far than he?

Had Mariam scorned to leave a due unpaid,
She would to Herod then have paid her love,
And not have been by sullen passion swayed;
To fix her thoughts all injury above
Is virtuous pride. Had Mariam thus been proved,
Long famous life to her had been allowed.

ACT V, SCENE I

[Enter] Nuntio.

Nun.   When, sweetest friend, did I so far offend
   Your heavenly self, that you, my fault to quit,
   Have made me now relator of her end,   1880
   The end of beauty, chastity and wit?
   Was none so hapless in the fatal place,
   But I, most wretched, for the queen to choose?
   'Tis certain I have some ill-boding face,
   That made me culled[108] to tell this luckless news.   1885
   And yet no news to Herod; were it new
   To him unhappy t'had not been at all.
   Yet do I long to come within his view,
   That he may know his wife did guiltless fall;
   And here he comes.

Enter Herod.

            Your Mariam greets you well.[109]   1890
Herod.   What? Lives my Mariam? Joy, exceeding joy;
   She shall not die.
Nun.   Heaven doth your will repel.
Herod.   Oh do not with thy words my life destroy,
   I prithee tell no dying tale; thine eye
   Without thy tongue doth tell but too too much.   1895
   Yet let thy tongue's addition make me die;
   Death welcome comes to him whose grief is such.
Nun.   I went amongst the curious gazing troop,
   To see the last of her that was the best,
   To see if death had heart to make her stoop,   1900
   To see the sun-admiring Phoenix nest.
   When there I came, upon the way I saw
   The stately Mariam not debased by fear;
   Her look did seem to keep the world in awe,
   Yet mildly did her face this fortune bear.   1905

Herod. Thou dost usurp my right, my tongue was framed
   To be the instrument of Mariam's praise.
   Yet speak: she cannot be too often famed:
   All tongues suffice not her sweet name to raise.
Nun. But as she came, she Alexandra met, 1910
   Who did her death (sweet queen) no whit bewail,
   But as if nature she did quite forget,
   She did upon her daughter loudly rail.
Herod. Why stopped you not her mouth? Where had she words
   To darken[110] that, that heaven made so bright? 1915
   Out sacred tongue, no epithet affords
   To call her other than the world's delight.
Nun. She told her that her death was too too good,
   And that already she had lived too long.
   She said, she shamed to have a part in blood 1920
   Of her that did the princely Herod wrong.
Herod. Base pick-thank devil. Shame, 'twas all her glory,
   That she to noble Mariam was the mother.
   But never shall it live in any story,
   Her name, except to infamy I'll smother. 1925
   What answer did her princely daughter make?
Nun. She made no answer, but she looked the while,
   As if thereof she scarce did notice take,
   Yet smiled, a dutiful though scornful smile.
Herod. Sweet creature, I that look to mind do call, 1930
   Full oft has Herod been amazed withal.
   Go on.[111]
Nun. She came unmoved, with pleasant grace,
   As if to triumph her arrival were,
   In stately habit, and with cheerful face,
   Yet every eye was moist, but Mariam's, there. 1935
   When justly opposite to me she came,
   She picked me out from all the crew;[112]
   She beckoned to me, called me by my name,
   For she my name, my birth and fortune knew.
Herod. What, did she name thee? Happy, happy man, 1940

> Will thou not ever love that name the better?
> But what sweet tune did this fair dying swan
> Afford thine ear; tell all, omit no letter.
>
> *Nun.* Tell thou my lord, said she.
> *Herod.*   Me, meant she me?
> Is't true; the more my shame. I was her lord.   1945
> Were I not made her lord, I still should be;[113]
> But now her name must be by me adored.
> Oh say, what said she more? Each word she said
> Shall be the food on which my heart is fed.
> *Nun.* Tell thou my lord thou sawst me lose my breath.   1950
> *Herod.* Oh, that I could that sentence now control.
> *Nun.* If guiltily eternal be my death —
> *Herod.* I hold her chaste even in my inmost soul.
> *Nun.* By three days hence if wishes could revive,
>   I know himself would make me oft alive.   1955
> *Herod.* Three days; three hours, three minutes, not so much,
>   A minute in a thousand parts divide;[114]
>   My penitence for her death is such,
>   As in the first I wished she had not died.
>   But forward in thy tale.
> *Nun.*   Why on she went,   1960
>   And after she some silent prayer had said,
>   She did as if to die she were content,
>   And thus to heaven her heavenly soul is fled.
> *Herod.* But art thou sure there doth no life remain?
>   Is't possible my Mariam should be dead?   1965
>   Is there no trick to make her breathe again?
> *Nun.* Her body is divided from her head.
> *Herod.* Why yet methinks there might be found by art
>   Strange ways of cure, 'tis sure rare things are done
>   By an inventive head, and willing heart.   1970
> *Nun.* Let not, my lord, your fancies idly run.
>   It is as possible it should be seen
>   That we should make the holy Abraham live,
>   Though he entombed two thousand years hath been,
>   As breath again to slaughtered Mariam give.   1975

The Tragedy of Mariam

  But now for more assaults prepare your ears.
Herod. There cannot be a further cause of moan,
  This accident shall shelter me from fears.
  What can I fear? Already Mariam's gone,
  Yet tell e'en what you will.
Nun.   As I came by 1980
  From Mariam's death, I saw upon a tree
  A man that to his neck a cord did tie,
  Which cord he had designed his end to be.
  When me he once discerned, he downwards bowed,
  And thus with fearful voice he[115] cried aloud: 1985
  Go tell the King he trusted ere he tried,
  I am the cause that Mariam causeless died.
Herod. Damnation take him, for it was the slave
  That said she meant with poison's deadly force
  To end my life that she the crown might have, 1990
  Which tale did Mariam from her self divorce.
  Oh pardon me, thou pure unspotted ghost,
  My punishment must needs sufficient be,
  In missing that content I valued most,
  Which was thy admirable face to see. 1995
  I had but one inestimable jewel,
  Yet one I had, no monarch had the like,
  And therefore may I curse myself as cruel,
  'Twas broken by a blow myself did strike.
  I gazed thereon and never thought me blessed, 2000
  But when on it my dazzled eye might rest,
  A precious mirror made by wondrous art,
  I prized it ten times dearer than my crown,
  And laid it up fast folded in my heart.
  Yet I in sudden choler cast it down, 2005
  And pashed[116] it all to pieces; 'twas no foe
  That robbed me of it; no Arabian host,
  Nor no Armenian guide hath used me so;
  But Herod's wretched self has Herod crossed.
  She was my graceful moiety, me accursed, 2010
  To slay my better half and save my worst.

But sure she is not dead, you did but jest,
To put me in perplexity a while;
'Twere well indeed, if I could so be dressed;
I see she is alive, methinks you smile. 2015
Nun. If sainted Abel yet deceased be,
'Tis certain Mariam is as dead as he.[117]
Herod. Why then go call her to me, bid her now
Put on fair habit, stately ornament,
And let no frown o'ershade her smoothest brow 2020
In her doth Herod place his whole content.
Nun. She'll come in stately weeds to please your sense,
If now she come attired in robe of heaven;
Remember you yourself did send her hence,
And now to you she can no more be given. 2025
Herod. She's dead, hell take her murderers; she was fair.
Oh, what a hand she had, it was so white,
It did the whiteness of the snow impair,
I never more shall see so sweet a sight.
Nun. 'Tis true, her hand was rare.
Herod. Her hand? Her hands! 2030
She had not singly one of beauty rare,
But such a pair as here where Herod stands,
He dares the world to make to both compare.
Accursed Salome, hadst thou been still,
My Mariam had been breathing by my side: 2035
Oh never had I, had I had my will,
Sent forth command, that Mariam should have died.
But Salome thou didst with envy vex,
To see thyself outmatched in thy sex.
Upon your sex's forehead Mariam sat, 2040
To grace you all like an imperial crown,
But you fond fool have rudely pushed thereat,
And proudly pulled your proper glory down.
One smile of hers, nay not so much, a look,
Was worth a hundred thousand such as you. 2045
Judaea, how can thou the wretches brook
That robbed from thee the fairest of the crew?

The Tragedy of Mariam

> You dwellers in the now-deprived land,
> Wherein the matchless Mariam was bred,
> Why grasp not each of you a sword in hand,   2050
> To aim at me your cruel sovereign's head?
> Oh, when you think of Herod as your king,
> And owner of the pride of Palestine,
> This act to your remembrance likewise bring,
> 'Tis I have overthrown your royal line.   2055
> Within her purer veins the blood did run,
> That from her granddam Sarah she derived,
> Whose beldame age the love of kings hath won;
> Oh, that her issue had as long been lived!
> But can her eye be made by death obscure?   2060
> I cannot think but it must sparkle still,
> Foul sacrilege to rob those lights so pure,
> From out a temple made by heavenly skill.
> I am the villain that have done the deed,
> The cruel deed, though by another's hand;   2065
> My word though not my sword made Mariam bleed,
> Hircanus' grandchild died[118] at my command,
> That Mariam that I once did love so dear,
> The partner of my now-detested bed.
> Why shine you, sun, with an aspect so clear?   2070
> I tell you once again, my Mariam's dead.
> You could but shine, if some Egyptian blows,[119]
> Or Ethiopian dowdy lose her life;
> This was, then wherefore bend you not your brows,
> The king of Jewry's fair and spotless wife.   2075
> Deny thy beams, and moon, refuse thy light,
> Let all the stars be dark, let Jewry's eye
> No more distinguish which is day and night,
> Since her best birth did in her bosom die.
> Those fond idolators the men of Greece   2080
> Maintain these orbs are safely governed,
> That each within themselves have gods apiece,
> By whom their steadfast course is justly led.
> But were it so, as so it cannot be,

They all would put their mourning garments on; 2085
Not one of them would yield a light to me,
To me that is the cause that Mariam's gone.
For though they fain their Saturn melancholy,
Of sour behaviours, and of angry mood,
They fain him likewise to be just and holy, 2090
And justice needs must seek revenge for blood.
Their Jove, if Jove he were, would sure desire,
To punish him that slew so fair a lass;
For Leda's beauty set his heart on fire,
Yet she not half so fair as Mariam was. 2095
And Mars would deem his Venus had been slain,
Sol to recover her would never stick;
For if he want the power her life to gain,
Then physic's god is but an empiric.
The queen of love would storm for beauty's sake, 2100
And Hermes too, since he bestowed her wit;
The night's pale light for angry grief would shake,
To see chaste Mariam die in age unfit.
But oh, I am deceived, she passed them all,
In every gift, in every property; 2105
Her excellencies wrought her timeless fall,
And they rejoiced, not grieved, to see her die.
The Paphian goddess did repent her waste,
When she to one such beauty did allow;
Mercurius thought her wit his wit surpassed, 2110
And Cynthia envied Mariam's brighter brow.
But these are fictions, they are void of sense,
The Greeks but dream, and dreaming falsehoods tell:
They neither can offend nor give defence,
And not by them it was my Mariam fell. 2115
If she had been like an Egyptian black,
And not so fair, she had been longer lived;
Her overflow of beauty turned back,
And drowned the spring from whence it was derived.
Her heavenly beauty 'twas that made me think, 2120
That it with chastity could never dwell.

But now I see that heaven in her did link,
A spirit and a person to excel.
I'll muffle up myself in endless night,
And never let mine eyes behold the light.
Retire thyself, vile monster, worse than he
That stained the virgin earth with brother's blood.
Still in some vault or den enclosed be,
Where with thy tears thou mayest beget a flood,
Which flood in time may drown thee; happy day,
When thou at once shalt die and find a grave.
A stone upon the vault someone shall lay,
Which monument shall an inscription have.
And these shall be the words it shall contain:
Here Herod lies, that hath his Mariam slain.

Chorus.

Whoever hath beheld with steadfast eye
The strange events of this one only day,
How many were deceived? How many die,
That once today did grounds of safety lay?
It will from them all certainty bereave,
Since twice six hours so many can deceive.

This morning Herod held for surely dead,
And all the Jews on Mariam did attend,
And Constabarus rise from Salom's bed,
And neither dreamed of a divorce or end.
Pheroras joyed that he might have his wife,
And Babus' sons for safety of their life.

Tonight our Herod doth alive remain,
The guiltless Mariam is deprived of breath,
Stout Constabarus both divorced and slain,
The valiant sons of Babus have their death.
Pheroras sure his love to be bereft,
If Salome her suit unmade had left.

Herod this morning did expect with joy,
To see his Mariam's much-beloved face.　　　　　　2155
And yet ere night he did her life destroy,
And surely thought she did her name disgrace.
Yet now again, so short do humours last,
He both repents her death and knows her chaste.

Had he with wisdom now her death delayed,　　　　2160
He at his pleasure might command her death.
But now he has his power so much betrayed,
As all his woes cannot restore her breath.
Now doth he strangely, lunaticly rave,
Because his Mariam's life he cannot save.　　　　　2165

This day's events were certainly ordained
To be the warning to posterity.
So many changes are therein contained,
So admirable strange variety,
This day alone, our sagest Hebrews shall　　　　　2170
In after times the school of wisdom call.

Finis.

NOTES

[1] 'Mistress Elizabeth Cary' was the author's sister-in-law, the wife of Philip Cary, brother of Cary's husband Henry Cary. This dedicatory poem is found only in two extant copies of *Mariam*.
[2] This line and the line about Apollo seem to refer to a lost work set in Sicily and dedicated to Henry Cary. The *Life* does not mention this work, but John Davies's poem to Cary refers to 'the scenes of Syracuse and Palestine'; Syracuse is a city in Sicily.
[3] A1R of the Huntington Library copy contains a list of 'The Names of the Speakers'; this title makes the play's status as a closet drama clear. I have used this list and have added some helpful details in square brackets. The spelling of the names of characters varies considerably in the text; I have normalized them so that the following spellings are always adopted; Babus, Constabarus, Silleus. All characters' names appear in full here, though some are abbreviated in the text.
[4] The principal source for the play is Thomas Lodge's translation of Josephus, *The Famous and Memorable Works of Josephus*, printed by G. Bishop, S. Waterson, P. Short and Thomas Adams, 1602; Cary makes particular use of Mariam's story as given in *Josephus of the Antiquity of the Jews*, Book xv, Chapters ix–xi, but the story is also given in Josephus, *History of the Jewish War*, also translated by Lodge, I. 431–45.
[5] 'grand-daughter': 'daughter' in text – that this is an error is demonstrated in the next paragraph, where Hircanus is described as the grandfather of Mariam's brother.
[6] Hircanus was the last legitimate ruler of Maccabean descent; Herod is from Idumaea, the Edomite territory south of Judaea forcibly converted to Judaism near the end of the second century BC.
[7] This line appears two syllables short.
[8] 'lowlyest' in text.
[9] 'maide' in text. The BL copytext has 'minde' as a manuscript emendation and I have followed this.
[10] 'vaunt-courier': a soldier or horseman sent out in advance of the main body; hence one sent out to announce the approach of another.
[11] 'murthers' in text.
[12] Herod is an Idumaean or Edomite and so a descendant of Esau, whereas Hircanus and Aristobolus are the legitimate heirs of David and therefore descendants of the younger brother Jacob.
[13] 'fain'd' in text.
[14] 'Edom' is the name given to Esau, meaning 'the red' (Genesis 25:30).
[15] 'Mariam' in text.

[16] The original assigns this speech to the messenger, but the speaker must be Mariam.
[17] 'passed' in text.
[18] Mariam and Alexandra are here discussing two different Alexanders: 'My Alexander', mentioned by Mariam, is her eldest son, at this point Herod's declared heir, rather than Antipater, the son of his first wife Doris; the Alexander 'of David's blood' to whom Alexandra refers is Mariam's father, son of Hircanus.
[19] 'slight' in text.
[20] 'leeke' in text.
[21] A reference to the battle of Actium; this is the first of two extended references to the story of Antony and Cleopatra. Both Samuel Daniel's *Tragedy of Cleopatra* and Mary Sidney, Countess of Pembroke's 1592 translation of Garnier's *Marc-Antoine* might have been fresh in Cary's mind as possible exempla.
[22] 'fumish': hot-tempered, irascible.
[23] 'suspitious' in text.
[24] I.e. Mariam (the head) should not contend with her social and moral inferior Salome (the foot).
[25] 'allyes' in text.
[26] 'Arabian' in text.
[27] 'for' in text.
[28] 'principles' in text.
[29] 'home' in text.
[30] Proverbs 12:4: 'A virtuous woman is a crown to her husband: but she that maketh ashamed is as rottenness in his bones'.
[31] 'swine' in text.
[32] The Gibeonites tricked Joshua and the Israelites into signing a peace treaty with them by pretending to be from a far country. Once Joshua discovered the trick, he made the Gibeonites 'hewers of wood and drawers of water for the congregation, and for the altar of the Lord' (Joshua 9:3–27).
[33] The land of Ham: Egypt.
[34] 'vowd' in text.
[35] 'Of' in text.
[36] This line is a syllable short; 'kindreds' in text.
[37] An echo of the Magnificat, Mary's prayer after the Annunciation (Luke 1:46–55).
[38] I.e. prevent Graphina's smile.
[39] I.e. should Herod's body become reunited with his soul.
[40] 'need' in text.
[41] 'operpast' in text.
[42] 'safely' in text.
[43] 'leer': to look askance at.
[44] 'falchion': a sword.
[45] This line appears two syllables short.
[46] 'Constab:' in text.
[47] 'live' in text.
[48] 'Julions' in text.

The Tragedy of Mariam

[49] 'phisnomy': physiognomy.
[50] 'Your' in text.
[51] Dunstan suggest 'oaths', but the metaphor may be of rain in the desert rather than many raindrops.
[52] 'expectation' in text. Expectation makes the line eleven syllables.
[53] 'Salom' in text.
[54] See Matthew 23:27: 'for ye are like unto whited sepulchres, which indeed appear beautiful outward, but are within full of dead men's bones, and of all uncleanness.'
[55] I.e. before one or both of them is killed.
[56] This stage direction appears in the text as part of Constabarus' speech: 'I, I, they fight'.
[57] 'so' in text.
[58] 'way' in text.
[59] 'bares' in text.
[60] This line appears two syllables short.
[61] 'Constan:' in text.
[62] Ophir is a mentioned a number of times as a source of gold in the Old Testament.
[63] I.e. Tyre, a rich Phoenician trading-port sacked after a long siege by Alexander the Great.
[64] 'no' in text.
[65] 'Consta:' in text.
[66] 'Consta:' in text.
[67] 'he' in text. Dunstan suggests 'we', but the subject of the final line must be singular as it stands.
[68] 'Consta:' in text.
[69] 'bides' in text.
[70] The text attributes this line to Sohemus.
[71] 'triple earth': Mariam refers here to Antony's interest in her; Antony was a member of the triumvirate, who ruled Rome between them. The line is reminiscent of Shakespeare's description of Antony, 'triple pillar of the world' (*Antony and Cleopatra* I. i. 12), but almost certainly predates it.
[72] Dunstan suggests 'Alexandra' here, but Alexander is the name of Mariam's son, and in the context of the play, especially the discussion between Alexandra and Mariam in Act I, Scene ii, it seems unlikely that Sohemus would give power to a woman.
[73] 'pray' in text.
[74] 'then' in text.
[75] This line appears before the stage direction in the text, but makes more sense after it.
[76] 'grief' in text. The Capitoline geese saved Rome when it was besieged by the Gauls by giving the alarm during a surprise attack at night.
[77] 'you' in text.
[78] 'Salom' in text.
[79] 'Salom' in text.
[80] I.e. the crown
[81] The rhyme-line is missing.

[82] Herod is addressing the butler.
[83] The first 'I' is missing in the text.
[84] 'Yet never wert thou chast' in text.
[85] 'heavy' in text.
[86] 'look' in text.
[87] I.e. 'I call Mariam a usurper, and thus defame her'.
[88] 'bove' in text.
[89] Note the evident image of the death of Christ, the sacrificial lamb.
[90] 'caules' in text.
[91] Achitophel: David's treacherous counsellor, who deserted to Absalom; when his advice was disregarded, he hanged himself (2 Samuel 15–17).
[92] Dunstan amends this to 'man' for the sake of the metre.
[93] 'he' in text.
[94] Cham: a corrupt form of Khan, usually applied to the ruler of the Tartars, Mongols and Chinese. Here Cary seems to be implying that these rulers kept women in particular subjection; she is perhaps thinking of harems, but the reference sits oddly within its Biblical context.
[95] 'refell' in text.
[96] 'Fanchions' in text. See note 39.
[97] The BL copy is amended in MS to read 'why let my [life] be [pain]'.
[98] Birds were caught for the table by smearing sticky lime on the leaves of branches. Salome implies that Mariam's beauty is a snare, a theme she develops further.
[99] This line appears two syllables short.
[100] Possibly refers to Salome's deceitful use of cosmetics to create a false appearance of beauty, but may also refer to the rhetorical 'painting' she gives of Mariam's ugliness.
[101] Bethsabe: Bathsheba, wife of Uriah, desired by king David, who had her husband killed so that he could marry her.
[102] The humble Jew: Esther, who married Ahasuerus, king of Persia and thus saved the Jewish people.
[103] 'At' in text.
[104] Paphos's queen: Aphrodite/Venus, goddess of love and beauty.
[105] Sarah, wife of Abraham; a female-centred rewriting of visions of heavenly bliss in Abraham's bosom. She was Mariam's ancestor and Mariam expects to be reunited with her in paradise (see also ll. 2056–8).
[106] 'I' in text.
[107] Probably Mount Gerizim; Deuteronomy 12:29; 27:12–26. Moses tells the Israelites that when they enter Canaan, six tribes shall stand upon Mt Gerizim to bless the people, and the other six upon Mt Ebal to pronounce curses. Cary has confused the cursing mountain with the blessing mountain.
[108] 'culled': chosen, selected.
[109] The text places this half-line before Herod's entrance.
[110] 'darke' in text.
[111] The text gives 'go on' to the messenger, but it makes more sense from Herod.
[112] This line appears two syllables short.
[113] Dunstan suggests amending 'made' to 'mad', but the line makes sense as

The Tragedy of Mariam

it stands, given Herod's grief-stricken derangement; Herod contrasts his public role as Mariam's ruler (and hence his responsibility for her execution) with his private role as her husband.

[114] 'divided' in text.
[115] 'she' in text.
[116] 'pashed': smashed.
[117] Abel: son of Adam and Eve, murdered by his brother Cain from jealousy; hence an image of slaughtered innocence and a type of Christ. Herod eventually represents himself as Cain (ll. 2126–7).
[118] 'did' in text.
[119] 'blows': blowsy woman, hence prostitute.

THE
HISTORY
OF
The LIFE, REIGN, and DEATH
OF
EDWARD II.
King of England,
AND
LORD of *IRELAND*.
WITH
The Rise and Fall of his great Favourites,
GAVESTON and the *SPENCERS*

Written by E. F. in the year 1627.
And Printed verbatim from the Original.

Qui nescit Dissimulare, nequit vivere, perire melius.[1]

LONDON

Printed by *J. C.* for *Charles Harper*, at the Flower-de-luce in *Fleet-street*; *Samuel Crouch*, at the Princes Arms in *Popes-Head Alley* in *Cornhill*; and *Thomas Fox*, at the Angel in *Westminster*-hall. 1680.

THE PUBLISHER TO THE READER

Reader,

Thou hast here presented to thy view the life and death of Edward the Second, one of the most unfortunate princes that ever swayed the English sceptre. What it was that made him so, is left to thee to judge, when thou hast read his story. But certainly the falseness of his queen, and the flattery of those court-parasites, Gaveston and the Spencers, did contribute not a little thereto.

As for the gentleman that wrote this history, his own following Preface to the Reader will give some short account, as also of the work itself, together with the design and time of its writing, which was above fifty years since.[2] And this we think we may say (and persuade ourselves that upon the perusal thou wilt be of the same opinion), that he was every way qualified for an historian.[3] And bating a few obsolete words (which show the antiquity of the work), we are apt to believe those days produced very few who were able to express their conceptions in so masculine a style.[4]

We might easily enlarge in our commendations of this excellent history; but it needs not; and therefore we leave it to thee to read and judge.

THE AUTHOR'S PREFACE TO THE READER

To out-run those weary hours of a deep and sad passion, my melancholy pen fell accidentally on this historical relation; which speaks a king, our own, though one of the most unfortunate; and shows the pride and fall of his inglorious minions.

I have not herein followed the dull character of our historians, nor amplified more than they infer, by circumstance. I strive to please the truth, not time; nor fear I censure, since at the worst, 'twas but one month mis-spended; which cannot promise aught in right perfection.[5]

If so you hap to view it, tax not my errors; I myself confess them.

20 Feb. 1627   E.F.

THE REIGN AND DEATH
OF EDWARD THE SECOND

Edward the Second, eldest son of Edward the First and Eleanor the virtuous sister of the Castilian king, was born at Carnarvon;[6] 'and in the most resplendent pride of his age, immediately after the decease of his noble father, crowned king of England.[7] The principal leaders of the rebellious Welshmen, Fluellen and Meredith, being taken and executed, the combustions of the Cambro-Britains were quieted and settled in a uniform obedience. The Scots, by the resignation of Balliol, the execution of Wallis, the expulsion of Bruce their pretended king, were reduced to their first monarchy, and brought to an absolute subjection, at such time as he took upon him the regiment of this then glorious kingdom. If we may credit the most ancient historians that speak of the princes and passages of those times, this royal branch was of an aspect fair and lovely, carrying in his outward appearance many promising predictions of a singular expectation. But the judgement, not the eye, must have the preeminence in point of calculation and censure. The smoothest waters are for the most part most deep and dangerous; and the goodliest blossoms, nipped by an unkindly frost, wither, or produce their fruit sour or unwholesome; which may properly imply, that the visible calendar is not the true character of inward perfection; evidently proved in the life, reign and death of this unfortunate monarch. His story speaks the morning fair, the noontide eclipsed, and the sad evening of his life more memorable by his untimely death and ruin. He could not have been so unworthy a son of so noble a father, nor so inglorious a father of so excellent a son, if either virtue or vice had been hereditary. Our chronicles, as they parallel not him in his licentious errors, so do they rarely equal the wisdom and valour of the one that went before, and the other that immediately succeeded him. Neither was this degenerate corruption in him transcendent from the womb that bore him, since all writers agree his mother to be one of the most pious and illustrious pieces of female goodness that is registered in those memorable stories of all our royal wedlocks. But the divine ordinances are inscrutable, and not to be questioned; it may else seem justly worthy admiration, how so crooked a plant should spring from a tree so great and glorious. His younger years discovered a softly, sweet and mild temper, pliable enough to the impressions of virtue; when he came to write man, he was believed over-liberally wanton, but not extremely vicious. The royal honour of his birthright was scarcely invested in his person, when time (the touchstone of truth) shows him to the world a mere imposture; in conversation light, in condition wayward, in will violent, and in passion furious and irreconcilable.[8]

Edward, his valiant and prudent father, had, by the glory of his victorious arms, and the excellency of his wisdom and providence, laid him the sure foundation of a happy monarchy; making it his last and greatest care to continue it so in his succession.[9] This caused him to employ his best understanding and labour for the enabling of his son, that he might be powerful, fit and worthy to perfect this great work, and preserve it. And from this consideration he leads him to the Scotch Wars, to teach him the right use of arms, which are to be managed as well by discretion as valour, and the advantage of time and opportunity, which lead human actions by the hand to their perfection. Here he likewise instructs him with those more excellent rules of knowledge and discipline, that he might exactly know what it was, and how to obey before he came to command. Lastly, he unlocks the closet of his heart, and lays before him those same *arcana imperii*[10] and secret mysteries of state, which are only proper to the royal operations, and lie not in the road of vulgar knowledge; yet letting him withal know, that all these were too weak to support the burden of a crown, if there be not a correspondent worth in him that wears it. With these grave principles the prudent father opening the way soon perceives he had a remaining task of a much harder temper; with an unwilling eye he beholds in his son many sad remonstrances which intimate rather a natural vicious inclination, than the corruption of time, or want of ability to command it. Unless these might be taken off and cleansed, he imagines all his other cautions would be useless and to little purpose. The pruning of the branches would improve the fruit little, where the tree was tainted in the root with so foul a canker. Too well he knew how difficult a thing it was to invert the course of nature, especially being confirmed by continuance of practice, and made habituary by custom; yet he leaves no means unattempted, being confident that wedlock, or the sad weight of a crown, would in the sense of honour call him in time off to thoughts more innocent and noble. Tenderness of fatherly affection abused somewhat his belief, and made him give his disorderly actions the best construction, which suggests their progression to flow from heat of youth, want of experience, and the wickedness of those that fed him with so base impressions; which, with all those sweet and mild entreaties that spring from the heart of an essential love, he strives to reclaim, intermixing withal as great a paternal severity as might properly suit the condition of a judicious father, and the dignity of the heir apparent of so great and glorious a kingdom. And to make him more apt and fit to receive and follow his instructions, he takes from him those tainted humours of his leprosy, that seduced the easiness of his nature, and misled his unripe knowledge, too green to master such sweet and bewitching temptations. Gaveston his Ganymede, a man as base in birth as in condition, he commandeth to perpetual exile.[11] This siren (as some write) came out of Gascony; but the author whom I most credit and follow, speaks him an Italian;[12] not guilty of any drop of noble blood; neither could he from the height of his hereditary hope, challenge more than a bare ability to live; yet his thoughts were above measure ambitious and aspiring, and his confidence far greater than became his birthright. Nature, in his outward parts had curiously expressed her workmanship, giving him in shape and beauty so perfect an excellence, that the most curious eye could not discover any manifest error, unless it were in his sex alone, since he had too much for a man, and perfection enough to have equalled the fairest female splendour that breathed within the confines of this kingdom.[13] Though in the abilities of the brain he were short of a deep and solid knowledge, yet he had understanding enough to manage his ways to their best advantage; having a smooth tongue, a humble look, and a winning behaviour, which he could at all times fashion and vary according to the condition of time and circumstance, for the most advantage. The youthful prince having fixed his wandering eye upon this pleasing object, and finding his amorous glances entertained with so gentle and well-becoming a modesty, begins dearly to cherish the growing affections of this new foreign acquaintance; who applies himself wholly to win him to a deeper engagement. A short passage of time had so cemented their hearts, that they seemed to beat with one and the self-same motion; so that the one seemed without the other, like a body without a soul, or a shadow without a substance. Gaveston, the more to assure so gracious a master, strives to fit his humour, leaving his honour to his own protection, seconding his wanton disposition with all those bewitching vanities of licentious and unbridled youth, which in short time, by the frequency of practice, begets such a confidence, that they fall from that reserved secrecy which should shadow actions so unworthy, professing freely a debauched and dissolute kind of behaviour, to the shame and sorrow of the grieved king and kingdom. This hastened on the sentence of his banishment, that thought himself then most secure in the assurance of the prince's favour. The melancholy apparitions of their parting gave the world a firm belief that this enchanting mountebank had in the cabinet of his master's heart too dear a room and being. The king, knowing such impressions are easily won, but hardly lost, strives to take him off by degrees, and labours to make him waive the memory of that dotage which with a divining spirit he foresaw in time would be his ruin. But death overtakes him before he could bring this so good a work to full perfection. The time was come that exacts the tribute of nature, commanding him to resign both his estate and kingdom. When he felt those cold fore-running harbingers of his nearly-approaching end, he thus entreats his son and lords, whose watery eyes engirt his glorious deathbed:

Edward,
The time draws near that calls me to my grave,
You to enjoy this kingdom.[14] If you prove good,
With happiness 'tis yours, and you will so preserve it;
If otherwise,
My pains and glory will be your dishonour.
To be a king, it is the gift of nature;
And fortune makes him so that is by conquest;
But royal goodness is the gift of heaven,
That blesses crowns with an immortal glory.
Believe not vainly that so great a calling
Is given to man to warrant his disorder.
It is a blessing, yet a weighty burden,
Which (if abused) breaks his back that bears it.
Your former errors, now continued,
Are no more yours,
They are the king's, which will betray the kingdom.
The sovereign's vice begets the subject's error,
Who practise good and ill by his example.
Can you in justice punish them for that
Whereof yourself are guilty? But you perhaps
May think yourself exempt, that are above
The law. Alas, mistake not; there are injunctions higher
Far than are your own, will crave a reckoning,
To be beloved secures a sweet obedience,
But fear betrays the heart of true subjection,
And makes your people yours but by compulsion.
Majestic thoughts, like elemental fire,
Should tend still upwards; when they sink
Lower than their sphere, they win contempt and hatred.
Advance and cherish those of ancient blood

And greatness; upstarts are raised with envy,
Kept with danger.
You must preserve a well-respected distance,
As far from pride, as from too loose a baseness.
Master your passions with a noble temper;
Such triumphs make the victor conquer others.
See here the ruins of a dying sceptre,
That once was, as you are, a youthful blossom.
I have not lived to see this snowy winter,
But that I weaned my heart from vain temptations;
My judgement, not my eye, did steer my compass,
Which gave my youth this age that ends in glory.
I will not say, you too too long have wandered,
Though my sad heart hath drooped to see your error.
The time now fitly calls you home; embrace it:
For this advantage lost, is after hopeless.
Your first-fruit must make good your worth; if that miscarry,
You wound your subjects' hopes and your own glory.
Those wanton pleasures of wild youth unmastered,
May no more touch the verge of your affections.
The royal actions must be grave and steady,
Since lesser lights are fed by their example:
So great a glory must be pure transparent,
That hand to hand encounters time and envy.
Cast off your former comforts; if they sway you,
Such an unnoble precedent will shake
Your peace, and wound your honour.
Your wanton minion I so lately banished,
Call you not back, I charge you on my blessing;
For his return will hasten your destruction.
Such cankers may not taste your ear or favour,
But in a modest and chaste proportion.
Let true-born greatness manage great employments;
They are most fit that have a native goodness.
Mushrooms in state that are preferred by dotage
Open the gap to hate and civil tumult.
You cannot justly blame the great ones' murmur,

If they command that are scarce fit to serve them;
Such sudden leaps must break his neck that ventures
And shake the crown which gives his wings their motion.
And you, my lords, that witness this last summons,
You in whose loyal hearts your sovereign flourished,
Continue still a sweet and virtuous concord;
Temper the heat of my youthful successor,
That he may prove as good, as great in title.
Maintain the sentence was by me pronounced;
Keep still that viper hence that harbours mischief;
If he return, I fear 'twill be your ruin.
It is my last request; I, dying, make it,
Which I do firmly hope you will not blemish.
I would say more, but ah! my spirits fail me.

With this, he fainting, swoons; at length recovers,
And sadly silent, longs to hear their answer.
His weeping son and heavy drooping barons
Do mutually protest a strict observance,
And vow to keep, with truth, this grave injunction.
His jealous spirit is not yet contented,
until they bind it with an oath, and swear performance.[15] Scarce was it ended, when he mildly leaves the world, more confident than he had cause, as a short passage of time made plain and evident. Dead men's prescriptions seldom tie the living, where conscience awes not those that are entrusted. *Mortui non mordent*:[16] which gives to human frailty a seeming uncontrolled power of such injustice. To trust to vows or oaths, is equal hazard; he that will wound his soul with one, can waive the other. If virtue, goodness and religion tie not, a deathbed charge and solemn oath are fruitless. Here you may see it instanced. This great king, as wise as fortunate, living, had the obedience of a father and a sovereign; who, scarcely cold in his mother earth, was soon lost in the memory both of son and subject. His funeral-tears (the fruits of form rather than truth) newly dried up, and his ceremonial rights ended, his heir assumes the crown and sceptre; while all men's eyes were fixed to behold the first

virgin-works of his greatness: so many glorious and brave victorious conquests having given this warlike nation life and spirit fit for present action. The youthful king, being in the bravery of his years, won a belief in the active soldier, that so apt a scholar as he had showed himself in the art military during the Scottish wars, would handsel the maidenhead of his crown with some outringing alarum that might waken the neighbour-provinces, and make them know his power.[17] But his inglorious aims were bent another way, neither to settle his own, or conquer others. He had within his breast an unnatural civil war which gains the first preeminence in his resolution. His care is to quiet these in a course wholly unjust, and most unworthy his proper goodness. Seeing himself now free and absolute, he thinks it not enough, unless his will as well as his power, were equally obeyed. Being a son and a subject, his conformity had witnessed his obedience; being now a sovereign and a king, he expects a correspondence of the selfsame nature. The sad restrictions of his dying father, so contrarious to his aims, trouble his unquiet thoughts, where the idea of his absent love did hold so firm a footing.[18] With ease he can dispense with his own engagement, but fears the lords, whom he conceits too firmly fixed to waver. He dares not communicate the depth of his resolution, being a secret of too great weight to be divulged; he thinks entreaty an act too much beneath him; and to attempt at random, full of hazard. In these his restless passions, he outruns the honeymoon of his empire, looking asquint upon the necessary actions of state that required his more vigilant care and foresight. This kind of reclused behaviour makes him unpleasant to his lords, and nothing plausible to the inferior sort of subjects, who expect the beginning acts of a crown to be affable and gracious, which wins ground by degrees on vulgar affections, making the way sure to a willing obedience. But he esteems this as a work of superogation, believing the bare tie of duty was enough, without confirmation; all his thoughts are entirely fixed upon his Gaveston: without him he cannot be, yet how to get him handsomely, without a scar, is quite without his knowledge. He concludes it in his secret revolutions too great an injustice, that confines the king from the free use and possession of his nearest and dearest affection; and cannot imagine it to be reason, that his private appetite should subscribe to public necessity. (Falls into the height of melancholy) In these kind of imaginary disputations, he brings himself to the height of such an inward agitation, that he falls into a sad retired melancholy; while all men (as they justly might) wondered, but few did know the reason.[19] Amongst these, a page of his chamber, one that had an oily tongue (a fit instrument for such a physician), adventures the care of this diseased passion. This green statesman, with a foreright look, strives rather to please than to advise, caring not what succeeds so he may make it the stair of his preferment.[20] The court-corruption engenders a world of these caterpillars, that to work their own ends value not at one blow to hazard both the king and kingdom. The error is not so properly theirs as their masters', who do countenance and advance such sycophants, leaving the integrity of hearts more honest (that would sacrifice themselves in his service in the true way of honour) wholly condemned and neglected, which hath begotten so many desperate convulsions, that have (as we may find in our own stories) deposed diverse glorious kings from their proper dignity and lawful inheritance.[21] There are too many frequent examples what mischief such parasitical minions have wrought to those several states they lived in, and certainly such revolutions succeed by a necessary and inevitable justice, for when the royal ear is so guided there ensues a general subversion of all law and goodness, as you may behold here evidently in this unfortunate king, who willingly entertains this fawning orator, that thus presents his counsel:

Are you a king (great sir) and yet a subject?[22]
Can you command, and yet must yield obedience?
Then leave your sceptre.
The law of nations gives the poorest their affections;
Are you restrained? It is your own injustice
That makes your will admit this separation:
If you command, who dares control your actions,

Which ought to be obeyed, and not disputed?
Say that your wayward lords do frown, or murmur,
Will you for this forbear your own contentment?
One rough majestic glance will charm their anger.
Admit great Edward did command obedience,
He then was king, your sovereign and your father;
He now is dead, and you enjoy his power:
Will you yet still obey and serve his shadow?
His vigour dulled with age could not give laws
To suit your youth and spirit,
Nor is it proper that the regal power
Be made a stranger to his own contentment
Or be debarred from inward peace and quiet.
Did you but truly know what 'tis to be a monarch,
You'd be so to yourself as well as others.
What do you fear, or what is it restrains you?
A seeming danger, more in show than substance.
Wise men that find their aims confined to hazard,
Secure the worst before they give them action.
You have a kingdom's power to back, a will to guide it:
Can private fear suggest to shake it?
Alas, they cannot, if yourself were constant;
Who dares oppose, if you command obedience?
I deny not, if you be faint or stagger,
You may be crossed or curbed by that advantage
That gives their moving-heart show of justice.
You understand yourself, and feel your passions;
If they be such as will not brook denial,
Why do you dally, or delay to right them?
The more you paise your doubts, the more they double,[23]
And make things worse than they or are or can be;
Appearing like yourself, these clouds will vanish,
And then you'll see or know your proper error.
Will you vouchsafe my trust, I'll fetch him hither
Whose absence gives you such a sad distraction;
You may the while secure his entertainment
With such a strength may warrant your proceedings.

'Twere madness to ask leave to act transgressions
Where pardon may be had when they are acted.
If you do seek consent from your great barons
They'll dare deny, which is nor fault nor treason,
And in that act you foil your hopes and action,
Which gives their opposition show of justice.
But 'tis in vain to plead the grounds of reason
Since 'tis your will must give the resolution:
If that be fixed, there needs no more disputing,
But such as best may bring it to perfection.

When this smooth physician had prescribed so fit a balsamum for so foul a wound, the king seems infinitely pleased in his relation; he had hit his desires in the master-vein, and struck his former jealousy between wind and water, so that it sunk in the instant. His lovesick heart became more free and frolic, which sudden mutation begat as great a wonder. The operations of the fancy transport sometimes our imagination to believe an actual possession of those things we most desire and hope for; which gives such a life to the dejected spirits of the body, that in the instant they seem clothed in a new habit. Such was the condition of this wanton king, that in this bare overture conceits the fruition of his beloved Damon, and apprehends this golden dream to be an essential part of his fantastic happiness.[24] He heaps a world of promises and thanks on the relator, letting him know he waits but a fitting opportunity to give this project life and action. It is a politic part of court wisdom to insinuate and lay hold of all the befitting opportunities that may claw the prince's humour that is naturally vainglorious or vicious; there is not a more ready and certain way of advancement, if it do shake hands with modesty, and appear with an undaunted, impudent boldness. He that will be a courtier and contains himself within the modest temperance of pure honesty, and not intrude himself before he be called, may like a seamark serve to teach other men to steer their course, while he himself sticks fast, unmoved, unpitied. All the abilities of nature, art, education, are useless if they be tied to the links of honesty, which hath little or no society in the rules of state or pleasure, which as they are unlimited, walk in the byway from all that is good or virtuous.

If this butterfly had truly laid before his unhappy master, what it had been to break the injunctions of a dying father, to falsify such vows and oaths so solemnly sworn, and to irritate the greatest peers of the kingdom with so unworthy an action (which had been the duty of a servant of his master's honour truly careful), he had felt the reward of such plain dealing, either with scorn, contempt, or passion; whose flattering falsehood wins him special grace and favour, and gains the title of an able agent.

Some few days pass, which seemed o'er long, before the king exacts a second trial. In the interim, to take away all jealousy, he enters into the business of the kingdom, and with a seeming serious care surveys each passage, and not so much as sighs, or names his Gaveston; doubting if in his way he were discovered there might be some cross-work might blast his project. He knew how easy 'twas (if once suspected) to take away the cause might breed a difference. What could so poor a stranger do that might protect him against or public force or private mischief, either of which he knew would be attempted, before the lords would suffer his reprisal? When all was whisht and quiet, and all men's eyes were fixed upon the present, he calls his trusty Roger to his private presence, and after some instructions throws him his purse, and bids him haste; he knew his errand.[25]
The wily servant knows his master's meaning
And leaves the court, pretending just occasion,
Proud of employment, posting on his journey.
The king having thus far gone, must now go onward;
He knew that long it could not be concealed;
Such actions cannot rest in sleepy silence;
Which made him think it fit to be the first reporter.
This made him send and call his council,
Who soon are ready, and attend his summons;
Where he makes known the fury of his passions
And tells the way that he had taken to ease them.[26]
So strange an act begets as great a wonder;

They *una voce* labour to divert him,
And humbly plead his father's last injunction,
To which their faiths were tied by deep engagement.
They urge the law that could not be dispensed with
Without a public breach of his proscription.
They speak the vows and oaths they all had taken,
Which in consenting would make them false and perjured.
This working nothing, they entreat him he would awhile adjourn his resolution; time might happily find out a way might give him content, and yet might save their honours. His jealous fear suspects this modest answer;
A temporizing must increase his sorrow,
While they so warned might work a sure prevention.
Being thus at plunge, he strives to make it sure
And win his will, or loose his jurisdiction.
Though he were naturally of a suspicious and timorous nature, yet seeing now the interest of his power at stake on the success of this overture, he lays aside his effeminate disposition, and with angry brow, and stern majesty, doth thus discourse his pleasure:

Am I your king? If so, why then obey me,
Lest while you teach me law, I learn you duty.[27]
Know I am firmly bent, and will not vary.
If you and all the kingdom frown, I care not;
You must enjoy your own affections, I
Not so much as question or control them,
But I that am your sovereign must be tutored
To love and like alone by your discretion.
Do not mistake, I am not now in wardship,
Nor will be chalked out ways to guide my fancy.
Tend you the kingdoms and the public errors;
I can prevent mine own without protection.
I should be loth to let you feel my power,
But must and will, if you too much enforce me.
If not obedience, yet your loves might tender
A kind comfort, when 'tis your king that seeks it.

But you perhaps conceit you share my power;
You neither do nor shall, while I command it;
I will be still myself, or less than nothing.

These words, and the manner of their delivery, bred a strange
distraction, in which he flings away with a kind of loose scorn;
for their refusal
His valiant heart had yet his proper motions,
Which tossed it to and fro with doubtful hazard.
They sadly silent sit, and view each other,
Wishing some one would show undaunted valour,
To tie the bell about the cat's neck that frights them;
But none appears. They yet were strangers
To their own party and the king's conditions.
Their late dead master's ways were smooth and harmless,
As free from private wrongs as public grievance,
Which had extinguished all pretence of faction
And made them meet as friends without assurance;
This wrought them with more ease to treat the business.
Each one doth first survey his own condition,
Which single could do little, and yet expressed might cause his proper ruin; next they measure the king's will and power, with his command; against which in vain were contestation, where wants united strength to make it sure. Lastly they examine what could at worst ensue in their consenting, since it was as possible to remove him being here as stop him coming. The king, advertised by a private intelligencer (a fit instrument in the body of state, in the society and body of a council) of their staggering irresolution, and finding his pills had so kind an operation, lays hold of the advantage, and would not let the iron cool before he wrought it. This brings him back with a more familiar and mild look, and begets a discourse less passionate, but more prevailing. Temperately he lays before them the extremity of his inward trouble, which had so engrossed his private thoughts that he had been thereby enforced to estrange himself from them, and neglected the rights due to his crown and dignity. He lets them know the depth of his engagement, which had no aim repugnant

to the public good, nor intention hurtful to their proper honours, and to conclude, he entreats them (if any of them had been truly touched with a disease of the same quality) that they would indifferently measure his condition by their own sufferings. So fair a sunshine following at the heels of so sharp a tempest wrought a sudden innovation; their yielding hearts seek to win grace, rather than hazard his displeasure;[28] yet to colour so apparent a breach of faith to their dead master, they capitulate certain conditions, which might seem to extenuate (if not take off), the stain of their dishonour; as if matter of circumstance had been a sufficient motive for the breach of an oath so solemnly and authentically sworn. The king, resolved to purchase his peace (whose price was but verbal), is nothing sparing to promise all and more than was demanded; which they credit over-hastily, though they could not be so light of belief as to imagine that he would keep his word with the subject, that wilfully incurs a perjury against his own father; yet in case of necessity it was by general consent agreed, rather to subscribe, than to endanger the peace of the kingdom by so unkind and unnatural a division. The king giving to each of them particular thanks (having thus played his master's prize) departs wondrously content and jocund; they seem outwardly not displeased, that had obtained as much as they could desire, and hoped the end would be fair, if not fortunate. The eye of the world may be blinded, and the severity of human constitutions removed, but so great a perjury seldom escapes unpunished by the divine justice, who admits no dalliance with oaths, even in the case of necessity, as it evidently appears in the sequel of this story; where you may behold the miserable ruin that his principal and efficient cause had from this beginning. It had been far more honourable and advantageous to the state if this young wanton king had point-blank found a flat denial, and been brought to have tugged at the arm's end; the injustice of the quarrel, which might in time have recollected his senses, and brought him to the true knowledge what a madness it was, for the loose affection of so unworthy an object, to hazard his own dignity, and alien[29] the love of the whole kingdom. But it is the general disease of greatness, and a kind of royal fever, when they fall upon an indulgent dotage, to patronize and advance the corrupt ends of their minions, though the whole society of state and body of the kingdom run in a direct opposition; neither is reason, law, religion, or the imminency of succeeding danger weight enough to divert the stream of such inordinate affections, until a miserable conclusion give it a fatal and just repentance. It were much better, if with a provident foresight they would fear and prevent the blow before they feel it. But such melancholy meditations are deemed a fit food for penitentials, rather than a necessary reflection for the full stomach of regal authority. The black clouds of former suspicion being thus vanished, nothing now wants to make perfect the royal desires, but the fruition of this long-expected purchase. The smooth servant that had so pleasingly advised was not less careful in the execution of his promise. He knew haste would advance the opinion of his merit; this makes him soon outrun his journey, and find the star of his directions, to whom he liberally relates the occasion of his coming, which he confirms by the delivery of his master's letter, wherein was drawn to the life the character of his affection, and the assurance of his safety and intended promotion. Gaveston being ravished with so sweet and welcome a relation, entertains it with as much joy, as the condemned prisoner receives his pardon at the place and hour of execution. His long-dejected spirits apprehend the advantage of so hopeful an opportunity, and spur him on with that haste, that he hardly consents to one night's intermission for the repose of this weary messenger. No sooner had the morning watchman given his shrill summons of the approaching daylight but he forsakes his weary bed and hastens straight to horseback, and being not well assured of his reception in the kingdom, being a banished man by so juridical a sentence, he esteems it too weak an adventure to expose himself to the hazard of the roadway, where he might with ease be intercepted. This leads him to disguise himself and seek a secret passage, which he as readily finds, all things concurring to improve his happiness, if he had had judgement and temper enough to have given it a right use. Every minute he esteems ill lost, till he might again be re-enfolded in the sweet and dear embraces of his royal master.

Time, that outruns proud fate, brings him at last to the end of his desires, where the interview was accompanied with as many mutual expressions, as might flow from the tongues, eyes and hearts of long-divided lovers.[30] This pair thus again reunited, the court puts on a general face of gladness, while wiser heads with cause suspect the issue. They esteem it full of danger, to have one man alone so fully possess the king's affections, who if he be not truly good, and deep enough to advise soundly, must often be the cause of error and disorder. This strange piece had neither nobility of birth, ability of brain, or any moral goodness, whereby they might justly hope he would be a stay to the unbridled youth of their sovereign. A precedent experience during the government of their dead master had given them a perfect knowledge that he was more properly a fit instrument for a brothel than to be steersman of the royal actions; yet there was now no prevention; they must hope the best and attend the issue.

Edward having thus regained his beloved favourite could not shadow or dissemble his affection, but makes it eminent by the neglects of the state affairs, and the forgetfulness of the civil and ordinary respect due to his great barons.[31] They wait condemned, and cannot gain the threshold, while this new upstart's courted in the royal chamber. This kind of usage won a sudden murmur, which calls them off to close and private meetings; there they discourse their griefs and means to right them; they sift each way might break this fond enchantment, or lessen this great light obscured their lustre. When they had canvassed all the stratagems of state, and private workings, they deemed it the most innocent and fair way, to win the king to marry; the interest of a wife was thought the most hopeful inducement to reclaim these loose affections that were prostituted without or sense or honour. She might become a fit counterpoise to qualify the pride of such a swelling greatness.

The major part soon jump in this opinion; the rest are quickly won that feared the sequel.[32] On this they all together present themselves and their request, and show the reasons, but touch not the true ground why they desired it. After some pause the king approves their motion, yet bids them well consider it was the greatest action of his life, which as it principally concerned his particular contentment, so did equally reflect on the general interest of the whole kingdom. If they could find him out such a wedlock as might add strength and honour to the crown, and be withal suitable to his liking, he would readily embrace it, and value it as a blessing. So fair a beginning encourageth them to move for Isabel the French king's daughter, one of the goodliest and fairest ladies of that time. The king readily inclines to have it treated; on which an honourable embassage is sent to make the motion. They are nobly received and willingly heard that bore this message, and the conditions easily reconciled to a full agreement. This brings them home with a like noble company, fully authorized to receive the king's consent and approbation.

This conclusion thus made, sends our new lover into France, to fetch his mistress; where he is received like himself, feasted, and married with a great deal of joy and pleasure.[33] The solemnity ended, and a farewell taken, he hastens homewards, returning seized of a jewel, which not being rightly valued, wrought his ruin. Infinite was the joy of the kingdom, evident in those many goodly expressions of her welcome. The excellency of so rare a beauty could not so surprise the heart of this royal bridegroom, but that he was still troubled with the pangs of his old infirmity. It was in the first praeludium of his nuptials a very disputable question whether the interest of the wife or favourite was most predominant in his affections; but a short time discovers that Gaveston had the sole possession of his heart and power to keep it.[34] To level their conditions, and make the terms between them more even, he ties this fair bullock in a yoke of the same nature, marrying him to a lovely branch of the house of Gloucester, whose noble heart struggled infinitely, yet durst not contradict the king's injustice.[35] He holds his blood disparaged by so base commixtion. To take away that doubt, the new-married man is advanced to the earldom of Cornwall, and hath in his gift the goodly castle and lordship of Wallingford, so that now in title he had no just exception, and for conditions, it must be thought enough his master loved him. To show himself thankful, and to seem worthy of such gracious favour, Gaveston applies himself wholly to the king's humour, feeding it with the variety of his proper appetite, without so much as question or contradiction. Not a word fell from his sovereign's tongue, but he applauds it as an oracle, and makes it as a law to guide his actions. This kind of juggling behaviour had so glued him to his master that their affections, nay their very intentions, seemed to go hand in hand; insomuch that the injustice of the one never found rub in the consent of the other. If the king maintained the party, the servant was ever fortunate, his voice was ever concurrent, and sung the same tune to a crotchet. The discourse being in the commendation of arms, the echo styles it an heroic virtue; if peace, it was a heavenly blessing; unlawful pleasures, a noble recreation; and actions most unjust, a royal goodness. These parasitical glozes[36] so betrayed the itching ear that heard them, that no honour or preferment is conceited great and good enough for the relator. A short time invests in his person or disposure all the principal offices and dignities of the kingdom; the command of war, and all military provisions, were committed solely to his care and custody;[37] all treaties foreign and domestic had by his direction success or ruin; nothing is concluded touching the government or royal prerogative, but by his consent and approbation. In the view of these strange passages, the king appeared so little himself, that the subjects thought him a royal shadow without a real substance.[38] This pageant, too weak a jade for so weighty a burden, had not a brain in itself able enough to manage such great actions; neither would he entertain those of ability to guide him, whose honest freedom might have made him go through-stitch with more reputation.[39] He esteems it a gross oversight, and too deep a disparagement, to have any creature of his own thought wiser than himself; he had rather his greatness (than hazard such a blemish) should lie open to the malice of time and fortune. This made him choose his servants as his master chose him, of a smooth fawning temper, such as might cry ayme,[40] and approve his actions, but not dispute them. Hence flew a world of wild disorder; the sacred rules of justice were subverted, the law's integrity abused, the judge corrupted or enforced, and all the types of honour due to virtue, valour, goodness, were like the pedlar's pack, made ware for chapmen. Neither was it conceived enough thus to advance him beyond proportion, or his birth and merit, but he must carry all without disputing. No-one may stand in his way, but tastes his power. Old quarrels are ripped up, to make his spleen more extant.

The grave Bishop of Chester, a man reverend for years, and eminent for his profession and dignity, is committed, and could be neither indifferently heard or released, upon the mere supposition that he had been the cause of his first banishment.[41] These insolences, carried with so great a height, and expressed with so malicious a liberty, were accompanied with all the remonstrances of a justly-grieved kingdom. The ancient nobility, that disdained such an equal, accuse the injustice of the time that makes him their superior.[42] The grave senators are grieved to see the places, due to their worths, possessed by those unworthy and unable. The angry soldier, that with his blood had purchased his experience, beholds with sorrow buffoons preferred, while he like the ruins of some goodly building, is left to the wide world, without use or reparation. The commons, in a more intemperate fashion, make known their griefs, and exclaim against so many great and foul oppressions. The new-made earl both saw and knew the general discontent and hatred, yet seeks not how to cure or stop this mischief; his proud heart would not stoop or sink; his greatness, which might perhaps have qualified the fury, with an ill-advised confidence outdares the worst of his approaching danger, and is not squeamish to let the kingdom know it.

The slumbering barons, startled with the murmur
That echoed nought but fear and quick confusion,
At length awake and change their drowsy temper,
condemning their long patience, that was so far unfit their blood and greatness. Lincoln, Warwick and Pembroke, whose noble hearts disdained to suffer basely, resolve to cure the state, or

make the quarrel fatal. This mushroom must be cropped, or arms must right the kingdom. Yet before they will attempt by force, they'll feel their sovereign's pulses, who drowned in sensual pleasure dreams not of their practice. This resolution leads them to the court, where with some suit they gain admittance; where to the king brave Lincoln thus discoursed their grievance:

> See here (my liege) your faithful though dejected servants,[43]
> that have too long cried ayme to our afflictions; we know you
> in yourself are good, though now seduced;
> The height is such, we fear a coming ruin.
> Let it not taint your ears to hear our sorrow,
> Which is not ours alone, but all the kingdom's,
> That groan and languish under this sad burden.
> One man alone occasions all this mischief;
> 'Tis one man's pride and vice that crusheth thousands;
> We hope you will not bolster such a foul disorder
> And for one poor worthless piece betray a kingdom.[44]
> The heavens forbid so great and fond injustice.
> You are your own, yet we believe you ours;
> If so, we may what you forget remember.
> Kings that are born so should preserve their greatness;
> Which goodness makes, not all their other titles.
> Your noble father, dying, bound our honours,
> Yet we subscribed a breach at your entreaty;
> You promised then a fair and grave proceeding;
> But what succeeds: the worst of base oppression.
> So long as we had hope, our tongues were silent;
> We sat and sighed out our peculiar sufferings.
> But when we see so fond and lewd progression,
> That seems to threaten you and all your subjects,
> You cannot blame us if we seek to right it.
> Would your impartial eye survey the present state of this late
>   glorious kingdom
> You there shall see the face of shame and sorrow.
> No place is free; both court and country languish;

All men complain, but none find help or comfort.
Will you for him, not worth your meanest favour,
Consent the ruin of so brave a nation?
Alas sir, if you would, we may not bear it;
Our arms that guard your life shall keep your honour.
'Tis not unjust if you yourself enforce it
The time admits no respite. For God's sake sir, resolve us;
Since you must part with him or us, then choose you whether.

The king, amazed with this strange petition,
Believes it backed with some more secret practice;
He knew their griefs were just, yet loth to right them;
He hoped this tempest would o'erblow, he might advise his answer.
But when he saw them fixed to know his pleasure,
He then believes it was in vain to struggle.
He knew their strength that had combined to seek it,
And saw he was too weak for contradiction.
This made him yield he should be once more banished.
Though his wretchless[45] improvidence had laid him open to this advantage, yet he was still master of his ancient kingcraft, which made him smoothly seem to pass it over, as if he well approved this sequestration, which he resolves to alter as he pleased, when he had made the party sure might back his actions; till then he slubbers o'er his private passion.[46] The lords, whose innocent aims had no end but reformation, depart content, yet wait upon the issue.
A second time this monster is sent packing,[47]
And leaves the kingdom free from his infection.
Ireland is made the cage must mew this haggard,
Whither he goes as if to execution.[48]
With a sad heart he leaves his great protector,
Vowing revenge if he may live to act it.
This weak statesman here gives a sure testimony of the poverty of his brain, that in the time of his prosperity and height had not made sure one foreign friend, to whom he might have had a welcome access in time of his expulsion.[49] But he had handled

matters so, that he was alike hateful here and abroad, insomuch that he believes this barbarous climate his surest refuge. But he being gone, all things seemed well reconciled; the state was quiet, and men's hopes were suitable to their desires, which seemed to promise a quick and speedy reformation. But the vanity of this belief vanished away like a shadow, and the intermission was little less intemperate than the former agitation. This wily serpent continues so his foreign correspondence, that the king was little bettered by his absence; which made it evident that death alone would end his practised mischief. Their bodies were divided, but their affections meet with a higher inflammation. The intervacuum of their absence hath many reciprocal passages, which interchangeably fly betwixt them. The king receives not a syllable but straight returns with golden interest. Infinitely are they both troubled with their division, but far more with the affront of the presuming barons, that had extorted it by force, yet with entreaty. The king esteemed this kind of proceeding too great an indignity to be pocketed; yet since it had the pretence of his safety and the general good, there was not apparent justice enough to call it to an after-reckoning. But alas, that needed not; for his effeminate weakness had left him naked of that royal resolution that dares question the least disorderly moving of the greatest subject. He was constant in nothing but his passions, which led him to study more the return of his left-handed servant than how to make it good, effected. He lays aside the majesty of a king, and thinks his power too slender; his sword sleeps like a quiet harmless beast while his tongue proves his better champion. He sends for those that have been the principal agents in the last sentence, and treats with them severally; knowing that hairs are plucked up one by one, that are not moved by handfuls; encountering them thus single, hand to hand, what with his hypocritical entreaties and mildewed promises, he soon gets from their relenting hearts a several consent answerable to his desires. When by untying the bundle he had disunited the strength of their confederacy, he then with confidence makes it a general proposition; which takes so, that the repeal of Gaveston's banishment passed current without exception.[50]

The king's intent and the approbation of the lords is scarcely known before (like an Irish hubbub, that needs nothing but noise to carry it) it arrived in Ireland.[51] Upon the wings of passion, made proud by the hope of revenge and a second greatness, he flies swiftly back to the fountain of his first preferment. Once more the breach is soldered, and this true-love's knot enjoys his first possession. But there wanted yet that deep reach and provident foresight that should have given it assurance. The king had neither enabled himself to carry things in their former height by main strength, neither had he wrought his disordered affections to a conformity, or a more stayed temper. His female Mercury lessens not his former ambition, but returns the selfsame man, only improved with the desire of revenge, which was naked of the means to act it; so that it was quickly perceived that the kingdom must feel another fit of her convulsion. The mutual corruptions of these two, went with an equal improvidence, which gave the lords their advantage, and them too late a cause of repentance.

Immediately on his reception, the king falls into a more dangerous relapse of his former dotage; which so fully engrossed him that all discourse and company seemed harsh and unpleasant, but such as came from the mellow tongue of his minion, who invents many new enchantments to feed and more engage his frenzy. All the dissolute actions of licentious youth are acted *cum privelegio*.[52] This bred such a grief and distemper in the sorrowing heart of the subject that a general cloud of sadness seemed to shadow the whole kingdom. Those former strict admonitions were not powerful enough to bridle this distemper, not so much as for a fair income; the one becomes at the first dash more fond, the other more insolent: those whom before he only scorned he now affronts with public hatred, letting them know his spleen waits but advantage. He fills his sovereign's ears with new suspicion, and whets him on to act in blood and mischief.[53]

It is a dispute variously believed, what climate hatched this vulture. I cannot credit him to be an Italian when I observe the map of his actions, so far different from that politic nation; they use not to vent publicly their spleens, till they do act them. He that will work in state, and thrive, must be reserved; a downright way that hath not strength to warrant it is crushed and breaks with his own weight, without discretion. Those that are in this trade held their craftsmasters, do speak those fairest whom they mean to ruin, and rather trust close work than public practice. Wise men made great disguise their aims with vizards, which see and are not seen, while they are plotting. Judge not by their smooth looks or words, which hath no kindred with the hearts of Machiavellian statesmen. Who trusts more to his will than wit may act his passion; but this man's malice is within protection. Where mischief harbours close and undiscovered, it ruins all her rubs without suspicion; a pill or potion makes him sure, that by plain force might have outlived an army. Such ends thus wrought, if once suspected, a neat state lie can parget o'er with justice.[54] But those ancient times were more innocent, or this great favourite more ignorant. He went on the plain way of corrupted flesh and blood, seeking to enchant his master, in which he was a perfect workman, and the contempt of his competitors, in which he was as wilful as fearless; but in the managing of his proper greatness, there he appears like himself, a mere imposture, going on with a full career, not so much as viewing the ground he went on.

The royal treasure he exhausts in pride and riot;[55] the jewels of the crown are in the Lombard;[56] that same goodly golden table and trestles of so great and rich a value he surreptitiously embezzles; and nothing almost left, that might either make money, or improve his glory. No man might now have the king's ear, hand or purse, but he's the mediator; his creatures are advanced, his agents flourish, and poorest grooms become great men of worship. The king hath nothing but the name, while his vicegerent hath the benefit and execution. All that appertains unto the crown and royal dignity are wholly in his power, so that he might justly be thought the lessee if not the inheritor of the prerogative and revenue. The sense of grief and duty that had long contested in the lion-hearts of the nobility are now reconciled. These strange presumptions had banished all possibility of a longer sufferance; they vow to make this monster shrink, and let his master know it. On this, well and strongly attended, they wait upon the king, and not with mild or fair entreaties, they boldly now make known their wrongs, and call for present justice. Edward with a steady eye beholds their looks, where he sees registered the characters of a just indignation, and the threatening furrows of ensuing danger. He stands not to dispute the quarrel, lest they should tear the object of their anger from his elbow; without all show of inward motion, he tells themselves had power to act what was most fitting, to whom he had assigned the care should keep his person, and assure the kingdom. They beyond their expectation finding the wind in that door, give not his inconstant thoughts time to vary, but command their antagonist off to a third banishment. He deprived of heart and strength is enforced to obey, having not so much liberty as to take a solemn farewell. Now is he sent for Flanders; the jurisdiction of the king's dominions are esteemed no fit sanctuary to protect so loose a liver.[57] They leave him to prey and practice on the Dutch, whose caps steeled with liquor had reeling craft enough to make him quiet.

This perhaps bred a supposition that he was now forever lost; the king made show as he were well contented, and men were glad to see this storm appeased, that seemed to threaten an intestine ruin. This happiness was but imaginary, but it is made perfect by one more real; Windsor presents the king an heir apparent; which happy news flies swiftly through the kingdom, which gives it welcome with a brave expression.[58] The royal father did not taste this blessing with such a sense of joy as it deserved; whether 'twas his misgiving spirit, or the absence of his lost jewel, he sadly silent sighs out the relation; such a deserving joy could not win so much as a smile from his melancholy brow, grown old with trouble. The appearance of his inward agitation was such that the greatest enemies of his dotage were the most compassionate of his sufferings. Such a masculine affection and rapture was in those times without precedent, where love went in the natural strain, fully as firm, yet far less violent. If the circumstances of this passionate humour, so predominant in this unfortunate king, be maturely considered, we shall find them as far short of possibility as reason; which have made many believe, that they had a supernatural operation and working, enforced by art or witchcraft.[59] But let their beginning be what it will, never was man more immoderately transported, which took from him in this little time of his third absence the benefit of his understanding and spirits so fully, that he seems rather distracted than enamoured, more properly without reason, than ability to command it. In the circumference of his brain he cannot find a way to lead him out of this labyrinth, but that which depended more of power than wisdom. Bridle his affections he could not, which were but bare embryos without possession; alter them he cannot, where his eye meets not with a subject powerful enough to engage him; what then rests to settle this civil discord, but restitution, which he attempts in spite of opposition. Gaveston comes back; the king avows, and bids them stir that durst, he would protect him.[60] Princes that falsify their faiths, more by proper inclination than a necessary impulsion, grow not more hateful to foreign nations than fearful and suspected to their own subjects. If they be tainted with a known guilt, and justify it, 'tis a shrewd presumption of a sick state, where the head is so diseased. A habit of doing ill, and a daring impudence to maintain it, makes all things in a politic wisdom lawful. This position in the end cozens the professor, and leaves him in the field open to shame and infamy. And it stands with reason, for if virtue be the roadway to perfection, the corruption of a false heart must certainly be the path to an unpitied ruin.

The enraged barons seeing great Cornwall return, are sensible of their dishonour, and think it too great a wrong to be dispensed with, yet they will have the fruit of their revenge through-ripe, before they taste it. He appears no changeling, but still pursues the strains of his presumption.[61] The actions of injustice seldom lessen. Progression is believed a moral virtue. He that hath a will to do ill, and doth it, cannot look back but on the crown of mischief. This makes him not disguise his conceptions, but show them fully, having withal this excellent virtue, that would be never reconciled where he once hated.

The lords observing his behaviour, think time ill lost in so weighty a business; they draw their forces together before the king could have a time to prevent or his abuser to shun it.

The gathering together of so many threatening clouds presaged the storm was a-coming; Gaveston labours to provide a shelter, but 'twas too late; the time was lost that should assure the danger. All that he could effect by his own strength, or the royal authority, he calls to his assistance (but such was the general distaste of the kingdom, he could not gain a strength might seem a party). The court he knew would be a weak protection against their arms, whose tongues had twice expelled him. This made him leave it, and with such provision as so short a time could tender, commit himself to Scarborough Castle. This piece was strong, and pretty well provided, but proved too weak against so just a quarrel. His noble enemies being informed where they should find him, follow the track, and soon begirt this fortress.[62]
He seeks a treaty, they despise conditions,
Knowing he none would keep that all had broken.
All hope thus lost, he falls into their power
From whom he had no cause could hope for mercy.
The butterflies, companions of his sunshine,
That were his fortune's friends, not his, forsake his winter
And basely leave him in his greatest troubles.
The tide of greatness gained him many servants;
They were but hangers-on, and mere retainers,
Like rats that left the house when it was falling.
The spring adorned him with a world of blossoms
Which dropped away when first they felt this tempest.
Forsaken thus, the cedar is surprised
And brought to know the end of such ambition.
The prey thus ta'en, short work concludes his story,
Lest that a countermand might come to stop
Their verdict, Gaverseed is made the fatal place
That sacrificed his life to quench their fury.[63]

Thus fell the first glorious minion of Edward the Second, which appearing for a time like a blazing star, filled the world with admiration, and gave the English cause to blame his fortune, that lived and died, nor loved, excused or pitied. In the wanton smiles of his lovely mistress, he remembers not that she was blind, a giglet and a changeling; nor did he make himself in time a refuge might be his safeguard.[64] If she had proved unconstant, such a providence had made the end as fair as the beginning. But these same towering summer birds fear not the winter till they feel it; and then benumbed they do confess their error. Height of promotion breeds self-love; self-love opinion; which undervalues all that are beneath it.

Hence it proceeds that few men, truly honest,
Can hold firm correspondence with so great a minion;
His ends go not their ways, but with cross-capers,
Which cares not how, so these attain perfection.
Servants that are confined to truth and goodness
May be in show, but not in trust, their agents.
He that will act what pride and lust imposeth
Is a fit page to serve so loose a master.
Hence it proceeds, that still they fall unpitied
And those they choose for friends do most supplant them.

To secure an ill-acquired greatness that is begot with envy, grows in hatred, as it requires judgement, claims a goodness to keep it right, and grave direction. Those that are truly wise, discreet and virtuous will make him so that pursues their counsel; upon which rock he rests secure untainted.

But this is country-doctrine courts resent not,
Where 'tis no way to thrive, for them are honest.[65]
A champion conscience without bound or limit,
A tongue as smooth as jet that sings in season,
A bloodless face that buries guilt in boldness:
These ornaments are fit to clothe a courtier.
He that wants these, still wants a means to live,
If he must make his service his revenue.
He that a child in court grows old, a servant
Expecting years or merit should prefer him
And doth not by some byway make his fortune,
Gains but a beard for all his pains and travel,

Unless he'll take a purse, and for reward a pardon.
Though many rise, it is not yet concluded
They all are of so base corruption
Which would produce a sudden ruin.[66]
The greater peers by birth inherit fit place in this election. The king's favour, or their intercession, may advance a deserving friend or kinsman; extraordinary gifts of nature, or some excellency in knowledge may prefer him that enjoys them; all these beams may shine on men that are honest. But if you cast your eye upon the gross body of the court, and examine the ordinary course of their gradation, it will plainly appear, that twenty creep in by the back gate, while one walks up by the street-door. But leaving those to their fortune, and that cunning conveyance must guide their destiny; when the sad tidings of this unhappy tragedy came to the king's ears, his vexations were as infinite as hopeless, and his passion transports him beyond the height of sorrow, which leads him to this bitter exclamation:

Could they not spare his life, O cruel tigers?[67]
What had he done, or how so much offended?
He never shed one drop of harmless blood
But saved thousands.
Must he be sacrificed to calm their anger?
'Twas not his fault, but my affection caused it;
Which I'll revenge, and not dispute my sorrow.
They, if I live, shall taste my just displeasure
And dearly pay for this their cruel error.
Till now I kept my hand from blood and fatal actions;
But henceforth I will act my passions freely,
And make them know I am too much provoked.
Blood must have blood, and I will spend it fully
Till they have paid his wandering ghost their forfeit.[68]
And thou, O sweet friend, who living I so lovest,
From thy sad urn shall see thy wrong requited.
Thy life, as I mine own did dearly value
Which I will lose, but I'll repay their rigour.

This said, he withdraws him to his melancholy chamber, and
makes himself a recluse from the daylight.
His manly tears bewray his inward sorrow,
And make him seem to melt with height of passion.
He could not sleep, nor scarce would eat, or speak but faintly,
which makes him living die with restless torment.
His lovely queen (not sorry that this bar was taken away, which
stopped the passage betwixt her husband's love and her affections)
Is truly pensive at this strange distraction,
Which seemed without the hope of reconcilement.
His nearer friends, amazed to see his passion,
Resolve to set him free or lose his favour;
Boldly they press into his cell of darkness
And freely let him know his proper error.
They lay before him how vain a thing it was to mourn or sorrow
for things past help, or hope of all redemption. His greatness
would be lost in such fond actions
And might endanger him and eke the kingdom.
If he but truly knew what desperate murmurs
Were daily whispered by his vain distemper,
He would himself appear to stay the danger
And to excuse the barons' act, so hateful.
They touch upon the earl's intemperate carriage,
Which threatened them and all the kingdom's ruin;
They show his insolence and misbehaviour, which having honour so far above his birth, and wealth above his merit, was ne'er contented. Lastly, they tell him plainly, unless he would resume more life and spirit, they feared the subject would make choice of one more able.

    The unworthy touches of his minion, though but sparingly given, nipped him to the soul, but when he heard the tenor of their last conclusion, it roused him up for fear of deposition. This brings him forth in show and look transformed, but yet resolved not to forget this trespass. The operations in his heart were not so great and weighty but that his lords were full as close and wary. So fair a warning piece gave them their summons, in time to make a strength might keep them sure. They cannot now recoil, or hope for favour; their arms must make their peace, or they must perish. These circumstances made them preserve so well a respected distance that well the king might bark, but durst not bite them. He was resolved, 'tis true, but not provided, and therefore holds it wisdom to be silent; the time he hoped would change, and they grow careless; when they should know such wrongs are not forgotten. But now brave Lincoln, one of the principal pillars of the barons' faction, follows his adversary to the grave, but with a mild and fairer fortune.[69] This reverend piece of true nobility was in speech and conversation sweet and affable, in resolution grave and weighty; his aged temper active and valiant above belief, and his wisdom more sound and excellent in inward depth than outward appearance. When those pale harbingers had seized his vital spirits, and he perceived the thought of life was hopeless, he gives Thomas of Lancaster, his son-in-law, this dying legacy:

My son (quoth he), for so your wedlock makes you,[70]
Hear and observe these my last dying precepts.
Trust not the king; his anger sleeps, but dies not;
He waits but time, which you must likewise tender,
Else in the least neglect be sure you perish.
Make good my place among the lords, and keep
The kingdom from foul oppression, which of late is frequent.
Your sovereign cares not how the state be guided
So he may still enjoy his wanton pleasures;
Have you an eye to those that seek to wrong him.
Be not deceived with his sugared language;
His heart is false, and harbours blood and mischief.
Keep yourselves firm and close; being well united
You are secure; he will not dare to touch you.
If he again fall on a second dotage,
Look to it in time, 'twill else be your confusion.
His minion's death lies in his heart concealed,
Waiting but time to act revenge and terror.
He shadows o'er, but cannot hide his malice

with a double string to his bow; the one of ancient title, the other of conquest. The nobility of Scotland and all the inferior ministers of state, seeing the great effusion of blood spent in this quarrel, which continued, seemed to threaten a general devaluation of their country, submit themselves to the English government, and are all solemnly sworn to obey it. Edward thus in possession, confirms it by seizing the property of all the royal jurisdiction into his own hand, removing such officers as were not agreeable to his will and liking, and giving many goodly estates and dignities to divers of his faithful servants that had valiantly behaved themselves in this service. The form of government by him established was peaceably obeyed, and continued during his life; neither was it questioned in the beginning government of his unhappy successor. But the wary Scots, more naturally addicted to a phoenix of their own nation, seeing into the present dissensions and disorders of the kingdom, thought it now a fit time to revolt to their old master, who like a crafty fox harbours himself under the French king's protection (the ancient receptacle and patron for that nation). No sooner is he advertised that the gate was open and unguarded, and that his well-affected subjects wished his return, but back he comes, and is received with a full applause and welcome. All oaths, obligements, and courtesies of the English, are quite cancelled and forgotten; and this long-lost lion is again reinvested in the royal dignity. As soon as he had moored himself in a domestic assurance, he then like a provident watchman begins to raise a strength that might oppose all foreign invasion, which he foresaw would thunder from the borders. This martial preparation flies swiftly to the king and council of England, where it appears like a great body upon a pair of stilts, more in bulk than the proportion of the strength that bore it. The pillars of the state, which wisely foresaw how great an inconvenience it would be to suffer such a member to be dissevered, that in the contestation with France would make the war a mattachine or song of three parts,[73] persuade their sovereign it was not proper for his greatness to suffer such an unworthy subversion of his father's constitutions, and to lose the advantage of so fair a part of his revenue.

Edward, that had outslept his native glory, had yet a just compunction of this dishonour, which seemed to rob him of a portion of his inheritance, purchased at too dear a value. He lays by his private rancour, and settles himself to suppress this sudden and unlooked-for commotion, waking from that sensual dream which had given him so large a cause of sorrow. Scarcely would he give his intentions such an intermission, as might attend the levy of his army, which he had summoned to be ready with all speed and expedition. The jealous lords, startled with this alarum, conceiting it but some trick of state to catch them napping, they suspect these forces, under pretence of public action, might be prepared to plot a private mischief. The king they knew was crafty, close and cunning; and thought not fit to trust too far to rumour. This makes them stand upon their guard, and keep assemblies, pleading for warrant the selfsame ground of rising.

But when their spies in court had given them knowledge
That all was sure, they need not fear their danger,
And that they daily heard the northern clamour
That echoed loudly with the Scottish motions,
They draw their forces to the king's; who thus united,
In person leads them to this hopeful conquest.[74]
But forehand reckonings ever most miscarry;
He had those hands, but not those hearts which fought his
 father's fortune.

Scarce had he passed and left the English borders but he beholds an army ready to affront him, not of dejected souls, or bodies fainting, but men resolved to win or die with honour. Their valiant leader heartens on their courage, and bids them fight for life, estate and freedom, all which were here at stake; which this day gains, or makes hereafter hopeless. Edward, that expected rather submission, or some honest terms of agreement, finding a check given by a pawn, unlooked for, plays the best of his game, and hopes to win it. He condemns their condition and number, slighting their power; and in the memory of his father's conquests thinks his own certain. But the success of battles runs not in a blood, neither is gained by confidence, but discretion and valour. No one thing hurts more in a matter of arms than presumption; a coward that expects no mercy is desperate by compulsion, and the most contemptible enemy proves most dangerous when he is too much undervalued. You may see it here instanced, where a rabble multitude of despised bluecaps encounter, rout and break the flower of England; Eastriveline doth yet witness the fatal memory of this so great disaster. There fell brave Clare, the Earl of Gloucester, the valiant Clifford, and stout Mawle, with above fifty knights and barons.[75] This bloody day, which had spilt so great a shower of noble blood, and cropped the bravest blossoms of the kingdom, sends the king back to Berwick with a few straggling horse, whose well-breathed speed outrun the pursuing danger. So near a neighbourhood to so victorious an enemy is deemed indiscretion, where the prize was believed so richly worth the venture. This sends away the melancholy king jaded in his hopes, and dull with his misfortune. If we may judge by the event, the condition of this man was truly miserable; all things at home under his government were out of rule and order, and nothing successful that he undertook by foreign employment; but where the ground is false the building cannot stand. He planted the foundation of his monarchy on sycophants and favourites, whose disorderly proceedings dried up all that sap that should have fostered up the springing goodness of the kingdom, and made him a mere stranger to those abilities that are proper to rule and government. Kings ought to be their own surveyors, and not to pass over the whole care of their affairs by letter of attorney to another man's protection. Such inconsiderate actions beget a world of mischief, when there are more kings than one in one and the selfsame kingdom; it eclipseth his glory, and derogates from his greatness; making the subject groan under the unjust tyranny of an insolent oppression. No man with such propriety can manage the griefs and differences of the subject, as the king, who by the laws of God, men and nature hath an interest in their heart and a share in their affections. When they are guided by a second hand, or heard by a relator, money or favour corrupts the integrity, and overrules the course of justice, followed at the heels with complaint and murmur, the mother of discontent and mischief.

The unexpected return of the general of this ill-succeeding enterprise filled the kingdom with a well-deserved sorrow, and is welcomed with a news as strange, though not so full of danger. Poydras, a famous impostor, a tanner's son, and born at Exeter, pretends himself with a new strain of lip-cozenage, to be the heir of Edward the First, by a false nurse changed in his cradle for the king now reigning.[76] All novelties take in the itching ears of the vulgar, and win either belief or admiration. This tale, as weak in truth as probability, was fortunate in neither, only it exalts this imaginary king to his instalment on Northampton gallows, where he ends the hour of his melancholy government with as strange a relation,[77] which suggests that for two years space, a spirit in the likeness of a cat had attended him as the chief groom of his chamber, from whom in many secret conferences he had received the truth and information of the mystery, with assurance it would bring him to the crown of England.[78] It was as great a fault in the master to believe as for the servant to abuse; yet the desire of the one to change his tan-vat[79] for a kingdom was not much out of square, nor the lying of the other, since he continued but his trade which he had practised from the beginning. It is a foul offence and oversight in them that have not devils of their own to hunt abroad and seek where they might gain them by purchase. If it be a mystery of state to know things by prediction of such virtuous ministers, methinks they were much better kept, as this tanner kept his, rather as a household servant than a retainer; which may in time bring them to a like preferment.[80] Such agents may seem lambs, but in the end they will be found as savage as tigers, and as false as the chameleons. Till now our wanton king had never felt the true touch of a just grief, but men's misfortunes alter their impressions; he inwardly and heartily laments his own dishonour, yet strives to hide and conceal his sorrow, lest those about him might be quite dejected. It was a bitter corrosive to think how oft his royal father had displayed his victorious colours, which knew not how to fight unless to conquer. How often had he overrun this neighbour nation, and made them take such laws as he imposed? How many times had he overthrown their greatest armies, and made them sue they might become his subjects? The memory of this doth vex his spirits, and makes him vow revenge and utter ruin. He calls to council all his lords and leaders, and lays before them the ancient glory of the kingdom, the late misfortune and his proper errors, and lastly his desire to right his honour. They, glad to hear the king in the sense of so general a disgrace touched with so noble a strain, do spur it on before it cooled, or the Scots should grow too proud of their new glory. The former loss had touched so near the quick that there is now a more wary resolution. Dispatches are sent out for a more exact and full provision; a mature consideration is thought necessary before it come to action. York is made the cabinet for this grave council; there the king soon appears, attended by all the bravest and ablest spirits of the kingdom.[81] The act of the first conference tends to the security of Berwick, the street-door of the North, and principal key of the borders.[82] This care with a full provision is committed to the fidelity and valour of Sir Peter Spalden, who undertakes the charge, being plentifully furnished, and promiseth defence against the united power of Scotland. This unfortunate king was as unhappy in counsel as in action. A short time shows this unworthy knight to the world false and perfidious. Robert le Bruce, that had this strength as a mote in his eye, conceived it by force almost impregnable. This made him seek to undermine it by corruption, and aloof off to taste the palate of this new governor.[83] The hook was no sooner baited but the trout falls a-nibbling; ready money and a specious promise of an expected preferment makes this conspiracy perfect, which at one blow sells the town, with all its warlike provisions, and the treacherous keeper's reputation and honour. The Pope, who with a pious and a truly compassionate eye beheld the misery of this dissension, and the unnatural effusion of so much Christian blood, seeks to reform it; and to this effect sends over two of his cardinals to mediate a peace, and to compose, if it might be, the differences in question.[84] They being arrived in England come down into the north to the king, by whom they are with great ceremony, according to the fashion of those religious times, received and welcomed. They discourse to him the occasion of their employment, and incline him with many excellent and virtuous motives to embrace a peace with Scotland. The greenness of the disgrace, and the late wound yet bleeding new, kept him in a long demurrer. Yet the holy and mild prosecution of these holy fathers won him at length to their mediation, with a proviso that he were not too far prejudiced in interest and honour. With this answer they take their leave, and prosecute their journey to Scotland, but with an example full of barbarous inhumanity they are in the way surprised and robbed.[85] Infinitely is the king incensed with this audacious act, which threw so foul a stain upon the whole nation, which causeth a strict inquisition for the discovery of these malefactors, which are soon known and taken. Middleton and Selby, both knights, expiate the offence with their shameful execution.[86] The persons of ambassadors amongst the most savage nations are free from rapine, but being clothed in the habit of religion and such a greatness, and going in a work so good and glorious, certainly it was an act deserved so severe a punishment. Immediately at the heels of this follows another example less infamous, but far more full of danger. Sir Jocelyn Denvil, having wasted his estate, and not able to lessen the height of his former expenses, gets into his society a regiment of ruffians, terming themselves outlaws.[87] With these he infests the north with many outrageous riots, insomuch that no man that had anything to lose could be secure in his own house from murder, theft and rapine. A little time had brought this little army, rolling like a snowball, to the number of 200; all the diseased flux of the corrupted humours of those parts fly to this impostume.[88] An attempt so impudent and daring flies swiftly to the king's knowledge. Report, that seldom lessens, makes the danger far greater than it deserved. The royal ear conceits it little better than a flat rebellion, whose apprehension felt itself guilty of matter enough to work on. This made an instant levy, and as ready a dispatch for the suppression of the flame, while it

The History of the Life, Reign and Death of Edward II

but burnt the suburbs. Experience soon returns; the fear is found greater than the cause; the principal heads and props of this co[...] severity of that law, w[...] olutely disclai[...] epth of this c[...] more perilo[...] nt had aliene[...] face of discor[...] ed daily more [...] he regal weak [...] usion. If this [...] general inclin[...] was constant [...] revolt of the [...] a farther time [...] rtunity of effe[...] of justice. It i[...] nd all the members surrer by [...] nd man is prone to error; yet if they manage their distempers with wisdom or discretion, so that they lie not open to public view and censure, they may be counted faults, but not predictions. But when the heart is gangrened, and the world perceives it, it is the fatal mark of that infection, which doth betoken ruin and destruction. The cardinals are now come back, the hopes of peace are desperate; the Scots are on the sunny side of the hedge, and will have no conditions but such as may not be with honour granted.[89] Edward inflamed, will have no further treaty; this makes them take their leave and hasten homeward. Their losses liberally are requited, and many goodly gifts bestowed at parting. Being come to Rome, they inform His Holiness of the success of their journey, who takes ill the contumacy of the perfidious Scots, and excommunicates both that king and kingdom.[90] But this thunderbolt wrought a small effect; where honesty had so little an acquaintance, religion must needs be a great stranger. The loss of Berwick, and the disgrace of his first overthrow, calls the king to adventure a revenge, which he thinks he had too long adjourned. He makes it a disputable question, whether he should besiege Berwick or invade Scotland, but the consideration thereof is referred till the moving of the army, which is advanced with all speed possible. Men, arms and money, with all such other provisions as were as well fit to continue the war as begin it, are suddenly ready in full proportion. The army attends nothing but the king's person, or some more lucky general to lead it. In the knowledge he loseth no time but appears in the head of his troops, and leads them on, making an armed hedge about Berwick, before his enemies had full knowledge of his moving.[91] The council of war thought it not expedient to leave such a thorn in the heel of so glorious an army. The Scots thought it too great a hazard to attempt the breach so strong a body, so excellently entrenched and guarded; the memory of former passages made them entertain this war with less heat, but with a more solid judgement. Berwick they knew was strong by art and nature, and fully provided to hold the English play, till want and the season of the year did make them weary. This made them leave the roadway and continue the war more by discretion than by valour. But during these passages, the divine justice sends down the other three fatal executioners of his wrath: plague, dearth and famine; no part is free, but hath his portion of one or all of these so cruel sisters.[92] To make this misery more perfect, the wily Scots taking the advantage of the king's fruitless encamping before Berwick, like a land-flood overrun the naked borders, and boldly march forward into the country, with fury, blood and rapine.[93] The stuff that should stop this breach was absent with the king, so that they find no rub in their eruption. The archbishop of York, a reverend old man, but a young soldier, able enough in his element, but ignorant in the rules of martial discipline, resolves to oppose this unruly devastation; he straightways musters up his congregations, and gives them arms, that knew scarce use of iron.[94] Soon had his example collected up a multitude, in number hopeful; but it was composed of men fitter to pray for the success of a battle than to fight it. With these and an undaunted spirit, he affronts his enemies and gives them an encounter, making

Milton-upon-Swale more memorable by the blood of this disaster.⁹⁵ His victorious and triumphing enemies christened this unhappy conflict in derision, The White Battle. Many religious men, with loss of their lives, purchased here their first apprenticeship in arms, and found that there was a dangerous difference betwixt fighting and praying. The intent of this grave bishop was certainly noble and worthy, but the act was inconsiderate, weak and ill-advised. It was not proper to his profession to undertake a military function, in which his hope in reason answered his experience; neither did it agree with the innocency and piety of his calling to be an actor in the effusion of blood, though the quarrel were defensive, but by compulsion. But questionless he meant well, which must excuse his action. Too great a care improperly expressed doth often lose the cause it strives to advantage. In all deliberations of this nature, where so many lives are at stake, there should be a deep foresight even in matter of circumstance; and the quality as well of our own, as of our adversaries, duly considered; else with a dangerous error we leave the success to the will of fortune, who in nothing is more tickle and wanton, than in the event of battles, which are seldom gained by multitude, the mother of confusion. To be a general is an act of greatness, and doth require a great and perfect knowledge, ripe by experience and made full by practice. It is not enough to dare a fight, which is but valour, but to know how and when, which makes it perfect. Discretion and judgement sometimes teach advantage, which make (the weight being light) the scale more even. I will not deny but the most expert leader may have all these, and yet may lose a battle; since (as all things are) this great design is guided by a divine providence; and many accidents may happen betwixt the cup and the lip while things are in action. But he that hath a well-grounded and warrantable reason for his engagement may lose the day and yet preserve his honour. Wise men do censure errors, not events of actions, which show them good or bad, as they be grounded.⁹⁶ The news of the defeat of this spiritual army, like the voice of a night-raven, had no sooner croaked his sad echo in the king's ear, but he straight raiseth his army, weakened with famine and lessened with sickness.⁹⁷ The prigging Scots seeing his going-off, judge his retreat little better than a plain flight, which gave them heart to set upon the fag-end of his troops, which they rout and break, to the astonishment of the whole army.⁹⁸ This done, they return, and think it honour enough they had done the work they came for. The king doubles his pace homewards; instead of triumph, glad to have got loose from so imminent a danger. This blank return filled the kingdom with a fretting murmur, and foreign nations thought their valour changed, which had so oft before o'ercome this nation. Mated with grief, oppressed with shame and sorrow, Edward exclaims against his wayward fortune, that made his greatness, like the crab, go backward; while he seeks to improve, the opinion of his worth he impairs, and grows still leaner; and when he shuns a taint, he finds a mischief. Sadly he now resolves no more to tempt her; he lays aside his arms, for harms to feed his humour. His vanities (companions of his greatness) had slept out the night of these combustions; he now awakes them, with a new assurance they should possess their former mansion. His wandering eyes now ravage through the confines of his great court, made loose by his example.⁹⁹ Here he seeks out some piece or copper-metal, whom by his royal stamp he might make current.¹⁰⁰ He finds a spacious choice, being well-attended, but 'twas by such as made their tongues their fortunes; vainglory here found none to cure it, and the sick heart ne'er felt the touch of wormwood.

The agents were composed of the just temper,
As was the spring that gave their tongues their motion;
Such a harmonious consort fits the organ,
That loved no flats nor sharps, or forced division.
No language pleased the king (the servants know it),
But that which was as smooth as gold new-burnished.
Old ancient truth was, like a threadbare garment,
Esteemed a foul disgrace to clothe a courtier.
Sincerity was no fit master for these revels,
Nor honest plainness for a seat in council.
This made this king, this court and glorious kingdom

Fall by degrees into a strange confusion.

The infidelity of servants, clothed in hypocrisy, betrays the master, and makes his misery greater or less dangerous, according to the qualities of their employments. It is an excellent consideration for the majesty of a king, in election, to reflect on goodness, truth and ability, for his attendance, more than the natural parts or those that are by art and cunning made pliable to his disposition. The first prove the props of greatness, the other the instruments of danger and disorder; which makes the master at best pitied, but most commonly hated and suspected. Neither is it safe for the royal ear to be principally open to one man's information, or to rest solely on his judgement. Multiplicity of able servants that are indifferently (if not equally) countenanced, are the strength and safety of a crown, which gives it glory and lustre. When one man alone acts all parts, it begets a world of error, and endangers not only the head, but all the members.

Edward could not but know that a new president over his royal actions, must make his subjects his but at a second hand; yet he is resolved of a new choice, of such a favourite as might supply and make good the room of his lost beloved Gaveston. Hence sprung that fatal fire which scorched the kingdom with intestine ruin. He was put to no great trouble to seek a foreign climate; he had variety of his own, that might be easily made capable enough for such a loose employment. He had a swarm of sycophants that gaped after greatness, and cared not to pawn their souls to gain promotion; amongst these his eye fixed on Spencer, a man till then believed a naked statesman; he was young, and had a pleasing aspect; a personage though not super-excellent, yet well enough to make a formal minion.[101]

The ladder by which he made his ascent, was principally thus; he had been always conformable to the king's will, and never denied to serve his appetite in every his ways and occasions; which was virtue enough to give him wealth and title. Some others think this feat was wrought by witchcraft, and by the spells of a grave matron, that was suspected to have a journeyman devil to be her loadstone; which is not altogether improbable, if we

behold the progression; for never was servant more insolently fortunate, nor master unreasonably indulgent. Their passages are as much beyond belief as contrary to the rules of reason. But leaving the discourse of the cause, the king applauds his own workmanship, and dotes infinitely on the nonage of this imposture, which seeing the advantage, labours to advance it; and though in his own nature he were proud, harsh, and tyrannous, yet he clothes himself in the habit of humility, as obsequious to his master as smooth and winning to his acquaintance; knowing that a rub might make the bowl fall short while it was running; heat of blood, and height of spirit, consult more with passion than judgement; where all sides are agreed, quick ends the bargain.
Spencer must rise, the king himself avows it;
And who was there durst cross their sovereign's pleasure?
The resolution known, like flocks of wild geese,
The spawn of court-corruption fly to claw him.
The great ones that till now scarce knew his offspring,
Think it an honour to become his kinsmen.
The officers of state, to win his favour,
Forget their oaths, and make his will their justice.
Lord, how the vermin creep to this warm sunshine,
And count each beam of his a special favour!
Such a thing is the prologue of a beginning greatness
That it can metamorphose all but those who hate it.

The king, though he were pleased with this new structure, yet his inward resolutions were not altogether free from agitation. He beheld the lords and kingdom now quiet, and the Scotch tragedy worn out of memory; he was not without cause doubtful whether this new act might not cause a new distraction.
He calls to mind the ground of his first troubles,
And found it had with this a near resemblance.
He looks upon the sullied state scarce cleansed,
And feared this leap might cause a new pollution.
These thoughts, like misty vapours, soon dissolved,
And seemed too dull to feed his lovesick fancy.
His hatred to the barons bids him freely venture,

That in their moving he might so oppress them,
Which on cool blood might seem too great injustice.
Gaveston's death lay in his heart impostumed,
Not to be cured but by a bloody issue.
From this false ground he draws his proper ruin,
Making phantasms seem as deeds were acted.
Such castles in the air are poor conceptions,
That sell the skin before the beast be killed.
The barons were no children, he well knew it;
The hope was little might be got with striving,
Where all the kingdom was so much distasted;
But he prized high his own, condemning theirs,
Which wrought their death, and after his misfortune.

Being resolved to countenance his will with more haste than advisement, he honours the subject of his choice with the Lord Chamberlain's place, professing freely he thought him worthy, and would maintain him in it. This foreright jump going so high, made all men wonder, and soon suspect him guilty of some secret virtue. Scarce had this new great lord possession of the white staff, but he forgets his former being, and sings the right nightcrow's tune of upstart greatness, and follows his predecessor's pattern to the life, but with a far more strength and cunning. He was not born a stranger or an alien, but had his birth and breeding here, where he is exalted; and though he had not so much depth to know the secrets, yet understands the plainsong of the state, and her progressions, which taught him his first lesson, that infant greatness falls where none support it. From this principle, his first work is employed to win and to preserve an able party. To work this sure, he makes a monopoly of the king's ear; no man may gain it but by his permission; establishing a sure intelligence within the royal chamber; not trusting one, but having sundry agents, who must successively attend all motions.[102] By this he wedgeth in his sentinels at such a distance that none can move, but he receives the larum. The first request he makes his sovereign (who ne'er denied him) was that he would not pass a grant, till he surveyed it; for this he makes a zealous care the cover; lest by such gift the subject might be grieved, the king abused.

This stratagem unmasked gave perfect knowledge;
Whoever leapt the horse he held the bridle,
Which reined his foes up short, while friends unhorsed them;
And raised as he pleased all such as bribed or sought him.
To mix these serious strains with lighter objects,
He feeds the current of his sovereign's vices
With store of full delights, to keep him busied,
Whilst he might act his part with more attention.
He quarrels those whom he suspects too honest,
Or at the least not his more than their master's,
And quickly puts them off, that there may be entry
For such as he prefers, his proper creatures;
So that a short time makes the court all of a piece at his
    commandment.
Those whom he feared in state would cross his workings,
He seeks to win by favour or alliance;
If they both fail, he tenders fairly,
To lift them higher by some new promotion,
So he may have them sure on all occasions;
And with these baits he catched the hungry planets.
Some that he finds too faithful for surprisal,
These he sequesters,
Mounting his kindred up to fill their places.
The queen, that had no great cause to like those sirens,
That caused her grief, and did seduce her husband,
He yet presumes to court with strong professions,
Vowing to serve her as a faithful servant.
She, seeing into the quality of the time,
Where he was powerful, and she in name a wife,
In truth a handmaid,
Doth not oppose, but more increase his greatness,
By letting all men know that she received him.
To win a nearer place in her opinion,
He gains his kindred places next her person;
And those that were her own, he bribes to back him.
The court thus fashioned, he levels at the country,
Where he must gain his strength, if need enforced it.

Here he must have an estate, and some sure refuge; this he contrives by begging the custody of divers of the principal honours and strength of the kingdom. But these were no inheritance which might perpetuate his memory, or continue his succession. He makes a salve for this sore; and to be able to be a fit purchaser of lands, by the benefit of the prerogative he falls a selling of titles, in which it was believed he thrived well, though he sold many more lordships than he bought manors. By this means yet he got many pretty retiring-places for a younger brother, within the most fertile counties of the kingdom. This for the private, now to the public; he makes sure the principal heads of justice, that by them his credit might pleasure an old friend, or make a new at his pleasure. If in this number any one held him at too smart a distance, prizing his integrity and honour before so base a traffic, he was an ill member of state, and either silenced, or sent to an Irish or Welsh employment.[103] It is enough to be believed faulty, where a disputation is not admitted. The hare knows her ears be not horns, yet dares not venture a trial, where things must not be sentenced as they are, but as they are taken. The commanders that sway most in popular faction, as far as he durst or might without combustion, he causeth to be conferred on his friends and kindred; and above all things he settles a sure correspondence of intelligence in all the quarters of the kingdom, as a necessary leading president. He fills the people's ears with rumour of foreign danger, to busy their brains from discoursing domestic errors; and sends out a rabble of spying Mercuries, who are instructed to talk liberally to taste other men's inclinations, and feel the pulses of those that had most cause to be discontented.[104] For the ancient nobility, which was a more difficult work to reduce to conformity, laying aside the punctilios of his greatness, he strives to gain them as he won his master; but when he found them shy and nice to make his party,

He slights them more and more, to show his power,
And make them seek to entertain his favour.
And to eclipse their power by birth and number,
He finds the means to make a new creation,

Which gave the rabble gentry upstart honours,
As children do give nuts away by handfuls;
Yet still he hath some feeling of the business.
Lastly he wins the king to call his father to the court, who with the shoal of all his kin are soon exalted, while he makes all things lawful that correspond his will, or master's humour. He thus assuming the administration of the royal affairs, his master giving way to all his actions, the incensed lords grown out of patience appoint the rendezvous of a secret meeting at Sharborough, where they might descant their griefs with more freedom, yet with such a cautelous secrecy, that this harpy with his lyncean eyes could not perceive their anger.[105] As soon as they were met, Thomas of Lancaster, the most eminent of this confederacy, in a grave discourse lays before them the iniquity of the time, the insolency of this new Ganymede, and the king's intemperate wretchlessness, which made the kingdom a prey to all manner of injustice. Hereford adviseth that they should all together petition the king, that he would be pleased to look into the disorders, and grant a reformation. Mowbray, Mortimer, and the rest soar a higher pitch, which Clifford thus expresseth.

My lords,
It is not now as when brave Lincoln lived,
Whom Edward feared, and all the kingdom honoured.[106]
Nor is this new lord a Gaveston, or naked stranger,
That only talked and durst not act his passions.
We now must have to do with one of our own country,
Which knows our ways and how to intercept them.
See you not how he weaves his webs in court and country,
Leaving no means untried may fence his greatness?
And can you think a verbal blast will shake him,
Or a set speech will sink his daring spirit?
No, he is no fantastic Frenchman
But knows as well as we where we can hurt him.
His pride is such, he'll ne'er go less a-farding;
But he must fall a key, or we must ruin.[107]
Women and children make their tongues their weapons;

True valour needs no words, our wrongs no wrangling.
Say this unconstant king hear our petition,
Admit he promise to redress our grievance;
This sends us home secure and well-contented,
Until the plot be ripe for our destruction.
If you will needs discourse your cause of grievance
Be yet provided to make good your error;
A wise man gets his guard, then treats conditions,
Which works a peace with ease and more assurance.
All treaties vain, our swords must be our warrant,
Which we may draw by such a just compulsion.
Those ready, then attempt your pleasure,
And see if words can work a reformation.
I am no tongue-man, nor can move with language;
But if we come to act, I'll not be idle;
Then let us fall to arms without disputing;
We'll make this minion stoop, or die with honour.

This rough speech, uttered with a soldier-like liberty by one so truly noble and valiant, inflamed the hearts of such as heard them.[108] They concur all in a general approbation, and thereupon they fall to present levies. Mortimer, a brave young active spirit, with his retinue, gains the maidenhead of this great action. He enters furiously upon the possession of the Spencers, spoiling and wasting like a professed enemy.[109] This outrage flies swiftly to the owners, and appears before them like Scoggin's crow, multiplied in carriage.[110] They as soon make the king the sharer of their intelligence, and increase it to their best advantage. Edward, sensible of so audacious an affront, thought it did yet rather proceed from private spleen than public practice; which made him in the tenderness of the one, and malice to the other, by proclamation thus make known his pleasure:[111] that the actors of this misdemeanour should immediately appear personally, and show cause whereby they might justify their actions, or forthwith to depart the kingdom, and not to return without his special license. When the tenor of this sentence was divulged, and come to the knowledge of the confederate lords, they saw their interest was too deeply at stake to be long shadowed. In the obedience of such a doom, the primity of their plot must receive a desperate blemish.[112] They therefore resolve as they had begun, so to make good and maintain the quarrel; they reinforce their forces, and draw them into a body strong enough to bolster out their doings, and to bid a base to the irresolute wanton king and his inglorious favourite, whose platforms were not yet so complete, as that they durst adventure the trial of so strong a battery. Yet the more to justify their arms (which in the best construction seemed to smatch of rebellion), they send unto the king a fair and humble message, the tenor whereof lets him know, that their intentions were fair and honest; and that the arms thus levied were to defend his honour, and not offend his person.[113] The sufferings of the kingdom were so deep and weighty that all was like to run to present ruin, unless he would be pleased to cure this fever. In all humility they desire he would sequester from his presence, and their usurped authority, those instruments which acted this disorder, and that their doings might receive a test by a fair trial. To this if he give way, they would attend him with all the expressions of a loyal duty; but if his heart were hardened for denial, then they entreat his pardon that would not be spectators of the general mischief which drew too swiftly on by this distemper. The king receiving so peremptory a message, thinks this fair gloss a kind of by-your-leave in spite of your teeth. He saw readily how the game went, and was loth to strike the hive for fear the swarm should sting him. Dearly he doted on his minion, yet conceived it fitter he should a little suffer, than they both should ruin, which probably might soon ensue if they prevailed. He had no power provided to withstand them, nor was he sure that time would make it stronger; the lords were well beloved, their quarrel pleasing, while he had nothing but the name of king, might hope assistance. Now he condemns bitterly his improvidence, that had not secured his work before he acts it. Spencer, that saw himself thus quite forestalled, and his great foresight in a manner useless, since those whom he had made were but a handful, and those of the poorer sort of weaker spirits, that stow themselves in tempests under hatches, knew 'twas too late to think of opposition; and therefore persuades his irresolute master to subscribe to the present necessity, yet so that these angry hornets might not be their own carvers. He knew, or at least believed, his faults were not yet capital, yet could not tell what construction might be given, if those which were his enemies were admitted to be his sole judges, and therefore made rather choice to be at the mercy of a parliament, than at their disposing. He was not without hope to be able to make an able party in this assembly, where at worst he knew he should be sentenced, rather by spleen than fury. This resolution by the king approved, an answer is returned to the lords; that his Majesty, having examined the contents of their petition, found therein a fair pretext of justice and reason, and that if their allegations were such as were by them pretended, himself would with as much willingness as they could desire, join in the act of reformation.[114] But for as much as private passion masked itself sometimes under the veil of public grievance, and particular ends had the pretext of general reformation, he thought it expedient to make this rather a parliamentary work, than the act of his prerogative, or their enforcement; which was more for their proper honours, and the good of the whole kingdom; which resolution if they thought fit to entertain, he wished them to lay down their arms, which were the marks rather of an intended violence, than a real desire of justice; that done, in the knowledge of their approbation, he would speedily cause his summons to be sent out for the calling together of this great assembly. The reception of this answer was not displeasing to the barons, who desired those might be the judges that had equally smarted with the stripes of this affliction; yet they conceived it not wisdom to disband their forces on a bare supposition; which could not be yet continued, without too much charge, and too great jealousy. To reconcile this, they divide themselves, every one retaining to himself a guard sufficient to assure his person, and so dispose the rest, that they might be ready on the least item. Things standing thus, the writs and proclamations for election are sent out, in which there was as much time won as might be taken without suspicion. Now is there stiff labouring on all sides (though not visibly, yet with underhand working) to cause a major part in this election; which the lords wisely foreseeing (as the mainspring that must keep all the wheels in the right motion) had beforehand so provided for, that the engines of the adverse party served rather to fright than make a breach in the rule and truth of this election. The subjects sensible of the disorders of the kingdom, and seeing into the advantage which promised a liberty of reformation, make choice of such as for their wisdom and integrity deserved it, rejecting such as sought it by corruption, or might be in reason suspected. This made the undertakers fall short and wide of the bowhand.[115]

The day of appearance being come, the jealous lords would not rely so much on the king's good nature, but that they come up like themselves, bravely attended with several crews of lusty yeomen, that knew no other way to win their landlords' favour but with fidelity and valour.[116] These, for distinction, and that they might be known all birds of a feather, are suited in cassocks with a white guard athwart; which gave this the name of the Parliament of White Bends. Spencer, seeing the retinue of his adversaries, makes himself a rampire of all his servants, friends, and kindred.[117] The jealous citizens, that sometime look beyond their shop-board, seeing such a confluence from all parts of the kingdom, and so ill-inclined, had a kind of shivering phantasy, lest while these strong workmen fell a-hammering, the corporation might become the anvil. The mayor, to prevent the worst, doubleth the guards, and plants a strong watch to keep the gates and suburbs. Now according to the usual custom, the Speaker is presented, and the king himself doth thus discourse his pleasure, which they attend ere they begun this session.

My lords, and you the commons of the nether-house![118]
I have at this time called you hither,
To crave your aid, advice, and best assistance.
I am informed my subjects are abused,
And that the kingdom's welfare daily suffers.
Such actions I maintain not, nor will suffer.
Sift out the depth of this, and find the authors;
Which found, I'll punish as yourselves think fitting.

A kingdom's weight depresseth so his owner,
That many faults may scape his eye unquestioned;
Your body is the perspicil that shows him[119]
What errors be, and how he may prevent them,
Which leads both king and subject to a settled quiet.
Be not too curious in your inquisition,
Which wastes but time, and feeds diseased passion;
Nor may you make those faults that are not,
Which savours more of envy than of justice.
Actions of state you may not touch but nicely,
They walk not in the road of vulgar knowledge;
These are high mysteries of private workings,
Which foreright eyes can never see exactly;
You cannot blindfold judge their form or substance.
As all times are believed, these may be guilty;
Yet let your judgement make them so, not private fancy,
Which is the nurse that suckles up confusion.
So grave a senate should not be the meeting
Where men do hunt for news to feed their malice.
Nor may you trench too near your sovereign's actions,
If they be such as not concern the public;
You would not be restrained that proper freedom,
Which all men challenge in their private dwellings;
My servants are mine own, I'll sift their errors,
And in your just complaint correct their vices.
Seek not to bar me of a free election,
Since that alone doth fully speak my power;
I may in that endure no touch or cavil,
Which makes a king seem lesser than a subject.
I know those I affect are more observed,
And envy waits their actions, if not hatred;
'Twere yet injustice they for this should suffer,
Or for my love, not their own errors, perish.
What one among you would not be exalted
Or be to me as he whom now you aim at?
Reason and nature tie me to their limits,
Else might you share it in a like proportion.

Ambition, that betrays poor man's affections,
Stares always upwards, sees nothing beneath it,
Till striving to o'erthrow some lofty steeple,
It stumbling falls in some foul sawpit.
Perhaps the court is guilty of some errors,
The country is not free from worse oppressions,
Yet these are waived, as acts unfit your knowledge,
Which rob and tear the poor distressed commons,
Who must be still possessed; my greater agents
Are the contrivers of this public mischief,
While you by these make good your proper greatness.
This should not be, if you conceit it rightly;
'Tis far from justice and a due proportion,
One man should fall, and thousands stay unpunished,
That are more guilty far of foul transgression.
If you would sift, and with unpartial dealing
Sweep from the kingdom such unjust oppressors,
It were a work of goodness worth your labour,
Would leave to aftertimes a brave example.
But these assemblies think those acts improper,
Which may reflect upon the proper freehold
Of those that are most nice, and apt to censure.
I now desire (it is your sovereign speaks it)
You will reform this kind of strange proceeding;
Prejudicate not any till you find him faulty,
Nor shoot your darts at one, where more are guilty.
In such a number diversely affected,
There are, I fear, too many thus affected
That this advantage fits their private rancour,
Making the public good the stale and subject, [120]
Which aims unveil'd at naught but innovation.
These busy-brains, unfit to be lawmakers,
Let graver heads restrain by their discretions;
Else I must make them know and feel my power.
I will support and still assist your justice,
But may not suffer such a fond distemper.
Your privilege gives warrant, speak in freedom;

Yet let your words be such as may become you;
If they fly out to taint my peace or honour,
This sanctuary may not serve to give protection;
If so, some discontent, or ill-affected spirit
May challenge power to vent a covert treason.
But your own wisdoms, I presume, will guide you
To make this such, that I may often call you.
What more is fit, or doth remain untouched,
You still shall understand in your progression,
Wherein let virtue lead, and wisdom rule your temper.

The king having ended, the several members of this goodly body draw together, where notwithstanding this grave admonition full of implicit direction, they fall roundly to their business. For form's sake, they awhile discourse the petty misdemeanours of the kingdom, to make a fairer introduction into the main end of their assembly. A few balls being tossed and bandied to and fro, they begin to crack the nut where the worm lay that ate the kernel. No sooner was the vote of the house discovered, but informations fly in like points, by dozens; no business is discoursed which touched the dishonour of the king, the grief of the kingdom, or the oppression of the subject, but straight flies upward and makes a noise that all had one beginning. The general thus far questioned, the particulars come to a reckoning, wherein Spencer is pointblank charged with insolency, injustice, corruption, oppression, neglect of the public, and immoderate advancement of his own particular.[121] Those few faint friends he had gotten into this number, more to express their own abilities, than with a hope of prevailing, hearing these thundering aspersions, rise up to justify, or if that fall short, to extenuate the faults of their glorious patron; but their oratory proved, just like the cause they strive to defend, full of apparent falsehood. Those nimbler spirits that haunt the ghosts of corrupted greatness, seek not to undermine this great building, whose structure had so hasty and rotten a foundation, but prove in reason, justice and necessity, that it ought to be demolished, since it was the spring that polluted all the lesser fountains. The places of judicature being still marted, the purchaser must sell his judgements; which was a commerce fit for those that had the worst, and were most dissident. The simoniacal trading for spiritual promotions, as it dishonoured the dignity, so it must exalt such as knew better how to shear their flocks than feed them.[122] Bartering of honour for private lucre would ruin the glory of antiquity in blood, and in another age, as prodigal as this, make lords as common as drovers.[123] Possession of so many great offices, as it was an injury to those of more deserving, so might it in time become a monopoly for every new-made upstart. Settling the strengths and military provision in the command of one so much insufficient, must open the way to foreign loss, or domestic mischief. Planting of the principal officers of the commonwealth by one man's corrupt distribution, must bring all to his guidance, and the kingdom to confusion. Admission of the royal ear to one tongue only, ties all the rest, and resembles the council-chamber to a school where boys repeat their lessons. These passages discoursed and aphorismed at large in the House; at the private committee, diverse fouler suspicions and aggravations are treated with a greater freedom; which being again with their several proofs reported before the whole body, by the general doom he is pronounced guilty. This daring favourite, seeing the violence of the tide, begins to fear it; and letting his anchor fall, hulls out the full sea in the royal harbour; he strikes his topsail, yet condemns the winds that cause the tempest,

And quarrels with their power must be his judges.

This takes away all hope of reconcilement,

And more inflamed their hearts that did pursue him.

They know he now must fall, or they must ruin.

Lions may not be touched, till they be sure,

Lest breaking loose, they tear those gins that catch them.

This consideration begets a solemn messenger, well attended with diverse seconds, to make a full relation both of their verdict and whole proceedings.

    The Lords being prepossessed by their own knowledge of all the actions of this false impostor, after a conference and grave discussion, pronounce their sentence: that the Spencers, father and son, should both be forthwith sent to live in exile.[124] This done, a grave declaration is made by both Houses and presented to the king, expressing the tenor of their doom, and reasons moved them to it. The king, as weak in his distractions, as wilful in advantage, sees now there was no striving, unless he would adventure his own hazard by such denial. No time is now left for dispute; he ratifies the sentence, and present execution swiftly follows judgement. Immediately are these two great courtiers carried with more attendants than they cared for unto the port of Dover, and straightways shipped to seek some other fortune. The son is no whit dejected, but bears up bravely; he knew his master's love, and scorned their malice. Parting, he takes a silent farewell full of rancour, which vows revenge, and hopes to live to act it. The aged father, whose guilt was less, and sorrow greater, deserved in justice pity and compassion; his snowy winter melts in tears, and shows his inward grievance; bitterly he taxeth his son's pride, and his own vanity, exclaiming against the rigour of his fortune, that had in the last act of his age cast him so cruelly from his inheritance, and at the very brink of the grave estranged him from his birthright. He confesseth the improvidence of his error, which being raised by byways, sought to keep it. Lastly, he wisheth his behaviour had been such that in this change might give him help or pity; but it is the inseparable companion of greatness fraudulently gotten, not by desert or virtue, it prefers falsehood, and a kind of shifting juggling, before a winning truth or goodness, which draws with it a firm assurance. Of all others, it is the most erroneous fond opinion, which conceits affections may be won and continued in a subordinate way. They are the proper operations of the soul, which move alone in their own course, without a forced compulsion. Other ways may serve as temporary provisions, but he that by a just desert, and credit of his own worth, hath won the love of good men, hath laid himself a sure foundation; this makes his honour his own, and the succession permanent to his continuing praise and glory. These imperious servants thus removed, the elder, in obedience of his doom, makes a foreign climate witness his submission.

The younger, of a more impatient and turbulent spirit, makes

the spacious sea the centre of his dwelling.[125] He would not trust
to any other nation, since his own climate so unkindly left him.
The king, yet scarcely weaned from his sorrow,
Makes yet fair weather to the parting barons:
He thanks them for their care and great discretion,
Which he would still acknowledge and remember.
Thus kings can play their parts, and hide their secrets,
Making the tongue the instrument of sweetness,
When that the heart is full of bitter gall and wormwood.
They knew he juggled, yet applaud his goodness,
And give him back an answer justly suiting;
Their tongues seemed twins, their hearts had both one temper,
Which at the length occasioned all their ruin.
And thus with the enacting of some few ragged laws, he dissolves this meeting. Now is the lost chamberlain furrowing up the watery sides of angry Neptune, wafting about the skirts of his first dwelling; falling short in the possibility of revenge of those he hated, he vows to make the harmless merchant feel it. What by surprise, and what by purchase, he had made himself strong at sea, and well-provided; with which he scours the coast, and robs all comers, making a prize of all he rifled.
Sometimes he slips into the private harbours,
And thence brings out the ships were newly-laden;
Such work to those that trade by sea, breeds strange
Amazement. A piracy so strong and daring,
Soon makes the terror great, the clamour greater;
The council table's covered with petitions,
The royal ear is cloyed with exclamations;
All still enforce that trade must sink and founder,
Unless the king the sooner did prevent it.
Edward well knew their griefs, and did believe them;
But saw withal it was his Spencer caused them,
Whom he too well affected to pursue with danger.
He thinks it reason to ease his grievance ere he right the subject;
Let them expect and bite upon the bridle,
That they may taste the error of their judgement.
Necessity in time would make them seek their quiet,

The means whereof he thinks not fit to motion.
Yet still he thunders out his show of anger,
And gives directions that shipping should
Be rigged and manned, well furnished
To bang this pirate off from his oppression,
Whom he would take, or lose the Royal Navy;
Yet underhand he countermands these precepts,
Pretending present want for such provision
As might make good at full this expedition;
Which should be done securely, though delayed.
While thus the rage grows out of this disorder,
All plaints prove fruitless, there was no provision.
The flock of merchants all appear before him,
Letting him know the state they stood in:[126]
Their stocks his custom must impair and minish,
Unless some present course repress this pirate.
The king gave answer. He laments and pitied
Their loss, his wants and private dangers,
Which in the instant was of such a nature
That he had cause to fear his proper safety.[127]
The malcontents, that fish in troubled waters,
Were plotting new combustions to act their malice;
He understood their workings strong and cunning,
Which he was forced to stop with haste, or lose the garland.
This was the cause he could not yet go onward
To help their griefs, which shortly he intended;
Till which, he wished their grave deliberations
Could fall upon some way might stop the current,
And take off Spencer from so cursed proceeding,
Which he believed he acted by enforcement,
Rather than will to wrong his fellow-subjects.

The citizens, as naturally talkative as suspicious, parting from the king, forget their losses, and fall to a liberal discoursing upon the king's words, what the plot of this great treason might be. They were not without a kind of jealous suspicion, lest the city might share in the sufferance, if it came to be acted. A little time brought the news to be the common discourse of every barber's shop and conduit. To make the suspicion more authentical, the king makes a strong guard about his person, sending forth directions to his friends and all his well-affected subjects, that they should enable themselves with the best strength they could, and to be ready on occasion upon an hour's warning. To lull the watchful lords asleep, he addresses unto them his particular letters, full of humanity and gentleness,[128] desiring as he most reposed on their loves and fidelity, so that they would (if the necessity required), be ready to assist him against a crew of disordered persons, who were secretly contriving both the ruin of himself, the ancient nobility, and the kingdom; their plot was not yet ripe and he conceived it in the reason of state, fit to have the birds flush before he caught them. The lords, that in the first rumour suspected it had some reflection on their particular, or a mere noise without ground or substance, on the receipt of this letter alter their opinion, and believe there was some real cause of this suspicion. They knew the king was wretchless, dull, and sleepy, and did not use to wake but when it thundered; they think him short in depth of so much judgement, as with a jig of state might catch them naked. His letter seemed a character of truth, but not of cunning; this kept them free from doubt,[129] but not from danger.

They send back an answer graciously received; themselves, their strengths and states should wait his pleasure.[130] These passages thus spent, the citizens, that like no laws but those of profit, do lay their heads together to find out a way how to dispose things, so that they might trade with safety. A cunning engineer (one of the king's own making) avows there was no means but one to make things sure, which was to move the king to call the Spencers home and reconcile them. The sequel was not fearful, since this trial would make them know themselves, and be more quiet; if not, they yet might be in distance where they might be surprised if they offended. This proposition finds consent and liking in the grave brain of the deep corporation; instead of punishment so well deserved, the thief must be preferred, to free the passage; yet to excuse their error, they saw the king had an itching inclination that way, and were not without a hope that Spencer being by their means recalled, would, of a professed enemy, become a sure friend to the city. This gave them heart to draw up their petition, and immediately to present it to the king; who having that he looked for, in outward show seemed nothing well contented.[131] He bids them examine well the nature of their petition, which run in a direct line in opposition against a parliamental sentence, and would incense the reconciled barons, against whose strength he could not well oppose, but it must hazard him and all the kingdom. Yet if their wisdoms did think fit, in their assured assistance he would venture, since he preferred their good before his private. Though Spencer had transgressed his will and pleasure, yet their entreaty should dispense his error, in hope he would become a new-made subject. They cry, 'God bless your grace; revoke your judgement, you shall command our lives to back your goodness.' Edward thus far on his way, causeth a declaration to be made, containing the request of his faithful subjects, and beloved royal chamber of London, at whose importunate entreaty he thought fit, out of his grace and tenderness of the general good, to recall the Spencers, who had given sufficient caution for their future good bearing.[132] This known, soon brings them back to grace and favour; their petty thefts at sea must have a sure way to trade in; they must return to shave and rob the kingdom, 'twas thought more fit, than they should rob the merchants.[133] 'Tis strange to see what shift this poor king made to work his own undoing. But when religion's lost, and virtue banished, and men begin to trade with slights and falsehood, the end proves fatal, and doth lead them blindfold into the ways that work their own destruction. The actions of a crown are exemplar, and must be perfect, clean, upright and honest; their errors die not with them, but are registered in the story of their lives with infamy or honour; which consideration may in justice beget a sincerity and cautelous respect from acting under the pretence of policy, those stratagems which seem, but are not, fruit of royal goodness. A like care must be had in the limitation of affections, so that they enforce him not to those ways which at one blow take from him his judgement and his honour. The power majestic is or should be bounded; and there is a reciprocal correspondence, which gives the king the obedience, the subject equal right and

perfect justice, by which they claim a property in his actions; if either of these fall short, or prove defective by wilful error, or by secret practice, the state's in danger of a following mischief.[134] The Spencers thus returned are reinvested into their former high and wonted greatness; the burnt child fears the fire; they know their danger, and not attend the storm until they feel it. Their master's plot they second, and closely gain a strength for present action. That done, they appear with confidence, and by main strength seek to crush those of the adverse faction. Sir Bartholomew Baldsmere is the first that tastes the prologue; they seize upon his castle of Leeds without a law or title; he sues to have his own, but is rejected.[135] Their peremptory return, and the abrogation of that law that sent them packing, was provocation enough; there needed not a second motive to inflame the angry barons; but when they understood the unjust oppression of their confederate, and the daily levies that were underhand made, then they conceive it time to look about them. They find the fruit of dalliance, and visibly see into the king's plot, which had abused them; condemning their credulity and coldness, that had not spoiled the brood while it was hatching. The king, who had so oft been catched, was now more wary; and resolving to be aforehand with his business prepares his forces. He knew his arms, not tongue, must plead his quarrel; another error in his guard, he suspects, would make him liable to a more cursed proceeding.
His favourite, that had his spies in every corner,
Is soon informed the potion was a-brewing
Would give him physic, if he did not prevent it.
The gathering clouds portend a sudden darkness,
Which threaten showers of blood and civil mischief.
He thinks his guilt above the rate of favour,
And vows to wade in blood, or die, or vanquish.
To suffer still, and not to act, he counts it weakness,
Which makes him strive to be the first invader.[136]
He wins the king to march with those strong forces
Their foresight had prepared, being soon united.
The first exploit seizeth the two Mortimers,

That with an unadvised security had played
Over their old game anew on his possessions.[137]
Their strength was great enough for an incursion,
But far too weak to cope with such an army.
Their resolution was to give the larum,
And then retreat to knit with their confederates;
But they were intercepted ere they feared it,
And made the Tower the prize of their adventure.
Thus sometimes it falls out, who acts injustice,
Is catched in the same net himself was weaving.
The lords with this report are strangely startled,
They see themselves forestalled in their own working;
Arms now they know must be their warrant,
Or else their lives must pay a bitter forfeit.
Their forces were not yet fully ready, yet they march on,
resolved to wait the king's approach at Burton.
Time, that runs swift to mischief, slow to goodness,
At length conjoins their strength and several levies,[138]
Which were not great, and yet believed sufficient
To give a canvas to the royal army,
Which as their couriers told them, was not mighty.
Soon are they brought to view each other's countenance;
Where friend against friend, and son against the father,
Brother against the brother, stood embattled;
Such mischief follows still a civil discord.
The king's force far exceeds in strength and number,
Which made the terms of hazard far unequal.
The adverse part, perceiving well the danger
Which they were in, if they abide the trial,
Condemn their own belief, and servants' falsehood,
Who had so far fallen short in their discovery.
But now a second deliberation is entertained, which adviseth them to decline the battle, and to make a retreat, till they were reinforced. This resolution taken from the present suspicion, was not more dishonourable than dangerous; it gave confidence to their enemies, and dejected their own party, willing rather to try their hands than their heels where the peril seemed indifferent.

But the reasons given in excuse were grave and weighty. The Earl of Lancaster had sent Sir Thomas Holland to raise his northern friends and tenants; who was marching up strongly and well-provided, so that if they could have adjourned the battle off to his arrival, it would have made the terms more hopeful, if not equal. It is in the rule of war esteemed a weakness to affront an enemy for a set battle, with too great disproportion in number; but to recoil without a marvellous, discreet and orderly proceeding is now more than laying the disheartened troops to a present slaughter; the experiment whereof was here apparent. The lords rise, but ill, and in disorder, more like a flight than a discreet retiring. Valence, Earl of Pembroke, that did command in chief under the king, sees this confusion, and straight lays hold of such a fair advantage. He chargeth hotly on the rear, which straight was routed; the barons make a head, but are forsaken; which makes them fly to seek their proper safeguard. With much ado they get to Pontefract, whither the broken troops at length repair for succour.[139] Holland entrusted performs the work he went for, and marched with speed hoping to give a rescue; but when he saw that their affairs were desperate, he thinks it his best play to change his master, and leads his troops to get the king's protection. As it deserved, it gains a gracious welcome. Thus all things tend to their confusion; one mischief seldom comes, but many thunder. The despairing barons finding themselves hotly pursued, repair to council, where many ways are moved, and none embraced, save that same fatal one which wrought their ruin. They leap, like fishes, from the pan that scorched them, into the raging flames that soon consumed them. The castle of Dunstanburgh was believed a strength tenable, until their friends do raise a second army, or they at worst might treat some fair conditions; they march to gain this hold, but are prevented. Sir Andrew Harclay meets them at Boroughbridge, and guards the passage; Hereford and Clifford seek to force it, and like enraged lions here act wonders; twice had their angry swords made the way open, but fresh supplies oppressed them still with number, till wearied, not o'ercome, they yield to fortune, and by a glorious death preserve their honour. When these brave arches fell, the building tottered; though Mowbray made awhile a brave resistance, till his heroic blood, not valour, failed him. The surprisal of Lancaster, and many other noble knights and barons, perfects this overthrow and ends these civil tumults.

The prey thus seized, the Spencers long to taste it; and like to furious tigers, act their passions. They give not their incensed master time to deliberate on that work which was so weighty, which had the lives of such great peers in balance. They whet on, and exasperate the king's revenge, that needs no instigation. Soon is the work resolved, where deep revenge hath mastered humane judgement, and reason doth subscribe to private malice. Valence, a stout and noble gentleman, hating such a barbarous cruelty, seeks to divert it, and mildly thus entreats the royal favour.[140]

To win a battle (sir) it is [a] glory;
To use it well, a far more glorious blessing.
In heat of blood to kill, may taste of valour,
Which yet on cooler terms may touch of murder.
Laws were not made to catch offences, but to judge them;
which are dispensed with where the cause is weighty,
Else none may live where many are delinquent.
Celestial powers have blest you with a conquest,
And do expect to see how you will use it.
For your own goodness sake, make known your virtue;
Be like to him that gave you this great blessing,
And then your mercy will exceed your justice.
The savage beasts but kill to kill their hunger;
And will you act in blood to please your fancy?
The heavens forbid the royal heart should harbour
A thought that justly may be deemed cruel.
Your sword victorious is imbrued with honour,
Let it not ravage where is no resistance;
To spill where you may save, proclaims your goodness.
I'll not excuse their faults, or plead their merits,
Which both are lesser far than is your mercy;
Let not such branches so untimely wither,

Which may in time be your defence and shelter.
Kings are but men, that have their fates attend them,
Which measure out to them, what they to others.
Blood is a crying sin that cries for vengeance,
Which follows swiftly those that vainly shed it.
Black apparitions, fearful dreams, affright them
Whose guilty souls are stained with deeds of darkness.
Oh, let your purer thoughts be unpolluted,
That they may live to show your grace and virtue,
And after ages speak your worth in glory.

The king had scarce the patience to hear out the conclusion of a theme so contrarious to his resolution and humour; yet weighing the integrity and well-deserving of the man that spake it, to justify himself and to give him satisfaction, with an angry brow he makes this sudden answer.
Valence, but that I know you truly love me,
Your words do touch too near your sovereign's honour.[141]
Shall I, seduced by a female pity,
Compassion those that do attempt my ruin?
Such actions may be goodness, no discretion;
How many times have I declined my power,
To win them home by mercy, not by justice?
What hath my mildness won, but flat rebellion,
Which had it took, where then had been their virtue?
Say I should spare their lives and give them freedom,
Each slight occasion colours new eruption,
And I may then too late repent my kindness.
When my poor Gaveston was ta'en, where was their mercy?
They made their arms their law, their swords their justice.
He had no guilt of treason or rebellion;
His greatest fault was this: his sovereign loved him;
And shall I spare those that for my sake wrought his ruin?
No, blood must have blood, their own law be their trial;
Let justice take her course; I'll not oppose it.
The deeds of charity must so be acted,
That he that gives be not abused by giving.

Who saves a viper that attempts to sting him,
If after stung deserves nor help nor pity.
What could they more have done than they have acted,
Unless to kill the king they so much hated;
And shall I pardon these sought my destruction,
And make them fit to act a new rebellion?
If it be virtue, 'tis a poor discretion.
No, I will make them sure, that their example
May others teach the just reward of treason.
Dead men do neither bark nor bite the living.

Instantly he flings away, and to the general grief of the whole army signeth a dispatch for present execution, without so much as the exception of any one particular of all the great ones whom this last conflict had thrown at his mercy. Lancaster is beheaded at Pontefract, and two and twenty others, of noble blood, and great eminency, in other parts of the kingdom; so that there was scarce a city of any note but was guilty of this bloody massacre.[142] So many excellent lives, so ingloriously lost, had been able to have commanded a victorious army while it had triumphed in some foreign conquest. Thomas of Lancaster, a man good and virtuous, though unfortunate, kept faithfully the death-bed promise he made his father, Lincoln; but erring in the time and manner, he tasted his prediction. The king, that was before so apparently guilty of many puny vices, by this act loseth all their memory, and dyes himself in grain with the true colour of a cruel tyrant. The reeking blood of so many brave subjects so untimely spilt had a quick and bitter reckoning, to the final destruction of him and all the actors. In the operations of so great a weight, though the colour of justice seem a warranty, yet mercy should have preceded rigour, since they were not all alike guilty. In point of extremity, it is more safe and honourable to do less than we may rather than all we may; the one makes known our goodness, the other the cruelty of our nature, which with a loathed fear thrusts a zealous and true love out of possession in the hearts of those that behold and observe our actions. Had these lords been of a disposition equally cruel, Spencer had not lived to triumph in their misery, nor they to taste his malice; for it is clear, when they had him at their mercy, that they sought not blood, but reformation, and assuredly in this their last act, which was rather defensive than otherways, their intentions towards the crown were innocent. In all respects (saving the levy of their arms, which was done only to support it with more honour) as things fell out afterwards, it had been happy for the king if he had lost this battle, and they had prevailed; for winning it was the beginning of all his ensuing misery, of which the fundamental cause (as appeareth in the sequel) originally sprung; that this bridle being taken away, he fell to those dissolute actions and injurious kind of oppression, that his government became hateful and his name odious; which wrought in time the general revolt of the whole kingdom. Fear, and the suspicion of the following danger, kept both him and his familiars in a better temper; for though they were fully as vicious, yet they were less confident, and more reserved; which, this barricado taken off, finds neither bound nor limit.

Certainly, in the regiment of a kingdom, it is a discreet and wise consideration in court and council to maintain a divided faction, yea, and interchangeably so to countenance them, that the one may be still a fit counterpoise to the other.[143] The king by this means shall be served with more sincerity and diligence, and informed with more truth and plainness. Where one particular man or faction is alone exalted and only trusted, his words, be they never so erroneous, find seldom contradiction, and his unjust actions pass unquestioned; all men under him seeking to rise by him, sing the same tune; the flock ever bleats after the voice of the bell-wether; which stands with a politic wisdom, since in opposition they purchase but disgrace and ruin. By these means the royal ear is abused, and the minion's acts are more daring and insolent, who cares ever more how to conceal cleanly, than to be sparing in doing the actions of injustice. By this the judgement of the king is impaired, the honour of the crown abused, the commonwealth suffers daily more and more, which by degrees aliens and estrangeth the heart of the subject. The greater the height is, the stronger is the working to preserve it, which for the most part is attended with those same state actions of impiety and injustice; hence spring murmur and hatred, exasperated by a continuing oppression which ends for the most part in a desperate conclusion. Though the fury of this victorious king had so fully acted his tragedy, yet the Mortimers were spared; but it was rather out of forgetfulness than pity, whose deaths had been more available than all those which in so great haste had tasted his fury.[144] Some think that the queen's intercession got the respite of their execution, mainly followed by Spencer, who in that act irreconcilably lost her favour; by the subsequent effect it seems probable enough; but howsoever it was wrought, it appears he was reserved to be one of the fatal executioners of the divine justice, which taught his persecutor that same ancient Roman law of *talionis*, and gave his unfortunate master so sad a cause of a just repentance.[145] The kingdom after these bloody hurly-burlies and strong convulsions, begins now to be a little settled, only it was filled with grief and expectation where these aims would end that ran on with such violence. The principal pillars of the common good being taken away, and those that remained being frighted and disheartened, gave such a liberty to the now great officers, that the whole interest of the state was believed little better than the fruits of an absolute conquest. All men suffer basely, yet no man dares oppose or question it.

The king secured, approves his Spencer's actions,
And makes the regal power the servant's warrant.
Hence springs the insolency of unjust oppressions,
And those unlawful ways to drain the subject,
Which leave no means might fill the royal coffers.
The grieved kingdom languished with these burdens;
The great ones suffer basely, courting his vices,
Which like a tree o'ergrown, of immense greatness,
Shadowed their growth, and did suppress their merit.
They fawn upon the time, and view each other
As ships salute at sea, whose voyage differs;
They were become strangers to themselves and to their fellows,
Which stop the passage to so just a quarrel.
The private end was now the thing in fashion,

The public was forsaken as a monster.
The commons, whose home-bred looks are the true index of all that dwells within, and honest plainness, do more than murmur out these oppressions. They gape to catch the turning tide, and would have moved,
But find no-one would give them heart or leading.
Oft do they make attempts, but yet discreetly,
To try if they could find a staff to lean to;[146]
But 'twas in vain, the law was such a terror,
That he that stirs and sticks was sure of drowning.
Now do the learned sages see their error,
That hung themselves in chains so great and many,
Making a lime-twig for each several feather;[147]
Now do they blame those laws themselves enacted,
Not like a watch, but as a paper army,
To keep the good still in the worst condition;
As if the multiplicity had been the glory,
Where laws are made to catch, not ease the subject.
If that great volume of the law draw forth his engines,
What subject can untouched escape his rigour?
Spencer, that knew himself thus hated, and that the general cry proclaimed his baseness, sinks not his height, nor would go less a-farding; but makes his mischief like himself, still foul, but greater; with reason yet suspects and fears the sequel. His mistress sat on thorns, which made her startle; he knows the wheel would turn, almost without touching. This calls his wits together, and puts them on the rack for a confession, what was the way might best assure this danger.[148] The king's weak humour, naturally wanton, he makes more vicious and apparent guilty, hoping to make him alike hateful, that in the change they both might run one fortune. A pretty policy, that makes it lawful to wound his master, that thereby he may scape the hand of justice, or at the least may make the hazard equal! The king, he knew, was too indulgent, but not tender, or of a heart enough to work the safety of his servants, as he observed in the case of his predecessor Gaveston, and his own late experience. To give him a more real engagement, and pin himself fast by

necessity, he eggs him on to all those actions that were more than most odious in practice, and hateful in the eye of the subject; feeding him in the meantime with a vain belief that the kingdom was generally ill-affected, and sought his deposition; which there was no better way to repress than by holding them short, and making severity rather than paternal love the handmaid of his sceptre. In all the actions of state, whatsoever carried a fair gloss, or proved well, he takes it upon his proper care and diligence; if the success were ill, or not prosperous, it must be esteemed either the will, weak advice, or fortune of his master; in all complaints that spake unjust oppression, he seemed to share the grief, but made the cause the king's, not his which must obey him; he gilds his proper actions o'er with shows of kindness, sullying the royal with his grossest errors, who sat and slept, or winked at these disorders. This was the substance of his first conceptions; but yet this was too weak to make a groundwork on which he might rely his false proceedings. Time daily changed, and new occurrents happen
Might win another faction to pursue him;
For to prevent this fear, he fetched a compass,
And leaves the beaten way of blood and malice;
Such of the great ones as were yet remaining,
And out of reason might be most suspected,
Or did but cross his way, by private practice
He sends to feed the worms and kiss their mother,
Who knew not her own children so transformed.
When that the blossoms dropped away (the garden's glory),
The season being sweet, and mildly pleasant,
All men admired but quickly knew the reason;
Some unkind hand had tainted that which fed them.[149]
This was too much, but yet he wades in deeper.
His brain is subtle, cunning, wary;
An active stirring wit, a quick invention,
A heart grown proud in mischief, full of falsehood,
That dwelt within a conscience knew no bounder;[150]
From these he hammers out another project
That works upon the king as well as subject.

This hath two forms, though of a different temper,
Yet both resembled nearly in dependence.
The first must keep the crown in fear, the kingdom busied
With foreign danger or domestic trouble;
The second holds it still in want, the coffers empty,
To keep the subject poor as they supply it.
Security in one might keep him careless,
And peace with plenty make the other wanton.
From these, being marshalled with a sound discretion,
He thinks the way was easy to assure his greatness;
Within his breast alone was locked the secrets
Of the prime plots of state and weighty business;
The counsellors, that were but merely ciphers,
Knew but the strains of slight and vulgar motions;
He sat alone at helm, and steered the compass,
Which fancies in his thoughts a vain impulsion;
He must be still employed, or all would ruin;
If in the agitations of the king or kingdom
Puzzled with motions of the present danger,
He could assure each party from these harpies,
It needs must add much to his faith and wisdom,
And make his station far more strong and sure;
The resty minds that kick at present greatness,[151]
May then turn craven, and approve his judgement;
He that conceits he could command the planets,
Doubts not to make such trifles light and easy.
His principles thus laid, he falls to action;
With a loose scorn he continues the French correspondence,
Slighting their treaties and desire of friendship;
The marriage of a sister was not powerful
To set things right betwixt these warlike nations;
There was no open war, but private grudges,
Which made the state uncertain, robbed the merchant;
Heart-burning on all sides, while both strain courtesy
Who should begin to set the balance even.
The Scots that were not sure, but yet were quiet,
He irritates afresh for new combustions;

But this was done with such a neat conveyance,
That all men see the smoke, yet feel no fire.
And to the lords at home that stood spectators,
He pares off from his greatness some few chippings,
And gives them here and there to feed their longings;
That they might thus be still, if not contented,
He gives away his female kindred for new friendship,
And makes the portion great, though nothing yet in title;
Which turned the world backward in appearance,
While January and June were dancing Trenchmore.[152]
Those fixed stars that moved not with this comet,
But kept aloof, and did preserve their distance,
These he condemns, and scorns with such proud usage,
That they may seek his grace, or seem to threaten
Some jealous danger to his fearful master.
Great impositions daily are divulged,
And some imposed are not fully levied,
To make the commons fear, not feel their ruin.
No circumstance is left, that but induced
To make the sovereign fear, the subject hate him.
The king, whose arms ne'er thrived, but in the conflict
Which winning lost his honour, caused his downfall,
Was in the memory of his former unfortunate proceedings sufficiently awed; and being now given over to the sensuality of his delights, entertains quickly the least apprehension of fear, if his supervisor did present it so that this part of his work was no great difficulty; and the second was not more uneasy. The royal treasure is profusely spent without account or honour, being but the fountain that served to water the drought of himself, his herd of hungry kindred, and the swarm of flesh-flies that became his creatures. The ancient plate is without the art of arithmetic multiplied into a world of little pieces; the jewels of the crown do leap beyond the sea, and are ta'en prisoners till they pay their ransom; the revenue royal being now grown weary, by proclamation would exchange his landlord; the prerogative, the type of sovereignty, forgets his patron, and cleaves to the fingers of some musty farmer. This want was great in

show, but more in substance, which made the surgeon seek to gain a plaster; the poverty of these institutions answer not the workman's expectation, for the remedy began to seem as fearful as the disease. These profuse prodigalities, instead of a counterfeit, brought in such a real necessity of such a height, that without a speedy supply it must beget a desperate hazard. Many several projections are made, but they fall wholly short, and like pistols charged with powder make a noise, but hit not that they aim at; the hope was dead, unless the old and right way parliamental did give it life and spirit. Spencer knew well enough that such assemblies
Was like a ringworm on the neck of greatness;
A court that in the bulk of high corruption
Would breed a palsy or a hectic fever;
The subject here he knew would see his inside,
Which single durst not quinch, much less encounter.[153]
He doubts the king would hardly be supplied,
Unless he were exposed to try their mercy;
Yet there's no other means, he must adventure.
This thus resolved, he leaves it not at random,
Or doth resign his state alone to fortune,
But wisely makes the way before he run it.
With a reserved secrecy he hides the platform,
Till that his practice might receive perfection.
He hurries forth strange news of foreign dangers,
To draw the people's eyes from private workings;
He makes a show as if all things went current,
And shadows o'er the royal wants with plenty,
Yet closely wills his friends and those his creatures
To get them place betimes in this great meeting.
All such as were the king's entirely, these he instructeth with the selfsame counsel, and courts all such as he believes are powerful to advance his ends, or else procure him danger; and to let all the world know he stood right in his master's affections, he gets his father, himself, and Sir Andrew Harclay, a chip of the same block, made Earls of Winchester, Bristol and Carlisle; Baldock a mean man altogether unworthy, unless it

were for being a disciple of so virtuous a patron, is made Lord Chancellor of England. The solemnity of this goodly creation ended, and the plot now ripe for execution.

The bruit of a parliament flies through the kingdom, and is followed at the heels with writs for present election.[154] The time limited for appearance was short, which speedily drew the great body together, bleeding with the fresh memory of the loss of so many of his brave and glorious members. All ceremonies are laid aside, or handled briefly, so that the time now serves to fall upon the business. Their pulses being felt aloof off, and their temper tried, there was a full discovery that the major part was sure, the rest were heartless. Then comes the king's demand, with fair pretences, which pleads the greatness of his charge and present uses; and shows he had on the strength of his revenue maintained the Scottish wars without assistance, which had exhausted so the royal treasure, that now he is enforced to try his subjects. This motion is soon seconded by such apt scholars as learnt to get the king's or Spencer's favour; others that had a hope to share the booty speak it great reason to assist their sovereign. The commons justly grieved with their oppressions would fain have made a head to stop this current; but 'twas in vain, here was too weak a party, and wants a heart to put it to a trial; this swayed the king the sixth penny of the temporality, and ends this meeting.[155] When the knowledge of this grant came into the country, it bred a general murmur, and quite estranged their loves from their subjection, cursing those times that caused so sad a burden. Upon the neck of this (if we may give credit to those historians, that all agree and publish this relation) were many fearful and prodigious sights, which mazed the people; amongst which this one was most remarkable: the sun for six hours' space showed himself in perfect blood, and sanguined over.[156] The ensuing times that retained it in their memory, and applied it as a prediction of the sequel, believed it did foreshow the king's destruction, which followed swiftly; others conceit it as a wonder showed from heaven, as a sure token of the just displeasure for the loss of the noble Earl of Lancaster and his adherents, whose blood implored justice and sharp vengeance. Thus in amazement man becomes a prophet.

The Scots, that love not rest, delight in prigging; and considering the distractions of the English, thought it a fit time to fall to action, and with a double blow to vent their malice;[157] one strikes upon the borders, which they boldly enter, but are repulsed with little loss or damage.[158]

The other doth invade their neighbour-Irish,
Where they receive with grief a worser welcome.
Bruce, the king's brother, general of this army,[159]
And all his troops, are killed and broken; scarce one was left
To carry back the news of this disaster.
The king, resenting this new provocation,
And all the former mischiefs they had wrought him,
Resolves once more to tempt his froward fortune;
But 'twas not his own valour, Spencer moved it,
That had his aim beyond his master's meaning;
He knew this was the way to waste that treasure,
Which else might breed a fearless fullness;
If it succeeded well, the gain and honour
Would be his share, as well as his that won it,
Since his advice had fathered first the action.
Admit it should prove ill, he then was guiltless,
It must be deemed alone his sovereign's fortune,
Whose destiny was such to be still luckless;
However yet, 'twould keep him so in action,
He might at all times yield the groaning subjects
A short account how he had spent their money.

Upon this, a summons is sent out to call together all the captains and men of war; provisions are daily made to wait upon so constantly a resolved journey. The former misfortune had taught him to undertake this action strong and soundly; the black ox had trod upon his foot, that well he knew the danger.

The king's intentions known, brings him together
All the remaining bravery of the kingdom;
They knew that there was money store to pay the soldier,
Which gives him life to fight and seek occasion.
The cream of all this strength must guard his person,

The History of the Life, Reign and Death of Edward II   161

The other fill the rear, and make the vanguard;
With these he marcheth forward and invadeth Scotland,
Making that nation justly fear the sequel.[160]
But whether it were the infidelity of those about him, the will of Him that is the guide of battles, or the proper destiny of this unfortunate king, this great preparation produced no effect answerable to the general expectation; he is enforced to retire without doing any one act worthy his memory, or the greatness of such an expedition. The wary Scots, that had kept themselves in their strengths and places of advantage, seeing the storm almost past, follow aloof off, and in a watched opportunity set upon the tail of his army, surprising all his stuff and treasure.[161] This loss sends him home to entertain a defensive war, which came from the coast he least expected; whether justly, or to transfer the guilt of his own unhappiness upon the treachery or falsehood of another. The new-made Earl of Carlisle is accused, condemned, and put to a shameful execution.[162] The grounds against him were probable, not certain; howsoever, he was believed to have attempted, like Judas, the sale of his master, which must be taken a sole motive of the inglorious retreat of this so brave an army. The principal reason that may lead us to the opinion that he was guilty, may be taken from the solemnity of his trial, and the severity of the sentence, which upon so grave and full a hearing deprived him both of life and honour in a ceremonious way, whereof till this there appears no former precedent. His old friend Spencer, whose ends he had faithfully served, left him at plunge, being as it seems well content now he had (as he thought) rooted his own greatness, to be free of his ambition, which he feared might rather supplant than support it. A common course of such as rise by their own or other men's corruption; they love a while their props, but after fear them; when with some dog-trick they pick some feigned occasion, private or public, for to send them packing. If you survey it well, it stands with reason; for such as they to serve their ends would act in baseness, in the least change may do so for another that in appearance must succeed his fortune; besides, where the reward seems shorter than the merit, fills one with grief, the other with

suspicion; which two can never long hold correspondence; and
kings themselves, that do abet the treason, do seldom love but
always fear the traitor. But now old quarrels sleep, here comes
a new one that ushered in the way to Edward's ruin.

 The French king Louis being dead, John next succeeds him; a
prince youthful and hot, full ripe for action. He privately
informed of the ill-usage of his sister, and that the king was
wholly led by his proud minion, whose actions witnessed he was
ill-affected to hold firm peace but with his own conditions,
thinks it fit time to break the league which had so weak
assurance. On this he makes an attempt upon the frontiers of
Guienne, and sends a solemn message he would no more
continue peace with England.[163] Edward, that had not yet
digested his Scottish pills, was much displeased to hear so
cursed a declaration from a brother.

Spencer, the spring that gave this difference motion,
Did little dream it would be his destruction;
He wished these princes might fall out and quarrel,
But yet not so, that it should come to action.
He deemed it not amiss his sovereign master
Should hear of war from France, but not to feel it.
The French were of another mind; they saw us beaten,
And discontent within ourselves, full of confusion;
Which gave them hope the time would fitly serve them
To reunite this piece to her first honour.
Thus kings play fast and loose with their advantage;
Affinity and oaths are weak restrictions;
Where profit holds the plough, ambition drives it.

Edward piercing narrowly into the danger, taxeth bitterly the
infidelity of his brother, and begins to examine his own condition, whereby he might accordingly order his affairs, either to
entertain the war, or embrace peace, the hopes whereof were
not yet desperate. He finds himself in the affections of his own
feared and hated; his coffers emptied by the Scottish surprisal,
and the sinews of his late parliamentary supplying shrunk in his
provision and prodigality. A second supply, unless conditional,
was doubtful; the kingdom was grown too wise to be again

anticipated in election; and lastly, he calls to mind the severity of that misfortune that waited so his military actions, that the subjects were diffident of success where he was either general or a party. In this distraction, while he remains irresolute, he seeks the advice of his cabinet council, the closet of his secrets; he thinks him alone worthy to communicate the depth of his misery, and to give the resolution.[164] Spencer, that had his underhand aims, out of a virtuous modesty appears not till he is called; which succeeding as he knew out of course and necessity it must, pleads his own disability in an affair so great and weighty, desiring his Majesty that his father and the chancellor might be admitted into this deliberation, whose maturity of years and ripeness in knowledge might be relied on with more assurance.[165] The reason of this reply, in show full of wisdom and care, had a plot with two faces, like the old description of Janus; the one looked upon his father and faithful friend, whom by this means he thought to advance in credit; the other was more to countenance his own particular, which had a part to play, that must be (as he thought) his masterpiece. No word of his sounds harshly, nor found contradiction in his sovereign's ear, who made his tongue a guide to lead his actions; they are freely admitted and fall to consultation, where the condition of the present affairs is fully opened, and sundry propositions made to reconcile them. But these all prove defective in some material point or other, that according to the pack, Spencer might hit the nail on the head, and by their applause make his project more solid and authentical.

Ever since the breach that happened between him and the queen concerning Mortimer, there had been a strong heart-burning, and many distasteful expressions of the ill inclination she bore him. He knew her to be a woman of a strong brain, and stout stomach, apt on all occasions to trip up his heels, if once she found him reeling; and was not without some discreet suspicion, that she was as well contriving inward practice, as she had been closely forward in the instigation of her brother. To make her sure, and to pare her nails before she scratched him, he thinks occasion had presented him with a fit opportunity,

which he intended not to lose without a trial; from which
ground he thus expresseth his conceptions:

Things standing as they do, (royal sir) there is but one way left
    to right them;
But how that way may like you, that I know not.
You are not fit for war, if you consider
Your proper weakness, bare of strength or money.
To seek, not sue for peace is no dishonour,
But shows a pious will to perfect goodness.
A servant's care, I not deny, may work it;
But this will ask instruction, time and leisure,
Which your condition cannot fitly limit.
Such treaties, for the most part, so are settled;
But 'tis with long dispute, and many windings,
By which we must grow worse, and they still stronger.
If they once find that we pursue it hotly,
They'll raise their height to win their own conditions,
Which may be far unfit your state and greatness.
I know you love the queen too much to spare her,
And I am loath to touch the string should cause it.[166]
But since great works are fittest for great actors,
I wish to her alone this brave employment.
Her wisdom and her love so well united,
Will work (I doubt not) peace as you desire;
So fair a pleader cannot be denied
In that request, which chiefly made her wedlock.
And since I am all yours, vouchsafe your pardon,
If I in reason discourse it farther;
Admit that he deny, her journey sort not,
You still are where you were, with some advantage;
If he refuse your love, you may his sister,
Which is then with him where he so may keep her
Till things are reconciled, and quarrels ended.
Reason of state must master your affections,
Which in this act will tell you 'tis unfitting
She should be here, that may inform her brother

From time to time of all your secret councils.
Say that your love and her obedience tie her,
And keep the scale still even, 'tis a hazard
Which wise men dare not trust in female weakness;
Admitting that her goodness do assure it,
This cannot warrant yet her silent servants,
Who may be sent with her perhaps of purpose,
Or after bribed to sift and show your workings.
Councils are seldom so reserved but that they glimmer
Some little light that leads to their intentions;
Which if they fly to those they touch unacted,
Find swift prevention ere their worth be valued.
These things considered, I do speak it freely,
'Tis fit the queen alone should undertake it;
Which lessens well the charge of your great household,
And brings you peace, or makes you else a freeman
From those domestic cares that shake your quiet.

This act ended, Baldock the chorus, who equally hated the queen, seconds it with a learned approbation; and the old roost-cock in his country language, which was the only tongue he was guilty of, tells the king briefly, he should be sure of peace at home or abroad.[167] The king with an attentive ear hears this relation, and could not but believe his Spencer spake it; nor did he dote so much upon his wedlock, but he could be contented well to spare her, whose eyes did look too far into his pleasures. But yet his wandering soul had strange impressions, which struck him deeply with a sad prediction, and made him faintly yield, but yet delay it.

This overture being come to the queen's ear, and withal the knowledge how this gypsy had marshalled his cunning practice, and had prescribed the way for her escape. which she herself intended, and in her private thoughts had laboured with the best powers of her understanding; she seemed wondrously well-pleased, and offers to undertake and to assure the business.[168]

Their several ends, far wide of one another,
Do kindly meet and knit in the first prologue;
Where craft encounters cunning, it sometimes happens

One and the selfsame hood doth fit the head-piece
Of diverse actors, diversely affected;
Hence it proceeds the plot's more surely acted,
When each side does believe his proper issue.
There is not such a cut-throat for a cozener,
As that which in his own trade doth cross-bite him;
The bee gets honey where the spider poison;
And that may kill physicians, cures their patients.
Such are the qualities of statesmens' actions,
That labour to contrive another's mischief,
And in their own way find their own destruction.

Love and jealousy, that equally possessed the queen, being intermixed with a stronger desire of revenge, spurs her on to hasten on this journey. She saw the king a stranger to her bed, and revelling in the wanton embraces of his stolen pleasures, without a glance on her deserving beauty. This contempt had begot a like change in her, though in a more modest nature, her youthful affections wanting a fit subject to work on, and being debarred of that warmth that should have still preserved their temper, she had cast her wandering eye upon the gallant Mortimer, a piece of masculine bravery without exception;[169] had those his inward gifts been like his outside, he had not been behindhand in reception, but with a courtly, brave respect, full meets her glances. A silent rhetoric, sparkling love, finds quick admittance; such private trading needs few words or brokage. But his last act had mewed him in the Tower, where he was fast from sight of his great mistress love, that makes some men fools, makes others wary.[170] Had Mortimer's design been known, his head had paid for it; which Spencer's malice long and strongly aimed at, but that the queen had begged a solemn respite, which Edward would not break at his entreaty. The cage of his restraint was strong, and guarded; yet 'twas too weak to cloister his ambition, which did suspect, but never feared his freedom; which he attempts, but yet was not so sure that he durst trust it. In the meantime, with a sweet correspondency, and the interchange of many amorous letters, their hearts are brought together, and their several intents perfectly known; hers, to prosecute her journey; his, to purchase his freedom, and to wait upon her, or else to lose his life if it miscarry. It was a strange adventure in the queen, in this inquisitive and dangerous time, to hazard her honour under the fidelity of a messenger; but she was well-beloved, paid liberally, and was not more careful in her election, than wary in the employment; which makes things difficult in themselves, prove facile and easy. No sooner had she knowledge of the plot for his escape, but by all her best means she confirms and strengthens it, and in the meantime advances her own affairs by all ways possible. She courts her adversary with all the shows of perfect reconcilement. But new delays interpose; the king had certainly some inward motive that presaged his ruin, and that this wife of his must be the actor; which brought him slowly on to set her forward. Spencer, that by his own could judge her cunning, suspects her plea of haste and sudden kindness, and now begins to grow a little colder, till he had better sounded her intentions; which by his spies he could not so discover, but that she seemed as pure and clear as crystal.

Yet Edward would not give consent she should be a-gadding; time passed away; she labours hard, but fruitless, till at length she found she was abused.[171] Guienne must be rather lost, than she should wander. Her heart so strongly fixed upon this journey, was torn as much with anger as with sorrow. Reason at length o'ercame her sex's weakness, and bids her rather cure than vent her passion. The opportunity thus snatched from her hopes, she seems well pleased, and glad to stay at home; no inward motion seemed to appear, that might beget suspicion. Spencer, that was as cunning as a serpent, finds here a female wit that went beyond him, one that with his own weapons wounds his wisdom, and taught him not to trust a woman's lip-salve, when that he knew her breast was filled with rancour. When the nap of this project was fallen off, and Spencer with the king were seeking for some other bush to stop this gap, her judgement was so fortunate as to pretend a journey of devotion to St Thomas of Canterbury; which by her jealous overseers (being a work of piety) is wholly unsuspected.[172] All things

prepared, by a faithful messenger she gives her beloved servant
Mortimer knowledge of the time, and her intention.
Then with the prince her son and comfort,
That must be made the stale of this great action,
She fearless ventures on this holy journey.
The king was well content that she should be absent,
And pray to whom she would within the kingdom;
Her jealous eyes so watchful, had enforced him
To take by stealth what now he gets in freedom.
Spencer is not displeased, but well contented,
That wished she would remain an absent pilgrim.
A short time bringing her to the shrine of her pretensions,
She makes as short a stay but hasteth forward.
Mortimer, informed the plot was now in action,
Puts on his practice for a present trial.
Some say that with a sleeping drink he charmed his keepers;
I rather think it drink that made them sleepy.
Whatever 'twas, by this he stole his freedom,
And slyly scapes away, unseen, untaken.
At the seaside he finds his royal mistress
And the young prince prepared to go a-shipboard;
The Earl of Kent and Bishop of Hereford ready to attend them;
And he now comes to make the comfort perfect.
All things succeeding thus fortunately, they lose no time, but
embark, and weigh their anchor.[173] Winchelsea had the honour
of their last farewell, that did provide them shipping.
Their sails hoist up, the heavens they find propitious,
The blustering winds were quiet, and Neptune bears them
Without a rugged brow of angry billows;
A pleasing foreright gale (as kept of purpose)
Fills up their sails, and brings them safe to Boulogne.
Thus did our pilgrims scape the pride and malice
Of him which little dreamed of this adventure.
His craft and care, that taught him all those lessons of cunning
greatness, here fell apparent short of all discretion, to be thus
over-reached by one weak woman. For her escape, it skilled not,
nor could hurt him; it was the rising son with cause he feared;

which who would have trusted with a mother, justly moved by their disorder? Where now were all his spies, his fawning agents, that fed his ear with every little motion that did but crack within the kingdom? Now it thundered, they were asleep, as was their minion-master, else he would sure have seen, and soon prevented so lame a project, that paced afoot so long a walk, so softly. But when the glorious power of heaven is pleased to punish man for his transgression, he takes away the sense and proper power by which he should foresee and stop his danger.

This news flies swiftly to the king, who entertains it with a sad heart, as justly it deserved.[174] The Spencers, with the crew of their dependents, are nettled with a tale that starts their greatness; they think the plot was surely laid, that took so rightly; and in the makers' wit, condemn their judgement, that led them by the hand to what they acted. Mortimer, whom Spencer deadly hated, was well allied, and strong in friends and kindred; he had a cause in hand would win assistance, when that a queen and an heir apparent backed it. But now 'twas past prevention; 'tis a virtue to make the best of that we cannot fly from.

Edward, whose yielding heart at first misgave him, grows sadly dull, and seems to read his fortune; his melancholy thoughts have no impressions but such as were engraved within his conscience. To take him off, Spencer condemns the danger, extenuating their best hopes, which were but fixed upon the French, a nation light and inconstant, whom money would take off if force should fail him.[175] He tells him he had cause to smile, not mourn, that was so freed of such a chamber-mischief, that was more to be feared at home, than with her brother. Lastly, he prays him to be like himself, a monarch, that well might bend, and yet not yield to fortune; 'twas now high time to order so his business, that there might be no farther fear of danger. Baldock the chancellor sets to a helping hand to revive his spirits, which seemed so much dejected; and briefly thus discoursed his better judgement:

Sir, if you now should droop, or show a faintness,
When your occasions do expect your valour,
Your subjects will believe you know more danger

Than they or see or fear; which must be followed
With a dull coldness over the whole kingdom;
Which what it may enforce, you may consider.
'Tis easy to o'ercome a weak resistance,
Which yielding fears the stroke before 'tis coming,
But nobler hearts are ever most triumphant
When they are round beset with greatest perils.
Alas, what can the queen a wandering woman compass,
That hath nor arms, nor means, nor men, nor money?
Think you her brother will so back her passion,
As to expose himself to such a hazard?
France knows our arms too well, too much to tempt them,
Or come within our distance in our dwellings;
Admit he should, what can he do to England,
Which hath a wooden wall will wet his courage?[176]
Louis, that had made him a sure party
Within the kingdom long before he landed,
When civil tumults had embroiled our forces,
Found here so sharp and hotly cursed a welcome,
As left your predecessor soon his first possession.[177]
He came in his own right, and yet forsook it;
Can you then fear they'll venture for another,
Or hazard war that look for no advantage?
Put case they do, have you your forces ready,
You need not fear the French, or any other;
But you must then by your own sprightful carriage
Give life and courage to the valiant soldier,
That fights your quarrel, and his proper honour;
Like to a careful steward, still provided
To give the new-come guest a handsome welcome.
And if I err not, 'tis not much improper
You let the kingdom know the queen's departure,
How far it swerves from duty, love or reason.
Dangers that be far off, may be prevented,
With time, advice, and with a better leisure;
Yet 'tis discretion to catch the foretop of a growing evil;
Look to your ports; your navy well provided,

No foreign force can wrong your peace or quiet.
For those within door that may breed suspicion,
The ways are easy to secure their moving.
Yet all this is too little if you stagger,
Or with a drowsy coldness seem disheartened:
'Tis life and action gives your people mettle.
For God's sake then (great sir) leave off this passion,
Which wrongs your greatness, and doth maze your servants,
That see no cause but merely your opinion.

This speech thus ended, the king forceth himself, against his disposition, and clothes his cheeks with smiles, his brow with gladness; with a more freedom he discourseth plainly the present state of this entangled business.
A declaration is sent out to all the kingdom,
That taints the honour of the queen, but more his judgement.[178]
The ports are all stopped up, that none should follow;
A medicine much too late; a help improper,
To shut the stable door, the steed being stolen.
But 'tis the nature of a bought experience,
To come a day too late, the market ended.
The navy is sent out to guard the frontier,[179]
And watch and ward is kept throughout the kingdom.
These and many other grave instructions
Are recommended to the Spencers' wisdom,
Whom it concerned as deeply as their welfare.
They think not fit to trust the care to others,
But do become themselves the supervisors;
Which for a time of force enforced their absence;
In which short intermiss, the king relapseth to his former error,
Which gave him many sad and deep impressions;
He thinks the breach of wedlock a foul trespass;
But to condemn her he so much had wronged,
Deserved as much as they could lay upon him;
But he was guilty in a higher nature;
He had upheld his parasites to brave her
With too too fond a base presumptuous daring;

He feared his cruel actions, stained with blood,
Would challenge a quick and sad requital, equal vengeance;
He saw the subjects full of grief and passion,
Apt and desirous to embrace rebellion;
And few or none declared themselves to aid him,
Unless 'twere such as stirred by mere compulsion,
Or private interest of their own safety.
Such dull conceits did so engross his fancy,
That he almost despaired of his own fortune.
His minions, now returned from their employment,
Had much ado to level these deep reckonings,
Which lay so heavy on his guilty conscience;
Yet at the length he gained his wonted temper,
And acteth o'er afresh his former errors.

The customary habit of transgression is like a corn that doth infest his owner; though it be pared and cut, yet it reneweth, unless the core be rooted out that feeds his tumour. The guilty conscience feels some inward motions, which slashing lightly, shave the hair of mischief; the scalp being naked, yet the roots remaining, they soon grow up again, and hide their baldness. The operations of the soul of true repentance grubs up the very depth of such vile monsters, and leaves alone the scars of their abuses.

The French king having notice of his sister's arrival, entertains it with a wondrous plausible and seeming show of gladness.[180] After she had well refreshed herself and her little son (as yet a stranger to the riding of so long a journey upon a wooden horse), with an honourable attendance, befitting more her estate, birth and dignity, than the present miserable condition she was in, she is waited on to Paris; all the great ones and bravery of that kingdom are sent to give her welcome, and to bring her to the king's presence. When she beheld the sanctuary of her hopes, her dearest refuge, she falls upon her knee, and with a sweetly-becoming modesty, she thus begins her story. Her royal brother, unwilling to suffer such an idolatry from her, that had a father, mother, brother, husband so great and glorious, takes her up in his arms, when thus she speaks her sorrow:

Behold in me (dear sir) your most unhappy sister,[181]
The true picture of a dejected greatness,
That bears the grief of a despised wedlock,
Which makes me fly to you for help and succour.
I have, with a sufferance beyond the belief of my sex, outrun a world of trials;
Time lessens not, but adds to my afflictions;
My burden is grown greater than my patience.
Yet 'tis not I alone unjustly suffer:
My tears speak those of a distressed kingdom,
Which, long time glorious, now is almost ruined.
My blushing cheek may give a silent knowledge,
I too much love and honour the cause of my afflictions, to express it.
Yet this in modesty I may discover;
My royal husband is too much abused;
His will, his ear, his heart is too too open
To those which make his errors their advantage.
The hope of his return is lost; he still must wander,
While such bewitching sirens are his leaders.
But why do I include them as a number?
'Tis only one; the rest are but his creatures.
How may of his brave and nobler subjects
Have sold their lives to purchase him his freedom?
All expectation fails; domestic quarrels
Have ta'en away their lives that strove to help it;
Unless you please your arms shall disenchant him,
He still must be abused, his kingdom grieved.
I had not else thus stolen to crave your favour.
Made to your hand, you have a way is glorious,
To let the world behold and know your virtue.
Fortune presents you with a just occasion
To crown your glory with an equal goodness.
Would you dispute it, can there be a motive
More weighty than to succour these poor ruins
Which else must lose their portions, being birthright?
See here, and view but with a just compassion,

Two royal plants depressed and like to wither,
Both branches of the flower-de-luce, the root you sprang from;
Which, but in you, have neither hope nor comfort.
Would your impartial wisdom but consider
How good a work it is to help distresses,
A wronged sister cannot be forsaken,
And an heir of such a crown be left unpitied.
In such an act of goodness and of justice,
Both heaven and earth will witness your true valour,
And your poor handmaid joy in such a brother.
Let it not breed suspicion that I seek you
With such a weak, forsaken, poor attendance;
I was enforced to steal away at random,
And durst not by my number be distrusted,
By those with Argus eyes observed my actions.[182]
Though I am here, and those behind that love me,
Besides the justice of my cause, the strongest motive,
I bring the hearts of a distressed kingdom,
That if you set me right will fight my quarrel.
Their truth needs no suspect; you have for warrant
Their queen and mistress, with their king that must be.
Then, gracious sir, extend your royal virtue.
I challenge by that purer blood, assistance
Whereof my birthright gives me equal portion.
Let not succeeding ages in your story
Read such a taint, that you forsook a sister,
A sister justly grieved, that sought your succour.

Her willing tongue would fain have moved farther;
But here the fountain of her eyes poured forth their treasure;
A shower of crystal tears enforced her silence;
Which kind of rhetoric won a noble pity.
The passions of the mind being sweetly moved, the heart grows great, and seems to sympathize their agitations, which produceth a ready willingness, that calls to action the foot, the hand, the eye, the tongue, the body, till that the engines slack that cause this vigour; and then they all revert to their first temper.

The queen's discourse and tears so far prevailed:
The king and all his peers are deeply moved;
Their longing hearts beat strongly for expression,[183]
Which might assure her, they embraced her quarrel,
And with their lives would venture soon a trial.
Her brother bids her cast her cares to his protection,
Which would make Edward know and feel his errors;
His greater subjects offer her their service,
And vow to be companions of her fortune.
The general voice of France proclaimed a fury
Strained to the height, to punish her oppressors.
This overture for a while is so hotly pursued that she (poor queen) with an abused confidence believed things as they seemed in show, true, perfect, real. 'Tis not alone her error, but a disease all flesh and blood embraceth; with ease we credit what we wish and hope for, yet where so great a consequence waits on the action, there is just cause to fear and doubt the sequel.
Though that our aims be just, discreet and hopeful,
Yet if they be confined to certain hazard,
Or do reflect upon the private danger;
Of that same second hand that is engaged,
Reason in justice strengthens the suspicion.
To right the queen, and to restore her heir;
To ease the subject, punish the oppressor;
All these are works thus far seem good and easy.
But these not will, but power and strength must compass,
Against a potent king in his own kingdom;
Which if it fell out well, returned with honour;
If ill, endangered France with an invasion,
Which might perhaps prove fatal and unhappy.
Wise men are moved in passion, not in judgement,
Which sifts the depth and core of such great actions,
Weighing the danger and advantage, with the hazard and dependence;
Which if they turn the scale, or make them even,
Takes off the edge of their propense[184] affections,
Which cause assuaged the heat of this employment.

Spencer, whose watchful eye was fixed on Paris,
By his perspectives sees the glorious welcome
That waits upon the queen and her attendants;[185]
He hears no other news, but what provisions
Were made in France to serve for war in England.
He is not frighted, or a whit distempered;
He knew the French were giddy, light, inconstant,
Apter for civil broils than foreign triumphs;
Beginning more than men, but in conclusion
Weaker and more uncertain far than women.
He taxeth yet his own improvidence,
That gave the angry queen so fair advantage;
'Twas not the power of France he feared, nor all their threatenings,
But the intestine danger, which seemed fearful.
He knew the subjects' hearts were quite estranged,
Which did expecting long for some combustion.
Severity of laws had kept them under;
'Twas not in duty but by mere compulsion,
Which backed by foreign aid, and such brave leaders,
Would break their chains upon the least alarum.
To take off France, he straight selects his agents,
Such as well knew the ways of these employments,
And lades them o'er with gold, and sound instructions,
Bidding them freely bribe, and promise mountains,
Till they had undermined and crossed the queen's proceedings.[186]
He bids them charily observe the quality of time, and place, and person,
Proportioning their rates with such discretion,
That those which most could hurt were deepest laden.
These pinnaces of state thus freighted, arrive at Paris,
Where the heat was almost cooled before their coming;
Yet they go on to make the business surer.
They set upon the pillars of the state, and feel their pulses;
Who wrought like wax against the glorious sunshine
Of brighter angels, which came showering downwards,
And struck them dumb and deaf for opposition.[187]

The History of the Life, Reign and Death of Edward II

Gold in an instant changed the council's temper,
And conquered without blows their valiant anger.
The queen's distressed tears are now forgotten;
They gave impressions, these a real feeling;
Words are but wind, but here's a solid substance,
That pierced not the ear, but hearts of her assistants.
The plot full ripe, to make it yet more perfect
They set upon the king, and show the danger.
To force by sea a passage into England,
Was a design as truly weak as hopeless,
Where wants a navy and the full provision
Might give a sure retreat, or certain landing.
To cope at home with such a potent kingdom,
Required an army full of strength and mighty,
Which must be still supplied with men and money;
Which, not ready here in such abundance,
A woman's passion was too weak a motive
To levy arms alone on that occasion,
Which brings no other gains but merely honour.
The English nation were not so affected
Unto their mistress's quarrel, as to venture
Legal revenge, or else intestine rapine;
Which they must hazard, if they lose, or vanquish.
Lastly, a bare relation of a female passion enforced the cause;
Which whether true or false was yet in question;
The plaintiff had been heard, but no defendant.
These were the reasons which are daily tendered
To take the French king off from his intentions;
Which loved to talk of war, but not to act it.
A small persuasion quickly fills his stomach,
That could not well digest a war with England.
Young kings that want experience have not judgement
To touch the marrow of their proper business,
And sound the depths of councils; for advisers
May be abused, and bought and sold to mischief,
While servants raise their gain from their dishonour.
This being so frequent, 'tis a royal virtue,

That hears and sees but gives no resolution
In things of weight, till he have reconciled
His own with judgement to the council's reasons;
If that it be above his reach that is in question,
Let him not so rely upon the great ones,
That their words prove a law, which have their workings,
That aim more at their ends, than his advancement.
As kings have councillors of state to ease their burden, so should
they have a second help to guard their honour; a lesser body of
selected good ones, whose wisdoms privately inform him rightly
of what in goodness is most fit his judgement.
State actions fill the purse, but foul the conscience,
And policy may bloom the profit, blights the honour,
Which kings should keep as tender as their eyesight.
Though thus the squares that fed her hopes were altered,
The queen is still led on with promised succours,
Which at the upshot meet with new excuses.
She seeing these delays, and vain protractions,
Begins to doubt and fear there was some juggling;[188]
Yet bears it strongly with a noble patience,
Showing no discontent or least suspicion;
Hoping at worst that here in safety
She and her son might anchor out their troubles.
The posts that daily fly 'twixt France and England
Had liberally informed the state of French occurrents.[189]
Spencer, informed the gap was stopped on that side,
Provides to quiet all at home if he could work it;
He sets upon the discontented barons,
That hated him and envied more his fortunes;
He courts their favour, and imparts promotions
That might betray them, more with show than profit;
He makes the gentry proud, by giving titles
That feed ambitious minds, but not content them;
And takes off from the people light oppressions,
But keeps afoot the greatest grievance,
That kept them down from hope to shake his greatness.
All sides do entertain it with a seeming gladness,

Though well they knew it was enforced kindness.
While each part thus dissembles their intentions,
The navy was called home; a charge was useless,
Where was no fear might cause a foreign danger;
The ports were opened, and the watch surceased
That day and night attended on the frontier.
This haste, as 'twas too sudden, wants assurance;
The rising sun was absent, and still looked for,
While the declining dipped his cheek in darkness.
To ease this care, the queen is strongly tempted
By such as seemed her friends, but were his agents,
To reconcile herself unto her husband,
Whom henceforth she might rule as she thought fitting.
When this fell short, she is at least entreated
To send back her young son, the kingdom's comfort;
Which took it ill he should be made a stranger,
Or in the power of a foreign nation.
These sweet enchantments move no whit her yielding,
That too well knew the serpent that begat them;
Her son sent back, they had the prey they looked for,
And she must lack the prop must keep her upright.

This project failing, they fall upon a new one. The king frames a letter to his Holiness, full of humility and fair obedience,[190] yet craving help, and bitterly complaining that Isabel his wife had fled his kingdom, pretending a mere voyage of devotion, and had stolen away his son, his only comfort, attended by a crew of traitorous rebels, that strove to break the peace of Christian princes; amongst which one being ta'en in actual treason, had escaped his prison by a lewd enchantment, whom he had cause to fear abused his wedlock. Lastly, the French king, his ally and brother, received and kept them, being often summoned to desist and leave them. The pack of this complaint so well contrived, was not opposed by the French king's council, who could be well content, that by commandment their importuning guests were fairly quitted; necessity would colour actions of unkindness, if household laws were broke, or those of nature. This letter runs from hence to Paris, from thence to Rome, by that same practic agent,[191] that in this interlude had won the garland; he bears a picklock with him, that must open the gates that were fast shut to guard the conclave; his first arrival finds a fair reception. Where money makes the mart, the market's easy. These goodly glozes gilded o'er with shadows, must win belief where there was none to answer. Had they been just and true, the fact was odious, and might in justice challenge reformation; it was enough that here it is believed so, the fact was fully proved, the reason smothered. The cardinals, that freely felt the English bounty, persuade the Pope it was both just and pious, so great a misdemeanour should be questioned, that gave the Christian word so lewd example. On this flies out a present admonition to the French king, that straight he free his kingdom of this his sister-queen, and her adherents, on pain of disobedience, interdiction.[192]

While this device was moulding, out of England the queen receives a large but secret summons, that all her friends were ready to attend her with all things fitting on her first arrival.[193] More than the plagues of Egypt did oppress them, which they nor could nor would endure longer. They bid her hasten her return; though her provision were not enough, their swords should fight her quarrel. She with a joyful heart receives this offer, which like a precious balm closed up the wounds of her sad thoughts, made dull with her suspicion. More to advance this weighty work declining, she tells the king the tenor of this tender.[194] His clouded brow, the character of passion, discovered soon the signs of alteration, which yet seemed more of pity than of anger; he had but then read his Italian summons, which he plucks forth, and casts his drooping sister, bidding her view, and wisely there consider, what danger he was in by her protection.[195] The amazed queen, when she beheld the sentence, instead of help, would rob her of her refuge, she falls upon her knee imploring pity, if not to give her aid, to right her honour, which was eclipsed with so foul a slander. A shower of mellow tears, as mild as April's, thrill down her lovely cheeks, made red with anger; dearly she begs at least but so much respite until his Holiness might be informed, her innocence was such sought no favour, but that the law should give upon full hearing. She does implore him that he would compare her adversaries' malice with his cunning, who not contented with her deep oppression, sought to betray at once her hope and honour, wrought with such art, and such a close conveyance, that here her judgement had outrun her trial.

He nothing sorry for so fair a warrant that took him off from charge and future hazard, and yet withal would cover such unkindness, seems to lament the cause, and his condition, that of necessity must yield obedience; he could not for her sake at one blow hazard the danger of himself and his whole kingdom. Not to forsake her wholly, he persuades her to entertain a peace;[196] the king her husband should yield to her conditions; he'll effect it that had a power to force it in his denial; which he would venture, if the world gainsaid it. 'Let him', quoth he, 'then use you ill, or not receive you, I'll make him know I can and will revenge it; small time is left you to consider or dispute it; advise with speed, and let me know your answer.'

The amazed queen, abandoned and forsaken, relates at full this far unlooked-for passage unto the bishop, Kent and Mortimer. Their valiant hearts make good their mistress's sorrows, and tell her they would set her right without the Frenchmen; bidding her not consent to her returning, though it were soldered up with showers of kindness.[197] She well enough did know her husband's humour, which would observe no vow, no oath, no promise; if Spencer once more seized her in his clutches, she should be surely mewed, and kept from gadding. Mortimer contains not in this strain his passion, but breaks into the bitterness of anger, taxing the French as base, unkind, perfidious, that knew not what belonged to love or valour.[198] The queen, that knew the danger, mildly calms him, letting him truly understand his weakness, that in such provocation might beget surprisal, when they must be sent back without prevention.[199] Though that her heart were fired, and swollen with anger, she temporiseth so, 'twas undiscovered. A whispering murmur, muttered from the courtiers, says that she should be sent with speed for England; she feigns to make provision for her journey, yet unresolved which way to scape, or whither; yet with this preparation she beguiled the French that had cozened her; for they had bargained to see her safe at home, and redelivered. Being thus irresolute, of means, of friends, of succour unprovided; the master failing, she attempts the servants, who sing their master's tune by rote verbatim; they cannot give her single help or comfort. Declining misery that once is sinking, finds itself shunned like some infectious fever, and goes alone in shades and silent darkness. Fortune's bright sunshine walks with more professors, than her resplendence hath or beams or streamers; but if her glory sink, or be eclipsed, they shun her fall, as children do a serpent. And yet such trials guide not wretched man's election. Affection (that forsakes in choice the judgement) is led alone by form, and not by substance; which does betray with ease where it is trusted. If virtue guide the chooser, the beginning is mutual goodness, which still ends in glory. The very height and depth of all affliction cannot corrupt the worth of such a friendship, that loves the man more than it loves his fortunes. The raging storms and winds may blow and batter, yet still this goodly rock makes good his station. The correspondency of firm affections is purely innocent, sincerely grounded; if private ends or worldly aims o'erweigh them, they then are but a mere commerce and traffic, which hold no longer than the bargain is driving. Where truth apparently doth warrant love and friendship, it lives and dies, but never changeth colour. But to proceed: the queen in this distraction finds past her hope an unexpected comfort; this heaven can do, when flesh and blood's at weakest. Robert of Artois, a man both wise and valiant, that loved goodness for her own sake, not for fashion, at her first coming tendered her his service.[200] He was a well-resolved steady statesman, not led by compliment, or feigned professions; he had been absent during all this passage; returning, hears and pities her condition, blaming her nation's falsehood, and her misfortune, which he resolves to help out with his best counsel; he seeks and finds the queen, whom, sadly musing, he interrupts, and thus revives her spirits:

Great queen, it is the most excellent part of wisdom, with an equal virtue to entertain the different kinds of fortune;[201] this peregrination of ours is a mere composition of troubles, which seem greater or less, as is the quality of that heart that bears them. I must confess, you have too great a portion, the justice of your grief doth truly speak it; but tears and sorrow are not means to right them. Just heaven doth graciously behold and pity those that do with an active hope implore it, and work as well as pray, the deeds of goodness; your tender sex, and former great condition, have been a stranger to these bitter trials; a little time will make them more familiar, and then you will confess your passion's error. They soonest perish yield to their afflictions, and see no journey's end that tire with burden. For your own virtue's sake, resume your spirits; your sorrows are not such as you believe them. Behold in me, your true and faithful servant, a resolution fixed to run your fortune; you may no longer hazard your abode or being in this unworthy and unthankful climate, paved o'er and closely made to your destruction. Wherefore if my advice may sway your judgement, let speed and care prevent so sure and great a danger. Near to this place the empire hath his confines, where many princes are may yield you succour; at worst, you there may find a sure protection, which in your native soil is more than doubtful. I will not yet presume to teach your judgement, that can much better sway your own condition. Only I lay before you truly my conceptions, which have no other aim than for your safety. Your wisdom may direct your best advantage, which I will second with my life and fortunes.

Infinitely was the queen joyed with his relation, which weighing the quality of the man that spake it, seemed justly worth embracing.[202] She finds it was sincere, not light or verbal, which makes itself a partner of her sorrows; she doubles many thanks, and gentle proffers of true requital, which her son performed when he himself was forced to leave his country. Straight she provides to follow his directions, and with a wary and secret carriage, settles herself for her intended journey; yet still gives out she means to go for England, whither she sends a post to treat conditions, with letters smoothly writ in all submission;

and courting Spencer with a world of kindness, she lets him know
that she relied solely upon his love to be the mediator. Unto her
royal brother she discourseth, that now she understood the peace
was finished, which made her first a stranger to her husband, who
now would hasten home to make it perfect. And to the council,
which well she knew were bribed, to send her back perforce if she
denied it, she more and more extols and praiseth Spencer, as if
'twere he alone had wrought her welfare.[203] The English thus
abused, the French deluded, both are secure; she was providing
homewards, which made the one remiss, the other careless; else
she, forestalled, had found her project harder. In this her course
she sees but small appearance, and few such hopes as might
induce assurance; yet she resolves to hazard all, and wander,
rather than to return thus unprovided. Could she in reason look
for any assistance from strangers, when her brother had denied it?
Or could she think the Germans would be faithful, when her own
birthright had for gain betrayed her? Alas, she could not; yet
enforced, must venture that in her hopes could find no other
refuge.[204] Necessity, the law of laws, makes cowards valiant, and
him content that hath no choice to guide him; which from the
barrenest ground expects some harvest, that else in danger would
despair and perish. All things prepared, and her attendants ready,
she takes a solemn leave, and thanks her brother, assuring him she
nothing more desired, than that she might but live to quit his
kindness. His answer, like his gifts, was short and little. And thus
she leaves the court, in show contented; with a sad heart, a watery
eye, a passion highly inflamed, she journeys forward till she came
nearer where the boundaries parted. The limits of ungrateful
France she then forsaking, gives them this parting blow, to ease
her sorrow:

Farewell (quoth she), farewell, thou glorious climate,
Where I first saw the world, and first did hate it;[205]
Thou gavest me birth, and yet denyest me being;
And royal kindred, but no friends were real.
Would I had never sought thy help or succour,
I might have still believed thee kind, not cruel;

But thou to me art like a graceless mother,
That suckles not, but basely sells her children.
Alas! What have I done, or how offended,
Thou shouldst deny my life her native harbour?
Was't not enough for thee in my distresses
To yield no comfort, but thou must expel me,
And which was worse, betray me to my ruin?
The poorest soul that claims in thee a dwelling
Is far more happy than thy royal issue.
But time will come thou wilt repent this error,
If thou remember this my just prediction;
My offspring will revenge a mother's quarrel,
A mother's quarrel just and fit for vengeance.
Then shalt thou seek and sue, yet find more favour
From him thy foe, than I could win, a sister.

With this she weeping ends, and paceth forward, the wheel of fortune turning; grief grown greater, few real friends attend it, false forsake it; infidelity, the plague of greatness, is commonly at full, when hope doth lessen; and strives to make the tide of sorrow greater. Stapleton, Bishop of Exeter, who till now had faithfully followed the queen's party, and made himself a sharer of her action, with an unnoble precedent doth now forsake her, seeing the French hopes vanished, and those remaining hopeless;[206] examining the grounds of her adventure, almost as short in hope as in assurance, he slyly steals away to his old master, which wins him grace, but lost his life and honour. Some think him from the first not sound or real, but a mere stalking-horse for Spencer's cunning; but this hath no congruity with reason. The queen's departure unknown and unsuspected, in which he was a prime and private actor, had he at first been false, had been prevented; at least the prince's, which had marred the project. Neither can I believe so mean or basely of that same reverend-honour of his calling, that it would be a conduit-pipe to feed the stomach of such a tainted, foul, polluted cistern. By this treachery the resolutions of the queen are fully discovered; the landscape of her travels soon surveyed, begets a more [c]ontempt than fear of danger. The coldness of the French king being understood, their flat denial yet contents not Spencer, who did expect his bargain for his money. Had he had but the prince, they had dealt fairly, while he was being in their proper power. But they, to justify themselves, profess it freely the queen had gone beyond them with their cunning; they thought she had been homeward bound, as she divulged. Thus women's wit sometimes can cozen statesmen. Now are the German natures sifted, and their motions, who fight but ill for words, and worse for nothing. Their constitutions dull and slow, were fitter to guard a fort, than to invade a kingdom. The queen was bare of money, void of credit; which might beget them valour, her assistance. These were conceptions pleased our minion's fancy.

Time, that at length outstrips the longest journey, hath brought our English pilgrims into Hainault. The earl, a man was truly good and noble, resolved so royal guests deserved as brave a welcome, esteeming it a virtue fit his greatness, to be the patron of majestic ruins.[207] He had a brother, youthful, strong and valiant, one that loved arms and made them his profession; this man observed the queen and sees her sorrow, which deeply sunk, and moved a swift compassion.[208] When he beheld a misery so great and glorious, a structure of such worth, so fair and lovely, forsaken, unfrequented, and unfurnished, by the cursed hand of an unworthy landlord, he vows within himself to help repair it. He tells her, he pitied her misfortune; his heart as well as eye did bear him witness. He promised her his service and assistance, which he would both engage in this her quarrel; and seems right glad of such a fair occasion to show his valour in so brave a quarrel.[209]

So fair a morning made the evening hopeful; by those sweet looks of her distressed beauty, and the best language of so rich a pleader, she doth confirm his well-disposed affection, whose willing offer seemed more than courtship. The gallant Hainaulder engaged, makes preparation to set upon this glorious work, this great employment.[210] Pity, that strains the nerves of virtuous passions, moves faster far, when that which gives it motion doth relish beauty, justice, goodness. The tongue that harshly pleads his own compassion, is for the most part entertained with like respondence; when humble sweetness, clothed in truth and plainness, invites the ear to hear, the heart to pity. Who by a crooked fortune is forced to try and to implore the help of strangers, must file his words to such a winning smoothness, that they betray not him that hears or speaks them; yet must they not be varnished o'er with falsehood, or painted with the terms of art or rhetoric; this bait may catch some gudgeons, but hardly him that hath a solid judgement.[211] 'Tis more improper where we sue for favour, to rustle boisterously, or grumbling murmur some unsavoury prayers; which seems to threaten rather a kind of force, than hope of pity. So begging soldiers fright a country farmer.

The earl being a man well broken in the affairs of state, having a knowledge of this his brother's resolution, thinks it tasted more of heat than sound discretion; he condemns his haste, and blames his promise;[212] and sending for him, with a grave, yet mild discourse, doth thus present the danger:

To undertake a war, is far more weighty,
Than hand-to-hand to fight a single combat;
The one needs many strengths, the other skill and valour.
Who thinks with his own arm to gain a conquest,
May sell his life, and yet not purchase honour.
I pity, as you do, this royal lady
And would assist her too, if I were able;
But to attempt where is no hope to vanquish,
Makes foes of friends, and friends far more unhappy.
France has refused, a strong and warlike nation;
That king, a brother, wisely waives the quarrel;
He knows the English strength, and so digests it,
That he'll not undertake a war so hopeless.
Think you yourself more prudent, strong or able
Than is the power and strength of France united?
Or can you dream the English may be conquered
By a few forward youths that long for action?
Do not mistake the work of your adventure,
Which is too sad and great for greater princes.

I do commend your forward valour, noble pity;
It shows a virtuous zeal, and will to goodness.
But measure well the act ere you begin it;
Your valour else must have a lame repentance.
Where is the sinew of the war that must maintain it?
Nor she nor you have arms, or means, or money;
And sure words will not conquer such a kingdom.
Yet if you will be fixed, on God's name venture,
I'll help you what I can, I'll be no party.
True valour dwells not with an overdaring,
But lives with those that fight by just discretion,
Where there is hope at least, if not advantage.
Could you but credit the beginning, that in reason
The world might think it had a touch of judgement,
I must confess I should approve your valour;
But you can only countenance your first motion
With confidence beyond the moon or planets.
Then leave betimes, before you be engaged,
Which after must much more impair your honour.
We'll both assist her with our purse and forces,
Yet do it so the quarrel seem not ours.

Sir John with a quiet and attentive patience hears out his brother, knowing his admonitions sprung from an honest heart and grave experience, yet thinks robbed by age of youthful vigour, from which belief he draws this sudden answer:

Sir,
If all the world forsake this noble lady,
My single arm alone shall fight her quarrel;[213]
I have engaged my faith, and will preserve it,
Or leave my bones within the bed of honour.
No after-age shall taint me with such baseness,
I gave a queen my vows, and after broke them.
Such precedents as these we seldom meet with,
Nor should they be so slenderly regarded.
The mother and her son, the heir apparent
Of such a kingdom, plead in justice pity;

Nor shall she basely be by me forsaken.
Reasons of state I know, not your own nature,
Do take you off from such a glorious action,
Which your own virtue tells you is full of goodness.
Then sit you still, cry ayme, I'll do the business.
Inglorious France may shame in his refusal,
Nor will I follow such a strain of baseness.
Although no sister, 'tis a queen that seeks it;
A queen that justly merits love and pity.
I have some followers, means and some friends and state to stick too;
I'll pawn them all ere she shall be forsaken.
I know I can in safety bring her thither,
And she hath there her friends, will bid her welcome.
That king hath lost his subjects' hearts, grown sore with grievance;
His minion's hatred will be our advantage.
Admit the worst, her expectations fail her,
We then can make retreat without dishonour.
But Edward then may chance revenge the quarrel;
We have those pawns, will make our own conditions;
The king in the remainder being ours,
They'll buy our peace, and not incense our anger.
I'll not deny, 'tis good to weigh the hazard,
But he that fears each danger shall do nothing,
Since every human action hath suspicion.
I am resolved your love shall still command me;
Yet give me leave to be mine own elector.
I cannot blanch this act which I am tied to,
Without the taint of shame and foul dishonour,
Which I will rather die than once consent to,
Although yourself and all the world persuade me.

These words spoken so full home, with such a brave resolution, stopped all reply, and farther contradiction. The queen, who had already a French and an Italian trick, was jealous lest she here should taste a Flemish one.[214] The earl's speech had given her a doubtful belief that he had been tempered withal, seeing his first temper so much cooled. She knew well enough, if money could prevail, it would be tendered freely; and she must then be bought and sold to mischief. Many of her domestic spies were here attending, as she well knew and saw, to work her ruin. Spencer 'tis true had sent his agents hither with like instructions, and their bills of lading; but here they find their pains and labour fruitless.[215] The earl was himself, not led by counsel, and had a heart of steel against corruption, though he was loth to back alone this quarrel; which did proceed from want, not will to help her. Yet he abhorred the very thought of selling his fame and honour by so foul injustice. Yet those that had the charge were not so hopeless, but that a little time might hap to work it. As all courts have, his had a kind of people, and these were great ones too, that boldly warrant and undertake to undermine their master; which daily fed them more and more with money, while they give only words instead of payment. The briber trades but on poor advantage, that buys but hope, and that at best uncertain, which often fails, although 'tis dearly purchased. And reason good, since this may be a maxim; corrupted minds, that to do the actions of injustice will prejudice the soul and conscience, by the contracting of a wicked enterprise for gain or lucre, will never refuse, in hope of a greater advantage, to sell themselves to a second mischief.

But now the queen's doubts increasing, and her longing grown to the height of her expectation, she is enforced with more importunity to hasten on the advancement of her journey.[216] She makes her winning looks (the handmaids of her hopes) express their best ability, more to inflame the heart of her protector. But, alas, these motives need not; ambition of glory, the natural operations of pity, and the honest care of his engagement, had made him so truly hers, and careful of this design, that he leaves no means or opportunity unattempted, that might set it forward. Already had he gotten together three hundred well-resolved gallants, that vow to live and die in this fair quarrel. Here was the body of this preparation, the pillar that this enterprise must stick to. Confidence is certainly, in the actions of this nature, a singular virtue, and can work wonders; else we cannot but believe this little army scarce strong enough to conquer such a kingdom. The queen's hopes must in reason have been very desperate, if her domestic expectation had not been greater than her foreign levy. But more could not be had, without some doubt, more hazard, and a longer protraction; and these are believed sufficient to try their fortune, if not to master it. They stay not therefore to attend the gaining of a multitude, which might at their arrival rather beget suspicion, than win assistance. If the intelligence kept touch, they were sure of men enough, and they had leaders.

Spencer's purloining brokers, seeing the flood coming, which yet would, as they thought, at best prove but a neap-tide, since they sailed in the deepest mystery of their employment (for here was room for no corruption), resolve yet not to make their labour altogether fruitless, but to give their great master a true touch of their willingness and ability; the remainder of that money which fell short in the masterpiece, they employ to gain a true and full understanding of the height and quality of this army, and principally to what part it was directed. Gold, that makes all things easy, fails not in this his forcible operation; which brings unto them the information of the men, arms, and number, with the quality of the navy that was to waft them, and the very haven intended for their place of landing. Though, the circumstances duly considered, the bulk of this enterprise was in itself contemptible enough; yet to improve their own diligence, they extenuate and lessen it in their advertisement; they send away a forerunning post, to anticipate the doubt, and forestall the danger. But now all provisions are ready, and attend the moving of these hopeful adventurers. The queen with a lively look, the presager of her future fortune, takes a solemn leave of her kind host with many hearty thanks, which must stand for payment till she had recovered the ability to free the reckoning; which after she as truly performed, by matching the king her son to a daughter of the house of Hainault.[217]

At Dordrecht the prince and she with their retinue are a-shipboard, whence they depart and steer their course for Dongport haven, which was the place resolved on for their landing;[218] that part being held the fittest and the readiest to give them succour. The heaven, that favoured their design, was more propitious, and from their present fear procures their safety. Spencer being largely informed of their intentions, had made a sound provision, to give them a hotter welcome than they could withstand or look for, had their directions held as they had meant them. Scarce had they run the morning's watch, the skies grew cloudy, a sullen darkness spread all o'er the welkin; the blustering winds break loose with hollow roaring, and angry Neptune makes his level mountains. The watery element had no green-sickness, but curled banks of snow that sparkle fury. These callenders at once assail the vessel, whose lading was the hope and glory of a kingdom; the wooden house doth like a mew triumphing, bestride the angry billow; and as a horse well-managed, doth beat his corvet bravely, without the hazard of his careful rider.[219]

The queen, that knew no floods, no tempests, but those which sprung from sighs and teats of passion, grows deeply frighted, and amazed with danger;[220] the little prince, that ne'er had felt such motions as made him deadly sick without disorder, takes it unkindly, and with sick tears laments the hansel of his first profession to be a soldier.[221] All are confused; the mariners dejected, do speak their tears in language seemed to conjure. Three days together tossed and tumbled they float it out in hope without assurance; in all which time the poor distressed vessel durst neither wear a band, or bear a bonnet. The violence at length being somewhat assuaged, and the bright sun appearing, smiling sweetly, they find themselves in view of land, but where they knew not, nor thought it fit by landing to discover. While thus irresolute they rest debating, a second doubt enforced their resolution; their victual was too short to feed their number till they could tack about for some new harbour; a fault without excuse in such employments, this made them venture forth at Harwich to try their fortune.[222] Unshipping of their men, their arms, their luggage, was long in action, and with much disorder; three days are spent in this, while they are forced to make the naked sands their strength and bulwark. This made great Spencer's error most apparent; the least resistance here, or show, or larum, had sent them back to sea, or else surprised them; a little strength at sea had stopped their passage, or made them lawful prize by such a purchase. But afterwits can help precedent errors, if they may be undone, and then new acted. Yet to excuse this oversight, in show so wretchless, 'twas his intelligence, not his judgement failed him. Knowing the weakness, he esteemed his vantage in suffering them to land secure and certain. He would not blanch the deer, the toil so near, which he was confident would give possession of those he had so long pursued and sought for. To raise a guard to wait upon each quarter, if it were wisdom, might be no discretion, as his affairs then stood; such motions promised rather a guard to bid them welcome, than resist them. As it would cause a fear, so 'twas a summons to such as were resolved to back their party. He made that place alone secure, where he expected, and they themselves resolved to make their landing; the rest he leaves at random, and to fortune, rather than make things worse by more commotion.

But now this weather-beaten troop marched boldly forward, finding as yet few friends, but no resistance; whoso had seen their body, might have deemed they had been come to rob some neighbour-village, rather than bent to bid the king to such a breakfast.[223] St Hamond's, an abbey of black monks, had the honour to give their long-lost mistress the first welcome. Here she receives a fair and free refreshing, and yet but a faint hope of present succour, without the which she knew her case was desperate. The bruit of this strange novelty was here divulged; which like a thunder-shower, or some land-water that had drowned the marshes, and o'erflowed the level, doth make the cattle run to seek for succour. But when they knew the bent of her intentions not fixed to rifle, but reform the kingdom, they come like pigeons by whole flocks to her assistance. Soon flew the news unto the grieved barons, whose itching ears attentive, longed to meet it. It doubled as it flew; and ere it touched them, three hundred Hainaults were ten thousand soldiers. They lose no time, for fear of some prevention. Henry of Lancaster, whose brother's death and proper grievance inflamed his heart with grief, his hand for vengeance, with a strong troop of friends and stout attendants, was the first great one that increased her party; while many other brave and noble spirits do second him themselves and all their forces.[224] By these supplies the queen and her great strangers are quickly cured, and freed from their first quartan that shaked their hopes with so much agitation.

The slumbering king had slept out all the prologue of this sad tragedy, which he suspects would end in blood and mischief. As in his pleasures, in this weighty business he had relied secure on Spencer's wisdom; but now the hollow murmur of his danger thundered so loud, that he enforced awakes, and sees nought but the face of a despairing sorrow. Each day brings news of new revolt, each hour a larum, that threatened guilty souls with blood and vengeance.[225] His startled council frighted, fainting, hopeless, fall to survey the strength of their pursuers; but while they are a-registering their forces, they are informed the storm grows strong and greater, and like a ball of snow increased by motion. Their proper weakness and the ill-affection of those which should defend their sovereign's quarrel, makes action doubtful, and the end as hopeless, so that no certain way remained to stop the current. Now is the error taxed, and judgement blamed, that neither barred the gates, nor stopped the entry, since in the house itself was no assurance. Now is the cruelty that judged the barons dearly repented, which was come for vengeance. Now is the tyranny of all that grievance which had abused the king, and robbed the kingdom, condemned by his own actors, as a motive in justice fit to be reformed and punished. Lastly, the purchase gained by such corruption as sold promotions, places, justice, honour, yields no assistance, but doth prove a burden, which bruised the hearts and thoughts of them that bore it. Affliction, fittest physic, sole commandress for all diseased minds, polluted bodies, when she doth sharply touch the sense of our transgressions, begets a sorrow and a sad repentance; making us know ourselves and our own weakness, which were mere strangers to our own conditions. This she effects in all; though full repentance be a work proper to a true contrition, which by amendment makes her power more perfect.

A mind that's prepossessed, by custom hardened, with a resolved will that acts injustice, observes the first part of her precepts; sadly sorry, yet 'tis not for his actions, but those errors laid him open to so cursed a trial. The point of satisfaction or amendment it thinks too deep a ransom, hard a sentence, which easeth not, but adds to his misfortune. If here might end the end of man's creation, this had some colour for such crafty wisdom; but where eternity of bliss or torment doth wait upon the soul, that leaves the body a prey to death, and to a base corruption, it is an act of madness to betray it with humane policy, without religion. Actions of goodness must be truly acted; not sacrificing part but all the offering, observing every point that is required to make up a repentance full and perfect. This lesson is too hard for those great babies that suck the milk of greatness, not religion. The fundamental part being fixed to get unjustly, believes a restitution more improper, which makes their cares and former labours fruitless, and in an instant blights an age of gleanings. These be the meditations of a statesman, grown plump and fat from other men's oppressions; they live in doubtful pleasures, die in terror; what follows after, they do feel forever.

Our counsellors, though they were deeply touched with cause, had yet no leisure but to deliberate their proper safety, which finds a poor protection, dull and hopeless. Their enemies rejoice, their friends turn craven, and all forsake the pit before the battle. Necessity, that treads upon their heels, admits no respite; they must resolve to fight, or fly, or suffer. This makes them choose that course which seemed most hopeful, to temporize, which might beget advantage. The fury of this storm in time would lessen; the giddy motions of the vulgar seldom lasted, which throng to all that tends to innovation. A king's distress once truly known, would win him succour, since those which break his peace not seek his ruin. With these vain hopes he seeks to guard the city, and make the Tower strong of all provision, knowing that he which hath but London sure, though all the rest be lost, may yet recover.

But Edward will not hear to keep the city; their multitude he feared would first betray him.[226] He knew they were a crew of weaker spirits, for fear would sell their fathers, or for profit; they never sift the justice, or the quarrel, but still adhere and stick to him that's strongest. Had he still kept this hold, and took the Tower, but with the strength he had, and might have levied, he then had bridled up the wavering city, and kept his adversaries at a bay too long and doubtful for their affairs, which were but yet uncertain. The guard of this place he commends to Stapleton, Bishop of Exeter. This charge did not properly suit with his profession, unless 'twere thought his tongue could charm obedience, but he already had been false, betrayed his mistress, and with more reason might be now suspected. It seems they had no choice, and strong presumptions the city would not long remain obedient. If so, the fact was worse and more unworthy, to leave so good a friend in such a hazard. The king, with Arundel and both the Spencers, with small attendance get them hence to Bristol.[227] His army was much less in his own kingdom, than those the queen had raised by foreign pity. This town was strong and able, well provided, and had a haven, whence in occasion they might venture further. But yet the king might have the same suspicion, which made him leave and quit the strength of London. Arundel and Winchester do undertake the city, Edward and Bristol would make good the castle; here was the refuge they resolve to stick to, which in the citizens' assurance seemed defensive.

The queen, understanding the royal chamber was forsaken and left to the custody of the bishop her old servant, that had given her the slip in her travels, quickly apprehends the advantage; addressing a fair but mandatory letter from herself and her son to Chickwell, then Lord Mayor, to charge him so to reserve and keep the city to their use, as he expected favour, or would answer the contrary at his peril.[228] Upon the receipt of this letter, he assembles the common council, and by a cunning-couched oration, the recorder makes known the contents; which is no sooner understood, but the general cry, that observed the tide turning, proclaim it reason to embrace the queen's party, who was so strongly provided to reform the disorders of the kingdom. Stapleton having gotten the knowledge of this passage, sends to the mayor for the keys of the gates, for the king's assurance, and his proper safety; who being incensed with the affront of this inconsiderate bishop, apprehends him, and delivers him to the fury of the enraged multitude; who neither respecting the gravity of his years, or the dignity of his profession, strike off his head, without either arraignment, trial or condemnation.[229] This brainsick and heady act had too far engaged them to reconcile them; they must now either adhere solely to the queen, or to taste a bitter penance. The king had an ill memory in point of desert, but the actions of so unjust a disorder he kept registered in brass, until he gained the opportunity of revenge; then he never failed it. It was a mad part, on so poor an occasion, to act so bloody a tragedy, which took away all hope of reconciliation, if the wheel had turned. However the squares had went, they were upon terms good enough, so long as they contained themselves in any temperate condition. But this was a way which incensed the one part, and not assured the other. But the actions of this same heady monster multitude never examine the justice, or the dependence, but are led by passion and opinion; which in fury leaves no disorder unacted, and no villainy unattempted. But certainly this was a mere cunning practice of the mayor, who being underhand made sure to the adverse party, resolved to make it of a double use; the one, to help on the opinion of his devotion to the queen, in the punishment of him that betrayed her; the other, by this action to make the citizens desperate of favour, and so more resolute; who else, being mutable as weathercocks, might alter on the least occasion. Let the consideration be what it will, the fact was inhumane and barbarous, that spilt, without desert or justice, the blood of such a reverend prelate; who yet had so much happiness, as to leave to his honour in the University of Oxford, a remarkable memorial of his charity and goodness. But now to seek out the reward of this virtuous service, four of the principal and most eminent burghers are selected to make known their proceedings and devotion; who are graciously received, entertained, and highly thanked, for their lawless bloody fact, which was styled an excellent piece of justice. Though the deed had been countenanced, in that it ran with the sway of the time, and the queen's humour, yet certainly no great cause of commendation appears, which is so more properly due to the hangman, which performs the grave ceremonies of his office by warrant, and the actual part on none but such as the law has made ready for his fingers.

Now is the queen settling her remove for Bristol, where the prey remained her haggard-fancy longed for.[230] She was unwilling to give them so much advantage, though she believed it almost impossible, as to hazard the raising of an army, or so to enable their provisions and defences, that it might adjourn the hope of making her victory perfect. She saw she had a great and royal army, well-provided, but how long it would hold so, she knew not; the principal strength and number consisting of the giddy commons, who like land-floods rise and fall in an instant; they had never yet seen the face of an enemy, nor did rightly understand what it was to bear arms against the king, whom they must here behold a party. These considerations hasten her on with more expedition. All the way as she went, she is entertained with joyful acclamations. Her army grows still greater, like a beginning cloud that doth forerun a shower. When she was come before this goodly city, and saw his strength, and the maiden bravery of their opposition, which gave her by a hot sally, led by the valiant Arundel, a testimony of her welcome, she then thinks that in the art of war there was somewhat more than mere imagination;[231] and justly feared lest the royal misery would beget a swift compassion; which was more to be doubted of him in his own kingdom, since she herself had found it in a foreign country. But smiling fortune, now become her servant, scarce gives her time to think she might be hindered. The townsmen, that knew no wars but at their musters, seeing themselves begirt, the market hindered, which was their chiefest and best revenue, begin among themselves to examine the business; they saw no likelihood of any to relieve them, and daily in danger of some sad surprisal. They saw their lives, wives, children, and state at stake for the defence of those that

The History of the Life, Reign and Death of Edward II

had oppressed them, and wronged the kingdom by their foul injustice. They measured the event of an unruly conquest, where many look for booty, all for pillage. This did so cramp their valiant hearts, that the convulsion seeks a present treaty. The queen, seeing a pusillanimity beyond her hopes, and a taint unlooked for, makes the use, and hits them on the blind side, and answers plainly, she will have no imparleance, no discoursing;[232] if they desired their own peace, and her assured favour, they then must entertain and follow her conditions; which if they but delayed, the next day following they should abide their chance, she would her fortune. This doom (as it sounds harshly) was deemed too heavy; but no entreaty could prevail, she would not alter.[233] They yet desire to know what she required; and that she grants, and thus unfoldeth: 'Your lives and goods', quoth she, 'shall rest untouched, nor shall you taste yourselves the least affliction, so you deliver up with speed your captains, and in the time prefixed resign the city.' A choice so short, so sharp, so peremptory, being related in the staggering city, breeds straight a supposition, not without reason, she had some certain practised plot within them, or else some way assured for her to force the city. They could have been content she had their captains, since it would set them free from fear and danger; but to be actors in so foul a treason, or sacrifice their guests that came for succour, this they conceit too false and poor a baseness. No more imparleance is allowed, or will be heard, no second motion; the breach in their faint hearts is so well-known, that nothing is allowed but present answer. This smart proceeding melts their leaden valour, which at the first had made so brave a flourish; and brings Arundel, Winchester and the town to her possession.[234]

When man's own proper portion is in question, and all he hath at stake, be it but doubtful, his eye doth more reflect on his own danger than on the laws of justice, friendship, honour. Charity, 'tis true, begins at home, but she's a virtue hath no society with fraud or falsehood; neither is the breach of faith, or touch of treason, allowed within the verge of her rich precepts. I do confess, necessity may drive him to such a bitter choice, that one must perish; but this should be, when things are so near hopeless, that there be more than words to give it justice. A wise and noble mind adviseth soundly upon the act, before it is engaged; but being so, it rather sleeps with honour, than lives to be the map of his thus tainted conscience. The interest of friends, of guests, of poor oppressed (though diversely they touch the patrons' credit) yet all agree in this one point of virtue, not to betray, where they have vowed assistance. Had these faint citizens not given assurance, had they not vowed to keep their faiths untainted, the other had not trusted nor enclosed themselves within so weak and false a safeguard. But they were most to blame, that would so venture their lives within the power of such a burrow, where they might know were none but suckling rabbits, that would suspect each mouse to be a ferret. Had they but had a guard, secured their persons, they might have awed them, or themselves have scaped.

Part of the party thus gotten, no time is lost to call them to a reckoning. Sir Thomas Wage, marshal of the army, draws up a short information of many large offences, which are solemnly read to the attentive army, with a comment of all the harsh aggravations might make them more odious. The confused clamour of the multitude, serves for judge, jury and verdict; which brings them to a sharp sentence to be forthwith hanged, and their bodies to remain upon the gallows. Revenge brooks no delay, no leisure malice. Old Spencer feels instantly the rigour of this judgement: the green before the castle is made the place of execution.[235] Nature that gave him life, had almost left him; her vigour was near spent, her beauty withered; he could not long have lived, if they had spared him. Ninety cold winters he had passed in freedom, and finds untimely death to end his story. He parts without complaint or long discoursing; he speaks these few words only, free from passion: 'God grant the queen may find a milder sentence when in the other world she makes her audit.' The king, and his unhappy son, the sad spectators of this heart-bleeding tragedy so full of horror, are with his dying farewell so amazed, that scarcely they had speech, or breath, or motion; so bitter a preludium made them censure their own conditions were as nearly fatal.[236] The king, a sovereign, father, and a husband, did hope these titles would be yet sufficient to guard his life, if not preserve his greatness; but these proved all too weak. Where crowns are gained by blood and treason, they are so secured. Spencer had not a grain of hope for mercy: the barons' deaths prejudged his coming fortune. The queen used not to jest where she was angry; his father's end assured her inclination and bade him rather venture any hazard, than that which must rely on female pity. With a world of melancholy thoughts he casts the danger, yet could not find a way that might prevent it. The castle in itself was strong, but weakly furnished. Time now he sees could promise no assistance; their adversaries were full bent to work their ruin, either by public force or private famine; so that in their abode was sure destruction. The king in this declared himself a noble master; he prized his servant's life as his own safety, which won them both to try their utmost hazard.

The queen, impatient to surprise this fortress, doth batter, undermine and still assail it;[237] but these were all in vain, and proved fruitless; the rampiers were too strong, too well defended. She threatens and entreats, but to small purpose; here were no citizens that might betray it. Alas, there needed none, as it succeeded; the proper owners wrought their own confusion; they leave their strength, and closely try their fortune, which made them board a bark rode in the harbour, in hope to get away undescried. This was the plot, or none, must work their freedom. But all things thrive alike with him that's falling.[238] The gale averse, they softly tide her onwards; the wind will not consent to give them passage, but rudely hurls them back to their first harbour. Thrice had they passed St Vincent's Rock, famous for Bristol diamonds, but in that reach are hurried back with fury. The elements of earth, of air, of water, conspired all at once to make them hopeless.

Sir Henry Beaumont quartered next the haven, being informed that this gadding pinnace had often attempted passage without reason, the wind contrarious, and the weather doubtful, suspects that her design was great and hasty; on this he seized her, and surveys her lading, which proved a prize beyond his expectation.[239] Within her hollow bulk, a cell of darkness, he finds this pair obscured, not undiscovered. The king hath gracious words, and all due reverence, but Spencer is condemned, and used with rigour. This ends the war, and gave the work perfection. Fortune, that triumphs in the fall of princes, like a stepmother rests not where she frowneth, till she have wholly ruined and o'erthrown their power, that do precede or else oppose her darlings.

The queen having thus attained to the full of her desire, resolves to use it to the best advantage. Ambition seized her strongly, yet resigneth to her incensed passion the precedence; her own good nature (though she might adventure) she would not trust so far, to see her husband; nor did she think it fit those valiant strangers begun the work, should view or see the captive. Such sights sometimes beget as strange impressions; instantly he is conveyed to Berkeley Castle, there to remain restrained, but well attended.[240] Spencer is hardly kept, but often visited; 'twas not with pity, which befits a prisoner, but with insulting joy, and base derision.[241] Their eyes with sight, and tongues with railing glutted, the act must follow that may stop the rancour, which gives him to the marshal locked in irons. He here receives the selfsame entertainment his aged father found; alone the difference, he had a longer time and sharper sentence. All things thus ordered, the queen removes for London, meaning to make Hereford her way, and the last journey of her condemned prisoner, that attends her each place she passeth by. A world of people do strain their wider throats to bid her welcome, with yelping cries that echoed with confusion. While she thus passeth on with a kind of insulting tyranny, far short of the belief of her former virtue and goodness, she makes this poor unhappy man attend her progress, not as the ancient Romans did their vanquished prisoners, for ostentation, to increase their triumph; but merely for revenge, despite, and private rancour. Mounted upon a poor, lean, ugly, jade, as basely furnished; clothed in a painted tabard, which was then a garment worn by condemned thieves alone; and tattered rascally, he is led through each town behind the carriage, with reeds and pipes that sound the summons to call the wondering crew together might abuse him; all the bitterest actions of disgrace were thrown upon him. Certainly this man was infinitely vicious, and deserved as much as could be laid upon him, for those many great and insolent oppressions, acted with injustice, cruelty and blood; yet it had been much more to the queen's honour if she had given him a quicker death, and a more honourable trial, free from these opprobrious and barbarous disgraces, which savoured more of a savage, tyrannical disposition, than a judgement fit to command, or sway the sword of justice.

Though not by birth, yet by creation he was a peer of the kingdom, and by the dignity of his place one of the most eminent; which might (if not to him in his particular, yet in the rights due to nobility and greatness) have found some more honourable a distinction, than to be made more infamous and contemptible than the basest rogue, or most notorious cutpurse. It is assuredly (give it what title you will) an argument of a villainous disposition, and a devilish nature, to tyrannize and abuse those wretched ruins which are under the mercy of the law, whose severity is bitter enough without aggravation.[242] A noble mind doth out of native goodness show a kind of sweetness in the disposition, which, if not the man, doth pity his misfortune, but never doth increase his sorrow by baser usage than becomes his justice. In Christian piety, which is the daystar that should direct and guide all human actions, the heart should be as free from all that's cruel, as being too remiss in point of justice. The life of man is all that can be taken; 'tis that must expiate his worst offences. The law must guide the way; justice, not fury, must be his judge; so far there is no error. But when a flux of torment follows judgement, which may be done in speech as well as action, it gives too many deaths to one offender, and stains the actors with a foul dishonour. To see such a monster so monstrously used, no question pleased the giddy multitude, who scarcely know the civil grounds of reason. The recollected judgement that beheld it, censured it was at best too great and deep a blemish to suit a queen, a woman and a victor. Whether her imposition, or his patient suffering, were greater, or became first weary, he now is brought to give them both an ending, upon a gallows highly built of purpose; he now receives the end of all his torments; the cruelty was such, unfit to be recorded. Whether it were the greatness of his heart, or it were broken, he leaves the world with such a constant parting, as seemed as free from fear, as fruitless plaining.[243]

Four days are scarcely ended, ere Arundel does taste the selfsame fortune.[244] Until the last combustion, I find no mention in the story of this noble gentleman, neither could I ever read any just cause why his life was thus taken from him, unless it were a capital offence not to forsake his master. It was then a very hard case, if it must be adjudged treason to labour to defend his king and sovereign, to whom he had sworn faith and obedience, suffering for preserving that truth and oath, which they had all treacherously broken, that were his judges. If it were deemed a fault deep enough to be taken in company with those that were corrupt and wicked, I see yet no reason why he alone should suffer, and those their other creatures were, permitted many of them unquestioned, some preferred, and none executed. But we may not properly expect reason in women's actions; it was enough the incensed queen would have it so, against which was no disputing.[245]

Her business thus dispatched, she comes to London, where she hath all the royal entertainment due to her greatness. The citizens do run and crowd to see her, that if the wheel should turn, would be as forward to make the selfsame speed to see her ruin. As soon as here she had settled her affairs, and made things ready, she calls a parliament and sends forth summons for the appearance, which as soon ensued.[246] Herein she makes her husband seal the warrant, who God knows scarcely knew what she was doing, but lived a recluse, well and surely guarded. When this grave assembly was come together, the errors and the abuses of the kingdom are laid full open; which touched the king with a more insolent liberty than might well become the tongues of those which must yet be his subjects. Many ways of reformation for form's sake are discussed, but the intended course was fully before resolved; yet is was fit there should be a handsome introduction. The issue at length falls upon the point of necessity, showing that Edward, by the imbecility of his judgement, and the corruption of his nature, was unfit longer to continue the government, which was so diseased and sick that it required a king more careful and active; as if the conferring it upon a green youth little more than an infant, had been warranty enough for these allegations; but they served turn well enough, where all were agreed, and there was not so much as a just fear of opposition. It ne'er was touched or expressed by what law, divine or human, the subject might depose, not an elective king, but one that lineally and justly had inherited, and so long enjoyed it: this was too deep a mystery, and altogether improper for their resolution. A short time at length brings them all to one mind, which in a true construction was no more than a mere politic treason, not more dangerous in the act than in the example. The three estates *una voce* conclude the father must be deposed, and his unripe son must be invested in the royal dignity.[247] Not a lord, bishop, knight, judge, or burgess, but that day left his memory behind him; they could not else so generally have forgot the oaths of their allegiance, so solemnly sworn to their old master, whom they had just cause to restrain from his errors, but no ground or colour to deprive him of his kingdom; who that day found neither kinsman, friend, servant, or subject to defend his interest. It is probable he could not be so generally forsaken, and not unlikely but that he had some in this assembly well-affected, which seeing the violence and strength of the current, knew their contestation might endanger themselves, and not advantage him in his possession. But this justifies them not, neither in their oaths, love, or duty, which should have been sincere and eminent. He that had here really expressed himself, had left to posterity an honourable memorial of his faith, worth, and valour. Never will the remembrance of that stout and reverend bishop die, who in the case of Richard the Second expressed himself so honestly and bravely. Civil respects, though they deeply touch in particular, warrant not the breach of public engagements; neither is it properly wisdom, but craft, infringeth the laws of duty or honesty. If that may be admitted, what perjury may not find an excuse, what rebellion not a justifiable answer? But it is clear, there may not be a wilful violation of oaths, though it tend deeply to our own loss and prejudice.[248]

The resolution being now fully concluded, that must uncrown this unhappy king, divers of both Houses are sent unto him to make the declaration; who being come into his presence, Truffel, the Speaker of the lower house, in the name of the whole kingdom, makes a resignation of all homage and fealty, and then doth read the sentence.[249] Edward, that had been aforehand informed, the better to prepare him, had armed himself with as much patience as his necessity could give him; with an attentive ear hears all full out; which done, he turns away without answering a word.[250] He knew it was in vain to spend time in discourse or contestation, which must be the ready way to endanger his life; and in his consenting with a dangerous example to his successors, he had both their power and his own guilt made evident to posterity; which might have made the practice more frequent and familiar. He had still a kind of hope that his adversaries[251] would run themselves out of breath, when there would be both room and time to alter his condition. Thus this unfortunate king, after he had with a perpetual agitation governed this kingdom eighteen years, odd months and days, lost it partly by his own disorder and improvidence, but principally by the treacherous infidelity of his wife, servants and subjects. And it is most memorable, an army of three hundred strangers entered his dominion, and took from him the rule and governance, without so much as blow given, or the loss of any one man, more than such as perished by the hand of justice.

Though in a sinking greatness all things conspire to work a fatal ruin, yet in our story this is the first precedent of this nature, or where a king fell with so little honour, and so great an infidelity, that found neither sword or tongue to plead his quarrel. But what could be expected, when for his own private vanities and passion he had been a continual lover and abetter of unjust actions, and had consented to the oppression of the whole kingdom, and the untimely death of so many noble subjects? It is certainly no less honourable than just, that the majesty of a king have that same full and free use of his affections, without envy or hatred, which every private man hath in his economic government. Yet as his calling is the greatest, such must his care be, to square them out by those same sacred rules of equity and justice; if they once transcend, or exceed, falling upon an extremity of dotage or indulgence, it then occasions those errors that are the certain predictions of an ensuing trouble, which many times proves fatal and dangerous. Let the favourite taste the king's bounty, not devour it; let him enjoy his ear, but not engross it; let him participate his love, but not enchant it. In the eye of the commonwealth if he must be a mote, let him not be a monster. And lastly, if he must practise on the subject, let it be with moderation, and not with rapine. If in either of these there be an excess, which makes the king a monarchy to his will, and the kingdom a prey to his passion, and the world take notice it be done by the royal indulgency, it begets not more hatred than multiplicity of error, which draw with them dangerous convulsions, if not a desperate ruin to that state where it hath his allowance and practice. As there ought to be a limitation in the affection of the one, so ought there to be a like curiosity in the quality of the other. Persons of meaner condition and birth exalted above proportion, as it taxeth the king's judgement, impaireth both his safety and honour. Neither is it proper, that the principal strengths and dignities should be committed to the care and fidelity of one man only; such unworthy and unequal distribution wins a discontent from the more capable in ability and blood, and carries with it a kind of necessary impulsion still to continue his greatness; else having the keys of the kingdom in his hand, he may at all times open the gates to a domestic danger, or a foreign mischief. The number of servants is the master's honour; their truth and faculties his glory and safety; which being severally employed and countenanced, make it at one and the selfsame time perspicuous in many; and being indifferently heard, do, both in advice and action, give a more secure, discreet and safe form of proceeding. Kings in their deliberations should be served with a council of state, and a council of particular interest and honour; the one to survey the policy, the other the goodness of all matters in question; both composed out of integrity, not corruption; these delivering truly their opinions and judgements, it is more easy for him to reconcile and elect. But when one man alone supplies both these places in private and public, all the rest follow the voice of the drone, though it be against their own conscience and judgement. The royal glory should be pure, and yet transparent, suffering not the least eclipse or shadow, which appears visibly defective, when it is wholly led by a single advice never so grave and weighty. Let the projection, if it be entertained, have the test of a council; but let the act and glory be solely the king's, which adds to the belief of his ability, and more assures his greatness. If the heart of majesty be given over to the sensuality of pleasure, or betrayed by his proper weakness, or the cunning of him he trusteth, yet let him not neglect the necessary affairs of a kingdom, or pass them over by bills of exchange to the providence of another. In such an act he loseth the prerogative of an absolute king, and is but so at secondhand and by direction. It is the practique, not the theorique of state, that wins and assures the subject. If the ability of that be confined or doubtful, it estrangeth the will of obedience, and gives a belief of liberty to the actions of disorder and injustice. Such an error is not more prejudicial in the imbecility than in the example. Royal vanities find a ready imitation, so that it becomes a hazard, that a careless king makes a dissolute kingdom. Man's nature is propensive to the worser part, which it embraceth with more facility and willingness, when it wins the advantage of the time, and is led by so eminent a precedent. From this consideration, natural weakness, or temporary imperfection, should be always masked, and never appear in public, since the court, state, and kingdom, practise generally by his example. As in affection, so in passion, there are many things equally considerable. I must confess, and do believe, that king worthy of an angelical title, that could master these rebellious monsters, which rob him of his peace and happiness. But this in a true perfection, is to flesh and blood most impossible; yet both in divinity and moral wisdom, [i]t is the most excellent masterpiece of this our peregrination, so to dispose them, that they wait upon the operations of the soul rather as obedient servants, than loose and uncontrolled vagabonds. Where the royal passions are rebellious and masterless, having so unlimited a power, his will becomes the law; his hand the executioner of actions unjust and disorderly, which end sometimes in blood, commonly in oppression, and evermore in a confused perturbation of the kingdom. The warranty of the law wrought to his temper, not that it is so, but that he must have it so, justifies him not, though he make a legal proceeding the justification of his tyranny; since the innocency of the subject seldom finds protection, where the fury of a king resolves his ruin. The rigour of human constitutions are to the delinquent weighty enough; let them not be wrested or inverted, which makes the king equally guilty, and the actor of his own passions, rather than those of justice or integrity. He should on earth order his proceedings in imitation after the divine nature, which evermore inclines more to mercy than justice. Lives cannot, being taken away, be redeemed; there ought then to be a tender consideration how they be taken, lest the injustice of the act challenge a vengeance of the same nature. As the quality of the act, so is the condition of the agent considerable in point of judicature; wherein there may be sometimes those dependencies, that it may be more honourable and advantageous to pardon, or delay execution, than to advance and hasten it. Howsoever, it is the more excellent and innocent way, to fall short of the better hand, and to suffer the severity of the law rather seem defective, than an apparent taint in the suffering disposition and goodness. The actions of repentance are registered in the table of our transgressions, where none to the guilty conscience appears more horrid and fearful, than those which by an inconsiderate haste or corruption of the will have been acted in blood and passion. So great a height as the majesty of a king, should be clothed with as sweet a temper, neither too precipitate, or too slow; neither too violent, or too remiss; but like the beating of a healthy pulse, with a steady and well-advised motion, which preserves a just obedience and fear in those which are vicious, and begets a love and admiration in all, especially such as so graciously taste his goodness.

I have dwelt too long in this digression; yet I must (though it a little delay the concluding part of this history) speak somewhat that is no less proper for him that shall have the happiness to enjoy so fair and large a room in the royal affections. There must be in him a correspondent worth, as well of wisdom and obedience as of sincerity and truth, which makes no other use of this so great a blessing, but to his sovereign's honour and his own credit; and not to advantage himself by the oppression of others, or improving the particular by the ruin of a kingdom. If the master's actions be never so pure and innocent, yet if out of affection he become the patron of the servant's misdemeanours and insolences, by protecting or not punishing, he makes himself guilty and shares both in the grievance and hatred of the poor distressed subject. The general cry seeing the stream polluted, ascribe it to the fountainhead, where is the spring that may reform and cleanse it. By this one particular error of protection, he that will read the history of our own, or those of foreign nations, shall find a number of memorable examples, which have produced deposition of kings, ruin of kingdoms, the effusion of Christian blood, and the general distemper of that part of the world, all grounded on this occasion.[252] Let him then that out of his master's love, more than his own desert, hath made himself a fortune, be precisely careful, that by his disorder he endanger not the stair and prop of his preferment; which he shall make firm and permanent, in making humility and goodness the adamant to draw the love both of his equals and inferiors. Such a winning sweetness assures their hearts, which in the least contempt or insolence are apt and ready to receive the impressions of envy and hatred, which if they once take root, end not in speculation, but actions either publicly violent, or privately malicious; both tending to his ruin and confusion. If he stray from this principle, striving to make an imperious height beget fear, and the opinion of that fear the rock whereon he builds his greatness, let him then know, that the first is the companion of trust and safety, the other a slave, that will break loose with opportunity and advantage. Neither hath it any touch of discretion, or society with wisdom, or moral policy, to glorify his new-acquired greatness with unnecessary amplifications, either in multiplicity of attendants, vanity of apparel, superfluity of diet, sumptuousness of structures, or any other ridiculous eminency, that may demonstrate his pride or ambition. Wise men deride it, fools applaud it, his equals envy it, and his inferiors hate it. All jumping at length in one conclusion, that his fortune is above his merit, and his pride much greater than his worth and judgement. But this presuming impudence ends not here; kings themselves may suffer for a time, but in the end they will rather change their affections, than to be dazzled and outshined in their own sphere and element.

Now is this young king crowned with a great deal of triumphant honour, but with a more expectation of what would become of this giddy world, which seemed to run upon wheels, by reason of so sudden and so great a revolution.[253] The queen and Mortimer in this his minority take upon them the whole sway and government of the kingdom.[254] The act wherein they expressed themselves and their new authority first, was the commitment of Baldock, the quondam Lord Chancellor, who hath the great seal taken from him, and was sent to Newgate.[255] It may be wondered why he was so long spared; they had use of his place, though not of his person; and had no power, if they had thrust him out, to have brought in another, or to have executed it by commission, unless they would admit it as an act of the old king, until the new were crowned. This cage was fit for such a coistrel;[256] but yet his place being so eminent, it was believed somewhat unworthy; yet succeeding time made it not much out of square, when Tresilian Lord Chief Justice was hanged, for interpreting the law against law and his own conscience, for the king's advantage.[257] Now the recollected spirits begin to parallel time present with that precedent, and to meditate upon that act which had disrobed and put down an anointed king, that had so long swayed the sceptre, to whom they had so solemnly sworn faith and obedience. They find the state little altered, only things are thought more handsomely carried, and the actors were somewhat more warrantable; yet the multitude, according to the vanity of their changeable hearts, begin already to be cropsick, wishing for their old master, and ready to attempt any new innovation.[258] Such is the mutability of the inconstant vulgar, desirous of new things, but never contented; despising the time being, extolling that of their forefathers, and ready to act any mischief to try by alteration the succedent; like Aesop's frogs, if they might have their own fancy, each week should give them a new king, though it were to their own destruction.[259] This occasions many unpleasing petitions and suits tendered to the new king and his protectors, for the releasement of Edward's imprisonment, or at least for more freedom, or a more noble usage. But these touch too near the quick to beget a sudden answer. As things stood, they neither grant nor deny, either of them carrying with it so dangerous a hazard. If he were free, they must shake hands with their greatness, and a flat denial would have endangered a sudden tumult. They give good words, and promise more than ever they meant to perform, yielding many reasons why they could not yet give a definitive resolution; this for the present satisfies.

The black monks are more importunate, and take not this delay for an answer; but being still adjourned over with protraction, they labour to bring that about by conspiracy, which they could not do by entreaty.[260] In their public exhortations they inveigh against the severity of the king's usage, and invite their auditory to set to a helping hand to the procurement of his freedom; they extenuate his faults, and transfer them to them that had the guidance of his affairs, and not to his own natural disposition; they tax the impropriety of the time, when the kingdom was under the government of a child and a woman; and spare no point that might advance compassion for the one, or procure a dislike of the other. Neither are they content with a verbal incitation, but fall to matter of fact, that others might move by their example. They make one of their number, named

Donhead, their captain; a good, stout, bold, and factious fellow; one that was daring enough, but knew better what belonged to church ornaments, than the handsome carriage of a conspiracy, that was to be managed by arms, and not by the liberty of the tongue; whose liberality claps him by the heels, where he not long after dies, before he had so much as mustered his convent.[261]

This gathering cloud thus dispersed without a shower, the queen and Mortimer, to take off the people from harping farther upon this string, send forth diverse plausible proclamations intimating a strict charge for the reformation of diverse petty grievances; and withal are divulged sundry probabilities of foreign dangers from France and Scotland, which were presently understood to be but mere fictions, in respect at the same instant she frees herself of her foreign aid, which in such an occasion might have as well served to defend the kingdom, as to invade it. They made, it is true, an earnest suit to be gone, having well feathered their nests, but if the fear had been such as was bruited, I think the queen both might and would have retained them. It may be their addiction to arms was weary of so long a vacation, or they were desirous to show themselves at home with honour, whence they had parted with so poor an expectation; and peradventure she was unwilling they should be witness of that unnatural tragedy, which she saw then broiling in Mortimer's breast, though not resolved on; which must have wounded her reputation in that climate, where she had won so great a belief of her wisdom, virtue and goodness. Liberally and nobly she requites every man, according to his merit and condition; but to Sir John of Hainault, whose heroic spirit gave the first life to this action, and to the oracle of her recovery, and all those of the better sort, she presents many rich jewels, and annuities of yearly revenue, according to the quality of the time in being. They hold themselves royally requited, and taking a solemn leave, are honourably accompanied to Dover, where they take their farewell of the kingdom, with a much merrier eye than when they first beheld it.[262]

Whoso shall wisely consider the desperate attempt of this little handful of adventurers, and their fortunate issue, may justly esteem it one of the most memorable passages of our time, since it was merely guided by pity and compassion; without pay, without provision, to attempt an act not more dangerous than hopeless; yet they gave it perfection, without so much as the loss of any one man; and returned home glorious in honour, rich in purchase; not gained by pillage, robbery or unjust rapine (the hope and revenue of war) but by the just reward due to their valour and virtue. The cause of so fair a progression, and so successful an end, may have diverse probabilities likely enough to ground our judgement; as the sincerity of the intention, the goodness of the work, and many other, which may be alleged. But the most essential may be drawn from this; they were (though but a small one) yet an entire body, composed of such as knew what appertained to arms and breeding; men that were virtuously inclined, and awed with the true sense of religion (in the wars of late years become a mere stranger) where no victory is esteemed dishonourable, no purchase unlawful.[263] Certainly our wars and our plantations nearly resemble, being both used as a broom to sweep the kingdom, rather than an enterprise to adorn it; which makes the event so unfortunate in war; which alone falls properly within the compass of this treaty, it being the greatest and most weighty work, that either gives honour or safety to a kingdom. They should be begun with justice, and managed as well with wisdom as valour; their beginning should be with a choice care, which makes the ending fortunate. The number of bodies is not the strength, their fury not the bulwark; it is the piety and true valour of an army, which gives them heart and victory; which how it can be expected out of ruffians and gaol-birds that are the scum of the commonwealth, I leave to your consideration. I commend his curiosity, that would not buy a piece of plate stolen from orphans, though he might have had it at an under-value, lawfully enough, but more his reason, which would not commix it with his own, for fear lest it might occasion a punishment upon his which were innocent, and not touched with a guilt that might in justice challenge vengeance. But in the military practice it is believed, so a man have shape and limbs, 'tis no matter though he have murdered his own father, or committed incest with his mother; it is his metal, not his conditions, gives him admittance. Hence spring treachery, that forsakes his colours; treason, that betrays the captain; and at the best, those actions of blood and murder that cry rather for vengeance than promise victory. A general, it is true, that hath his army made to his hand, cannot distinguish their conditions; the first act is the error of those entrusted; yet if he in the knowledge continue, and not punish the practice of so barbarous actions, though it be against an enemy, it must wound his honour, and endanger his safety, liable to the account of those transgressions, which are acted by those that are under his charge without a just punishment.[264] It is an observation remarkable, that a press coming into the country, there is a great deal of shift made in every town and village to lay hold of all the most notorious debauched rascals, to fill up the number;[265] these clear the coast, and are believed fit champions to fight for their sovereign's honour and the kingdom's safety; and the rather, because in want of pay (the ruin of an army) they are best able to live by their trade. But what follows? They are either led to the slaughter, or by the divine justice prove the ruin of the enterprise; or returning, practise private villainies with more confidence; or public mutinies, under pretence of want of wages.

But I will leave them to a reformation, and proceed to the tragedy of this unfortunate king, who is now taken from the Earl of Lancaster and delivered over by indenture to Sir Maurice Berkeley and Sir John Matravers.[266] They lead him back to the cage of his first imprisonment; carrying him closely, and with a reserved secrecy, lest his friends in the knowledge of his remove might attempt his freedom. And to make his discovery more difficult, they disfigure him, by cutting off his hair, and shaving of his beard.[267] Edward, that had been formerly honourably used, and tenderly served, is bitterly grieved with this indignity, and one day among the rest, when they came to shave him, which was attempted without fire, and a cold liquor, his eyes pour forth a stream of tears in sense of his misfortune,[268] which to the inquisitive actors gives this answer, 'He would have some warm water, in spite of all their malice.' Another time, in the presence of two or three of those that were as well set to be spies over him as to guard him, in a deep melancholy passion he thus discoursed his sorrow:

Is mine offence (quoth he) so great and grievous,[269]
That it deserves nor pity nor assistance?
Is Christian charity, all goodness lost;
And nothing left in subject, child or servant,
That tastes of duty? Is wedlock-love forgotten
So fully, all at once forsake me?
Admit my errors fit for reformation;
I will not justify myself, or censure others.
Is't not enough that it has taken from me
My crown, the glory of my former being,
But it must leave me void of native comfort?
I yet remain a father, and a husband;
A sovereign and a master lost, cannot deprive me
Of that which is mine own, till death dissolve me.
Where then is filial love? Where that affection
That waits upon the laws of God and Nature?
My wretched cares have not so much transformed me,
That I am turned to basilisk or monster.
What can they fear, that they refuse to see me,
Unless they doubt mine eyes can dart destruction?
I have no other weapons that may fright them;
And these (God wot) have only tears to drown them.
Can they believe or once suspect a danger
In visit of a poor distressed captive?
Their hardened hearts I know are not so noble,
Or apt to take a gentler mild impression,
By seeing these poor ruins thus forsaken;
What then occasions this so great a strangeness,
Or makes them jealous of so poor a venture?
Are they not yet content in the possession
Of all that once was mine, now theirs? But by what title,
Their arms can better tell, than can their conscience.
My misled harmless children are not guilty;

My wife betrays them, and false Mortimer;
Who else I know would run to see their father.
Justly I pay the price of former folly,
That let him scape to work mine own confusion.
Had he had his desert, the price of treason,
He had not lived to work me this dishonour.
But time will come my wrongs will be revenged,
When he shall fall with his own weight unpitied.
Thou wretched state of greatness, painted glory,
That falling find'st thine own the most perfidious;
Must thou still live, and yet not worthy
Of one poor look? It is a mere injustice:
Would they would take my life; 'tis that they aim at.
I will esteem it as an act of pity,
That, as I live, but hate mine own conditions.

Here with a deep sigh of scalding passions, his tears break loose afresh to cool their fury. All sadly silent while he rests perplexed, a stander by makes this uncivil answer, whom Mortimer had placed to increase his sorrow:
Most gracious sir, the queen your wife, and children,
Are justly jealous of your cruel nature;
They know too well your heat and former fury,
To come too near so great and sure a danger;
Besides, they are assured that your intentions
Are bent to work them hurt, or some foul mischief,
If they adventure to approach your presence.[270]

The queen my wife (quoth he), hath she that title,
While I that made her so am less than nothing?
Alas, poor wretched woman, can her invention, apt for mischief, fashion no one excuse but this so void of reason? Is there a possibility in her suspicion?
Can I, being so resolved, act a murder,
Or can their false hearts dream me so ill-minded?
I am, thou seest, a poor forsaken prisoner,
As far from such a power, as will to act it;
They too well know it, to suspect my nature.

But let them wonder on, and scorn my sorrow;
I must endure, and they will taste their error.
But fellow, thou that tak'st such saucy boldness
To character, and speak thy sovereign's errors,
Which thou shouldst cover, not presume to question;
Know, Edward's heart is as free from thine aspersions,
As thou or they from truth or moral goodness.
When he had ended these words, he retires himself to his chamber, sad and melancholy, thinking his case was hard and desperate, when such a paltry groom durst so affront him.

   The queen and Mortimer revelling in the height of their ambition, had yet a wary eye to the main, which they knew principally consisted in the sure keeping of their prisoner. They see their plausible income was but dully continued, there being a whispering murmur not so closely muttered, but that it came to their ears, which showed an absolute dislike of the manner of their proceedings. Though they had all the marks and essential parts of sovereignty, the name alone excepted, yet they had unquiet and troubled thoughts; what they wished they had obtained, yet there was still something wanting to give it perfection.[271] Such is the vanity of our imagination, which fashions out a period to our desires, that being obtained, are yet as loose and restless. Ambition hath no end, but still goes upward, never content or fully satisfied. If man had all that earth could give, and were sole monarch of the world, he yet would farther; and as the giants did make war with heaven, rather than lose those symptoms of his nature. Fear to preserve what is unjustly gotten, doth give the new-made great one agitation, which something limits his immense affections, that do believe he must still mount up higher, and else would swallow all within his compass. This made this pair stop here a while, to strengthen and more assure what was already gotten.
They knew the people giddy, false, inconstant;
A feather wagged would blow them to commotion.
They see the lords, that were their prime supporters,
Seeming content, in heart not satisfied;
The bough was lopped that shadowed o'er their greatness;

Another was sprung up as large and fearful,
Which though more noble, yet no less aspiring.
The drooping tongue of the dejected kingdom
Doth grumble out his expectations cozened.
The grievance still continues great and heavy,
Not changed in substance, but alone in habit;
A just compassion aggravates the clamour,
To see their former king so hardly used,
Short of his honour, merit, birth and calling.
These passages related, tingled the ears of our great Mortimer; he knew that all was now at stake, which unprevented must hurl them back again with worse conditions.[272]
No longer can he mince his own conceptions,
But plainly tells the queen the cause must perish,
Edward must die; this is the only refuge
Must make all sure, and cleanse this sad suspicion;[273]
So long as he remained, their fear continues,
As would the hope of them attempt their ruin.
The warranty of arms had a fair colour
That should be levied to attempt his rescue,
Which had a royal stamp to raise and make them current.
If such a project should be once in action,
It would be then too late to seek to cross it.
All men are apt to pity so great a king oppressed; and not so much look on what he had been, as what he is, and being restored he might be.

The queen, whose heart was yet believed innocent of such foul murder, is, or at least seems, highly discontented;[274] she acknowledges his present sufferings greater than his offences, or might become the king, her lord and husband; and holds this act of too too foul injustice, which styles her son a homicide and her a monster. The crimson guilt of such a crying action could not escape the cruel hand of vengeance; if it might be concealed from human knowledge, the all-knowing power of heaven would lay it open. She thinks it more than an act of blood, to kill a husband, and a king, that sometimes loved her. She thinks her son not of so ill a nature, as to slip o'er his father's death untouched, unpunished, when that he was grown up in power to sift it. These motives made her thus return her answer:

Let us resolve (dear friend) to run all hazards,[275]
Rather than this that is so foul and cruel;
Let us not stain our souls with royal blood and murder,
Which seldom scapes unseen, but never unpunished,
Especially for such a fear as is but casual.
While we are innocent, at worst our danger
Is but privation of this glorious shadow,
Which death can take, when we believe it surest;
But if we taint the inward part with such a tincture,
Our proper guilt will bring continual terror,
A fear that never dies, but lives still dying.
If Edward do get loose, what need we fear him,
That pulled him down when he was great, at highest?
Why should we then resolve his death or murder?
This help may serve when we are desperate
Of other remedies, which yet appear not.
To act so great a sin without compulsion,
Adds to the deed, and makes it far more odious;
Nor can it plead excuse if after questioned,
That hath no cause but merely supposition.
Say that he were a dead man, gone and hopeless,
Neither our fears or dangers are more lessened;
We are still subject to the selfsame hazard,
And have to boot our proper guilt to cause it.
Those that do hate or envy us can fashion
Other pretexts, as fair as this, to shake us;
Which we shall better crush while we are guiltless.
Then think upon some other course as sure, more harmless;
Ne'er can my heart consent to kill my husband.

Mortimer being nettled with this reply, so far wide of the aim which in his bloody thoughts he had so constantly resolved on, thought he would return the queen as bitter a pill, as she had given him to bite on; which makes him thus reply in anger:[276]

Madam, who hath the time to friend, and doth neglect it, is
justly falling scorned, and sinks unpitied.
Have you for this endured so bitter trials,
To be at length a foe to your own safety?
Did you outrun your troubles, suffering meanly,
But to return unto your first condition?
If it be so, I must approve your reasons,
And say your grounds were like your project, hopeful;
You see your glorious morning now turned cloudy,
The kingdom doth repine to see our greatness,
Yet have no hope but in the king deposed;
Who taken away, what fear can justly move us?
Your youthful son we'll rule till he grows older,
And in that time establish such a greatness,
As he shall hardly touch or dare to question.
To cast a world of doubts is vain and senseless,
Where we enforced must either act or perish;
And to be nice in that hath no election,
Doth waste our time, and not prevent the error.
If you stick fast in this your tender pity,
I must in justice then accuse my fortune,
That gave my heart to such a female weakness.
Is there a disproportion in this action,
To keep the crown with blood, that was so gotten?
Is there a more restraint to keep than get by treason?
If so, I yield, and will sit still and ruin.
Had Edward known or feared, he had prevented,
Nor you nor I had had the power to hurt him.
But he neglected time, and now repents it;
And so must we, if we embrace his error.
Fear is far less in sense than apparition,
And makes the shadow greater than the subject,
Which makes a faintness as the fancy leads it,
Where is small reason to be so affected.
You urge it cannot be concealed or hidden.
I not deny but it may be discovered;
Such deeds may yet be so contrived and acted,

That they prevent all proof, if not suspicion.
But why do I spend time in this persuasion?
Let him get free, whom we so much have wronged,
Let him examine our proceedings, sift our actions,
Perhaps he will forget, forgive, be reconciled.
And spare your tears, lest that your mighty brother
Should chance grow angry; if you lose your greatness,
You may if you be pleased abide the trial.
Mortimer's resolved, since you refuse his judgement,
You neither prize his safety nor his service,
And therefore he will seek some other refuge,
Before it be too late, and too far hopeless.

With this he flings away in discontentment,
As if he meant with speed to quit the kingdom.[277]
The amazed queen pursues and overtakes him,
Who seemed unwilling to prolong the treaty:
Stay, gentle Mortimer (quoth she), I am a woman;
Fitter to hear and take advice, than give it;[278]
Think not I prize thee in so mean a fashion,
As to despise thy safety or thy counsel.
Must Edward die, and is there no prevention?
Oh wretched state of greatness, frail condition,
That is preserved by blood, secured by murder!
I dare not say I yield, or yet deny it;
Shame stops the one, the other fear forbiddeth.
Only I beg I be not made partaker,
Or privy to the time, the means, the manner.[279]
With this she weeps, and fain would have recanted,
But she saw in that course a double danger.
Mortimer, that had now what he looked for, assures her he would undergo the act and hazard; which would not have moved, if not enforced by those strong motives of their certain danger. He requests alone the king might seal a warrant, that he may change anew his former keepers. Sir Maurice Berkeley, as it seems, had been aloof off treated with, but was not pliable, or apt to fasten; he was both careful of his charge, and master's safety; this takes

him suddenly from his custody.[280] Sir Thomas Towurlie supplies his place, with his old partner; they having received their new warrant, and their royal prisoner, carry him by sudden and hasty journeys to Corfe Castle, the place that in all the world he most hated.[281] Some say that he was foretold by a certain magician, who as it seems was his craftsmaster, that this place was to him both fatal and ominous. 'Twas ill in him to seek by such ill and unlawful means the knowledge of that which being known did but augment his sorrow. Whatsoever the cause was, his arrival here makes him deeply heavy, sad and melancholy; his keepers, to repel this humour, and to take him off from all fear and suspicion, feed him with new hopes and pleasant discourse, improving his former entertainment both in his diet and attendance; while his misgiving spirit suspects the issue. Though he would fain have fashioned his belief to give them credit, yet he had such a dull cloud about his heart, it could receive no comfort.

The fatal night in which he suffered shipwreck, he eats a hearty supper, but stays not to digest it; immediately he goes to bed, with sorrows heavy; as soon he takes his rest, and sleeps securely, not dreaming of his end so near approaching. Midnight the patron of this horrid murder being newly come, this crew of perjured traitors steal softly to his chamber, finding him in a sweet and quiet sleep, taking away his life in that advantage.

The historians of these times differ both in the time, place and manner of his death, yet all agree that he was foully and inhumanly murdered, yet so that there was no visible or apparent sign which way 'twas acted. A small tract of time discovers the actors, and shows evidently that it was done by an extremity of violence. They long escape not, though Mortimer's greatness for the present time keep them both from question and punishment, yet by the divine justice they all meet with a miserable and unpitied death, and the master workman himself in a few years after suffered an ignominious execution.

The queen, who was guilty but in circumstance, and but an accessory to the intention, not the fact, tasted with a bitter time of repentance, what it was but to be quoted in the margins of such a story. The several relations so variously expressed of their confessions, that were the actors and consenters to this deed, differ so mainly, that it may be better passed over in silence, than so much as touched, especially since if it were in that cruel manner, as is by the major part agreed on, it was one of the most inhuman and barbarous acts that ever fell within the expression of all our English stories; fitter rather to be passed over in silence than to be discoursed, since it both dishonoureth our nation, and is in the example so dangerous.[282] It seems Mortimer was yet a novice to Spencer's art, of that same Italian trick of poisoning, which questionless had wrought this work as surely, with a less noise, and fewer agents. It had been happy if such a villainy had never gained knowledge or imitation in the world; since it came to be entertained as a necessary servant of state, no man that runs in opposition, or stands in the way of greatness, is almost secure in his own house, or among his friends or servants. I would to God we had not fresh in our memory so many bleeding examples, or that this diabolical practice might stop his career with the mischief it hath already done; but so long as the close conveyance is deemed a politic virtue, and the instruments by power and favour are protected, what can be expected but that in short time it must fall under the compass of a trade or mystery, as fit for private murderers as statesmen?[283]

But leaving the professors of this execrable practice to their deserts and that guilt which still torments them; thus fell that unfortunate King Edward the Second, who by the course of age and nature might have outrun many years, had not his own disorder, the infidelity of his subjects, and the treachery of those that had deprived him of his kingdom, sent him to an untimely death and ruin. Many reasons are given, probable enough, to instance the necessity of his fall, which questionless may be the secondary means, but his doom was registered by the inscrutable providence of heaven, which with the selfsame sentence punished both him and Richard the Second his great-grandchild, who was coequally guilty of the same errors, that both betrayed them and the peace of their kingdom. Henry the Sixth, though he tasted of the same cup of deposition, yet there was more reason to induce it. Henry the Fourth his grandfather was a usurper, and had unjustly got the crown by pulling down the house of York, and exalting that of Lancaster, which in justice brings it back again to the right inheritor; yet were not those times innocent of those enormities which occasioned their confusion. It is most true that Henry himself was a sweet harmless conditioned man, religious, and full of moral goodness; but he was fitter for a cloister than a crown, being transported with a divine rapture of contemplation, that took him off from the care of all worldly affairs;[284] while Margaret his wife, daughter of Reynard that styled himself King of Naples and Jerusalem, acted her part with a like imitation; though she had not a Gaveston, a Spencer, or a Duke of Ireland, yet she had a Suffolk, and a Somerset, that could teach the same way to the destruction and deposition of her husband.

These three sympathized in their royal inheritance, in their depositions, deaths, and fortunes, and these alone, since the conquest of the Normans, unless we rank into the number Edward the Fifth, which must be with an impropriety, since he was by Richard his tyrannical uncle murdered before he was crowned. If we example him with them, we may it is true conclude his case most miserable, that lost the crown before he enjoyed it, or had the perfection of years to make known his inclination. The event that followed the others, especially the two precedent, may be fitly a caution and admonition to posterity, and teach them what it is to hazard a kingdom, and their own lives, by the continuing of a wilful error. Certainly we have had other kings fully as vicious, that have outlived their vices, not dying by a violent hand, but by the ordinary and easy course of nature; they were more cautelous and flexible, and were content in the more moderate use of their own vices.

The condition of this our Edward, the subject of this story, was not in itself more hurtful, than dangerous to the peace and tranquillity of the whole kingdom. If by heat of youth, height of fortune, or the corruptions of nature, the royal affections fly loosely and at random; yet if it extend no farther than the satisfaction of the private appetite, it may obscure the glory, but not supplant the strength and safety of a sceptre. But when it is not only vicious in itself but doth patronize it in others, not blushing or shrinking in the justification, it is a forerunning and presaging evidence, that threatens danger, if not destruction. It is much in a king, that hath so great a charge delivered over to his care and custody, to be himself dissolute, licentious, and ill-affected; but when he falls into a second error, making more delinquents kings, where one is too much, he brings all into disorder, and makes his kingdom rather a stage of oppression, than the theatre of justice, which opens the ready way to an ensuing misery. The heart of the subject as it is obliged, so it is continued by the majesty and goodness of the king; if either prove prostitute, it unties the links of affection; those lost, the breach of duty succeeds, which hunts after nothing but change and innovation. The bridle of the laws is too weak a restriction, especially when it is infringed by him, that is most bound to protect it. Neither can the king in justice blame or punish the breach, when he himself goes the way of subversion of those precepts, which should preserve his peace and obedience. It is so singular and so weighty a consideration, that a burden should never be imposed upon the subject by extent of the prerogative; that may beget a just grievance, besides the grief in payment; the novelty of the act incites to a tumultuous opposition. Where there is neither law to warrant, nor fit precedent to induce the injustice of the demand, such actions begin in complaint, which unredressed fall into an extremity, which draws with it a desperate hazard. If the tie of duty and allegiance preserve the obedience to the crown inviolate, let him beware that is the prime instrument, or seducer; for he must be persecuted with implacable hatred, which ends not until he be made a sacrifice to expiate and quench the fury, or the endangering of his master by his unjust protection. It is no less proper for the majesty and goodness of a king, in case of a general complaint, to leave those great cedars to the trial of the law and their own purgation; this makes known the integrity and equality of his justice, which should not be extended to the grubbing up of brambles and shrubs, while monstrous enormities of a greater height and danger scape unlopped. The accumulation of his favour, though it be a property of his own power, yet ought it in some measure to be satisfactory, as well in the present worth of him elected, as in his future progression; else in the continuance he winds himself into the danger of participating his hatred, as well as protection of his error. The eye of the subject waits curiously upon the sovereign's actions, which if they seem to degenerate from his wisdom and greatness, and preferring a private inconvenience before the redress of a public grievance, it by degrees varies the integrity of the heart, and begets a liberty of speech which falls often on the actions of revolt and tumult. Neither is it proper (if there must be a dotage in the royal affections) that the object of their weakness should sway and manage the affairs of state; such an intermixture begets confusion, and disorder, accompanied by envy, hatred, and a world of errors. If the king be never so innocent, yet in this course he cannot avoid the actions of injustice. Experience tells the right use of a favourite. A good cause in the integrity of time warrants itself, and needs no supporter; but imperfection, fraud, dishonesty, and weakness in true worth, fly to his protection, that by his strength they may prevail, which in equity and justice are merely corrupt and counterfeit. Money, friends or favour engageth him, and he his master; hence proceed all manner of oppression and disorder. Let the springhead be never so pure and unpolluted, yet such a diver makes it foul and muddy. A smooth tongue finding a favourable hearing, sets a fair gloss upon the blackest overture; love and a seeming goodness leads, where all seems current; which hatches daily broods of grief and mischief. Thus doth the kingdom suffer, so misguided. Had this unhappy subject of this story not been thus abused, had he been worser far, he had subsisted; but when for his inglorious minions, Gaveston and Spencer, who successively enjoyed him, he made the kingdom a prey to their insolence, he found both heaven and earth conspired his ruin. So great a fall these latter times produce not; a king in potent kingdom of his own, deposed by a handful of strangers, who principally occasioned it, without so much as any kinsman, friend or subject that either with his tongue or sword declared himself in his quarrel. But you may object, he fell by infidelity and treason, as have many other that went before and followed him. 'Tis true, but yet withal observe, here was no second pretendents, but those of his own, a wife and a son, which were the greatest traitors; had he not indeed been a traitor to himself, they could not all have wronged him. But my weary pen doth now desire a respite; wherefore leaving the perfection of this, to those better abilities that are worthy to give it a more full expression, I rest, until some more fortunate subject invite a new relation.

NOTES

[1] '*Qui nescit Dissimulare, nequit vivere, perire melius*': he who doesn't know how to dissemble, is unable to live, and is better off dead.
[2] Either the printers did not know that 'E. F.' was a woman, or they are being disingenuous.
[3] 'every' repeated in error in text.
[4] Cary uses numerous rare words in *Mariam* as well as here. The remarks about masculine style are ironic, whether or not the printer intended irony.
[5] A couplet, printed in prose, of the sort which occur frequently in the text.
[6] 'April 25 1284'; note in text.
[7] 'July 1307'; note in text.
[8] Note the shift to historic present, as in a dramatic synopsis; such abrupt changes of tense are common in *Edward II*.
[9] 'Edw[ard] I's care in educating his son'; note in text.
[10] '*arcana imperii*': the mysteries of empire.
[11] 'Banishes Gaveston'; note in text.
[12] 'Gaveston's original and character'; note in text. Woolf, p. 444, identifies the author who makes Gaveston Italian as the fourteenth-century *Vita et Mors Edwardi Secundi*; most accounts make Gaveston a Frenchman.
[13] This figuration of perfect male beauty as female looks back to Shakespeare's Sonnet 20 and Marlowe's portrait of Leander.
[14] 'Edw[ard] I's dying speech to the prince and barons'; note in text.
[15] 'They swear not to recall Gaveston'; note in text.
[16] '*Mortui non mordent*' : dead men don't bite.
[17] 'handsel': the first trial of something with the notion of its being auspicious of what is to follow.
[18] 'The young king troubled at his oath'; note in text.
[19] 'Falls into the height of melancholy'; note in text.
[20] 'The character and danger of court parasites'; note in text. 'Foreright': honest, straightforward.
[21] On court corruption in the court of James I, see Lynda Levy Peck, *Court Patronage and Corruption in Early Stuart England*, London: Unwin Hyman, 1990.
[22] 'A courtier's speech to the king, to recall Gaveston'; note in text.
[23] 'paise': appease.
[24] Damon: the lover of Pythias, and a disciple of Pythagoras. The story of Pythias' heroism in guaranteeing his friend's release from prison with his life does not seem relevant.
[25] 'The king sends for Gaveston'; note in text.
[26] 'Acquaints his council therewith; who labour to divert him'; note in text.
[27] 'His angry reply'; note in text.
[28] 'The council consent to recall Gaveston'; note in text.

[29] 'alien': alienate.
[30] 'Gaveston returns'; note in text.
[31] 'The king slights his barons'; note in text.
[32] 'They persuade him to marry'; note in text.
[33] 'The king marries'; note in text.
[34] 'praeludium': a preliminary, prelude.
[35] 'and marries Gaveston to Margaret, daughter of Gilb[ert] de Clare, Earl of Gloucester, by his wife Jane of Acres, daughter to Edw[ard] 1. Creates him Earl of Cornwall'; note in text.
[36] 'glozes': deceptive flatteries.
[37] 'And makes him chief minister of state'; note in text.
[38] 'real': an alternative spelling for 'royal', hence a pun.
[39] 'through-stitch': to stitch right through, thoroughly; hence, to succeed.
[40] 'ayme': obsolete form of ay me.
[41] 'Gaveston imprisons the Bishop of Chester'; note in text.
[42] 'The kingdom resent it'; note in text.
[43] 'Lincoln's speech to the king'; note in text.
[44] I.e. Gaveston. Note the courtiers' curious reluctance to name him, which may come from a refusal to acknowledge his new title.
[45] 'wretchless': reckless.
[46] 'slubbers': slobbers.
[47] 'Gaveston banished the second time and sent into Ireland'; note in text.
[48] 'mew this haggard'; a haggard is a wild hawk; mew is a technical term in falconry for caging a hawk.
[49] One of the many transitions to prose that read like a marginal comment on an extant chronicle. For the way the Renaissance read history, see Lisa Jardine and Anthony Grafton, 'How Gabriel Harvey read his Livy', *Past and Present* 129 (1990) pp. 32–78.
[50] 'Again recalled'; note in text.
[51] Note the references to Ireland, where the Carys had lately been living.
[52] 'cum priveligio': with privileges.
[53] A couplet, hence the odd syntax.
[54] 'parget': to cover or daub with plaster, to decorate.
[55] 'Abuses the king and kingdom'; note in text.
[56] 'the Lombard': a pawnshop.
[57] 'Gaveston banished the third time; goes into Flanders'; note in text.
[58] 'Edward of Windsor, afterwards Edw[ard] the 3, born 13 Oct[ober] 1312'; note in text.
[59] For Cary's youthful humanist scepticism about witchcraft, see the *Life*, pp. 5–6, where she proves a woman accused of witchcraft innocent. Cary canvasses the question of witchcraft again when considering Spencer's rise.
[60] Gaveston again returns'; note in text.
[61] 'The barons take up arms'; note in text.
[62] 'Seize Gaveston at Scarborough Castle'; note in text.
[63] 'and behead him'; note in text.
[64] 'giglet': a wanton woman, 1632. This is one of many words used by Cary before their first recorded usage in the OED.
[65] I.e. for those that are honest.

⁶⁶ Note the octosyllabic couplet; in *Mariam* too there are several lines which are two syllables short of pentameter.
⁶⁷ 'The king's exclamation on the news, vowing revenge'; note in text.
⁶⁸ This may be an allusion to Achilles and the death of Patroclus; Achilles is visited by the ghost of Patroclus before killing Hector.
⁶⁹ 'Henry Lacy, Earl of Lincoln, dies, 1310'; note in text.
⁷⁰ 'His dying speech to Tho[mas] Earl of Lancaster, his son-in-law'; note in text.
⁷¹ 'A parliament called'; note in text.
⁷² 'The Scots adhere to Bruce, 1313'; note in text.
⁷³ 'mattachine': a sword-dancer in fantastic costume.
⁷⁴ 'The king goes in person against the Scots, 1314'; note in text.
⁷⁵ 'The king defeated at Bannockburn near Striveling.'; note in text.
⁷⁶ 'Poydras of Exeter pretends himself king, and the king a changeling'; note in text.
⁷⁷ 'His strange confession'; note in text.
⁷⁸ This enchanting narrative mingles the notion of a witch's familiar with the folktale of Puss-in-Boots. There had been a few pretenders in Elizabeth's reign, notably an Essex man who claimed to be her son; Cary may have been remembering this.
⁷⁹ 'tan-vat': a tub or pit in which hides are laid in tanning.
⁸⁰ All this alludes to Edward's treatment of Gaveston, in tones of biting irony.
⁸¹ 'The king goes a second time against the Scots'; note in text.
⁸² 'Sir Peter Spalden made governor of Berwick'; note in text.
⁸³ 'Who betrays it to the Scots, 1318'; note in text.
⁸⁴ 'The Pope sends over two cardinals, to mediate a peace'; note in text. This enthusiasm for Papal interference in politics sounds a strongly recusant note; it would be unusual in 1627, and remarkable in 1680, coming from a Protestant.
⁸⁵ 'Who are robbed at Darlington'; note in text.
⁸⁶ 'Sir Gilbert de Middleton and Sir Walter de Selby executed for the same'; note in text.
⁸⁷ 'Sir Jocelyn Denvil with certain ruffians infest the north'; note in text.
⁸⁸ 'impostume': a purulent swelling or cyst.
⁸⁹ 'The Cardinals return'; note in text.
⁹⁰ 'The Pope excommunicates the Scotch king and kingdom'; note in text.
⁹¹ 'King Edw[ard] besieges Berwick'; note in text.
⁹² 'A great dearth, which lasted three years'; note in text.
⁹³ 'The Scotch overrun the borders'; note in text.
⁹⁴ 'The Archbishop of York opposeth them'; note in text.
⁹⁵ 'and is beaten at Milton-upon-Swale'; note in text.
⁹⁶ A couplet, hence the odd syntax.
⁹⁷ 'The king leaves Berwick'; note in text.
⁹⁸ 'prigging': thieving.
⁹⁹ A common criticism of James I was that he had made the entire court dissolute.
¹⁰⁰ 'King seeks a new favourite'; note in text.
¹⁰¹ 'Spencer taken into favour'; note in text.
¹⁰² 'Spencer's policy'; note in text.

[103] Cary had just returned from Ireland in 1627; in her period it was known as a graveyard of political reputation.

[104] Many of Spencer's devices seem to be drawn from Machiavelli's *The Prince*. Both the Elizabethan and Jacobean regimes used spies in this way, especially against Catholics, as Cary would have been well aware. Mercury was the messenger of the gods.

[105] 'The barons incensed'; note in text. 'Cautelous': crafty, tricky.

[106] 'Clifford's speech'; note in text.

[107] 'His pride is such . . . ruin': Spencer's pride won't allow him to drop his pretensions, but unless he does, we are ruined. 'Farding': make-up to conceal deformities.

[108] 'The barons take arms'; note in text.

[109] 'Mortimer spoils Spencer's possession'; note in text.

[110] 'Scoggin's crow': Scoggin was a court fool under Edward IV, and the name became proverbial; a collection of tales, *Scoggin's Jests*, was published in 1566.

[111] 'The king's proclamation thereon'; note in text.

[112] 'primity': beginning.

[113] 'The barons' message to the king'; note in text.

[114] 'The king's answer'; note in text.

[115] This is one of the passages which Woolf argues must be post-1660. However, elections were becoming more important in the 1620s, as Derek Hirst's work suggests; see his *The Representative of the People? Voters and Voting in England under the Early Stuarts*, Cambridge: Cambridge University Press, 1975, and Mark A. Kishlansky, *Parliamentary Selection: Social and Political Choice in Early Modern England*, Cambridge: Cambridge University Press, 1986.

[116] 'The barons appear with a strong guard'; note in text.

[117] 'rampire': rampart.

[118] 'The king's speech to the parliament'; note in text.

[119] 'perspicil': an optic glass or lens.

[120] 'stale': lure or deceptive device.

[121] 'The commons' charge against Spencer'; note in text.

[122] Simony: the sale of church offices. Cary offers a recusant rather than a Protestant critique of the Edwardian clergy.

[123] Possibly a reference to James I's notorious willingness to expand the nobility.

[124] 'The Spencers banished'; note in text.

[125] 'The son turns pirate'; note in text.

[126] 'The merchants petition the king against him'; note in text.

[127] 'The king's answer'; note in text.

[128] 'The king writes to the lords'; note in text.

[129] 'doubt': 'boubt' in text.

[130] 'The barons' answer'; note in text.

[131] 'The Londoners petition for Spencer's return'; note in text.

[132] 'The Spencers return'; note in text.

[133] Note the equation of the kingdom with the nobility; the merchants are sardonically excluded. This is typical of Cary's politics throughout, which oppose monarchical authority on grounds of aristocratic privilege rather than democracy; for her, tyranny is the rule of king or mob unchecked by the nobility, since mobs are assumed to support tyrants.

[134] This approaches a notion of rule by contract, but seems to break off by predicting difficulties rather than structural change.
[135] 'Sir Barthol[omew] Baldsmere's castle seized'; note in text.
[136] 'The king takes arms'; note in text.
[137] 'Seizes the two Mortimers'; note in text.
[138] 'The barons rise'; note in text.
[139] 'The barons beaten, fly to Pontefract'; note in text.
[140] 'Valens' speech in favour of the lords'; note in text.
[141] 'The king's reply'; note in text.
[142] 'Lancaster beheaded, and 22 more'; note in text. Cary backs even a noble rebellion directly against the monarch.
[143] 'Good policy to maintain a divided faction in court and council'; note in text. A commonplace of seventeenth-century *realpolitik*.
[144] 'available': of advantage, capable of producing a desired result. The Mortimers are the only rebels of whom Cary disapproves.
[145] The *lex talionis*: the law of retaliation; an eye for an eye and a tooth for a tooth.
[146] In Elizabethan and Jacobean periods it was routinely assumed that the common people would rebel only if they could find a noble leader to plan it for them, despite some evidence to the contrary.
[147] A reference to birdlime, a sticky substance smeared on leaves to trap birds for the table.
[148] 'Spencer's policy'; note in text.
[149] I.e. Spencer poisons some of the remaining nobles.
[150] 'bounder': boundary.
[151] 'resty': stubbornly refusing movement; sluggish, lazy.
[152] 'Trenchmore': a boisterous English country dance.
[153] 'quinch': quench, destroy.
[154] 'bruit': rumour, word. 'A Parliament called'; note in text.
[155] 'They give the king the sixth penny'; note in text.
[156] 'Prodigious sights'; note in text. Prodigies of this sort were also seen after Buckingham's murder in Cary's own time, and later multiplied lavishly around the death of Charles I.
[157] 'The Scotch invade the English borders and Ireland'; note in text.
[158] 'Are repulsed'; note in text.
[159] 'Their general slain'; note in text.
[160] 'The king invades Scotland'; note in text.
[161] 'The Scotch seize the K[ing's] treasure; note in text.
[162] 'Earl of Carlisle executed'; note in text.
[163] 'The French king breaks his peace with England'; note in text.
[164] 'The king adviseth with Spencer'; note in text.
[165] 'Spencer's answer'; note in text.
[166] 'He adviseth the queen be sent to France'; note in text. The relation between this scene and the events of *Mariam* is particularly clear. Both Isabel and Mariam are married to kings at war with their people; the loyalty of both becomes the subject of unjust suspicion.
[167] 'roost-cock': rooster or cockerel. The references to acts and choruses might indicate that the MS was an outline for an unfinished play; on the

other hand, Cary may be using the theatrical terms as the familiar metaphor of *theatrum mundi*, and in calling Baldock a chorus may mean no more than that he comments on events.

[168] 'She offers to go'; note in text.

[169] 'She casts a wandering eye on Mortimer'; note in text.

[170] 'Mortimer in the Tower'; note in text.

[171] 'The king will not consent to her going'; note in text.

[172] 'Pretending a journey of devotion'; note in text. Note the difference from Mariam; Isabel uses virtue to *deceive* her captors.

[173] 'She embarks for France with Mortimer'; note in text.

[174] 'The king sad at the news'; note in text.

[175] 'Spencer encourageth him'; note in text.

[176] 'wooden wall'; the navy, made of wooden ships. Cary is alluding to the Athenian navy; when the Persian army invaded Greece, the priestess of Apollo prophesied that Athens would be saved by wooden walls, and Themistocles interpreted this to mean ships.

[177] The future Louis VIII unsuccessfully invaded England in 1216–17, during the civil wars at the end of John's reign.

[178] 'The queen is tainted. The ports are stopped'; note in text.

[179] 'The navy sent out, and watch and ward everywhere'; note in text.

[180] 'The queen entertained in France with seeming gladness'; note in text.

[181] 'The queen's address'; note in text.

[182] Argus: in classical mythology, a hundred-eyed monster-watchman.

[183] 'The king and his peers moved at her discourse'; note in text.

[184] 'propense': inclined or biased.

[185] 'Spencer eyes the French... but fears them not'; note in text.

[186] 'He bribes them'; note in text.

[187] The angel was a golden coin.

[188] 'juggling': deceptions.

[189] 'occurrents': occurrences.

[190] 'King Edward complains to the Pope'; note in text.

[191] 'practic': practised, expert, particularly in conspiracy and deceit.

[192] 'The Pope admonishes the French king to quit the queen'; note in text. Note that only those around the Pope are bribed, and not the Pope himself.

[193] 'She is enticed to return into England'; note in text.

[194] 'She tells the French king'; note in text.

[195] 'He shows her the Pope's sentence'; note in text.

[196] 'Persuades her to peace'; note in text.

[197] 'She relates it to the bishop, Kent and Mortimer... who advise her not to return'; note in text.

[198] 'Mortimer storms'; note in text.

[199] 'The queen moderates'; note in text.

[200] 'Robert of Artois'; note in text.

[201] 'His speech'; note in text.

[202] 'Which infinitely joys the queen'; note in text.

[203] Again Isabel differs from Mariam in being virtuous but duplicitous and secret.

[204] This passage recalls Elizabeth of Bohemia, the 'Winter Queen', and her struggles to find support for her cause at the courts of James I, Charles I and

other European rulers. Elizabeth was Charles's sister. However, since she was fighting for Protestantism against Catholicism, it would be surprising if Cary were representing her here.

205 'Her farewell to France'; note in text. Edward III, Isabel's son by Edward II, defeated the French at the Battle of Crecy; Isabel is prophesying.
206 'The Bishop of Exeter forsakes the queen'; note in text.
207 'Is bravely welcomed by the earl'; note in text.
208 'His brother pities the queen'; note in text.
209 'and promises his service'; note in text.
210 'He makes preparation'; note in text.
211 'gudgeons': ones that will swallow anything; gullible persons.
212 'The earl condemns his haste'; note in text.
213 'His answer'; note in text.
214 'The queen jealous of treachery'; note in text.
215 'Spencer's agents frustrated'; note in text.
216 'The queen's doubts increasing, she importunes the hastening her journey... but without need'; note in text.
217 Edward III married Phillippa of Hainault.
218 'The queen embarks at Dor[drech]t'; note in text.
219 'callenders': an order of mendicant turkish dervishes; OED first records its use in 1634; 'mew': a seagull; 'corvet': curvet, a spring with the front legs off the ground.
220 'She is frighted at sea'; note in text.
221 'hansel': the first trial of something with the notion of its being auspicious of what is to follow.
222 'She lands at Harwich'; note in text.
223 'Marching forward she' is refreshed at St Hamond's Abbey'; note in text.
224 'Lancaster first joins her'; note in text.
225 'The king is despairingly sorrowful, his council startled'; note in text.
226 'The king suspects the city of London'; note in text.
227 'Betakes himself to Bristol'; note in text.
228 'The queen sends a mandatory letter to the Mayor of London, to keep the city for her and the prince'; note in text.
229 'Bishop Stapleton beheaded by the multitude'; note in text.
230 'The queen sets out for Bristol'; note in text.
231 'Whence a hot sally upon her'; note in text.
232 'A treaty desired by that city'; note in text. 'Imparleance': conference, discussion, also a delay in a lawcase for the parties to reach agreement. Cary's knowledge of legal terms may come from her father.
233 'Which being rejected, the queen gives them a peremptory summons'; note in text.
234 'It is yielded'; note in text.
235 'Old Spencer executed'; note in text.
236 'The king and young Spencer amazed'; note in text.
237 'The queen batters the castle'; note in text.
238 'The king and Spencer betake to a bark but are beaten back by the weather'; note in text.
239 'The bark seized'; note in text.

[240] 'The king sent to Berkeley castle'; note in text.
[241] Spencer insulted over'; note in text.
[242] 'The queen's cruelty'; note in text.
[243] 'Spencer hanged'; note in text. Cary has changed sides again, and now supports Edward and Spencer against Isabel. Cary may mean that Spencer may have been hanged, drawn and quartered as a traitor.
[244] 'Arundel the like'; i.e. hanged; note in text.
[245] Note that this passage, with its misogynist rhetoric, is very far removed from blank verse. It's tempting to suspect another hand sporadically at work from about this point; on the other hand, *Mariam* also contains slices of misogynistic discourse.
[246] 'The queen comes to London... She calls a parliament'; note in text.
[247] 'They conclude to depose the king'; note in text.
[248] Again straight prose, without a trace of blank verse, and again a reversal of earlier statements; whereas the account of the early years of Edward's reign stresses the privileges of the aristocracy infringed by monarchic autarchy, this defends absolutism in a context which does seem coloured by events, possibly the Gunpowder Plot if Cary is the author of this section. This event would give a recusant every reason to disassociate herself from notions of regicide.
[249] 'The Speaker makes a resignation of homage, and reads the sentence'; note in text.
[250] 'The king answers not'; note in text.
[251] The pages of the BL copy and of all other copies I have managed to see are misnumbered here; p. 132 is followed by p. 137, but the text is continuous, as is signified by the keyword 'would' at the bottom of p. 132 and its repetition as the first word of p. 137; Edward is still being described.
[252] This paragraph, again lacking any trace of verse, seems especially applicable to the Exclusion Crisis, and not to the pre-Civil War enthusiasm for Buckingham on the part of James I and Charles I, whose kingdom had not fallen in 1627 or in 1639. I suspect that it may have been 'updated' for 'relevance', perhaps by the printer, possibly from the parenthesis about delaying the conclusion of the history.
[253] 'The young king crowned'; note in text. Note the complete break in the text between paragraphs, uncharacteristic of Cary's usual segues, and suggesting again the possibility of interpolation in the previous paragraph.
[254] 'The queen and Mortimer bear sway'; note in text.
[255] 'They commit Baldock to Newgate'; note in text.
[256] 'coistrel': knave, varlet, base fellow.
[257] 'Tresilian Lord Chief Justice hanged'; note in text.
[258] 'cropsick': sick in the stomach; crop is a term for stomach. OED first records its use in 1624.
[259] Aesop's frogs: the frogs demand a king, and Zeus/Jupiter sends them a log; they complain that he is too quiet, so the irate deity sends them a stork who devours them all.
[260] 'The black monks impatient of the king's restraint'; note in text.
[261] 'They not only incite the people, but make Donhead their captain... Who is clapped by the heels and dies'; note in text.

[262] 'Sir John of Hainault and the rest well rewarded... They depart the kingdom'; note in text.
[263] Woolf professes to find in the 'the wars of late years' a reference to the Civil War (1642–6), but Grundy remarks that it could equally refer to the wars in Ireland, of which Cary had just had first-hand experience; this reading is surely strengthened by Cary's reference to plantations, which presumably refers to the settlement of English pioneers in Ireland and the consequent sequestration of Irish land. For Cary's involvement with the suffering Irish, see 'Introduction: Life'.
[264] The armies of the British in Ireland had a reputation for both disaster and atrocity.
[265] Press-gangs roamed the country and could impress men into any one of the armed services; for a satire on their corruption, see Shakespeare's *Henry IV, Part 1* and *Henry IV Part 2*; both these plays may be in Cary's mind here.
[266] 'The king taken from the Earl of Lancaster, and delivered to Sir Maurice Berkeley and Sir John Matravers'; note in text.
[267] 'They remove him in disguise'; note in text.
[268] 'The king grieved with indignities'; note in text.
[269] 'His complaint'; note in text.
[270] 'The king is uncivilly upbraided... His answer'; note in text.
[271] 'The queen and Mortimer unquiet still'; note in text.
[272] 'Mortimer's ears tingle'; note in text.
[273] 'He tells the queen, the king must die'; note in text.
[274] 'She seems discontented'; note in text.
[275] 'She returns her answer'; note in text.
[276] 'Mortimer nettled... His reply'; note in text.
[277] 'Mortimer flings away'; note in text.
[278] 'The queen's expostulation'; note in text.
[279] 'She unwillingly consents to the king's death'; note in text.
[280] 'The king's keepers changed'; note in text.
[281] 'He is removed to Corfe Castle'; note in text. The main text has 'Cork', but Corfe is clearly correct.
[282] As the last clause makes clear, Cary refrains from a graphic description of Edward's murder not out of delicacy (as Stauffer claims), but because such descriptions might be a 'dangerous' example for potential regicides. Shakespeare's *Richard II* was censored by the removal of the deposition scene for similar reasons.
[283] The 'bleeding examples' of poisoning which Cary sees as 'fresh in our minds' may refer to the Overbury poisoning case; in 1613 Frances Howard, Countess of Essex, poisoned Sir Thomas Overbury while he was imprisoned in the Tower, to put an end to his opposition to her plan to divorce her husband and marry the Earl of Somerset. The revelation of the murder two years later was the most reverberating scandal of James I's reign.
[284] Henry VI was venerated as a saint by the fifteenth-century Catholic Church, and only the Reformation interrupted the English campaign to have him canonized. See Eamonn Duffy, *The Stripping of the Altars: Traditional Religion in England 1400–1580*, New Haven: Yale University Press, 1992.

SALVE DEUS
REX JUDAEORUM.

Containing,

1 The Passion of Christ.
2 Eve's Apology in defence of Women.
3 The Tears of the Daughters of Jerusalem.
4 *The Salutation and Sorrow of the Virgin Mary.*

With diverse other things not unfit to be read.

Written by Mistress *Aemilia Lanyer*, wife to Captain *Alfonso Lanyer* Servant to the King's Majesty.

At LONDON
Printed by *Valentine Simmes* for *Richard Bonian*, and are to be sold at his Shop in Paul's Church-yard. *Anno* 1611.[1]

TO THE QUEEN'S

MOST EXCELLENT MAJESTY[2]

Renowned Empress, and great Britain's Queen,
Most gracious mother of succeeding kings;
Vouchsafe to view that which is seldom seen,
A woman's writing of divinest things:
Read it, fair Queen, though it defective be,   5
Your excellence can grace both it and me.

For you have rifled nature of her store,
And all the goddesses have dispossessed
Of those rich gifts which they enjoyed before,
But now great Queen, in you they all do rest.   10
If now they strived for the golden ball,
Paris would give it you before them all.[3]

From Juno you have state and dignities,
From warlike Pallas, wisdom, fortitude,
And from fair Venus all her excellencies,   15
With their best parts your highness is indued:[4]
How much are we to honour those that springs
From such rare beauty in the blood of kings?

The Muses do attend upon your throne,
With all the artists at your beck and call;   20
The sylvan gods and satyrs every one,
Before your fair triumphant chariot fall:
And shining Cynthia with her nymphs attend
To honour you, whose honour hath no end.

From your bright sphere of greatness where you sit,
Reflecting light to all those glorious stars
That wait upon your throne; to virtue yet
Vouchsafe that splendour which no meanness bars:
Be like fair Phoebe, who doth love to grace
The darkest night with her most beauteous face.[5]

Apollo's beams do comfort every creature,
And shines upon the meanest things that be;
Since in estate and virtue none is greater,
I humbly wish that yours may light on me:
That so these rude unpolished lines of mine,
Graced by you might seem the more divine.

Look in this mirror of a worthy mind,
Where some of your fair virtues will appear;
Though all it is impossible to find,
Unless my glass were crystal, or more clear:
Which is dim steel, yet full of spotless truth,
And for one look from your fair eyes it su'th.

Here may your sacred majesty behold
That mighty monarch both of heav'n and earth,
He that all nations of the world controlled,
Yet took our flesh in base and meanest berth:
Whose days were spent in poverty and sorrow,
And yet all kings their wealth of him do borrow.

For he is crown and crowner of all kings,
The hopeful haven of the meaner sort,[6]
It's he that all our joyful tidings brings
Of happy reign within his royal court:
It's he in extremity can give
Comfort to them that have no time to live.

And since my wealth within his region stands,
And that his cross my chiefest comfort is,

Yea in his kingdom only rests my lands,
Of honour there I hope I shall not miss:
Though I on earth do live unfortunate,
Yet there I may attain a better state. 60

In the meantime, accept most gracious Queen
This holy work Virtue presents to you,
In poor apparel, shaming to be seen,
Or once t'appear in your judicial view:
But that fair virtue, though in mean attire, 65
All princes of the world do most desire.

And sith all royal virtues are in you,
The natural, the moral and divine,
I hope how plain soever being true,
You will accept even of the meanest line 70
Fair virtue yields; by whose rare gifts you are
So highly graced, t'exceed the fairest fair.

Behold, great Queen, fair Eve's apology,[7]
Which I have writ in honour of your sex,
And do refer unto your majesty, 75
To judge if it agrees not with the text:
And if it do, why are poor women blamed,
Or by more faulty men so much defamed?

And this great lady I have here attired,
In all her richest ornaments of honour, 80
That you fair Queen, of all the world admired,
May take the more delight to look upon her:
For she must entertain you to this feast
To which your highness is the welcom'st guest.

For here I have prepared my paschal lamb, 85
The figure of that living sacrifice;
Who dying all the infernal powers o'ercame,
That we with him t'eternity might rise:

This precious passover feed upon, O Queen,
Let your fair virtues in my glass be seen.   90

And she that is the pattern of all beauty,[8]
The very model of your majesty,
Whose rarest parts enforceth love and duty,
The perfect pattern of all piety:
O let my book by her fair eyes be blest,   95
In whose pure thoughts all innocency rests.

Then shall I think my glass a glorious sky,
When two such glittering suns at once appear;
The one replete with sov'reign majesty,
Both shining brighter than the clearest clear: 100
And both reflecting comfort to my spirits,
To find their grace so much above my merits.

Whose untuned voice the doleful notes doth sing
Of sad affliction in a humble strain;
Much like unto a bird that wants a wing,   105
And cannot fly, but warbles forth her pain,
Or he that barred from the sun's bright light,
Wanting day's comfort doth commend the night.

So I that live closed up in sorrow's cell,
Since great Eliza's favour blest my youth;[9]   110
And in the confines of all cares do dwell,
Whose grieved eyes no pleasure ever vieweth.
But in Christ's sufferings, such sweet taste they have,
As makes me praise pale sorrow and the grave.

And this great Lady whom I love and honour,   115
And from my very tender years have known,[10]
This holy habit still to take upon her,
Still to remain the same and still her own,
And what our fortunes do enforce us to,
She of devotion and mere zeal doth do.   120

Salve Deus Rex Judaeorum

Which makes me think our heavy burden light,
When such a one as she will help to bear it;
Treading the paths that make our way go right,
What garment is so fair but she may wear it?
Especially for her that entertains, 125
A glorious Queen in whom all worth remains.

Whose power may raise my sad dejected muse,
From this low mansion of a troubled mind;
Whose princely favour may such grace infuse,
That I may spread her virtues in like kind. 130
But in this trial of my slender skill,
I wanted knowledge to perform my will.

For even as they that do behold the stars,
Not with the eye of learning but of sight,
To find their motions, want of knowledge bars 135
Although they see them in their brightest light.
So though I see the glory of her state,
It's she that must instruct and elevate.

My weak distempered brain and feeble spirits,
Which all unlearned have adventured this, 140
To write of Christ, and of his sacred merits,
Desiring that this book her hands may kiss.
And though I be unworthy of that grace,
Yet let her blessed thoughts this book embrace.

And pardon me, fair Queen, though I presume, 145
To do that which so many better can;
Not that I learning to my self assume,
Or that I would compare with any man.
But as they are scholars, and by art do write,
So nature yields my soul a sad delight. 150

And since all arts at first from nature came,
That goodly creature, mother of perfection,

Whom Jove's almighty hand at first did frame,
Taking both her and hers in his protection,
Why should not she now grace my barren muse,   155
And in a woman all defects excuse?

So peerless princess, humbly I desire,
That your great wisdom would vouchsafe t'omit
All faults; and pardon if my spirits retire,
Leaving to aim at what they cannot hit.   160
To write your worth, which no pen can express,
Were but t'eclipse your fame and make it less.

To the Lady Elizabeth's Grace[11]

Most gracious lady, fair Elizabeth,
Whose name and virtues puts us still in mind
Of her, of whom we are deprived by death;[12]
The phoenix of her age, whose worth did bind
All worthy minds so long as they have breath,   5
In links of admiration, love and zeal,
To that dear mother of our commonweal.

Even you fair princess next our famous Queen,
I do invite unto this wholesome feast,
Whose goodly wisdom, though your years be green,   10
By such good works may daily be increased,
Though your fair eyes far better books have seen;
Yet being the first fruits of a woman's wit,
Vouchsafe you favour in accepting it.

To all virtuous Ladies in general

Each blessed lady that in virtue spends,
Your precious time to beautify your souls;
Come wait on her whom winged fame attends
And in her hand the book where she enrols
Those high deserts that majesty commends.   5

Salve Deus Rex Judaeorum

Let this fair Queen not unattended be,
When in my glass she deigns herself to see.

Put on your wedding garments every one,
The bridegroom stays to entertain you all;
Let virtue be your guide, for she alone 10
Can lead you right that you can never fall,
And make no stay for fear he should be gone:
But fill your lamps with oil of burning zeal,
That to your faith he may his truth reveal.

Let all your robes be purple scarlet white, 15
Those perfect colours purest virtue wore,[13]
Come decked with lilies that did so delight
To be preferred in beauty, far before
Wise Solomon in all his glory dight,
Whose royal robes did no such pleasure yield, 20
As did the beauteous lily of the field.

Adorn your temples with fair Daphne's crown,
The never-changing laurel, always green;
Let constant hope all worldly pleasures drown,[14]
In wise Minerva's paths be always seen; 25
Or with bright Cynthia though fair Venus frown;
With Aesop cross the posts of every door
Where sin would riot, making virtue poor.

And let the Muses your companions be,
Those sacred sisters that on Pallas wait, 30
Whose virtues with the purest minds agree,
Whose godly labours do avoid the bait
Of worldly pleasures, living always free,
From sword, from violence and from ill report,
To these nine worthies all fair minds resort. 35

Anoint your hair with Aaron's precious oil,
And bring your palms of vict'ry in your hands,
To overcome all thoughts that would defile

The earthly circuit of your soul's fair lands;
Let no dim shadows your clear eyes beguile, 40
Sweet odours, myrrh, gum, aloes, frankincense,
Present that king who died for your offence.

Behold bright Titan's shining chariot stays,
All decked with flowers of the freshest hue,
Attended on by Age, Hours, Nights and Days, 45
Which alters not your beauty, but gives you
Much more, and crowns you with eternal praise.
This golden chariot wherein you must ride,
Let simple doves and subtle serpents guide.

Come swifter than the motion of the sun, 50
To be transfigured with our loving Lord,
Lest glory end what grace in you begun,
Of heav'nly riches make your greatest hoard,
In Christ all honour, wealth and beauty's won,
By whose perfections you appear more fair 55
Than Phoebus, if he seven times brighter were.

God's holy angels will direct your doves,
And bring your serpents to the field of rest,
Where he doth stay that purchased all your loves,
In bloody torments when he died oppressed, 60
There shall you find him in those pleasant groves
Of sweet Elizium, by the well of life[15]
Whose crystal springs do purge from worldly strife.

Thus may you fly from dull and sensual earth,
Whereof at first your bodies formed were, 65
That new regen'rate in a second birth
Your blessed souls may live without all fear,
Being immortal, subject to no death,
But in the eye of heaven so highly placed,
That others by your virtues may be graced.[16] 70

Where, worthy ladies, I will leave you all,
Desiring you to grace this little book;
Yet some of you methinks I hear to call
Me by my name, and bid me better look,
Lest unawares I in an error fall,   75
In general terms to place you with the rest,
Whom fame commends to be the very best.

'Tis true, I must confess (O noble fame)
There are a number honoured by thee,
Of which some few thou didst recite by name,   80
And willed my muse they should remembered be;
Wishing some would their glorious trophies frame,
Which if I should presume to undertake,
My tired hand for very fear would quake.

Only by name I will bid some of those,   85
That in true honour's seat have long been placed,
Yea even such as thou hast chiefly chose,
By whom my muse may be the better graced.
Therefore, unwilling longer time to lose,
I will invite some ladies that I know,   90
But chiefly those as thou hast graced so.

To the Lady Arabella[17]

Great learned lady, whom I long have known,
And yet not known so much as I desired,
Rare phoenix, whose fair feathers are your own,
With which you fly, and are so much admired.
True honour whom true fame hath so attired,   5
In glittering raiment shining much more bright,
Than silver stars in the most frosty night.

Come like the morning sun new out of bed,
And cast your eyes upon this little book,

Although you be so well accompanied,   10
With Pallas and the Muses, spare one look,
Upon this humbled king, who all forsook,
That in his dying arms he might embrace
Your beauteous soul and fill it with his grace.

To the Lady Susan, Countess Dowager of Kent, and daughter to the Duchess of Suffolk[18]

Come you that were the mistress of my youth,
The noble guide of my ungoverned days;
Come you that have delighted in God's truth,
Help now your handmaid to sound forth his praise;
You that are pleased in his pure excellency   5
Vouchsafe to grace this holy feast, and me.

And as your rare perfections showed the glass
Wherein I saw each wrinkle of a fault;
You the sun's virtue, I that fair green grass,
That flourished fresh by your clear virtues taught.   10
For you possessed those gifts that grace the mind,
Restraining youth, whom error oft doth blind.

In you these noble virtues did I note,
First, love and fear of God, of prince, of laws,
Rare patience with a mind so far remote   15
From worldly pleasures, free from giving cause
Of least suspect to the most envious eye,
That in fair virtue's storehouse sought to pry.

Whose faith did undertake in infancy,
All dang'rous travels by devouring seas[19]   20
To fly to Christ from vain idolatry,
Not seeking there this worthless world to please,
By your most famous mother so directed,
That noble duchess, who lived unsubjected.

From Rome's ridiculous prayer and tyranny, 25
That mighty monarchs kept in awful fear;
Leaving here her lands, her state, dignity;
Nay more, vouchsafed disguised weeds to wear.
When with Christ Jesus she did mean to go,
From sweet delights to taste part of his woe. 30

Come you that ever since have followed her,
In these sweet paths of fair humility;
Condemning pride pure virtue to prefer,
Not yielding to base imbecility,
Nor to those weak enticements of the world, 35
That have so many thousand souls ensnarled.

Receive your love whom you have sought so far,
Which here presents himself within your view;
Behold this bright and all-directing star,
Light of your soul, that doth all grace renew. 40
And in his humble paths since you do tread,
Take this fair bridegroom in your soul's pure bed.

And since no former gain hath made me write,
Nor my desertless service could have won,
Only your noble virtues do incite 45
My pen; they are the ground I write upon;
Nor any future profit is expected,
Then how can these poor lines go unrespected?

The Author's Dream[20] to the Lady Mary, the Countess Dowager
    of Pembroke[21]

Methought I passed through th'Edalyan groves
And asked the Graces, if they could direct
Me to a lady whom Minerva chose,
To live with her in height of all respect.

Yet looking back into my thoughts again,   5
The eye of reason did behold her there
Fastened unto them in a golden chain;
They stood, but she was set in honour's chair.²²

And nine fair virgins sat upon the ground,
With harps and viols in their lily hands;   10
Whose harmony had all my senses drowned,
But that before mine eyes an object stands,

Whose beauty shined like Titan's clearest rays;
She blew a brazen trumpet, which did sound
Through all the world that worthy lady's praise,   15
And by eternal fame I saw her crowned.

Yet studying if I were awake or no,
God Morphy²³ came and took me by the hand,
And willed me not from slumber's bower to go,
Till I the sum of all did understand.   20

When presently the welkin that before
Looked bright and clear, me thought was overcast,
And dusky clouds with boisterous winds great store
Foretold of violent storms which could not last.

And gazing up into the troubled sky,   25
Methought a chariot did from thence descend,
Where one did sit replete with majesty,
Drawn by four fiery dragons, which did bend

Their course where this most noble lady sat,
Whom all these virgins with due reverence   30
Did entertain, according to that state
Which did belong unto her excellence.

When bright Bellona,²⁴ so they did her call,
Whom these fair nymphs so humbly did receive,

A manly maid which was both fair and tall, 35
Her borrowed chariot by a spring did leave.

With spear, and shield, and cuirass on her breast,
And on her head a helmet wondrous bright,
With myrtle, bays and olive branches dressed,
Wherein methought I took no small delight. 40

To see how all the Graces sought grace here,
And in what meek yet princely sort she came;
How this most noble lady did embrace her,
And all humours unto hers did frame.

Now fair Dictynna[25] by the break of day, 45
With all her damsels round about her came,
Ranging the woods to hunt, yet made a stay,
When harkening to the pleasing sound of fame;

Her ivory bow and silver shafts she gave
Unto the fairest nymph of all her train; 50
And wondering who it was that in so grave,
Yet gallant fashion did her beauty stain:

She decked herself with all the borrowed light
That Phoebus would afford from his fair face,
And made her virgins to appear so bright, 55
That all the hills and vales received grace.

Then pressing where this beauteous troop did stand,
They all received her most willingly,
And unto her the lady gave her hand,
That she should keep with them continually. 60

Aurora[26] rising from her rosy bed,
First blushed, then wept to see fair Phoebe graced,
And unto Lady May these words she said
'Come, let us go; we will not be outfaced'.

'I will unto Apollo's waggoner, 65
A[nd] bid him bring his master presently,
That his bright beams may all her beauty mar,
Gracing us with the lustre of his eye.

'Come, come, sweet May, and fill their laps with flowers,
And I will give a greater light than she, 70
So all these ladies' favours shall be ours;
None shall be more esteemed than we shall be'.

Thus did Aurora dim fair Phoebus' light,
And was received in bright Cynthia's place,
While Flora all with fragrant flowers dight, 75
Pressed to show the beauties of her face.

Though these, methought, were very pleasing sights,
Yet now these worthies did agree to go,
Unto a place full of all rare delights,
A place that yet Minerva did not know. 80

That sacred spring where art and nature strived,
Which should remain as sov'reign of the place;
Whose ancient quarrel being new revived,
Added fresh beauty, gave far greater grace.

To which as umpires now these ladies go, 85
Judging with pleasure their delightful case;
Whose ravished senses made them quickly know,
'Twould be offensive either to displace.

And therefore willed they should forever dwell,
In perfect unity by this matchless spring, 90
Since 'twas impossible either should excel,
Or her fair fellow in subjection bring.

But here in equal sov'reignty to live,
Equal in state, equal in dignity,

That unto others they might comfort give, 95
Rejoicing all with their sweet unity.

And now methought I long to hear her name,
Whom wise Minerva honoured so much,
She whom I saw was crowned by noble fame,
Whom envy sought to sting, yet could not touch. 100

Methought the meagre elf did seek by ways
To come unto her, but it would not be;
Her venom purified by virtuous rays
She pined and starved like an anatomy.

While beauteous Pallas with this lady fair 105
Attended by these nymphs of noble fame,
Beheld those woods, those groves, those bowers rare,
By which Pergusa, for so hight the name

Of that fair spring, his dwelling place and ground,
And through those fields with sundry flowers clad 110
Of sev'ral colours, to adorn the ground,
And please the senses ev'n of the most sad.

He trailed along the woods in wanton wise,
With sweet delight to entertain them all;
Inviting them to sit and to devise 115
On holy hymns; at last to mind they call

Those rare sweet songs which Israel's king did frame[27]
Unto the father of eternity;
Before his holy wisdom took the name
Of great Messiah, lord of unity. 120

Those holy sonnets they did all agree,
With this most lovely lady here to sing;
That by her noble breast's sweet harmony,
Their music might in ears of angels ring.

While saints like swans about this silver brook, 125
Should hallelujah sing continually,
Writing her praises in the eternal book
Of endless honour, true fame's memory.

Thus I in sleep the heavenliest music heard,
That ever earthly ears did entertain; 130
And durst not wake, for fear to be debarred
Of what my senses sought still to retain.

Yet sleeping, prayed dull slumber to unfold
Her noble name, who was of all admired;
When presently in drowsy terms he told 135
Not only that, but more than I desired.

This nymph, quoth he, great Pembroke hight by name,
Sister to valiant Sidney, whose clear light
Gives light to all that tread true paths of fame,
Who in the globe of heav'n doth shine so bright; 140

That being dead, his fame doth him survive,
Still living in the hearts of worthy men;
Pale death is dead, but he remains alive,
Whose dying wounds restored him life again.

And this fair earthly goddess which you see, 145
Bellona and her virgins do attend,
In virtuous studies of divinity,
Her precious time continually doth spend.

So that a sister well she may be deemed,
To him that lived and died so nobly; 150
And far before him is to be esteemed[28]
For virtue, wisdom, learning, dignity.

Whose beauteous soul hath gained a double life,
Both here on earth and in the heav'ns above,

Till dissolution end all worldly strife 155
Her blessed spirit remains, of holy love,

Directing all by her immortal light,
In this huge sea of sorrows, griefs and fears,
With contemplation of God's powerful might
She fills the eyes, the hearts, the tongues, the ears 160

Of after-coming ages, which shall read
Her love, her zeal, her faith and piety;
The fair impression of whose worthy deed,
Seals her pure soul unto the Deity.

That both in heav'n and earth it may remain, 165
Crowned with her maker's glory and his love;
And this did Father Slumber tell with pain,
Whose dullness scarce could suffer him to move.

When I awaking left him and his bower,
Much grieved that I could no longer stay; 170
Senseless was sleep, not to admit me power,
As I had spent the night, to spend the day.

Then had god Morphy showed the end of all,
And what my heart desired, my eyes had seen;
For as I waked methought I heard one call 175
For that bright chariot lent by Jove's fair queen.

But thou, base cunning thief, that robs our spirits
Of half that span of life which years doth give;[29]
And yet no praise unto thyself it merits,
To make a seeming death in those that live. 180

Yea, wickedly thou dost consent to death,
Within thy restful bed to rob our souls;
In slumber's bower thou steal'st away our breath
Yet none there is that thy base stealths controls.

If poor and sickly creatures would embrace thee, 185
Or they to whom thou giv'st a taste of pleasure,
Thou fliest as if Actaeon's hounds did chase thee
Or that to stay with them thou hadst no leisure.

But though thou hast deprived me of delight
By stealing from me ere I was aware; 190
I know I shall enjoy the selfsame sight
Thou hast no power my waking spirits to bar.

For to this lady now I will repair,
Presenting her the fruits of idle hours;
Though many books she writes that are more rare, 195
Yet there is honey in the meanest flowers:

Which is both wholesome and delights the taste,
Though sugar be more finer, higher prized,
Yet is the painful bee no whit disgraced,
Nor her fair wax or honey more despised. 200

And though that learned damsel and the rest
Have in a higher style her trophy framed;
Yet these unlearned lines being my best,
Of her great wisdom can no whit be blamed.

And therefore, first I here present my dream, 205
And next, invite her honour to my feast;
For my clear reason sees her by that stream
Where her rare virtues daily are increased.

So craving pardon for this bold attempt,
I here present my mirror to her view, 210
Whose noble virtues cannot be exempt;
My glass being steel declares them to be true.

And madam, if you will vouchsafe that grace,
To grace those flowers that springs from virtue's ground;

Though your fair mind on worthier works is placed, 215
On works that are more deep and more profound,

Yet is it no disparagement to you
To see your saviour in a shepherd's weed,
Unworthily presented in your view,
Whose worthiness will grace each line you read. 220

Receive him here by my unworthy hand,
And read his paths of fair humility;
Who though our sins in number pass the sand
They all are purged by his divinity.

To the Lady Lucy, Countess of Bedford[30]

Methinks I see fair virtue ready stand,
T'unlock the closet of your lovely breast,
Holding the key of knowledge in her hand,
Key of that cabin where your self doth rest,
To let him in by whom her youth was blest, 5
The true-love of your soul, your heart's delight,
Fairer than all the world in your clear sight.

He that descended from celestial glory,
To taste of our infirmities and sorrows,
Whose heavenly wisdom read the earthly story 10
Of frail humanity which his godhead borrows;
Lo here he comes all stuck with pale death's arrows,
In whose most precious wounds your soul may read
Salvation, while he (dying Lord) must bleed.

You whose clear judgement far exceeds my skill, 15
Vouchsafe to entertain this dying lover,
The ocean of true grace, whose streams do fill
All those with joy that can his love recover;
About this blessed ark bright angels hover,
Where your fair soul may sure and safely rest, 20
When he is sweetly seated in your breast.

There may your thoughts as servants to your heart,
Give true attendance on this lovely guest,
While he doth to that blessed bower impart
Flowers of fresh comforts, deck that bed of rest   25
With such rich beauties as may make it blest:
And you in whom all rarity is found,
May be with his eternal glory crowned.

To the Lady Margaret, Countess Dowager of Cumberland[31]

Right honourable and excellent Lady, I may say with Saint Peter, 'Silver nor gold have I none, but such as I have, that give I you'; for having neither rich pearls of India, nor fine gold of Arabia, nor diamonds of inestimable value; neither those rich treasures, aromatical gums, incense and sweet odours, which   5
were presented by those kingly philosophers to the babe Jesus, I present unto you even our Lord Jesus himself, whose infinite value is not to be comprehended within the weak imagination or wit of man; and as Saint Peter gave health to the body, so I deliver you the health of the soul, which is this most precious   10
pearl of all perfection, this rich diamond of devotion, this perfect gold growing in the veins of that excellent earth of the most blessed paradise, wherein our second Adam had his restless habitation. The sweet incense, balsams, odours and gums that flow from that beautiful tree of life, sprung from the root   15
of Jesse, which is so superexcellent, that it giveth grace to the meanest and most unworthy hand that will undertake to write thereof; neither can it receive any blemish thereby, for as a right diamond can lose no whit of his beauty by the black soil underneath it, neither by being placed in the dark, but retains 20
his natural beauty and brightness shining in greater perfection than before; so this most precious diamond, for beauty and riches exceeding all the most precious diamonds and rich jewels of the world, can receive no blemish, nor impeachment, by my unworthy handwriting, but will with the sun retain his own   25
brightness and most glorious lustre, though never so many

blind eyes look upon him. Therefore good madam, to the most perfect eyes of your understanding I deliver the inestimable treasure of all elected souls, to be perused at convenient times; as also, the mirror of your most worthy mind, which may   30
remain in the world many years longer than your honour, or myself can live, to be a light unto those that come after, desiring to tread in the narrow path of virtue, that leads the way to heaven. In which way, I pray God send your honour long to continue, that your light may so shine before men, that they   35
may glorify your father which is in heaven; and that I and many others may follow you in the same track. So wishing you in this world all increase of health and honour, and in the world to come life everlasting, I rest.

To the Lady Katherine, Countess of Suffolk[32]

Although, great lady, it may seem right strange,
That I a stranger should presume thus far,
To write to you; yet as the times do change,
So are we subject to that fatal star,
Under the which we were produced to breath,   5
That star that guides us even until our death.

And guided me to frame this work of grace,
Not of itself but by celestial powers,
To which both that and we must needs give place,
Since what we have, we cannot count it ours.   10
For health, wealth, honour, sickness, death and all,
Is in God's power, which makes us rise and fall.

And since his power hath given me power to write,
A subject fit for you to look upon,
Wherein your soul may take no small delight,   15
When her bright eyes behold that holy one,
By whose great wisdom, love and special grace,
She was created to behold his face.

Vouchsafe, sweet lady, to accept these lines,
Writ by a hand that doth desire to do   20
All services to you whose worth combines
The worthiest minds to love and honour you;
Whose beauty, wisdom, children, high estate,
Do all concur to make you fortunate.

But chiefly your most honourable lord,   25
Whose noble virtues fame can ne'er forget;
His hand being always ready to afford
Help to the weak, to the unfortunate;
All which begets more honour and respect,
Than Croesus' wealth, or Caesar's stern aspect. 30

And rightly showeth that he is descended
Of honourable Howard's ancient house,
Whose noble deeds by former times commended,
Do now remain in your most loyal spouse,
On whom God pours all blessings from above,   35
Wealth, honour, children and a worthy love.

Which is more dear to him than all the rest,
You being the loving hind and pleasant roe,
Wife of his youth, in whom his soul is blest,
Fountain from whence his chief delights do flow. 40
Fair tree from which the fruit of honour springs,
Here I present to you the King of Kings.

Desiring you to take a perfect view
Of those great torments patience did endure;
And reap those comforts that belongs to you,   45
Which his most painful death did then assure,
Writing the covenant with his precious blood,
That your fair soul might bathe her in that flood.

And let your noble daughters likewise read
This little book that I present to you;   50

Salve Deus Rex Judaeorum

On heavenly food let them vouchsafe to feed;
Here they may see a lover much more true
Than ever was since first the world began,
This poor rich king that died both God and man.

Yea, let those ladies, who do represent   55
All beauty, wisdom, [honour], zeal and love,
Receive this jewel from Jehovah sent,
This spotless lamb, this perfect patient dove,
Of whom fair Gabriel, God's bright Mercury,
Brought down a message from the deity.   60

Here may they see him in a flood of tears,
Crowned with thorns, and bathing in his blood;
Here may they see his fears exceed all fears,
When heaven in justice flat against him stood,
And loathsome death with grim and ghastly look,   65
Presented him that black infernal book,

Wherein the sins of all the world were writ,
In deep characters of due punishment;
And nought but dying breath could cancel it,
Shame, death, and hell must make the atonement: 70
Showing their evidence, seizing wrongful right,
Placing heav'n's beauty in death's darkest night.

Yet through the sable clouds of shame and death,
His beauty shows more clearer than before;
Death lost his strength when he did lose his breath: 75
As fire suppressed doth shine and flame the more,
So in death's ashy pale discoloured face,
Fresh beauty shined, yielding far greater grace.

No dove, no swan, nor ivory could compare
With this fair corpse, when 'twas by death embraced, 80
No rose, nor no vermilion half so fair,
As was that precious blood that interlaced

His body, which bright angels did attend,
Waiting on him that must to heaven ascend.

In whom is all that ladies can desire, 85
If beauty, who hath been more fair than he?
If wisdom, doth not all the world admire
The depth of his, that cannot searched be?
If wealth, if honour, fame, or kingdom's store,
Who ever lived that was possessed of more? 90

If zeal, if grace, if love, if piety,
If constancy, if faith, if fair obedience,
If valour, patience, or sobriety,
If chaste behaviour, meekness, continence,
If justice, mercy, bounty, charity, 95
Who can compare with his divinity?

Whose virtues more than thoughts can apprehend
I leave to their more clear imagination
That will vouchsafe their borrowed time to spend
In meditating and in contemplation 100
Of his rare parts, true honour's fair prospect,
The perfect line that goodness doth direct.

And unto you I wish those sweet desires
That from your perfect thoughts do daily spring,
Increasing still pure, bright and holy fires, 105
Which sparks of precious grace by faith do spring;
Mounting your soul unto eternal rest,
There to live happily among the best.

To the Lady Anne, Countess of Dorset[33]

To you I dedicate this work of grace,
This frame of glory which I have erected,
For your fair mind I hold the fittest place,

Salve Deus Rex Judaeorum

Where virtue should be settled and protected;
If highest thoughts true honour do embrace
And holy wisdom is of them respected,
Then in this mirror let your fair eyes look
To view your virtues in this blessed book.

Blest by our saviour's merits, not my skill,
Which I acknowledge to be very small;
Yet if the least part of his blessed will
I have performed, I count I have done all.
One spark of grace sufficient is to fill
Our lamps with oil, ready when he doth call[34]
To enter with the bridegroom to the feast
Where he that is the greatest may be least.

Greatness is no sure frame to build upon;
No worldly treasure can assure that place;
God makes both even, the cottage with the throne,
All worldly honours there are counted base.
Those he holds dear, and reckons as his own,
Whose virtuous deeds by his especial grace[35]
Have gained his love, his kingdom and his crown,
Whom in the book of life he hath set down.

Titles of honour which the world bestows,
To none but to the virtuous doth belong,
As beauteous bowers where true worth should repose
And where his dwellings should be built most strong.
But when they are bestowed upon her foes,
Poor virtue's friends endure the greatest wrong;
For they must suffer all indignity,
Until in heav'n they better graced be.

What difference was there when the world began?
Was it not virtue that distinguished all?
All sprang but from one woman and one man,
Then how doth gentry come to rise and fall?

Or who is he that very rightly can
Distinguish of his birth, or tell at all,
In what mean state his ancestors have been
Before some one of worth did honour win?   40

Whose successors, although they bear his name,
Possessing not the riches of his mind,
How do we know they spring out of the same
True stock fo honour, being not of that kind?
It is fair virtue gets immortal fame,   45
'Tis that doth all love and duty bind;
If he that much enjoys, doth little good,
We may suppose he comes not of that blood.

Nor is he fit for honour, or command,
If base affections overrules his mind;   50
Or that self-will doth carry such a hand
As worldly pleasures have the power to blind,
So as he cannot see, nor understand
How to discharge that place to him assigned.
God's steward must for all the poor provide   55
If in God's house they purpose to abide.

To you, as to God's steward I do write,
In whom the seeds of virtue have been sown
By your most worthy mother, in whose right
All her fair parts you challenge as your own;   60
If you, sweet lady, will appear as bright
As ever creature did that time hath known,
Then wear this diadem I present to thee
Which I have framed for her eternity.

You are the heir apparent of this crown   65
Of goodness, bounty, grace, love, piety,
By birth it's yours; then keep it as your own,
Defend it from all base indignity;
The right your mother hath to it is known

Salve Deus Rex Judaeorum

Best unto you, who reaped such fruit thereby: 70
This monument of her fair worth retain
In your pure mind, and keep it from all stain.

And as your ancestors at first possessed
Their honours for their honourable deeds,
Let their fair virtues never be transgressed; 75
Bind up the broken, stop the wounds that bleeds,
Succour the poor, comfort the comfortless,
Cherish fair plants, suppress unwholesome weeds;
Although base pelf do chance to come in place,
Yet let true worth receive your greatest grace. 80

So shall you show from whence you are descended,
And leave to all posterities your fame;
So will your virtues always be commended,
And everyone will reverence your name;
So this poor work of mine shall be defended 85
From any scandal that the world can frame;
And you a glorious actor will appear
Lovely to all, but unto God most dear.

I know right well these are but needless lines,
To you, that are so perfect in your part, 90
Whose birth and education both combines;
Nay, more than both, a pure and goodly heart,
So well instructed to such fair designs,
By your dear mother that there needs no art;
Your ripe discretion in your tender years, 95
By all your actions to the world appears.

I do but set a candle in the sun,
And add one drop of water to the sea,
Virtue and beauty both together run,
When you were born, within your breast to stay; 100
Their quarrel ceased, which long before begun,
They live in peace, and all do them obey:

In you, fair madam, are they richly placed
Where all their worth by eternity is graced.

You goddess-like unto the world appear,   105
Enriched with more than fortune can bestow,
Goodness and grace, which you do hold more dear
Than worldly wealth, which melts away like snow;
Your pleasure is the word of God to hear,
That his most holy precepts you may know: 110
Your greatest honour, fair and virtuous deeds,
Which from the love and fear of God proceeds.

Therefore to you (good madam) I present
His lovely love, more worth than purest gold,
Who for your sake his precious blood hath spent,   115
His death and passion here you may behold,
And view this lamb, that to the world was sent,
Whom your fair soul may in her arms enfold:
Loving his love, that did endure such pain
That you in heaven a worthy place might gain.   120

For well you know this world is but a stage,
Where all do play their parts and must be gone;
Here's no respect of persons, youth, nor age,
Death seizes all, he never spareth one;
None can prevent or stay that tyrant's rage   125
But Jesus Christ the Just; by him alone
He was o'ercome; he open set the door
To eternal life, ne'er seen, nor known before.

He is the stone the builders did refuse,
Which you, sweet lady, are to build upon;   130
He is the rock that holy church did choose,
Among which number you must needs be one;
Fair shepherdess, 'tis you that he will use
To feed his flock, that trust in him alone;
All worldly blessings he vouchsafes to you,   135
That to the poor you may return his due.

And if deserts a lady's love may gain,
Then tell me who has more deserved than he?
Therefore in recompense of all his pain,
Bestow your pains to read, and pardon me,   140
If out of wants, or weakness of my brain,
I have not done this work sufficiently;
Yet lodge him in the closet of your heart,
Whose worth is more than can be showed by art.

To the Virtuous Reader

Often have I heard that it is the property of some women not
only to emulate the virtues and perfections of the rest, but also
by all their powers of ill-speaking to eclipse the brightness of
their deserved fame; now contrary to this custom, which men I
hope unjustly lay to their charge, I have written this small   5
volume or little book, for the general use of all virtuous ladies
and gentlewomen of this kingdom; and in commendation of
some particular persons of our own sex, such as for the most
part are so well known to myself and others, that I dare
undertake fame dares not to call any better. And this have I   10
done to make known to the world that all women deserve not
to be blamed, though some forgetting they are women them-
selves, and in danger to be condemned by the words of their
own mouths, fall into so great an error, as to speak unadvisedly
against the rest of their sex; which if it be true, I am persuaded 15
they can show their own imperfection in nothing more; and
therefore could wish (for their own ease, modesties and credit)
they would refer such points of folly to be practised by evil-
disposed men, who forgetting they were born of women, nour-
ished of women, and that if it were not by the means of women, 20
they would be quite extinguished out of the world, and a final end
of them all, do like vipers deface the wombs wherein they were
bred, only to give way and utterance to their want of discretion
and goodness. Such as these, were they that dishonoured Christ,

his apostles and prophets, putting them to shameful deaths. Therefore we are not to regard any imputations, that they undeservedly lay upon us, no otherwise than to make use of them to our own benefits, as spurs to virtue, making us fly all occasions that may colour their unjust speeches to pass current. Especially considering that they have tempted even the patience of God himself, who gave power to wise and virtuous women to bring down their pride and arrogance. As was cruel Cesarius by the discreet counsel of noble Deborah, judge and prophetess of Israel, and resolution of Jael, wife of Heber the Kenite; wicked Haman, by the divine prayers and prudent proceedings of beautiful Hester; blasphemous Holofernes, by the invincible courage, rare wisdom, and confident carriage of Judith; and the unjust judges, by the innocence of chaste Susanna; with infinite others, which for brevity's sake I will omit. As also in respect it pleased our Lord and Saviour Jesus Christ, without the assistance of man, being free from original and all other sins, from the time of his conception till the hour of his death, to be begotten of a woman, born of a woman, nourished of a woman, obedient to a woman; and that he healed women,[36] pardoned women, comforted women, yea, even when he was in his greatest agony and bloody sweat, going to be crucified, and also in the last hour of his death, took care to dispose of a woman; after his resurrection, appeared first to a woman, sent a woman to declare his most glorious resurrection to the rest of his disciples. Many other examples I could allege of diverse faithful and virtuous women, who have in all ages not only been confessors, but also endured most cruel martyrdom for their faith in Jesus Christ. All which is sufficient to enforce all good Christians and honourable-minded men to speak reverently of our sex, and especially of all virtuous and good women. To the modest censures of both which I refer these my imperfect endeavours, knowing that according to their own excellent dispositions they will rather cherish, nourish, and increase the least spark of virtue where they find it, by their favourable and best interpretations, than quench it by wrong constructions. To whom I wish with all increase of virtue, and desire their best opinions.

Salve Deus Rex Judaeorum

Sith Cynthia[37] is ascended to that rest
Of endless joy and true eternity,
That glorious place that cannot be expressed
By any wight clad in mortality,
In her almighty love so highly blest, 5
And crowned with everlasting sov'reignty;
Where saints and angels do attend her throne,
And she gives glory unto God alone.

To thee great Countess[38] now I will apply
My pen, to write thy never-dying fame; 10
That when to heav'n thy blessed soul shall fly
These lines on earth record thy reverent name.
And to this task I mean my muse to tie
Though wanting skill I shall but purchase blame.
Pardon (dear lady) want of woman's wit 15
To pen thy praise, when few can equal it.

And pardon (madam) though I do not write
Those praiseful lines of that delightful place
As you commanded me in that fair night
When shining Phoebe gave so great a grace, 20
Presenting paradise to your sweet sight,
Unfolding all the beauty of her face
With pleasant groves, hills, walks and stately trees,
Which pleasures with retired minds agrees.

Whose eagle's eyes behold the glorious sun 25
Of th'all creating providence, reflecting
His blessed beams on all by him begun;
Increasing, strengthening, guiding and directing
All worldly creatures their due course to run;
Unto his powerful pleasure all subjecting; 30
And thou (dear lady) by his special grace
In these his creatures dost behold his face.

Whose all reviving beauty yields such joys
To thy sad soul, plunged in waves of woe,
That worldly pleasures seem to thee as toys, 35
Only thou seek'st eternity to know,
Respecting not the infinite annoys
That Satan to thy well-stayed mind can show;
Ne can he quench in thee the spirit of grace
Nor draw thee from beholding heaven's bright face. 40

Thy mind so perfect by thy maker framed,
No vain delights can harbour in thy heart;
With his sweet love, thou art so much inflamed
As of the world thou seem'st to have no part;
So, love him still, thou need'st not be ashamed, 45
'Tis he that made thee, what thou wert and art,
Tis he that dries all tears from orphans' eyes,
And hears from heav'n the woeful widows' cries.

'Tis he that doth behold thy inward cares
And will regard the sorrows of thy soul; 50
'Tis he that guides thy feet from Satan's snares,
And in his wisdom doth thy ways control;
He through afflictions, still thy mind prepares,
And all thy glorious trials will enrol,
That when dark days of terror shall appear 55
Thou as the sun shalt shine; or much more clear.

The heav'ns shall perish as a garment old,
Or as a venture by the maker changed,
And shall depart, as when a scroll is rolled;
Yet thou from him shalt never be estranged, 60
When he shall come in glory, that was sold
For all our sins; we happily are changed,
Who for our faults put on his righteousness,
Although full oft his laws we do transgress.

Long may'st thou joy in this almighty love, 65
Long may'st thy soul be pleasing in his sight,

Salve Deus Rex Judaeorum

Long may'st thou have true comforts from above,
Long may'st thou set on him thy whole delight,
And patiently endure when he doth prove,
Knowing that he will surely do thee right: 70
Thy patience, faith, long-suffering, and thy love,
He will reward with comforts from above.

With majesty and honour is he clad,
And decked with light, as with a garment fair;
He joys the meek, and makes the mighty sad, 75
Pulls down the proud, and doth the humble rear.
Who sees this bridegroom never can be sad;
None lives that can his wondrous works declare:
Yea, look how far the east is from the west
So far he sets our sins that have transgressed. 80

He rides upon the wings of all the winds,
And spreads the heavens with his all-powerful hand;
Oh! Who can loose when the Almighty binds?
Or in his angry presence dares to stand?
He searcheth out the secrets of all minds; 85
All those that fear him shall possess the land.
He is exceeding glorious to behold,
Ancient of times; so fair and yet so old.

He of the watery clouds his chariot frames,
And makes his blessed angels powerful spirits, 90
His ministers are fearful fiery flames,
Rewarding all according to their merits.
The righteous for a heritage he claims,
And registers the wrongs of humble spirits;
Hills melt like wax in presence of the Lord, 95
So do all sinners, in his light abhorred.

He in the waters lays his chamber beams,
And clouds of darkness compass him about,
Consuming fire shall go before in streams,

And burn up all his en'mies round about. 100
Yet on these judgements worldlings never dream
Nor of these dangers never stand in doubt;
While he shall rest within his holy hill,
That lives and dies according to his will.

But woe to them that double-hearted be 105
Who with their tongues the righteous souls do slay;
Bending their bows to shoot at all they see,
With upright hearts their maker to obey;
And secretly do let their arrows flee,
To wound true-hearted people any way. 110
The Lord will root them out that speak proud things,
Deceitful tongues are but false slander's wings.

Froward are the ungodly from their birth,
No sooner born, but they do go astray;
The Lord will root them out from off the earth, 115
And give them to their en'mies for a prey;
As venomous as serpents is their breath,
With poisoned lies to hurt in what they may
The innocent: who as a dove shall fly
Unto the Lord, that he his cause may try. 120

The righteous Lord doth righteousness allow,
His countenance will behold the thing that's just;
Unto the mean he makes the mighty bow,
And raiseth up the poor out of the dust.
Yet makes no count to us, nor when, nor how, 125
But pours his grace on all, that put their trust
In him, that never will their hopes betray,
Nor lets them perish that for mercy pray.

He shall within his tabernacle dwell,
Whose life is uncorrupt before the Lord, 130
Who no untruths of innocents doth tell,
Nor wrongs his neighbour, not in deed, nor word,

Nor in his pride with malice seems to swell,
Nor whets his tongue more sharper than a sword,
To wound the reputation of the just;   135
Nor seeks to lay their glory in the dust.

That great Jehovah, king of heav'n and earth,
Will rain down fire and brimstone from above,
Upon the wicked monsters in their berth
That storm and rage at those whom he doth love.   140
Snares, storms and tempests he will rain, and dearth,
Because he will himself almighty prove;
And this shall be their portion they shall drink,
That thinks the Lord is blind when he doth wink.

Pardon (good madam)[39] though I have digressed   145
From what I do intend to write of thee,
To set his glory forth whom thou lov'st best,
Whose wondrous works no mortal eye can see;
His special care on those whom he hath blest;
From wicked worldlings, how he sets them free;   150
And how such people he doth overthrow
In all their ways, that they his power may know.

The meditation of this monarch's love,
Draws thee from caring what this world can yield;
Of joys and griefs both equal thou dost prove,   155
They have no force to force thee from the field;
Thy constant faith, like to the turtle dove
Continues combat, and will never yield
To base affliction; or proud pomp's desire
That sets the weakest minds so much on fire.   160

Thou from the court to the country art retired,
Leaving the world before the world leaves thee;
That great enchantress of weak minds admired,
Whose all-bewitching charms so pleasing be
To worldly wantons; and too much desired   165

Of those that care not for eternity
But yield themselves, a prey to lust and sin,
Losing their hopes of heav'n hell's pains to win.

But thou, the wonder of our wanton age
Leav'st all delights to serve a heav'nly king: 170
Who is more wise? or who can be more sage
Than she that doth affection subject bring;
Not forcing for the world, or Satan's rage,
But shrouding under the almighty's wing;
Spending her years, months, days, minutes, hours 175
In doing service to the heav'nly powers.

Thou fair example, live without compare
With honour's triumphs seated in thy breast;
Pale envy never can thy name impair
When in thy heart thou harbour'st such a guest; 180
Malice must live forever in despair;
There's no revenge where virtue still doth rest;
All hearts must needs do homage unto thee,
In whom all eyes such rare perfection see.

That outward beauty which the world commends[40] 185
Is not the subject I will write upon,
Whose date expired, that tyrant time soon ends;
Those gaudy colours soon are spent and gone,
But those fair virtues which on thee attends
Are always fresh, they never are but one: 190
They make thy beauty fairer to behold
Than was that queen's for whom proud Troy was sold.[41]

As for those matchless colours red and white,
Or perfect features in a fading face,
Or due proportion pleasing to the sight; 195
All these do draw but dangers and disgrace.
A mind enriched with virtue shines more bright,
Adds everlasting beauty, gives true grace,

Frames an immortal goddess on the earth,
Who though she dies, yet fame gives her new birth.   200

That pride of nature which adorns the fair,
Like blazing comets to allure all eyes,
Is but the thread, that weaves their web of care
Who glories most, where most their danger lies.
For greatest perils do attend the fair   205
When men do seek, attempt, plot and devise
How they may overthrow the chastest dame
Whose beauty is the white whereat they aim.

'Twas beauty bred in Troy the ten years' strife,
And carried Helen from her lawful lord;   210
'Twas beauty made chaste Lucrece lose her life,
For which proud Tarquin's act was so abhorred;[42]
Beauty the cause Antonius wronged his wife,
Which could not be decided but by sword;
Great Cleopatra's beauty and defects   215
Did work Octavia's wrong, and his neglects.

What fruit did yield that fair forbidden tree,
But blood, dishonour, infamy and shame?
Poor blinded queen, could'st thou no better see
But entertain disgrace instead of fame?   220
Do these designs with majesty agree?
To stain thy blood, and blot thy royal name.
That heart that gave consent unto this ill
Did give consent that thou thyself should'st kill.

Fair Rosamund,[43] the wonder of her time,   225
Had been much fairer, had she not been fair;
Beauty betrayed her thoughts aloft to climb,
To build strong castles in uncertain air,
Where th'infection of a wanton crime
Did work her fall; first poison, then despair,   230
With double death did kill her perjured soul,
When heavenly justice did her sin control.

Holy Matilda[44] in a hapless hour
Was born to sorrow and to discontent,
Beauty the cause that turned her sweet to sour, 235
While chastity sought folly to prevent.
Lustful King John refused, did use his power,
By fire and sword, to compass his content;
But friends' disgrace, nor father's banishment,
Nor death itself could purchase her consent. 240

Here beauty in the height of all perfection,
Crowned this fair creature's everlasting fame,
Whose noble mind did scorn the base subjection
Of fears or favours to impair her name;
By heavenly grace she had such true direction 245
To die with honour, not to live in shame;
And drink that poison with a cheerful heart
That could all heavenly grace to her impart.

This grace, great lady,[45] doth possess thy soul,
And makes thee pleasing in thy maker's sight; 250
This grace doth all imperfect thoughts control,
Directing thee to serve thy God aright;
Still reckoning him the husband of thy soul,
Which is most precious in his glorious sight,
Because the world's delights she doth deny 255
For him who for her sake vouchsafed to die.

And dying made her dowager of all;
Nay more; co-heir of that eternal bliss
That angels lost, and we by Adam's fall,
Mere castaways, raised by a Judas-kiss, 260
Christ's bloody sweat, the vinegar and gall,
The spear, sponge, nails, his buffeting with fists,
His bitter passion, agony and death
Did gain us heaven, when he did lose his breath.

These high deserts invites my lowly muse[46] 265
To write of him, and pardon crave of thee.

For time so spent I need make no excuse,
Knowing it doth with thy fair mind agree
So well, as thou no labour will refuse
That to thy holy love may pleasing be;
His death and passion I desire to write,
And thee to read the blessed soul's delight.

But my dear muse, now whither wouldst thou fly
Above the pitch of thy appointed strain?
With Icarus thou seekest now to try,
Not waxen wings, but thy poor barren brain,
Which far too weak, these silly lines descry;
Yet cannot this thy forward mind restrain,
But thy poor infant verse must soar aloft,
Not fearing threat'ning dangers happening oft.

Think when the eye of wisdom shall discover
Thy weakling muse to fly, that scarce could creep,
And in the air above the clouds to hover,
When better 'twere mewed up, and fast asleep;
They'll think with Phaeton thou canst ne'er recover,
But helpless with that poor young lad to weep,
The little world of thy weak wit on fire,
Where thou wilt perish in thine own desire.

But yet the weaker thou dost seem to be
In sex or sense, the more his glory shines,
That doth infuse such powerful grace in thee
To show thy love in these few humble lines;
The widow's mite, with this may well agree
Her little all more worth than golden mines,
Being more dearer to our loving Lord,
Than all the wealth that kingdoms could afford.

Therefore I humbly for his grace will pray,
That he will give me power and strength to write,
That what I have begun, so end I may,

As his great glory may appear more bright; 300
Yea in these lines I may no further stray,
Than his most holy spirit shall give me light;
That blindest weakness be not overbold,
The manner of his passion to unfold.

In other phrases than may well agree 305
With his pure doctrine and most holy writ,
That heaven's clear eye and all the world may see
I seek his glory rather than to get
The vulgar's breath, the seed of vanity,
Nor fame's loud trumpet care I to admit; 310
But rather strive in plainest words to show
The matter which I seek to undergo.

A matter far beyond my barren skill,
To show with any life this map of death,
This story, that whole worlds with books would fill, 315
In these few lines, will put me out of breath,
To run so swiftly up this mighty hill,
I may behold it with the eye of faith;
But to present this pure unspotted lamb,
I must confess I far unworthy am. 320

Yet if he please t'illuminate my spirit,
And give me wisdom from his holy hill,
That I may write part of his glorious merit,
If he vouchsafe to guide my hand and quill,
To show his death, by which we do inherit 325
Those endless joys that all our hearts do fill;
Then will I tell of that sad black-faced night
Whose mourning mantle covered heavenly light.

That very night our saviour was betrayed,[47]
Oh night! exceeding all the nights of sorrow, 330
When our most blessed Lord, although dismayed,
Yet would not he one minute's respite borrow,

But to Mount Olives went, though sore afraid,
To welcome night, and entertain the morrow;
And as he oft unto that place did go, 335
So did he now, to meet his long-nursed woe.

He told his dear disciples that they all
Should be offended by him that self night;
His grief was great, and theirs could not be small,
To part from him, who was their sole delight; 340
Saint Peter thought his faith could never fall,
No mote could happen in so clear a sight;
Which made him say, though all men were offended,
Yet would he never, though his life were ended.

But his dear Lord made answer, that before 345
The cock did crow, he should deny him thrice;
This could not choose but grieve him very sore,
That his hot love should prove more cold than ice,
Denying him he did so much adore;
No imperfection in himself he spies 350
But sayeth again, with him he'll surely die
Rather than his dear master once deny.

And all the rest (did likewise say the same)
Of his disciples at that instant time;
But yet poor Peter, he was most to blame, 355
That thought above them all by faith to climb;
His forward speech inflicted sin and shame
When wisdom's eyes did look and check his crime,
Who did foresee, and told it him before,
Yet would he needs aver it more and more. 360

Now went our Lord unto that holy place,
Sweet Gethsemaine, hallowed by his presence,
That blessed garden, which did now embrace
His holy corpse, yet could make no defence
Against those vipers, objects of disgrace, 365

Which sought that pure eternal love to quench.
Here his disciples willed he to stay
Whilst he went further, where he meant to pray.

None were admitted with their Lord to go,
But Peter and the sons of Zebedeus;   370
To them good Jesus opened all his woe,
He gave them leave his sorrows to discuss,
His deepest griefs he did not scorn to show
These three dear friends, so much he did entrust.
Being sorrowful, and overcharged with grief,   375
He told it them, yet looked for no relief.

Sweet Lord, how couldst thou thus to flesh and blood
Communicate thy grief? Tell of thy woes?
Thou knew'st they had no power to do thee good
But were the cause thou must endure these blows, 380
Being the scorpions bred in Adam's mud
Whose poisoned sins did work among thy foes
To re-o'ercharge thy overburdened soul,
Although the sorrows now they do condole.

Yet didst thou tell them of thy troubled state,   385
Of thy soul's heaviness unto the death,
So full of love, so free wert thou from hate,
To bid them stay, whose sins did stop thy breath,
When thou wert entering at so strait a gate,
Yea, entering even into the door of death,   390
Thou bidst them tarry there, and watch with thee,
Who from thy precious bloodshed were not free.

Bidding them tarry, thou didst further go,
To meet affliction in such graceful sort
As might move pity both in friend and foe,   395
Thy sorrows such, as none could them comport;
Such great endurements who did ever know,
When to th'Almighty thou didst make resort?

And falling on thy face didst humbly pray,
If 'twere his will that cup might pass away.

Saying, not my will, but thy will Lord be done.
When as thou prayedst, an angel did appear
From heaven, to comfort thee God's only son,
That thou thy sufferings might'st the better bear,
Being in an agony, thy glass near run,
Thou prayedst more earnestly, in so great fear,
That precious sweat came trickling to the ground
Like drops of blood thy senses to confound.

Lo, here his will, not thy will, Lord, was done
And thou content to undergo all pains,
Sweet lamb of God, his dear beloved son,
By this great purchase, what to thee remains?
Of heaven and earth thou hast a kingdom won,
Thy glory being equal with thy gains,
In ratifying God's promise on th'earth,
Made many hundred years before thy birth.

But now returning to thy sleeping friends
That could not watch one hour for love of thee,
Even those three friends, which on thy grace depends,
Yet shut those eyes that should their maker see;
What colour, what excuse or what amends
From thy displeasure now can set them free?
Yet thy pure piety bids them watch and pray,
Lest in temptation they be led away.

Although the spirit was willing to obey,
Yet what great weakness in the flesh was found!
They slept in ease, whilst thou in pain didst pray;
Lo, they in sleep, and thou in sorrow drowned;
Yet God's right hand was unto thee a stay,
When horror, grief and sorrow did abound;
His angel did appear from heaven to thee
To yield thee comfort in extremity.

But what could comfort then thy troubled mind
When heaven and earth were both against thee bent?
And thou no hope, no ease, no rest could'st find   435
But must restore that life, which was but lent;
Was ever creature in the world so kind
But he that from eternity was sent?
To satisfy for many worlds of sin,
Whose matchless torments did but then begin.   440

If one man's sin doth challenge death and hell
With all the torments that belong thereto;
If for one sin such plagues on David fell
As grieved him, and did his seed undo;
If Solomon, for that he did not well,   445
Falling from grace, did lose his kingdom too;
Ten tribes being taken from his wilful son
And sin the cause that they were all undone.

What could thy innocency now expect,
When all the sins that ever were committed   450
Were laid to thee, whom no man could detect?
Yet far thou wert of man from being pitied,
The judge so just could yield thee no respect,
Nor would one jot of penance be remitted,
But greater horror to thy soul must rise,   455
Than heart can think or any wit devise.

Now draws the hour of thy affliction near,
And ugly death presents himself before thee;
Thou now must leave those friends thou held'st so dear,
Yea, those disciples, who did most adore thee;   460
Yet in thy countenance doth no wrath appear,
Although betrayed to those that did abhor thee;
Thou did'st vouchsafe to visit them again
Who had no apprehension of thy pain.

Their eyes were heavy, and their hearts asleep,   465
Nor knew they well what answer then to make thee;

Yet thou as watchman had'st a care to keep
Those few from sin, that shortly would forsake thee;
But now thou bidst them henceforth rest and sleep,
Thy hour is come, and they at hand to take thee; 470
The son of God to sinners made a prey,
O hateful hour! O blest! O cursed day!

Lo, here thy great humility was found,
Being king of heaven, and monarch of the earth,
Yet well content to have thy glory drowned, 475
By being counted of so mean a birth;
Grace, love and mercy did so much abound,
Thou entertainedst the cross, even to the death;
And nam'dst thyself the son of man to be
To purge our pride by thy humility. 480

But now thy friends whom thou didst call to go,
Heavy spectators of thy hapless case,
See thy betrayer, whom too well they know,
One of the twelve, now object of disgrace,
A trothless traitor, and a mortal foe, 485
With feigned kindness seeks thee to embrace,
And gives a kiss, whereby he may deceive thee,
That in the hands of sinners he might leave thee.

Now muster forth with swords, with staves, with bills,
High priests and scribes, and elders of the land, 490
Seeking by force to have their wicked wills,
Which thou didst never purpose to withstand;
Now thou mak'st haste unto the worst of ills,
And who they seek, thou gently dost demand;
This didst thou Lord, t'amaze these fools the more, 495
T'enquire of that thou knew so well before.

When lo, these monsters did not shame to tell,
His name they sought, and found, yet could not know
Jesus of Nazareth, at whose feet they fell

When heavenly wisdom did descend so low 500
To speak to them; they knew they did not well,
Their great amazement made them backward go;
Nay, though he said unto them, 'I am he',
They could not know him whom their eyes did see.

How blind were they could not discern the light! 505
How dull! if not to understand the truth,
How weak! if meekness overcame their might;
How stony-hearted, if not moved to ruth;
How void of pity, and how full of spite,
'Gainst him that was the lord of light and truth; 510
Here insolent boldness checked by love and grace
Retires, and falls before our maker's face.

For when he spake to this accursed crew,
And mildly made them know that it was he;
Presents himself, that they might take a view; 515
And what they doubted they might clearly see;
Nay more, to reassure that it was true,
He said: 'I say unto you, I am he';
If him they sought, he's willing to obey,
Only desires the rest might go their way. 520

Thus with a heart prepared to endure
The greatest wrongs impiety could devise,
He was content to stoop unto their lure,
Although his greatness might do otherwise;
Here grace was seized on with hands impure 525
And virtue now must be suppressed by vice,
Pure innocency made a prey to sin,
Thus did his torments and our joys begin.

Here fair obedience shined in his breast,
And did suppress all fear of future pain; 530
Love was his leader unto this unrest,
Whilst righteousness doth carry up his train;

Mercy made way to make us highly blest,
When patience beat down sorrow, fear and pain;
Justice sat looking with an angry brow,   535
On blessed misery appearing now.

More glorious than all the conquerors
That ever lived within this earthly round;
More powerful than all the kings or governors
That ever yet within this world were found;   540
More valiant than the greatest soldiers
That ever fought to have their glory crowned;
For which of them that ever yet took breath,
Sought t'endure the doom of heaven and earth?

But our sweet saviour whom these Jews did name,   545
Yet could their learned ignorance apprehend
No light of grace to free themselves from blame;
Zeal, laws, religion now they do pretend
Against the truth, untruths they seek to frame;
Now all their powers, their wits, their strengths they bend   550
Against one silly, weak, unarmed man,
Who no resistance makes, though much he can,

To free himself from these unlearned men
Who called him saviour in his blessed name;
Yet far from knowing him their saviour then,   555
That came to save both them and theirs from blame;
Though they retire and fall, they come again
To make a surer purchase of their shame;
With lights and torches now they find the way
To take the shepherd whilst the sheep do stray.   560

Why should unlawful actions use the light?
Iniquity in darkness seeks to dwell;
Sin rides his circuit in the dead of night,
Teaching all souls the ready ways to hell;
Satan comes armed with all the powers of spite,   565

Heartens his champions, makes them rude and fell,
Like ravening wolves, to shed his guiltless blood
Who thought no harm, but died to do them good.

Here falsehood bears the show of formal right,
Base treachery has got a guard of men;   570
Tyranny attends, with all his strength and might,
To lead this silly lamb to lion's den;
Yet he unmoved in this most wretched plight
Goes on to meet them, knows the hour, and when;
The power of darkness must express God's ire,   575
Therefore to save these few was his desire.

These few that wait on poverty and shame
And offer to be sharers in his ills;
These few that will be spreaders of his fame,
He will not leave to tyrants' wicked wills,   580
But still desires to free them from all blame;
Yet fear goes forward, anger patience kills,
A saint is moved to revenge a wrong,
And mildness does what doth to wrath belong.

For Peter grieved at what might then befall;   585
Yet knew not what to do, nor what to think;
Thought something must be done: now, if at all,
To free his master, that he might not drink
This poisoned draught, far bitterer than gall,
For now he sees him at the very brink   590
Of grisly death, who gins to show his face
Clad in all colours of a deep disgrace.

And now that hand,[48] that never used to fight,
Or draw a weapon in his own defence,
Too forward is, to do his master right,   595
Since of his wrongs he feels so true a sense;
But ah! poor Peter! now thou wantest might,
And he's resolved, with them he will go hence;

Salve Deus Rex Judaeorum

To draw thy sword in such a helpless cause,
Offends thy Lord and is against the laws.

So much he hates revenge, so far from hate,
That he vouchsafes to heal whom thou dost wound;
His paths are peace, with none he holds debate,
His patience stands upon so sure a ground,
To counsel thee, although it comes too late;
Nay to his foes his mercies so abound
That he in pity doth thy will restrain,
And heals the hurt, and takes away the pain.

For willingly he will endure this wrong,
Although his prayers might have obtained such grace,
As to dissolve their plots though ne'er so strong,
And bring these wicked actors in worse case
Than Egypt's king on whom God's plagues did throng,
But that foregoing Scriptures must take place;
If God by prayers had an army sent
Of powerful angels, who could them prevent?

Yet mighty JESUS merely asked, why they
With swords and staves do come as to a thief?
He teaching in the temple day by day
None did offend or give him cause of grief.
Now all are forward, glad is he that may
Give most offence, and yield him least relief;
His hateful foes are ready now to take him,
And all his dear disciples do forsake him.

Those dear disciples that he most did love,
And were attendant at his beck and call,
When trial of affliction came to prove,
They first left him, who now must leave them all.
For they were earth, and he came from above,
Which made them apt to fly, and fit to fall;
Though they protest they never will forsake him,
They do like men, when dangers overtake them.

And he alone is bound to loose us all,
Whom with unhallowed hands they led along,
To wicked Caiphas in the judgement hall, 635
Who studies only how to do him wrong;
High priests and elders, people great and small,
With all reproachful words about him throng;
False witnesses are now called in apace,
Whose trothless tongues must make pale death embrace 640

The beauty of the world, heaven's chiefest glory,
The mirror of martyrs, crown of holy saints,
Love of th'Almighty, blessed angels' story,
Water of life, which none that drinks it faints,
Guide of the just, where all our light we borrow, 645
Mercy of mercies, hearer of complaints,
Triumpher over death, ransomer of sin,
Falsely accused; now his pains begin.

Their tongues do serve him as a passing-bell,
For what they say is certainly believed; 650
So sound a tale unto the judge they tell,
That he of life must shortly be bereaved;
Their share of heaven they do not care to sell,
So his afflicted heart be thoroughly grieved;
They tell his words, though far from his intent, 655
And what his speeches were, not what he meant.

That he God's holy temple could destroy
And in three days could build it up again;
This seemed to them a vain and idle toy;
It would not sink into their sinful brain; 660
Christ's blessed body, all true Christians' joy,
Should die, and in three days revive again:
This did the Lord of heaven and earth endure,
Unjustly to be charged by tongues impure.

And now they do all give attentive care, 665
To hear the answer which he will not make;

The people wonder how he can forbear
And these great wrongs so patiently can take;
But yet he answers not, nor doth he care
Much more he will endure for our sake; 670
Nor can their wisdoms any way discover
Who he should be that proved so true a lover.

To entertain the sharpest pangs of death
And fight a combat in the depth of hell
For wretched worldlings made of dust and earth 675
Whose hardened hearts with pride and malice swell;
In midst of bloody sweat and dying breath
He had compassion on these tyrants fell;
And purchased them a place in heav'n forever
When they his soul and body sought to sever. 680

Sin's ugly mists so blinded had their eyes
That at noon days they could discern no light;
These were those fools that thought themselves so wise,
The Jewish wolves that did our saviour bite;
For now they use all means they can devise 685
To beat down truth, and go against all right;
Yea now they take God's holy name in vain
To know the truth, which truth they do profane.

The chiefest hell-hounds of this hateful crew
Rose up to ask what answer he could make 690
Against those false accusers in his view,
That by his speech they might advantage take;
He held his peace, yet knew they said not true;
No answer would his holy wisdom make,
Till he was charged in his glorious name, 695
Whose pleasure 'twas he should endure this shame.

Then with so mild a majesty he spake,
As they might easily know from whence he came;
His harmless tongue doth no exceptions take,

Nor priests nor people means he now to blame;   700
But answers folly for true wisdom's sake,
Being charged deeply by his powerful name
To tell if Christ the son of God he be,
Who for our sins must die to set us free.

To thee, O Caiphas, does he answer give,   705
That thou hast said, what thou desir'st to know,
And yet thy malice will not let him live,
So much thou art unto thyself a foe;
He speaketh truth, but thou will not believe
Nor canst thou apprehend it to be so;   710
Though he express his glory unto thee,
Thy owly eyes are blind, and cannot see.

Thou rend'st thy clothes instead of thy false heart
And on the guiltless lay'st thy guilty crime;
For thou blasphem'st, and he must feel the smart;   715
To sentence death, thou think'st it now high time;
No witness now thou need'st, for this foul part
Thou to the height of wickedness canst climb,
And give occasion to the ruder sort
To make afflictions, sorrows, follies sport.   720

Now when the dawn of day gins to appear
And all your wicked counsels have an end,
To end his life, that holds you all so dear,
For to that purpose did your studies bend,
Proud Pontius Pilate must the matter hear,   725
To your untruths his ears he now must lend;
Sweet Jesus bound, to him you led away,
Of his most precious blood to make your prey.

Which when that wicked caitiff[49] did perceive,
By whose lewd means he came to this distress;   730
He brought the price of blood he did receive,
Thinking thereby to make his fault seem less,

Salve Deus Rex Judaeorum

And with these priests and elders did it leave;
Confessed his fault, wherein he did transgress;
But when he saw repentance unrespected 735
He hanged himself, of God and man rejected.

By this example, what can be expected
From wicked man, which on the earth doth live?
But faithless dealing, fear of God neglected;
Who for their private gain cares not to sell 740
The innocent blood of God's most dear elected,
As did that caitiff wretch, now damned in hell;
If in Christ's school he took so great a fall,
What will they do that come not there at all?

Now Pontius Pilate is to judge the cause 745
Of faultless Jesus, who before him stands,
Who neither hath offended prince nor laws
Although he now be brought in woeful bands;
O noble governor, make thou yet a pause;
Do not in innocent blood imbrue thy hands, 750
But hear the words of thy most worthy wife[50]
Who sends to thee to beg her saviour's life.

Let barb'rous cruelty far depart from thee,
And in true justice take affliction's part;
Open thine eyes, that thou the truth may'st see; 755
Do not the thing that goes against thy heart;
Condemn not him that must thy saviour be,
But view his holy life, his good desert.
Let not us women glory in men's fall
Who had power given to over-rule us all. 760

Till now your indiscretion sets us free,[51]
And makes our former fault much less appear;
Our mother Eve, who tasted of the tree,
Giving to Adam what she held most dear,
Was simply good, and had no power to see; 765

The after-coming harm did not appear;
The subtle serpent that our sex betrayed,
Before our fall so sure a plot had laid.

That undiscerning ignorance perceived
No guile, or craft that was by him intended; 770
For had she known of what we were bereaved,
To his request she had not condescended.
But she (poor soul) by cunning was deceived,
No hurt therein her harmless heart intended;
For she alleged God's word, which he denies, 775
That they should die, but even as gods, be wise.

But surely Adam cannot be excused;
Her fault though great, yet he was most to blame;
What weakness offered, strength might have refused,
Being lord of all, the greater was his shame; 780
Although the serpent's craft had her abused,
God's holy word ought all his actions frame,
For he was lord and king of all the earth,
Before poor Eve had either life or breath.

Who being framed by God's eternal hand 785
The perfect'st man that ever breathed on earth;
And from God's mouth received that strait command,
The breach whereof he knew was present death;
Yea, having power to rule both sea and land,
Yet with one apple won to lose that breath 790
Which God had breathed in his beauteous face,
Bringing us all in danger and disgrace.

And then to lay the fault on patience back,
That we (poor women) must endure it all;
We know right well he did discretion lack, 795
Being not persuaded thereunto at all.
If Eve did err, it was for knowledge sake;
The fruit being fair persuaded him to fall;

Salve Deus Rex Judaeorum

No subtle serpent's falsehood did betray him,
If he would eat it, who had power to stay him? 800

Not Eve, whose fault was only too much love,
Which made her give this present to her dear,
That what she tasted he likewise might prove,
Whereby his knowledge might become more clear.
He never sought her weakness to reprove, 805
With those sharp words which he of God did hear;
Yet men will boast of knowledge, which he took
From Eve's fair hand, as from a learned book.

If any evil did in her remain,
Being made of him, he was the ground of all; 810
If one of many worlds could lay a stain
Upon our sex, and work so great a fall
To wretched man, by Satan's subtle train,
What will so foul a fault amongst you all?
Her weakness did the serpent's words obey 815
But you in malice God's dear son betray.

Whom, if unjustly you condemn to die,
Her sin was small, to what you do commit;
All mortal sins that do for vengeance cry
Are not to be compared unto it; 820
If many worlds would altogether try
By all their sins the wrath of God to get,
This sin of yours surmounts them all as far
As doth the sun another little star.

Then let us have our liberty again, 825
And challenge to yourselves no sov'reignty;
You came not in the world without our pain,
Make that a bar against your cruelty.
Your fault being greater, why should you disdain
Our being your equals, free from tyranny? 830
If one weak woman simply did offend,
This sin of yours hath no excuse nor end.

To which (poor souls) we never gave consent;
Witness thy wife (O Pilate) speaks for all;
Who did but dream, and yet a message sent, 835
That thou should'st have nothing to do at all
With that just man, which, if thy heart relent,
Why wilt thou be a reprobate with Saul?
To seek the death of him that is so good,
For thy soul's health to shed his dearest blood. 840

Yea, so thou may'st these sinful people please,
Thou art content against all truth and right
To seal this act, that may procure thine ease,
With blood and wrong, with tyranny and might;
The multitude thou seekest to appease 845
By base dejection of this heavenly light,
Demanding which of these that thou should'st loose:
Whether the thief, or Christ, King of the Jews.

Base Barrabas the thief, they all desire,
And thou, more base than he, perform'st their will. 850
Yet when thy thoughts back to themselves retire,
Thou art unwilling to commit this ill.
Oh that thou couldst unto such grace aspire,
That thy polluted lips might never kill
That honour which right judgement ever graces, 855
To purchase shame, which all true worth defaces.

Art thou a judge, and asketh what to do
With one in whom no fault there can be found?
The death of Christ wilt thou consent unto,
Finding no cause, no reason nor no ground? 860
Shall he be scourged, and crucified too?
And must his miseries by thy means abound?
Yet not ashamed to ask what he hath done,
When thine own conscience seeks this sin to shun.

Three times thou ask'st, what evil hath he done? 865
And saist, thou find'st in him no cause of death;

Yet wilt thou chasten God's beloved son,
Although to thee no word of ill he saith?
For wrath must end what malice hath begun,
And thou must yield to stop his guiltless breath. 870
This rude tumultuous rout doth press so sore,
That thou condemnest him thou shouldst adore.

Yet Pilate, this can yield thee no content,
To exercise thine own authority,
But unto Herod he must needs be sent 875
To reconcile thyself by tyranny.
Was this the greatest good in justice meant,
When thou perceiv'st no fault in him to be?
If thou must make thy peace by virtue's fall,
Much better 'twere not to be friends at all. 880

Yet neither thy stern brow, nor his great place,
Can draw an answer from the holy one;
His false accusers, nor his great disgrace,
Nor Herod's scoffs: to him they are all one;
He neither cares, nor fears his own ill case, 885
Though being despised and mocked of every one;
King Herod's gladness gives him little ease,
Neither his anger seeks he to appease.

Yet this is strange, that base impiety
Should yield those robes of honour, which were due, 890
Pure white, to show his great integrity,
His innocency, that all the world might view
Perfection's height in lowest penury,
Such glorious poverty as they never knew;
Purple and scarlet well might him beseem, 895
Whose precious blood must all the world redeem.

And that imperial crown of thorns he wore
Was much more precious than the diadem
Of any king that ever lived before

Or since his time; their honour's but a dream 900
To his eternal glory, being so poor
To make a purchase of that heavenly realm:
Where God with all his angels lives in peace,
No griefs nor sorrows, but all joys increase.

Those royal robes, which they in scorn did give, 905
To make him odious to the common sort,
Yield light of grace to those whose souls shall live
Within the harbour of this heavenly port;
Much do they joy and much more do they grieve,
His death, their life, should make his foes such sport; 910
With sharpest thorns to prick his blessed face,
Our joyful sorrow, and his greater grace.

Three fears at once possessed Pilate's heart:
The first, Christ's innocency, which so plain appears;
The next, that he which now must feel this smart 915
Is God's dear son, for anything he hears;
But that which proved the deepest-wounding dart
Is people's threat'nings, which he so much fears,
That he to Caesar could not be a friend,
Unless he sent sweet JESUS to his end. 920

Now Pilate thou art proved a painted wall,
A golden sepulchre with rotten bones,
From right to wrong, from equity to fall;
If none upbraid thee, yet the very stones
Will rise against thee, and in question call 925
His blood, his tears, his sighs, his bitter groans;
All these will witness at the latter day
When water cannot wash thy sin away.[52]

Canst thou be innocent, that 'gainst all right
Wilt yield to what thy conscience doth withstand? 930
Being a man of knowledge, power and might,
To let the wicked carry such a hand

Before thy face to blindfold heav'n's bright light,
And thou to yield to what they did demand?
Washing thy hands, thy conscience cannot clear,
But to all worlds this stain must needs appear.

For lo, the guilty does accuse the just,
And faulty judge condemns the innocent,
And wilful Jews to exercise their lust,[53]
With whips and taunts against their Lord are bent;
He basely used, blasphemed, scorned and cursed,
Our heavenly king to death for us they sent;
Reproaches, slanders, spittings in his face,
Spite doing all her worst in his disgrace.

And now this long-expected hour draws near,[54]
When blessed saints with angels do condole;
His holy march, soft pace, and heavy cheer,
In humble sort to yield his glorious soul,
By his deserts the foulest sins to clear,
And in th'eternal book of heaven to enrol
A satisfaction till the general doom,[55]
Of all sins past, and all that are to come.

They that had seen this pitiful procession,
From Pilate's palace to Mount Calvary,
Might think he answered for some great transgression,
Being in such odious sort condemned to die;
He plainly showed that his own profession
Was virtue, patience, grace, love, piety,
And how by suffering he could conquer more
Than all the kings that ever lived before.

First went the crier with open mouth proclaiming,
The heavy sentence of iniquity,
The hangman next, by his base office claiming[56]
His right in hell, where sinners never die,
Carrying the nails, the people still blaspheming

Their maker, using all impiety;
The thieves attending him on either side,
The sergeants watching while the women cried.[57]

Thrice happy women that obtained such grace
From him whose worth the world could not contain, 970
Immmediately to turn about his face
As not remembering his great grief and pain,
To comfort you whose tears poured forth apace
On Flora's banks, like showers of April rain.
Your cries enforced mercy, grace and love 975
From him, whom greatest princes could not move

To speak one word, nor once to lift his eyes[58]
Unto proud Pilate, no nor Herod, king,
By all the questions that they could devise,
Could make him answer to no manner of thing; 980
Yet these poor women, by their piteous cries
Did move their lord, their lover and their king
To take compassion, turn about, and speak
To them whose hearts were ready now to break.

Most blessed daughters of Jerusalem, 985
Who found such favour in your saviour's sight,
To turn his face when you did pity him;
Your tearful eyes beheld his eyes more bright,
Your faith and love unto such grace did climb,
To have reflection from this heav'nly light; 990
Your eagles' eyes did gaze against this sun,
Your hearts did think, he dead, the world were done.

When spiteful men with torments did oppress
Th'afflicted body of this innocent dove,
Poor women seeing how much they did transgress, 995
By tears, by sighs, by cries entreat, nay prove,
What may be done among the thickest press;
They labour still these tyrants' hearts to move,

In pity and compassion to forbear
Their whipping, spurning, tearing of his hair.

But all in vain; their malice hath no end,
Their hearts more hard than flint or marble stone;
Now to his grief, his greatness they attend,
When he (God knows) had rather be alone;
They are his guard, yet seek all means to offend.
Well may he grieve, well may he sigh and groan
Under the burden of a heavy cross;
He faintly goes to make their gain his loss.

His woeful mother, waiting on her son,[59]
All comfortless in depth of sorrow drowned;
Her grief's extreme, although but new begun,
To see his bleeding body oft she swooned;
How could she choose but think herself undone,
He dying, with whose glory she was crowned?
None ever lost so great a loss as she,
Being son and father of eternity.

Her tears did wash away his precious blood,
That sinners might not tread it under feet
To worship him, and that it did her good
Upon her knees, although in open street,
Knowing he was the Jesse flower and bud[60]
That must be gathered when it smelled most sweet:
Her son, her husband, father, saviour, king,
Whose death killed death, and took away his sting.

Most blessed virgin, in whose faultless fruit,
All nations of the earth must needs rejoice,
No creature having sense though ne'er so brute
But joys and trembles when they hear his voice;
His wisdom strikes the wisest persons mute;
Fair chosen vessel, happy in his choice,
Dear mother of our Lord, whose reverend name,
All people blessed call, and spread thy fame.

For the Almighty magnified thee,
And looked down upon thy mean estate;
Thy lowly mind, and unstained chastity, 1035
Did plead for love at great Jehovah's gate,
Who sending swift-winged Gabriel unto thee,
His holy will and pleasure to relate,
To thee most beauteous queen of womankind,
The angel did unfold the maker's mind. 1040

He thus began: 'Hail Mary full of grace,[61]
Thou freely art beloved of the Lord,
He is with thee, behold thy happy case';
What endless comfort did these words afford
To thee that saw'st an angel in the place 1045
Proclaim thy virtue's worth, and to record
Thee blessed among women, that thy praise
Should last so many worlds beyond thy days.

Lo, this high message to thy troubled spirit
He doth deliver in the plainest sense; 1050
Says, 'Thou shouldst bear a son that shall inherit
His father David's throne, free from offence',
Calls him that holy thing, by whose pure merit
We must be saved, tells what he is, of whence,
His worth, his greatness, what his name must be, 1055
Who should be called the son of the most high.

He cheers thy troubled soul, bids thee not fear,
When thy pure thoughts could hardly apprehend
This salutation, when he did appear;
Nor couldst thou judge whereto those words did tend. 1060
His pure aspect did move thy modest cheer
To muse, yet joy that God vouchsafed to send
His glorious angel, who did thee assure
To bear a child, although a virgin pure.

Nay more; thy son should rule and reign for ever; 1065
Yea, of his kingdom there should be no end;

Over the house of Jacob, heaven's great giver
Would give him power, and to that end did send
His faithful servant Gabriel to deliver
To thy chaste ears no word that might offend,   1070
But that this blessed infant born of thee
Thy son, the only son of God should be.

When on the knees of thy submissive heart
Thou humbly didst demand how that should be?
Thy virgin thoughts did think none could impart   1075
This great good hap and blessing unto thee;
Far from desire of any man thou art,
Knowing not one, thou art from all men free;
When he, to answer this thy chaste desire,
Gives thee more cause to wonder and admire.   1080

That thou a blessed virgin should remain,
Yea that the Holy Ghost should come on thee
A maiden mother subject to no pain,
For highest power should overshadow thee;
Could thy fair eyes from tears of joy refrain   1085
When God looked down upon thy poor degree?
Making thee servant, mother, wife and nurse
To heaven's bright king, that freed us from the curse.

Thus being crowned with glory from above,
Grace and perfection resting in thy breast,   1090
Thy humble answer doth approve thy love,
And all these sayings in thy heart do rest;
Thy child a lamb, and thou a turtle-dove,
Above all other women highly blest,
To find such favour in his glorious sight,   1095
In whom thy heart and soul do most delight.

What wonder in the world more strange could seem
Than that a virgin could conceive and bear
Within her womb a son, that should redeem

All nations on the earth, and should repair 1100
Our old decays, who in such high esteem
Should prize all mortals, living in his fear,
As not to shun death, poverty and shame,
To save their souls and spread his glorious name.

And partly to fulfil his Father's pleasure, 1105
Whose powerful hand allows it not for strange,
If he vouchsafe the riches of his treasure,
Pure righteousness to take such ill exchange;
On all iniquity to make a seizure,
Giving his snow-white weed for ours in change, 1110
Our mortal garment in a scarlet dye,
Too base a robe for immortality.

Most happy news that ever yet was brought,
When poverty and riches met together,
The wealth of heaven, in our frail clothing wrought 1115
Salvation by his happy coming hither;
Mighty Messiah, who so dearly bought
Us slaves to sin, far lighter than a feather,
Tossed to and fro with every wicked wind,
The world, the flesh or devil gives to blind. 1120

Who on his shoulders our black sins doth bear
To that most blessed yet accursed cross;
Where fastening them, he rids us of our fear,
Yea, for our gain he is content with loss,
Our ragged clothing scorns he not to wear, 1125
Though foul, rent, torn, disgraceful, rough and gross,
Spun by that monster sin, and weaved by shame,
Which grace itself disgraced with impure blame.

How canst thou choose (fair virgin) then but mourn
When this sweet offspring of thy body dies, 1130
When thy fair eyes beholds his body torn,
The people's fury, hears the women's cries,

His holy name profaned, he made a scorn,
Abused with all their hateful slanderous lies,
Bleeding and fainting in such wondrous sort   1135
As scarce his feeble limbs can him support.

Now Simon of Cyrene passeth them by,
Whom they compel sweet JESUS' cross to bear
To Golgotha, there do they mean to try
All cruel means to work in him despair;   1140
That odious place, where dead men's skulls did lie,
There must our Lord for present death prepare;
His sacred blood must grace that loathsome field,
To purge more filth than that foul place could yield.

For now arrived unto this hateful place,[62]   1145
In which his cross erected needs must be,
False hearts and willing hands come on apace,
All pressed to ill, and all desire to see;
Graceless themselves, still seeking to disgrace,
Bidding him, if the son of God he be,   1150
To save himself, if he could others save,
With all th'opprobrious words that might deprave.

His harmless hands unto the cross they nailed,
And feet that never trod in sinner's trace,
Between two thieves, unpitied, unbewailed,   1155
Save of some few possessors of his grace,
With sharpest pangs and terrors thus appalled,
Stern death makes way, that life might give him place;
His eyes with tears, his body full of wounds,
Death last of pains his sorrows all confounds.   1160

His joints disjointed and his legs hang down,
His alabaster breast, his bloody side,
His members torn, and on his head a crown
Of sharpest thorns, to satisfy for pride;
Anguish and pain do all his senses drown,   1165

While they his holy garments do divide,
His bowels dry, his heart full fraught with grief,
Crying to him that yields him no relief.

This with the eye of faith thou mayst behold,[63]
Dear spouse of Christ, and more than I can write; 1170
And here both grief and joy thou mayst unfold,
To view thy love in this most heavy plight,
Bowing his head, his bloodless body cold,
Those eyes wax dim that gave us all our light,
His count'nance pale, yet still continues sweet, 1175
His blessed blood watering his pierced feet.

O glorious miracle without compare!
Last, but not least which was by him effected;
Uniting death, life, misery, joy and care,
By his sharp passion in his dear elected; 1180
Who doth the badges of like liveries wear,
Shall find how dear they are of him respected.
No joy, grief, pain, life, death, was like to his,
Whose infinite dolours wrought eternal bliss.

What creature on the earth did then remain[64] 1185
On whom the horror of this shameful deed
Did not inflict some violent touch or strain,
To see the Lord of all the world to bleed?
His dying breath did rend huge rocks in twain,
The heavens betook them to their mourning weed, 1190
The sun grew dark, and scorned to give them light
Who durst eclipse a glory far more bright.

The moon and stars did hide themselves for shame,
The earth did tremble in her loyal fear,[65]
The temple veil did rent to spread his fame, 1195
The monuments did open everywhere,
Dead saints did rise forth of their graves, and came
To diverse people that remained there

Salve Deus Rex Judaeorum

Within that holy city, whose offence
Did put their maker to this large expense.   1200

Things reasonable, and reasonless possessed
The terrible impression of this fact;
For his oppression made them all oppressed,
When with his blood he sealed so fair an act,
In restless misery to procure our rest.   1205
His glorious deeds that dreadful prison sacked,
When death, hell, devils using all their power,
Were overcome in that most blessed hour.

Being dead, he killed death, and did survive
That proud insulting tyrant, in whose place   1210
He sends bright immortality to revive
Those whom his iron arms did long embrace;
Who from their loathsome graves brings them alive
In glory to behold their saviour's face,
Who took the keys of all death's power away,   1215
Opening to those that would his name obey.

O wonder, more than man can comprehend,
Our joy and grief both at one instant framed,
Compounded; contrarieties contend
Each to exceed, yet neither to be blamed: 1220
Our grief to see our saviour's wretched end,
Our joy to know both death and hell he tamed,
That we may say: 'O death where is thy sting?
Hell, yield thy victory to thy conquering king'.

Can stony hearts refrain from shedding tears,   1225
To view the life and death of this sweet saint?
His austere course in young and tender years
When great endurements could not make him faint;
His wants, his pains, his torments and his fears,
All which he undertook without constraint,   1230
To show that infinite goodness must restore
What infinite justice looked for, and more.

Yet had he been but of a mean degree,
His sufferings had been small to what they were;
Mean minds will show of what mean moulds they be;   1235
Small griefs seem great, yet use doth make them bear;
But ah! 'tis hard to stir a sturdy tree;
Great dangers hardly put great minds in fear:
They will conceal their gifts which mighty grow
In their stout hearts until they overflow.   1240

If then an earthly prince may ill endure
The least of those afflictions which he bare,
How could this all-commanding king procure
Such grievous torments with his mind to square,
Legions of angels being at his lure?   1245
He might have lived in pleasure without care;
None can conceive the bitter pains he felt
When God and man must suffer without guilt.

Take all the sufferings thoughts can think upon,
In every man that this huge world hath bred;   1250
Let all those pains and sufferings meet in one,
Yet are they not a mite to that he did
Endure for us. Oh, let us think thereon,
That God should have his precious blood to shed,
His greatness clothed in our frail attire   1255
And pay so dear a ransom for the hire.

Lo, here was glory, misery, life and death,
An union of contraries did accord;
Gladness and sadness here had one berth.
This wonder wrought the passion of our Lord,   1260
He suffering for all the sins of all th'earth.
No satisfaction could the world afford,
But this rich jewel, which from God was sent
To call all those that would in time repent.

Which I present (dear lady) to your view,   1265
Upon the cross deprived of life or breath,

To judge if ever lover were so true,
To yield himself unto such shameful death.
Now blessed Joseph doth both beg and sue,[66]
To have his body who possessed his faith, 1270
And thinks, if he this small request obtains,
He wins more wealth than in the world remains.

Thus honourable Joseph is possessed,
Of what his heart and soul so much desired,
And now he goes to give that body rest, 1275
That all his life with griefs and pains was tired;
He finds a tomb, a tomb most rarely blest,
In which was never creature yet interred.
There this most precious body he encloses,
Embalmed and decked with lilies and with roses. 1280

Lo, here the beauty of heav'n and earth is laid,
The purest colours underneath the sun,
But in this place he cannot long be stayed,
Glory must end what horror hath begun;
For he the fury of the heavens obeyed, 1285
And now he must possess what he has won;
The Marys do with precious balms attend,[67]
But being come, they find it to no end.

For he is ris'n from Death t'eternal life,[68]
And now those precious ointments he desires 1290
Are brought unto him by his faithful wife
The holy church; who in those rich attires
Of patience, love, long-suffering, void of strife,
Humbly presents those ointments he requires:
The oils of mercy, charity and faith, 1295
She only gives that which no other hath.

These precious balms do heal his grievous wounds,[69]
And water of compunction washeth clean
The sores of sins, which in our souls abounds;

So fair it heals, no scar is ever seen, 1300
Yet all the glory unto Christ redounds,
His precious blood is that which must redeem;
Those well may make us lovely in his sight
But cannot save without his powerful might.

This is that bridegroom that appears so fair, 1305
So sweet, so lovely in his spouse's sight,
That unto snow we may his face compare,
His cheeks like scarlet, and his eyes so bright
As purest doves that in the rivers are,
Washed with milk, to give the more delight; 1310
His head is likened to the finest gold,
His curled locks so beauteous to behold,

Black as a raven in her blackest hue,
His lips like scarlet threads, yet much more sweet
Than is the sweetest honey-dropping dew 1315
Or honeycombs, where all the bees do meet;
Yea, he is constant, and his words are true;
His cheeks are beds of spices, flowers sweet,
His lips like lilies, dropping down pure myrrh,
Whose love before all worlds we do prefer. 1320

Ah! give me leave (good lady) now to leave[70]
This task of beauty which I took in hand;
I cannot wade so deep, I may deceive
Myself, before I can attain the land;
Therefore (good madam) in your heart I leave 1325
His perfect picture, where it still shall stand,
Deeply engraved in that holy shrine,
Environed with love and thoughts divine.

There you may see him as a God in glory,
And as a man in miserable case; 1330
There may you read his true and perfect story,
His bleeding body there you may embrace,

Salve Deus Rex Judaeorum

And kiss his dying cheeks with tears of sorrow,
With joyful grief you may entreat for grace;
And all your prayers and all your alms-deeds 1335
May bring to stop his cruel wounds that bleeds.

Oft times hath he made trial of your love,
And in your faith hath took no small delight,
By crosses and afflictions he doth prove,
Yet still your heart remaineth firm and right, 1340
Your love so strong, as nothing can remove,
Your thoughts being placed on him both day and night,
Your constant soul doth lodge between his breasts,[71]
This sweet of sweets, in which all glory rests.

Sometime he appears to thee in shepherd's weed 1345
And so presents himself before thine eyes,
A good old man, that goes his flocks to feed;
Thy colour changes, and thy heart doth rise;
Thou call'st, he comes; thou find'st 'tis he indeed,
Thy soul conceives that he is truly wise, 1350
Nay more, desires that he may be the book,
Whereon thine eyes continually may look.

Sometime imprisoned, naked, poor and bare,
Full of diseases, impotent and lame,
Blind, deaf and dumb, he comes unto his fair, 1355
To see if yet she will remain the same;
Nay, sick and wounded, now thou dost prepare
To cherish him in thy dear lover's name;
Yea, thou bestow'st all pains, all cost, all care
That may relieve him, and his health repair. 1360

These works of mercy are so sweet, so dear
To him that is the Lord of life and love,
That all thy prayers he vouchsafes to hear
And sends his Holy Spirit from above;
Thy eyes are opened, and thou seest so clear, 1365

No worldly thing can thy fair mind remove;
Thy faith, thy prayers, and his special grace
Doth open heaven, where thou behold'st his face.

These are those keys Saint Peter did possess,
Which with a spiritual power are giv'n to thee,   1370
To heal the souls of those that do transgress,
By thy fair virtues; which, if once they see,
Unto the like they do their minds address,
Such as thou art, such they desire to be:
If they be blind, thou giv'st to them their sight,   1375
If deaf or lame, they hear and go upright.

Yea, if possessed with any evil spirits,
Such power thy fair examples have obtained
To cast them out, applying Christ's pure merits,
By which they are bound, and of all hurt restrained;   1380
If strangely taken, wanting sense or wits,
Thy faith applied unto their souls so pained,
Healeth all griefs, and makes them grow so strong,
As no defects can hang upon them long.

Thou being thus rich, no riches dost respect,   1385
Nor dost thou care for any outward show;
The proud that do fair virtue's rules neglect,
Desiring place, thou sittest them below;
All wealth and honour thou dost quite reject,
If thou perceiv'st that once it proves a foe   1390
To virtue, learning and the powers divine,
Thou may'st convert, but never wilt incline

To foul disorder, or licentiousness,
But in thy modest veil dost sweetly cover
The stains of other sins, to make themselves,   1395
That by this means thou may'st in time recover
Those weak lost sheep that did so long transgress,
Presenting them unto thy dearest lover,

Salve Deus Rex Judaeorum

That when he brings them back into his fold,
In their conversion then he may behold 1400

Thy beauty shining brighter than the sun,
Thine honour more than ever monarch gained,
Thy wealth exceeding his that kingdoms won,
Thy love unto his spouse, thy faith unfeigned,
Thy constancy in what thou hast begun, 1405
Till thou his heavenly kingdom have obtained,
Respecting worldly wealth to be but dross,
Which if abused, doth prove the owner's loss.

Great Cleopatra's love to Antony,
Can no way be compared unto thine; 1410
She left her love in his extremity,
When greatest need should cause her to combine
Her force with his, to get the victory;
Her love was earthly and thy love divine;
Her love was only to support her pride, 1415
Humility thy love and thee doth guide.

That glorious part of death, which last she played,
T'appease the ghost of her deceased love,
Had never needed, if she could have stayed
When his extremes made trial and did prove 1420
Her leaden love unconstant and afraid;
Their wicked wars the wrath of God might move
To take revenge for chaste Octavia's wrongs,
Because she enjoys what unto her belongs.

No Cleopatra, though thou wert as fair 1425
As any creature in Antonius' eyes;
Yea, though thou wert as rich, as wise, as rare
As any pen could write, or wit devise;
Yet with this lady canst thou not compare,
Whose inward virtues all thy worth denies; 1430
Yet thou a black Egyptian dost appear
Thou false, she true, and to her love more dear.

She sacrificeth to her dearest love,
With flowers of faith, and garlands of good deeds;
She flies not from him when afflictions prove, 1435
She bears his cross, and stops his wounds that bleeds;
She loves and lives chaste as the turtle dove,
She attends upon him, and his flock she feeds;
Yea, for one touch of death which thou did'st try,
A thousand deaths she every day doth die. 1440

Her virtuous life exceeds thy worthy death,
Yea, she hath richer ornaments of state,
Shining more glorious than in dying breath
Thou didst, when either pride or cruel fate
Did work thee to prevent a double death; 1445
To stay the malice, scorn and cruel hate
Of Rome, that joyed to see thy pride pulled down,
Whose beauty wrought the hazard of her crown.

Good madam, though your modesty be such
Not to acknowledge what we know and find, 1450
And that you think these praises overmuch,
Which do express the beauty of your mind;
Yet pardon me, although I give a touch
Unto their eyes, that else would be so blind,
As not to see thy store, and their own wants, 1455
From whose fair seeds of virtue spring these plants.

And know, when first into this world I came,
This charge was giv'n me by th'eternal powers,
Th'everlasting trophy of thy fame,
To build and deck it with the sweetest flowers 1460
That virtue yields; then, madam, do not blame
Me, when I show the world but what is yours,
And deck you with that crown which is your due,
That of heav'n's beauty earth may take a view.

Though famous women elder times have known, 1465
Whose glorious actions did appear so bright,

Salve Deus Rex Judaeorum

That powerful men by them were overthrown,
And all their armies overcome in fight.
The Scythian women by their power alone[72]
Put king Darius unto shameful flight; 1470
All Asia yielded to their conquering hand,
Great Alexander could not their power withstand,

Whose worth, though writ in lines of blood and fire,
Is not to be compared unto thine;
Their power was small to overcome desire, 1475
Or to direct their ways by virtue's line;
Were they alive, they would thy life admire,
And unto thee their honours would resign;
For thou a greater conquest dost obtain,
Than they who have so many thousands slain. 1480

Wise Deborah that judged Israel,
Nor valiant Judith cannot equal thee;
Unto the first, God did his will reveal,
And gave her power to set his people free;
Yea, Judith had the power likewise to quell 1485
Proud Holofernes, that the just might see
What small defence vain pride and greatness hath
Against the weapons of God's word and faith.

But thou far greater war dost still maintain.
Against that many-headed monster sin, 1490
Whose mortal sting hath many thousand slain,
And every day fresh combats do begin;
Yet cannot all his venom lay one stain
Upon thy soul; thou dost the conquest win,
Though all the world he daily doth devour, 1495
Yet over thee he never could get power.

For that one worthy deed by Deborah done,
Thou hast performed many in thy time;
For that one conquest that fair Judith won,

By which she did the steps of honour climb,   1500
Thou hast the conquest of all conquests won,
When to thy conscience hell can lay no crime;
For that one head that Judith bore away,
Thou tak'st from sin a hundred heads a day.

Though virtuous Hester fasted three days' space,   1505
And spent her time in prayers all that while,
That by God's power she might obtain such grace
That she and hers might not become a spoil
To wicked Haman, in whose crabbed face
Was seen the map of malice, envy, guile,   1510
Her glorious garments though she put apart,
So to present a pure and single heart

To God, in sackcloth, ashes, and with tears;
Yet must fair Hester needs give place to thee,
Who hath continued days, weeks, months and years   1515
In God's true service, yet thy heart being free
From doubt of death, or any other fears;
Fasting from sin, thou pray'st thine eyes may see
Him that hath full possession of thine heart,
From whose sweet love thy soul can never part.   1520

His love, not fear, makes thee to fast and pray,
No kinsman's counsel needs thee to advise;
The sackcloth thou dost wear both night and day,
Is worldly troubles, which thy rest denies;
The ashes are the vanities that play   1525
Over thy head, and steal before thine eyes,
Which thou shak'st off when mourning time is past,
That royal robes thou may'st put on at last.

Joachim's wife, that fair and constant dame,[73]
Who rather chose a cruel death to die,   1530
Than yield to those two elders void of shame,
When both at once her chastity did try;

Salve Deus Rex Judaeorum

Whose innocency bore away the blame,
Until th'Almighty Lord had heard her cry
And raised the spirit of a child to speak,   1535
Making the powerful judged of the weak;

Although her virtue do deserve to be
Writ by that hand that never purchased blame,
In holy writ, where all the world may see
Her perfect life, and ever-honoured name;   1540
Yet was she not to be compared to thee,
Whose many virtues do increase thy fame;
For she opposed against old doting lust,
Who with life's danger she did fear to trust.

But your chaste breast, guarded with strength of mind,   1545
Hates the embracements of unchaste desires;
You loving God, live in yourself confined
From unpure love, your purest thoughts retires,
Your perfect sight could never be so blind,
To entertain the old or young desires   1550
Of idle lovers which the world presents,
Whose base abuses worthy minds prevents.

Even as the constant laurel, always green,[74]
No parching heat of summer can deface,
Nor pinching winter ever yet was seen   1555
Whose nipping frosts could wither, or disgrace;
So you (dear lady) still remain as queen,
Subduing all affections that are base,
Unalterable by the change of times,
Not following, but lamenting others' crimes.   1560

No fear of death, or dread of open shame,
Hinders your perfect heart to give consent;
Nor loathsome age, whom time could never tame
From ill designs, whereto their youth was bent;
But love of God, care to preserve your fame,   1565

And spend that precious time that God hath sent,
In all good exercises of the mind,
Whereto your noble nature is inclined.

That Ethiopian queen did gain great fame,
Who from the southern world did come to see 1570
Great Solomon, the glory of whose name
Had spread itself o'er all the earth, to be
So great that all the princes thither came,
To be spectators of his royalty;
And this fair queen of Sheba came from far, 1575
To reverence this new-appearing star.

From th'utmost part of all the earth she came,
To hear the wisdom of this worthy king,
To try if wonder did agree with fame,
And many fair rich presents did she bring; 1580
Yea, many strange hard questions did she frame,
All which were answered by this famous king,
Nothing was hid that in her heart did rest,
And all to prove this king so highly blest.

Here majesty with majesty did meet, 1585
Wisdom to wisdom yielded true content,
One beauty did another beauty greet,
Bounty to bounty never could repent;
Here all distaste is trodden under feet,
No loss of time, where time was so well spent 1590
In virtuous exercises of the mind,
In which this queen did much contentment find.

Spirits affect where they do sympathize,
Wisdom desires wisdom to embrace,
Virtue covets her like, and doth devise 1595
How she her friends may entertain with grace;
Beauty sometime is pleased to feed her eyes
With viewing beauty in another's face;

Both good and bad in this point do agree,
That each desireth with his like to be.

And this desire did work a strange effect,
To draw a queen forth of her native land,
Not yielding to the niceness and respect
Of womankind; she passed both sea and land,
All fear of danger she did quite neglect,
Only to see, to hear, and understand
That beauty, wisdom, majesty and glory,
That in her heart impressed his perfect story.

Yet this fair map of majesty and might
Was but a figure of thy dearest love,
Born t'express that true and heavenly light
That doth all other joys imperfect prove;
If this fair earthly star did shine so bright,
What doth that glorious sun that is above?[75]
Who wears th'imperial crown of heaven and earth,
And made all Christians blessed in his birth.

If that small spark could yield so great a fire,
As to inflame the hearts of many kings
To come to see, to hear and to admire
His wisdom, tending but to worldly things;
Then much more reason have we to desire
That heav'nly wisdom which salvation brings,
The sun of righteousness, that gives true joys,
When all they sought for were but earthly toys.

No travels ought th'affected soul to shun,
That this fair heavenly light desires to see;
This king of kings to whom we all should run,
To view his glory and his majesty;
He without whom we all had been undone,
He that from sin and death hath set us free,
And overcome Satan, the world and sin,
That by his merits we those joys might win.

Prepared by him, whose everlasting throne
Is placed in heaven, above the starry skies,
Where he that sat was like the jasper stone, 1635
Who rightly knows him shall be truly wise.
A rainbow round about his glorious throne;
Nay more, those winged beasts so full of eyes,
That never cease to glorify his name,
Who was, and will be, and is now the same. 1640

This is that great almighty Lord that made
Both heaven and earth, and lives for evermore;
By him the world's foundation first was laid,
He framed the things that never were before;
The sea within his bounds by him is stayed, 1645
He judgeth all alike, both rich and poor;
All might, all majesty, all love, all law
Remains in him that keeps all worlds in awe.

From his eternal throne the lightning came,
Thunderings and voices did from thence proceed; 1650
And all the creatures glorified his name,
In heaven, in earth, and seas, they all agreed,
When lo, that spotless lamb so void of blame,
That for us died, whose sins did make him bleed;
That true physician that so many heals, 1655
Opened the book and did undo the seals.

He only worthy to undo the book,
Of our charged souls, full of iniquity,
Where with the eyes of mercy he doth look
Upon our weakness and infirmity; 1660
This is that corner stone that was forsook,
Who leaves it, trusts but to uncertainty;
This is God's son, in whom he is well-pleased,
His dear beloved that his wrath appeased.

He that had power to open all the seals, 1665
And summon up our sins of blood and wrong,

Salve Deus Rex Judaeorum

He unto whom the righteous souls appeals,
That have been martyred, and do think it long,
To whom in mercy he his will reveals,
That they should rest a little in their wrong,　　　　1670
Until their fellow-servants should be killed,
Even as they were, and that they were fulfilled.

Pure-thoughted lady, blessed be thy choice[76]
Of this almighty, everlasting king;
In thee his saints and angels do rejoice,　　　　1675
And to their heav'nly Lord do daily sing
Thy perfect praises in their loudest voice;
And all their harps and golden viols bring
Full of sweet odours, even thy holy prayers
Unto that spotless lamb, that all repairs.　　　　1680

Of whom that heathen queen obtained such grace,
By honouring but the shadow of his love,
That great judicial day to have a place,
Condemning those that do unfaithful prove;
Among the hapless, happy is her case,　　　　1685
That her dear saviour spake for her behalf;
And that her memorable act should be
Writ by the hand of true eternity.

Yet this rare phoenix of that worn-out age,
This great majestic queen comes short of thee,　　　　1690
Who to an earthly prince did then engage
Her heart's desires, her love, her liberty,
Acting her glorious part upon a stage
Of weakness, frailty and infirmity;
Giving all honour to a creature, due　　　　1695
To her creator, whom she never knew.

But lo, a greater thou hast sought and found
Than Solomon in all his royalty;
And unto him thy faith most firmly bound

To serve and honour him continually;   1700
That glorious God, whose terror doth confound
All sinful workers of iniquity;
Him hast thou truly served all thy life,
And for his love lived with the world at strife.

To this great Lord thou only art affected,   1705
Yet came he not in pomp or royalty,
But in an humble habit, base, dejected,
A king, a God clad in mortality.
He hath thy love, thou art by him directed,
His perfect path was fair humility;   1710
Who being monarch of heav'n, earth and seas,
Endured all wrongs, yet no man did displease.

Then how much more art thou to be commended
That seek'st thy love in lowly shepherd's weed?
A seeming tradesman's son, of none attended,   1715
Save of a few in poverty and need,
Poor fishermen that on his love attended,
His love that makes so many thousands bleed;
Thus did he come, to try our faiths the more,
Possessing worlds, yet seeming extreme poor.   1720

The pilgrim's travels, and the shepherd's cares,
He took upon him to enlarge our souls,
What pride hath lost, humility repairs,
For by his glorious death he us enrols
In deep characters, writ with blood and tears,   1725
Upon those blessed everlasting scrolls,
His hands, his feet, his body and his face,
Whence freely flowed the rivers of his grace,

Sweet holy rivers, pure celestial springs,
Proceeding from the fountain of our life,   1730
Swift sugared currents that salvation brings,
Clear crystal streams, purging all sin and strife,

Fair floods, where souls do bathe their snow-white wings,
Before they fly to true eternal life,
Sweet nectar, and ambrosia, food of saints, 1735
Which whoso tasteth never after faints.

This honey-dropping dew of holy love,
Sweet milk, wherewith we weaklings are restored,
Who drinks thereof, a world can never move,
All earthly pleasures are of them abhorred; 1740
This love made martyrs many deaths to prove,
To taste his sweetness, whom they so adored,
Sweetness that makes our flesh a burden to us,
Knowing it serves but only to undo us.

His sweetness sweetened all the sour of death 1745
To faithful Stephen his appointed saint,
Who by the river stones did lose his breath,
When pains nor terrors could not make him faint;
So was this blessed martyr turned to earth,
To glorify his soul by death's attaint, 1750
This holy saint was humbled and cast down,
To win in heaven an everlasting crown;

Whose face replete with majesty and sweetness,
Did as an angel unto them appear,
That sat in council hearing his discreetness, 1755
Seeing no change, or any sign of a fear;
But with a constant brow didst there confess
Christ's high deserts, which were to him so dear;
Yea, when these tyrants' storms did most oppress,
Christ did appear to make his grief the less. 1760

For being filled with the Holy Ghost
Up unto heav'n he looked with steadfast eyes,
Where God appeared with his heavenly host
In glory to this saint before he dies;
Although he could no earthly pleasures boast 1765

At God's right hand sweet JESUS he espies;
Bids them behold heaven's open, he doth see
The son of man at God's right hand to be;

Whose sweetness sweetened that short sour of life,
Making all bitterness delight his taste, 1770
Yielding sweet quietness in bitter strife,
And most contentment when he died disgraced,
Heaping up joys where sorrows were most rife;
Such sweetness could not choose but be embraced,
The food of souls, the spirit's only treasure, 1775
The paradise of our celestial pleasure.

This lamb of God, who died and was alive,
Presenting us the bread of life eternal,
His bruised body powerful to revive
Our sinking souls, out of the pit infernal; 1780
For by this blessed food he did contrive
A work of grace, by this his gift external,
With heav'nly manna, food of his elected,
To feed their souls, of whom he is respected.

This wheat of heaven, the blessed angels' bread, 1785
Wherewith he feeds his dear adopted heirs,
Sweet food of life that doth revive the dead,
And from the living takes away all cares;
To taste this sweet Saint Lawrence did not dread
The broiling gridiron cooled with holy tears, 1790
Yielding his naked body to the fire,
To taste this sweetness, such was his desire.

Nay, what great sweetness did th'Apostles taste,
Condemned by council, when they did return,
Rejoicing that for him they died disgraced, 1795
Whose sweetness made their hearts and souls so burn
With holy zeal and love most pure and chaste;
For him they sought from whom they might not turn;

Salve Deus Rex Judaeorum

Whose love made Andrew go most joyfully
Unto the cross, on which he meant to die. 1800

The princes of th'Apostles were so filled
With the delicious sweetness of his grace,
That willingly they yielded to be killed,
Receiving deaths that were most vile and base,
For his name's sake; that all might be fulfilled 1805
They with great joy all torments did embrace;
The ugliest face that death could ever yield,
Could never fear these champions from the field.

They still continued in their glorious fight,
Against the enemies of flesh and blood, 1810
And in God's law did set their whole delight,
Suppressing evil and erecting good;
Not sparing kings in what they did not right,
Their noble acts they sealed with dearest blood;
One chose the gallows, that unseemly death, 1815
The other by the sword did lose his breath.

His head did pay the dearest rate of sin,
Yielding it joyfully unto the sword,
To be cut off as he had never been,
For speaking truth according to God's word, 1820
Telling King Herod of incestuous sin,
That hateful crime of God and man abhorred;
His brother's wife, that proud licentious dame
Cut off his head to take away his shame.

Lo, madam, here you take a view of those 1825
Whose worthy steps you do desire to tread,
Decked in those colours which our Saviour chose,
The purest colours both of white and red;
Their freshest beauties would I fain disclose,
By which our Saviour most was honoured;[77] 1830
But my weak muse deserveth now to rest,
Folding up all their beauties in your breast,

Whose excellence hath raised my spirits to write,
Of what my thoughts could hardly apprehend;
Your rarest virtues did my soul delight;
Great lady of my heart, I must commend
You that appear so fair in all men's sight;
On your deserts my muses do attend;
You are the Arctic star that guides my hand;
All what I am, I rest at your command.

FINIS

The Description of Cooke-ham[78]

Farewell (sweet Cooke-ham) where I first obtained
Grace from that grace where perfect grace remained;
And where the muses gave their full consent,
I should have power the virtuous to content;
Where princely palace willed me to indite   5
The sacred story of the soul's delight.[79]
Farewell (sweet place) where virtue then did rest,
And all delights did harbour in her breast;
Never shall my sad eyes again behold
Those pleasures which my thoughts did then unfold;   10
Yet you (great lady) mistress of that place,
From whose desires did spring this work of grace,
Vouchsafe to think upon these pleasures past
As fleeting, worldly joys that could not last,
Or as dim shadows of celestial pleasures,   15
Which are desired above all earthly treasures.
Oh how (methought) against you thither came
Each part did seem some new delight to frame!
The house received all ornaments to grace it,
And would endure no foulness to deface it.   20
The walks put on their summer liveries,
And all things else did hold like similes:
The trees with leaves, with fruits, with flowers clad,
Embraced each other, seeming to be glad,
Turning themselves to beauteous canopies   25
To shade the bright sun from your brighter eyes;
The crystal streams with silver spangles graced,
While by the glorious sun they were embraced;
The little birds in chirping notes did sing,
To entertain both you and that sweet spring;   30
And Philomela with her sundry lays,
Both you and that delightful place did praise.
Oh, how methought each plant, each flower, each tree
Set forth their beauties then to welcome thee;

The very hills right humbly did descend, 35
When you to tread upon them did intend.
And as you set your feet, they still did rise,
Glad that they could receive so rich a prize.
The gentle winds did take delight to be
Among those woods that were so graced by thee 40
And in sad murmur uttered pleasing sound,
That pleasure in that place might more abound;
The swelling banks delivered all their pride,
When such a phoenix once they had espied.
Each arbour, bank, each seat, each stately tree 45
Thought themselves honoured in supporting thee.
The pretty birds would oft come to attend thee,
Yet fly away for fear they should offend thee;
The little creatures in the burrow by
Would come abroad to sport them in your eye; 50
Yet fearful of the bow in your fair hand
Would run away when you did make a stand.
Now let me come unto that stately tree,
Wherein such goodly prospects you did see;
That oak that did in height his fellows pass, 55
As much as lofty trees, low-growing grass;
Much like a comely cedar, straight and tall,
Whose beauteous stature far exceeded all;
How often did you visit this fair tree,
Which seeming joyful in receiving thee, 60
Would like a palm tree spread his arms abroad,
Desirous that you there should make abode;
Whose fair green leaves much like a comely veil
Defended Phoebus when he would assail;
Whose pleasing boughs did lend a cool fresh air, 65
Joying his happiness when you were there;
Where being seated, you might plainly see
Hills, vales and woods, as if on bended knee
They had appeared, your honour to salute,
Or to prefer some strange unlooked-for suit;[80] 70
All interlaced with brooks and crystal springs,

A prospect fit to please the eyes of kings;
And thirteen shires appear all in your sight,
Europe could not afford much more delight.
What was there then but gave you all content, 75
While you the time in meditation spent,
Of their creator's power, which there you saw
In all his creatures held a perfect law,
And in their beauties did you plain descry
His beauty, wisdom, grace, love, majesty. 80
In these sweet woods how often did you walk
With Christ and his apostles there to talk;
Placing his holy writ in some fair tree,
To meditate what you therein did see;
With Moses you did mount his holy hill, 85
To know his pleasure and perform his will.
With lovely David you did often sing,
His holy hymns to heaven's eternal king.[81]
And in sweet music did your soul delight,
To sound his praises, morning, noon and night. 90
With blessed Joseph you did often feed
Your pined brethren when they stood in need.
And that sweet lady sprung from Clifford's race,[82]
Of noble Bedford's blood, fair stem of grace,
To honourable Dorset now espoused,[83] 95
In whose fair breast true virtue then was housed;
Oh what delight did my weak spirits find
In those pure parts of her well-framed mind;
And yet it grieves me that I cannot be
Near unto her, whose virtues did agree 100
With those fair ornaments of outward beauty,
Which did enforce from all both love and duty.
Unconstant fortune, thou art most to blame,
Who casts us down into so low a frame,
Where our great friends we cannot daily see, 105
So great a difference is there in degree.
Many are placed in those orbs of state,
Parters in honour, so ordained by fate,[84]

Nearer in show, yet farther off in love,
In which the lowest always are above.   110
But whither am I carried in conceit?
My wit too weak to conster of the great.[85]
Why not? although we are but born of earth,
We may behold the heavens, despising death;
And loving heaven that is so far above,   115
May in the end vouchsafe us entire love.
Therefore sweet memory, do thou retain
Those pleasures past, which will not turn again;
Remember beauteous Dorset's summer sports,[86]
So far from being touched by ill reports;   120
Wherein myself did always bear a part,
While reverend love presented my true heart;
Those recreations let me bear in mind,
Which her sweet youth and noble thoughts did find;
Whereof deprived, I evermore must grieve,   125
Hating blind fortune, careless to relieve.
And you, sweet Cooke-ham, whom these ladies leave,
I now must tell the grief you did conceive
At their departure; when they went away,
How everything retained a sad dismay;   130
Nay long before, when once an inkling came,
Methought each thing did unto sorrow frame;
The trees that were so glorious in our view,
Forsook both flowers and fruit, when once they knew
Of your depart, their very leaves did wither,   135
Changing their colours as they grew together.
But when they saw this had no power to stay you,
They often wept, though speechless, could not pray you;
Letting their tears in your fair bosoms fall,
As if they said: 'Why will ye leave us all?'   140
This being vain, they cast their leaves away,
Hoping that pity would have made you stay;
Their frozen tops, like age's hoary hairs,
Shows their disasters, languishing in fears;
A swarthy rivelled rine all overspread[87]   145

Their dying bodies, half-alive, half-dead.
But your occasions called you so away,
That nothing there had power to make you stay;
Yet did I see a noble, grateful mind,
Requiting each according to their kind;   150
Forgetting not to turn and take your leave
Of these sad creatures, powerless to receive
Your favour, when with grief you did depart,
Placing their former pleasures in your heart;
Giving great charge to noble memory,   155
There to preserve their love continually;
But specially the love of that fair tree,
That first and last you did vouchsafe to see;
In which it pleased you oft to take the air,
With noble Dorset, then a virgin fair;   160
Where many a learned book was read and scanned;
To this fair tree, taking me by the hand,
You did repeat the pleasures which had passed,
Seeming to grieve they could no longer last.
And with a chaste, yet loving kiss took leave,   165
Of which sweet kiss I did it soon bereave;
Scorning a senseless creature should possess
So rare a favour, so great happiness.
No other kiss it could receive from me,
For fear to give back what it took of thee;   170
So I ungrateful creature did deceive it,
Of that which you vouchsafed in love to leave it.
And though it oft had giv'n me much content,
Yet this great wrong I never could repent;
But of the happiest made it most forlorn,   175
To show that nothing's free from fortune's scorn,
While all the rest with this most beauteous tree,
Made their sad consort sorrow's harmony.
The flowers that on the banks and walks did grow,
Crept in the ground, the grass did weep for woe.   180
The winds and waters seemed to chide together,
Because you went away, they knew not whither.

And those sweet brooks that ran so fair and clear,
With grief and trouble wrinkled did appear.
Those pretty birds that wonted were to sing, 185
Now neither sing, nor chirp, nor use their wing;
But with their tender feet on some bare spray,
Warble forth sorrow, and their own dismay.
Fair Philomela leaves her mournful ditty,
Drowned in dead sleep, yet can procure no pity; 190
Each arbour, bank, each seat, each stately tree
Looks bare and desolate now, for want of thee;
Turning green tresses into frosty grey,
While in cold grief they wither all away.
The sun grew weak, his beams no comfort gave, 195
While all green things did make the earth their grave;
Each briar, each bramble, when you went away,
Caught fast your clothes, thinking to make you stay;
Delightful Echo, wonted to reply
To our last words, did now for sorrow die; 200
The house cast off each garment that might grace it,
Putting on dust and cobwebs to deface it.
All desolation then there did appear,
When you were going whom they held so dear.
This last farewell to Cooke-ham here I give; 205
When I am dead thy name in this may live,
Wherein I have performed her noble hest,
Whose virtues lodge in my unworthy breast,
And ever shall, so long as life remains,
Tying my heart to her by those rich chains. 210

FINIS

To the doubtful reader

Gentle reader, if thou desire to be resolved, why I give this title, *Salve Deus Rex Judaeorum*, know for certain, that it was delivered unto me in sleep many years before I had any intent to write in this manner, and was quite out of my memory, until I had written the Passion of Christ, when immediately it came into my remembrance, what I had dreamed long before; and thinking it a significant token, that I was appointed to perform this work, I gave the very same words I received in sleep as the fittest title I could devise for this book.

NOTES

[1] STC 15227. Entered in the Stationer's Register on 2 October 1610. This is the unique second Huntingdon copy, probably the first issue, and used here as the copytext. STC 15227.5 has a slightly different title page; the printer's name is set in four lines as AT LONDON/ Printed by Valentine Simmes for Richard Bonian, and are/ to be sold at his shop in Pauls Churchyard, at the/ sign of the Flower de Luce and/ Crown. 1611; in other respects it exactly resembles STC 15227, and it has not been reset except for the title page. All the remaining copies have this title page. On other variations between issues, see Introduction.

[2] Anne of Denmark, wife of James I, and mother of Prince Henry (d. 1612) and the future Charles I. Anne of Denmark was a patron of the arts and a participant in court masques. This allowed her participation in the public sphere, an area otherwise closed to her by the misogyny of the king. Lanyer alludes to these activities in the fourth stanza.

[3] At the judgement of Paris, Paris Prince of Troy was asked to choose the fairest of three godesses (Juno, Pallas Athena and Venus) by awarding a golden apple to one of them. He chose Venus, who had offered him the most beautiful woman in the world as a reward, rejecting Athena's offer of wisdom and Juno's offer of rule. This story was frequently moralized in the Renaissance as a choice between active, contemplative and sensual life.

[4] Court masques frequently compared both Anne and James to figures from classical myth and legend.

[5] See Ben Jonson, *The Masque of Blackness*, 1606.

[6] I.e. the poor.

[7] Lanyer foregrounds the apology for women in her preface to the queen, possibly because she expects Anne to be enthusiastic about a defence of women. 'The text' is the Bible.

[8] 'The Lady Elizabeth's Grace' (note in original); i.e. Elizabeth of Bohemia, daughter of James I and Anne of Denmark, born 1595. See the prefatory poem addressed to her, p. 246.

[9] Elizabeth I; comparisons between Elizabeth of Bohemia and Elizabeth I were common, and Lanyer develops the comparison in the succeeding poem. Lanyer's father Baptista Bassano was a court musician; he died in 1576, and seems never to have performed for Elizabeth I.

[10] This can hardly refer to Anne, who came to England when Lanyer was about 33 years old. It may refer to the Duchess of Kent, since Lanyer refers to the duchess as 'the noble guide of my ungoverned days', or may refer to the Virgin Mary.

[11] Elizabeth of Bohemia, later known as the Winter Queen after the loss of Bohemia in 1620. See Carola Oman, *Elizabeth of Bohemia*, London; Hodder and Stoughton, 1938.

[12] Elizabeth I. See note 9.
[13] 'The robes that Christ wore before his death'; note in text.
[14] 'In token of constancy'; note in text.
[15] Elizium: the Elysian fields. I have retained this spelling because of possible puns on Elizabeth.
[16] Lanyer here makes virtuous ladies into a panoply of saints who can save other women; this is a metaphor for the patronage relation, where the patron's favour can salvage inadequate verse.
[17] Arabella Stuart, born 1575, daughter of the Earl of Lennox, was at the end of Elizabeth's reign next in line to the throne after James VI, later James I. James I remained anxious about her, particularly when she announced her intention of marrying William Seymour, grandson of Lady Catherine Grey, heiress to the throne through the Suffolk line under Henry VIII's will. Having declared that she would not marry William without the king's consent, Arabella finally married him without it and in secret in July 1610; Arabella was imprisoned in the Tower, where she went mad and died in 1615. A highly educated woman, she may have had some protofeminist sympathies which, with her rank, may have prompted Lanyer's dedication. This poem is among the prefatory materials removed from the British Library copy of *Salve Deus*, possibly because of the arrest of Arabella in June 1611. See David N. Durant, *Arabella Stuart: A Rival to the Queen*, London: 1978, and Sara Jayne Steen, 'Fashioning an Acceptable Self: Arbella Stuart', in *Women in the Renaissance: Selections from English Literary Renaissance*, eds. Kirby Farrell, Elizabeth H. Hageman, and Arthur F. Kinney, Amherst: University of Massachusetts Press, 1990, pp. 136–53.
[18] Susan Bertie, married to Reginald Grey, *de jure* Earl of Kent, who died in 1573. In 1581 she married Sir John Wingfield of Withcall, a member of the Leicester-Sidney faction; this marriage may explain why the poem dedicated to her is followed by the poem on Mary Sidney. Lanyer's residence with her, mentioned in the first stanza, must have taken place before Lanyer's own marriage in 1592.
[19] This refers to Susan Bertie's mother's decision to flee England with her family during the reign of the Catholic queen Mary I; Catherine Bertie, Duchess of Suffolk was staunchly Protestant. The terms of the dedication associate Susan with her heroic mother, the Duchess of Suffolk.
[20] The dream-vision form for patronage poetry dates back to Chaucer's *Book of the Duchess*. For another dream-vision of the early seventeenth century by a woman writer, see Rachel Speght, *Mortalities Memorandum*, 1621.
[21] Mary Sidney, Countess of Pembroke, was the sister of Sir Philip Sidney and Robert Sidney of Penshurst, and wife of Henry Herbert, third Earl of Pembroke. She was herself a writer and translator, completing her brother Philip's collection of translations from the Psalms and translating Philippe du Mornay's *Discourse of Life and Death*, Petrarch's *Trionfo della Morte*, and Robert Garnier's French neoclassical tragedy *Marc Antoine*. She was the patron of (among others) Edmund Spenser, Fulke Greville, Thomas Nashe, Gabriel Harvey, Samuel Daniel, Michael Drayton, John Davies of Hereford, Ben Jonson and John Donne. She was a figure of major significance and may have been Lanyer's model of a woman writer, as Lewalski suggests. See Margaret

Patterson Hannay, *Philip's Phoenix: Mary Sidney, Countess of Pembroke*, New York and Oxford: Oxford University Press, 1991; Mary Ellen Lamb, 'The Countess of Pembroke's patronage', *ELR* 12.2, 1982, pp. 162–79.

[22] The lady is the Countess of Pembroke, who resolves the strife between art and nature through her own artistic labours, the Psalms. For the Sidney Psalms see *The Psalms of Sir Philip Sidney and the Countess of Pembroke*, ed. J. C. A. Rathmell, New York, 1963.

[23] 'The God of Dreams'; note in text. See Morpheus in Glossary.

[24] 'Goddess of War and Wisdom'; note in text.

[25] 'The Moon'; note in text.

[26] 'The Morning'; note in text. Actually Aurora is the dawn; many of Lanyer's mythological glosses are slightly inaccurate.

[27] 'The Psalms written newly by the Countess Dowager of Pembroke'; note in text.

[28] A remarkable assertion; Lanyer elevates Mary Sidney over her brother Philip. This may form part of her concern with the position of women.

[29] 'To Sleep'; note in text.

[30] Lucy Russell, Countess of Bedford was, together with Mary Sidney Countess of Pembroke, one of the most important woman patrons of the Renaissance; she was the patron of, among others, Ben Jonson, George Chapman, Samuel Daniel, Michael Drayton, and John Donne, who addressed seven verse letters to her. She was married to Edward, third Earl of Bedford, who was exiled from court after the Essex rebellion and later suffered partial paralysis after a fall; as a result, her role depended on herself and her connections with the Harington family; she was the sister of Sir John Harington. See Barbara K. Lewalski, 'Lucy, Countess of Bedford: Images of a Jacobean Courtier and Patroness' in *Politics of Discourse: The Literature and History of Seventeenth-Century England*, ed. Kevin Sharpe and Steven Zwicker, Berkeley: University of California Press, 1987, pp. 52–77, and Margaret M. Byard, 'The Trade of Courtiership: The Countess of Bedford and the Bedford Memorials: A Family History from 1585 to 1607', *History Today*, January 1979, pp. 20–28; Patricia Thomson, 'John Donne and the Countess of Bedford', *Modern Language Review* 44, 1949, pp. 329–40.

[31] Margaret Clifford, Dowager Duchess of Cumberland, was the daughter of Francis Russell, second Earl of Bedford, and married George Clifford, third Earl of Cumberland, in 1577. He was for several years virtually separated from his wife, though they were reconciled at his request on his deathbed. He left a will bequeathing all his northern estates to his brother, the new earl, ignoring a deed from the reign of Edward II which entailed the estates on his child regardless of sex. Margaret Clifford, and later Anne, engaged in endless litigation to secure Anne's right to these estates, but they only reverted to her when her uncle's male line had been exhausted. These protracted battles may explain why Lanyer chose to dedicate a defence of women to the Cliffords; the British Library copy of *Salve Deus* is plainly especially prepared for them, since other dedications are removed from it. See Introduction, and line 9ff. in the main poem, which dedicate it explicitly to the Dowager Duchess.

[32] Katherine Knevet Howard, Countess of Suffolk was the wife of Thomas Howard, Lord Admiral and Lord Chamberlain of the Household. In 1618,

Thomas and Katherine were disgraced and imprisoned for extortion and embezzlement. See Lynda Levy Peck, *Court Patronage and Court Corruption in Early Stuart England*, London; Unwin Hyman, 1990, pp. 181–4.

[33] Lady Anne Clifford, Countess of Dorset, was the daughter of Margaret Clifford, Dowager Duchess of Cumberland, to whom Lanyer also offers praise. Anne Clifford married Richard Sackville, Earl of Dorset, in 1609, and after his death married the younger son of another of Lanyer's dedicatees, Mary Sidney. She kept a diary; see D. J. H. Clifford, ed., *The Diaries of Lady Anne Clifford*, London: Alan Sutton, 1990.

[34] Alludes to the parable of the wise and foolish virgins; the foolish virgins fail to provide themselves with oil for their lamps, and so are locked out when the bridegroom comes. The bridegroom is Christ; the foolish virgins represent those unprepared for him.

[35] 'Especially grace' in original.

[36] Amended from 'woman' in original

[37] Cynthia: one of the names used for Elizabeth I by court poets like Sir Walter Ralegh.

[38] 'The Lady Margaret Countess Dowager of Cumberland'; note in text. See the prose dedication to her, and 'A Description of Cookeham'.

[39] 'To the Countess of Cumberland'; note in text.

[40] 'An invective against outward beauty unaccompanied with virtue'; note in text. Lanyer here explicitly refuses an epideixis derived from Petrarchan encomia to the beauty of women in favour of a rhetoric which foregrounds women's virtue.

[41] Helen of Troy.

[42] 'proud Tarquin's fact' in text.

[43] 'Of Rosamund'; note in text.

[44] 'Of Matilda'; note in text.

[45] 'To the Lady of Cumberland the Introduction to the passion of Christ'.

[46] 'A preamble of the author before the Passion'; note in text.

[47] 'Here begins the Passion of Christ'; note in text.

[48] 'those hands' in text.

[49] Judas.

[50] Pilate's wife had a prophetic dream in which she saw him condemning an innocent man to death; later tradition made her a secret Christian.

[51] Eve's apology; note in text.

[52] After condeming Christ, Pilate washed his hands in a basin, signifying that he took no responsibility for Christ's blood.

[53] The passion of Christ was often described through an antisemitic rhetoric, but it may be relevant to note here than Lanyer's father was of Jewish extraction; in the antisemitic atmosphere of Jacobean London, she may have felt a special wish to disassociate herself from her Jewish origins.

[54] 'Christ going to death'; note in text.

[55] General doom: the last judgement.

[56] Lanyer describes the execution in terms more appropriate to Jacobean London than to Palestine; this may simply be an updating, but may also implicitly critique the spectacle of execution in the seventeenth century.

[57] 'The tears of the daughters of Jerusalem'; note in text.

[58] 'To speak on word' in text.
[59] 'The sorrow of the Virgin Mary'; note in text.
[60] Rod of Jesse; i.e., member of the house of David.
[61] 'The salutation of the Virgin Mary'; note in text.
[62] 'Christ's death'; note in text.
[63] To my Lady of Cumberland'; note in text.
[64] 'The terror of all creatures at that instant when Christ died'; note in text.
[65] This passage prefigures Cookeham's seasonal mourning for the departure of the Cliffords, and makes them types of Christ.
[66] Joseph of Arimathea, the rich man who organized Christ's burial.
[67] Mary of Bethany, Mary Magdalen, and Mary the mother of Jesus.
[68] 'Christ's resurrection'; note in text.
[69] 'A brief description of his beauty upon the canticles'; note in text.
[70] 'To my Lady of Cumberland'; note in text.
[71] 'her breasts' in text. This may be Lanyer's interesting slip, for Christ is figured in maternal terms throughout this section.
[72] The Scythian women are Amazons.
[73] Susanna; see Glossary.
[74] The laurel is a symbol of chastity; see Daphne in Glossary.
[75] 'sonne' in text; there is a pun here on sun/son that can't be reproduced in modern spelling.
[76] 'To the Lady dowager of Cumberland'; note in text.
[77] 'Colours of confessors & martyrs'; note in text.
[78] The manor of Cookeham, a royal possession until 1818, is near Maidenhead, and was inhabited by the Countess of Cumberland's brother in 1603. Greer suggests that Lanyer's husband may have served with Cumberland's brother Lord William Russell of Thornleigh in Ireland (p. 51). The poem probably dates from 1609–10 (see subsequent notes), making it the first 'country-house' poem published in English and probably the first written; Jonson's 'To Penshurst' dates from before the death of Prince Henry in November 1612, but was not published until 1616, and is not known to have circulated in MS. The poem is not very like the description of place which Lanyer says the countess requested at the beginning of *Salve Deus*.
[79] I.e. *Salve Deus*.
[80] The conceit here is that the landscape becomes the countess's client; therefore like a client it might proffer a suit or request.
[81] David's hymns: the Psalms, believed to have been written by David.
[82] Lady Anne Clifford; see note 3.
[83] Lady Anne married Richard Sackville, Lord Buckhurst, third Earl of Dorset, on 25 February 1609. The poem clearly postdates the marriage.
[84] 'Parters': one who or that which parts; it is unclear whether honour is to be shared or is that which divides.
[85] 'conster': construe.
[86] May have involved masques, dancing and cardplaying as well as outdoor games. Lady Anne performed in both *The Masque of Beauty* (1609) and *The Masque of Queens* (1610) at court.
[87] 'rivelled': wrinkled; 'rine': rind, bark, or frost. The conceit is that the bark is a kind of frost.

Printed in the United Kingdom
by Lightning Source UK Ltd.
104760UKS00001B/6